FINDING JESUS IN THE GOSPELS

FINDING JESUS IN THE GOSPELS

A Companion to Mark,
Matthew, Luke and John

ROBERT KNOPP

AVE MARIA PRESS NOTRE DAME, INDIANA 46556

6/93

© 1989 by Ave Maria Press, Notre Dame, Indiana 46556

International Standard Book Number: 0-87793-405-3

Library of Congress Catalog Card Number: 89-84557

Cover and text design: Thomas W. Ringenberg

Printed and bound in the United States of America.

Books

To my nephew, Paul,
who found Jesus in the Gospels
and, in a sense, inspired this book

CONTENTS

INVITATION

"Seek and You Will Find"

Jesus Christ invites us: "Seek and you will find."

Seek what? "Fulfillment," say today's psychologists. We've been seeking it everywhere—in pleasure, money, gadgets, casual relationships. Long ago Augustine ran this gamut only to find that "our hearts are restless, Lord, until they rest in you." Only God knows how to fulfill our longing!

But we were never very good at seeking him; so he sought us. He became human to help us find the destiny for which he fashioned us: *himself*. We will never be fulfilled until we find God by finding Jesus Christ.

How will we find Jesus? He walked for a few years in Galilee, suffered and died in Jerusalem, rose from death and ascended into heaven—seemingly far out of our reach. But he can reach us, and he left us means to reach him: He formed disciples into a religious community. He commissioned them to teach all nations what he had taught and to baptize all who were willing to follow him as a people lovingly united in his church, his new body on earth. He sent the Holy Spirit, his Spirit, to dwell in this body, to guide its members in his way to the Father, and to inspire some of them to write down what he had said and done.

If, then, we really want to find Jesus, we must seek him in his church—its community, its sacraments, its scriptures, its service of others—and in our own experiences, especially in our most loving relationships. This book is intended to be a companion along one of these paths, the one by which the early church meant to lead us to a more

9

complete understanding and love of Jesus and his message—the gospels.

Many seekers have been looking into the scriptures. Many have joined study groups. But some have become frustrated with groups that seldom get beyond the personal opinion stage. They feel the need to fathom the basic meaning of gospels that seem subject to contradictory interpretations. Others who have never joined groups try to read the New Testament on their own, only to find its language foreign to their modern mentality. Bored, they lay it aside and seek Jesus elsewhere, or simply nowhere at all.

There are many books that offer help, from simple how-to books to detailed commentaries. Most commentaries are so heavy that few people systematically read them; they are used for occasional reference. The how-to books tell about the special reading skills necessary for reading scripture, but usually offer little help in acquiring them.

Ideally, we must read scripture itself with a ''companion'' at our side supplying necessary background, insight into the significance of the author's literary devices, the inner meaning of this phrase and the Old Testament echo in that, as well as making suggestions to convert our reading into prayer. Of course, the Holy Spirit is the ideal companion, but the Spirit also expects us to use our own ingenuity and any helpful human companion we can find. This book is intended to be such a reading companion, filling the gap between complicated commentaries and oversimplified how-to books.

This is not a book for scholars. Rather, it depends upon the scholars, without a clutter of reference notes. It makes use of some of the tremendous new insights that they have discovered in their painstaking study of background and context. But not every scholarly investigation will help us achieve our purpose—finding Jesus in the gospels. Attempts to reconstruct the sequence of events in Jesus' life, for instance, can become a distraction from our goal of seeing the kind of person he is.

In writing this companion-book for readers who want to concentrate their energy upon the great goal of finding Jesus, I hope to offer the background needed for reading with greater insight into the intentions of the biblical authors and the meaning of their works. I hope that this reading of the gospels will encourage both individual readers and groups to continue reading on their own with greater confidence and insight.

This book is not intended to be read by itself. Please read along with it the corresponding gospel passages, for it is scripture above all that we must read; no other book will serve as substitute for God's word to us. Christians of every age have agreed that when we pray, we speak to God, and when we read scripture, God speaks to us. When we pray we gradually learn to listen more than speak; when we read scripture we must also learn to listen to what God is saying to us in the reading, letting it form our thinking, our willing, our acting. Then our reading becomes a kind of sacramental act that brings Jesus to us in his word, his thought, his will, his actions—in his *presence*.

I owe a special debt of gratitude to several friends who offered valuable suggestions for improving my efforts, especially to Rev. John G. Leies, S.M., Rev. David Fleming, S.M., Rev. James Beighlie, C.M., my niece Kay Ashida, and my own dear wife, Marian.

I hope this book will help you find Jesus in the gospels.

PART I

Seeking Jesus in the Gospels

From the misty dawn of human life our ancestors sought the meaning of their lives. Their hearts would not let them feel satisfied with this earthly home. Their minds would not let them think that this little space and time were all they could hope for. They longed for a better life that would break the boundaries of earth and time, for a more lasting, even an *everlasting life*. If nature died in winter only to rise again to new life in spring, would not they who found themselves to be the crown of nature likewise have their springtime?

But their experience also told them that they were not the complete masters of nature. They looked up to the sky and the clouds that they could not control, and they instinctively believed that there must be a sky god. They looked out to the rolling sea and felt that there must be a sea god. Those who lived along the Nile or the Tigris believed in river gods. Our ancestors called upon their gods to save them from sky and sea and river.

Even more than their inability to explain natural phenomena, their experience of truth, beauty, goodness, and especially of love, could convince them that life is a precious gift from a supremely good and loving Being. Religion could raise their lives above the level of their earthly existence. But this same religion could also degenerate into prejudice, human sacrifice, war. Our ancestors were tempted to think that their very nature, reaching out toward being beyond themselves, even to a Supreme Being, was betraying them to believe in an impossible dream.

And then the dream came true! Nearly four thousand years ago, the Supreme Being spoke to a man, even renamed him Abraham in solemn covenant with him and his people, promising to be their God if they would be his chosen people.

Abraham's people preserved the story of this covenant relationship with Yahweh in their traditions, which they eventually wrote into the Hebrew scriptures. The Christians added the New Testament to form the Bible. Down through the centuries millions of people have considered the Bible to be a collection of books different from all others. Why have so many people thought the Bible to be inspired by God himself? And why have so many considered the gospels to be the core of the Bible?

God's Own Book Centers in the Gospels

It does not take much comparative reading to discover that the Bible is vastly different from all other books. For instance, the Genesis story of creation, though not scientific by modern standards, is incomparably superior to the creation stories of other ancient peoples. Compare this story with that of their Babylonian captors: In battle the god Marduk defeated the goddess Tiamat and split her in two to form the sea and the sky.

Just as simplistic was the Babylonian explanation of good and evil in the world: Good came from good gods, evil from bad gods. But the Jews, convinced that Yahweh alone was God of all, not only told a much better story; they produced a beautiful poem that characterized both Yahweh and his creation (Gn 1). Yahweh is good, so all that he makes is good, especially man and woman, and the relationship with which Yahweh blessed them. But in their desire to become gods themselves, they rebelled against Yahweh and his creation; their sin brought evil into the world.

A further comparison of how ancient peoples viewed their own histories reveals an equally vast difference between the Hebrew scriptures and all other ancient manuscripts. Many of these peoples attributed their military victories to their gods and glorified their past with legends and epics, such as the *Iliad*, replete with great deeds and myriad gods. But only the Jews saw their whole history as a romance with the One God, a romance in which they surprisingly admitted, despite their strong nationalistic pride, that they were often unfaithful though Yahweh was always faithful.

Of all peoples the Jews alone believed that the one God had

14

blessed them ever since that dim past when he made the covenant with their nomad father Abraham, promising them their very own land, a land that came to signify all that makes life meaningful. Yahweh renewed his covenant with Isaac and with Jacob, whom he renamed Israel. But Israel's sinful sons sold their own brother Joseph into slavery in Egypt; later, the Israelites were themselves enslaved in Egypt.

Ever-merciful Yahweh did not abandon them. Through Moses he freed them from Pharaoh, led them through the desert and gave them his ten commandments to guide them toward goodness, even holiness. Through Joshua he enabled them to conquer the land he had promised them.

Whenever they fell back into sin, Yahweh brought them to their senses by allowing them to fall prey to their enemies. And when they turned back to him, he restored their freedom. He gave them a great king, David, to whom he promised an heir who would be Yahweh's own son to rule forever. He sent them great prophets to guide their kings. Most of these kings ignored Yahweh, but the prophets proclaimed that he loved his people more than a good husband loves his wife. Even when Israel was unfaithful, ever-loving Yahweh would rescue it from its enemies and from its sinfulness.

But the injustices of Israel's kings and the idolatry of its people eventually brought it low again, this time into exile in Babylonia. Again Yahweh rescued Israel, bringing back a loyal remnant to rebuild Jerusalem and the temple. Israel waited and longed for its former greatness. Yet it also sinned, and so fell to the Greeks, to the Egyptians, and then to the Syrians, who persecuted Israel severely. Yahweh sent the valiant Maccabees to win a short time of relative freedom. But Israel continued to sin, and in 63 B.C. the Romans took control of its affairs.

For more than a century no prophet appeared. Yahweh was silent. And Israel was waiting, longing.

Suddenly, in a way utterly unexpected, Yahweh fulfilled all his promises! He sent his only Son to save not only Israel but the whole world. Jesus Christ, through his life, teaching, death, resurrection and sending of his Holy Spirit, offers all men and women salvation from sin and death.

This is the unique significance of the Bible. This is why so many people down through the centuries have sought its guidance and, receiving it, have considered the Bible as God's sacred word to humanity. There is one sure way to find out for ourselves. We simply have to read it frequently to nourish our spirit. As it speaks to the hidden depths of our heart, we will recognize in it the word of the Maker of that heart. And we will share the excitement of those first readers who found their faith expressed and nourished in these sacred books.

Christians find the Hebrew scriptures fulfilled in the New Testament, with its heart in the gospels. No other ancient book portrays a personage of such incomparable human, moral and religious stature as the Jesus of the gospels. His surpassing love exceeds the power of the human imagination to conceive. Jesus himself is the best argument for the divine inspiration of the Bible. Not only does he present God as our most loving Father and send us his Holy Spirit as our own dear Companion and Advocate; Jesus himself is the clearest, most convincing revelation of God.

The gospels were written for all who seek God by seeking Jesus. They are deceptively easy to read, for they encompass a depth that we can only too readily miss.

Is a Reading Companion Really Necessary?

We don't need a reading companion to help us understand the books of the Bible if by *understand* we mean "get something out of them." But what if *understand* means "interpret correctly"? The Bible itself warns us against the dangers of misunderstanding the sacred books: "In them [Paul's letters] there are some things hard to understand that the ignorant and unstable distort to their own destruction, just as they do the other scriptures" (2 Pt 3:15-16; *NAB*).

Are we not all relatively ignorant of the ways of God and unstable in our faith? If, then, we would heed this warning against distorting the biblical writer's meaning to our own harm, we must admit our need of help in reading the Bible. If we bring only our own preconceptions to it, we run the risk of reading into it our own thoughts; worse yet, we risk reading our own Jesus into the gospels instead of trying to find the Jesus they portray.

Jesus himself attests that even the learned can misread the word of God. When the Sadducees tried to ridicule the doctrine of the resurrection by asking him which of the seven brothers who had successively taken the same wife would be her husband after the resurrection, Jesus replied: "Are you not misled because you do not know the scriptures?" (Mk 12:24).

Our ordinary experience as Christians convinces us that it is only too easy to misunderstand scripture. Yet it is also true that without any special help, many people read the Bible with great interest and profit, sometimes even receiving from their reading a very personal message from God.

Some years ago a friend of mine saw his 3-year-old son run into the street and fall under the wheel of a passing bus. Doctors held out no hope for the boy's life. Husband and wife did what they were accustomed to do in every crisis: They opened their bible at random, asking God for help to know and accept his will. Their eyes fell upon the following passage:

> As he [Jesus] drew near to the gate of the city [of Nain], a man who had died was being carried out, the only son of his mother, and she was a widow. A large crowd from the city was with her. When the Lord saw her, he was moved with pity for her and said to her, "Do not weep." He stepped forward and touched the coffin; at this, the bearers halted, and he said, "Young man, I tell you, arise!" The dead man sat up and began to speak, and Jesus gave him to his mother (Lk 7:11-15).

When the doctors repeated their negative diagnosis, my friend and his wife declared their own conviction that the boy would live, for they believed that God had answered their prayer by speaking his personal word to them in his word of revelation. And so it happened! In a few months the boy's recovery was complete.

Before they could perceive a personal message, however, this couple had to understand in some degree the general meaning of the miracle story of Nain: Jesus has the compassion and power of God, for the Father reveals himself in Jesus and works through him. Only after grasping this general meaning could they hope that they were receiving the personal message that the Lord would exercise his power for them, just as he had for the widow of Nain.

Obviously there are dangers in trying to find this kind of personal message by reading scripture. To what extent did these parents begin their reading merely in the expectation of finding solace? After reading the story of Nain, was their conviction that the boy would recover simply lucky self-deception? If the boy had died, would they have lost their faith in Jesus? Such questions point up dangers, but faith is always a risk in its reaching out beyond ordinary human understanding. The answer to the prayer of these parents was really in their own hearts, implanted there by the reading. Who but those involved can discern whether it is their own or God's voice that speaks in their hearts? And to what extent can they be sure? Such uncertainties are reduced to insignificance by the abundant rewards of faith. The risks are further diminished by a good preparation for reading the Bible.

Rather than a spectacular cure, a personal message from scripture usually takes the form of an application of the passage to the reader's life. Consider the case of Augustine. As he relates in his *Confessions*, he was praying desperately for courage to leave his life of sin and become a Christian, yet feeling helpless to make a final decision. Suddenly he heard a child's voice shouting, ''Take and read! Take and read!'' Unfamiliar with such a phrase in children's games, he accepted the voice as a divine command, opened his Bible at random, and read:

> Let us conduct ourselves properly as in the day, not in orgies and drunkenness, not in promiscuity and licentiousness, not in rivalry and jealousy. But put on the Lord Jesus Christ, and make no provision for the desires of the flesh (Rom 13:13-14).

Augustine's heart was flooded with light and peace. He knew what he had to do and was filled with the courage to do it. This reading set him on the road to becoming *Saint* Augustine.

These are extraordinary examples of personal blessings granted through prayerful reading of scripture. But we are all capable of such prayerful reading; we should all read scripture to hear God's word encouraging us to apply what we read to our lives.

Personal Meanings Depend Upon Perception of General Meanings

Reading scripture for personal enrichment requires understanding of the general meaning of the passage involved; if it is misunderstood, the personal application may go astray. Another friend of mine took Jesus' words to the widow of Nain, ''Do not weep,'' so literally that he didn't shed a single tear for his dying mother, much as he loved her. Apparently he had not read Jesus' words in context and therefore had failed to realize that the widow herself did not take Jesus' words as a command to hold back her tears, but as an expression of sympathizing love. Far from coldly objecting to her tears, Jesus was compassionately responding to them. To think that he was forbidding tears for a loved one distorts the general meaning of the passage and severely reduces the reader's perception of Jesus' great sensitivity.

On the other hand, the person who refrained from tears at his mother's death may have seen in this passage more than its obvious meaning. Perhaps he had concluded that Luke is presenting Jesus at Nain as the powerful and merciful Lord capable of granting the ultimate consolation of bringing our loved ones not only back to this earthly life, but even into the eternal life of the resurrection. Such a meaning is in harmony with Luke's gospel taken as a whole and therefore a legitimate extended meaning of this passage, beyond ordinary interpretation—a deep personal insight that might very well justify tearless tranquility at a good mother's death.

There are, then, various beneficial ways of understanding passages of scripture, and often there are several layers of meaning. It is especially helpful to distinguish at least the two principal meanings discussed here: (1) a general *interpretation* that holds true for all readers; (2) a prayerful personal *application* of that meaning to one's own life.

We can hardly read scripture without looking for both general and personal meanings. Usually no special study is necessary in order to draw a personal application, at least in the sense of finding guidance for our decisions, attitudes and behavior. Ordinarily we need only a prayerful receptivity to the word and action of the Holy Spirit in our lives. But it is obvious that the rightness of the personal application depends in large part on the rightness of the interpretation, which, for many difficult passages, requires serious study. Interpretation is often illuminated by the work of scholars. Application is encouraged by the example of saints. To read scripture intelligently and profitably, we need the help of both saints and scholars.

Taking Advantage of the Work of Scripture Scholars

When we read the gospels we are dealing with books written nearly two thousand years ago. To read an ancient book intelligently, we must try to return in spirit to the time in which it was written in order to take into account the customs and mindset of the people to whom the ancient manuscript was originally addressed. This is a historical study of great difficulty from which we can excuse ourselves because enough has already been done by experts to allow us to profit immensely from their findings, some of which will be presented in this book.

19

Of the documents that were eventually combined to form the New Testament, none of the originals has survived the ravages of time and persecution. It would be surprising if even one had survived, for neither have any of the original manuscripts of the Greek and Latin classics of ancient times. This means that a comparative study must be made to determine which of the existing manuscripts of scripture, or combination of these manuscripts, offers the best hope of reproducing the text accepted by early Christians as canonical. Dedicated scholars have devoted their lives to this difficult science of textual criticism. They have reached enough agreement in essentials to merit our trust in their findings. And they assure us that ancient copyists have been so careful in their work that the differences among the oldest extant manuscripts of the New Testament are comparatively minor, rarely affecting the basic meaning of a passage and leaving untouched the overall meaning of the New Testament for the Christian faith.

The original language of the New Testament books is an ancient non-classical form of Greek. Here again, most of us will have to trust translators and the evaluation of dedicated scholars to point out the best of the many existing translations. One of the most heartening developments in the ecumenical movement is the increasing agreement among Protestant and Catholic linguists in their translations of the Bible; they have even worked together on some versions. However there is no general consensus that any existing version is the best in all respects. Some translations excel for liturgical use, others for study of the precise meaning of the text. One version is more accurate in its rendering of certain passages; another version, of other passages.

One of the most widely accepted modern English translations for use in the liturgy and in private or group reading is *The New American Bible*. With the pastoral experience of many years of actual use, a team of scholars has recently completed a revision of this translation of the New Testament "to provide a version suitable for liturgical proclamation, for private reading, and for purposes of study" (Preface to the Revised Edition). Its footnotes are especially helpful in offering the reader many insights of modern scholarship. Quotations in this book not otherwise indicated are from the revised edition of *The New American Bible*.

The art of reading literature, and especially ancient literature, requires considerable discernment and practice. It is a doubly difficult art, for it requires (1) the effort to understand the meaning that the author intended to convey to his original readers in their situation of life, and (2) the further effort to understand this meaning in terms of our current life situation. Yet, this is the art in which we must become proficient if we are to read the gospels for their full meaning.

To read each gospel with deeper insight we will enlist the assistance of dedicated scholars to enlighten us about the cultural and historical background out of which the author writes, the literary forms he uses, his theological perspective, and so on. But a book of modest proportions could never attempt to offer the historical background and literary analysis of every part of the gospels. We will therefore concentrate upon passages that offer us clearest insight into the personal identity of Jesus. Our efforts will deeply involve us in problems of biblical interpretation.

Modern Approaches to Interpreting the Gospels

Many passages of scripture have been given contradictory interpretations during the course of history. But within the past half century, Protestant and Catholic scholars have succeeded in arriving at a common approach to interpretation. There is now almost unanimous acceptance of the historical-literary method, which combines historical research on the customs and ways of thinking at the time of writing with literary analysis of the writings themselves.

The general use of this method has led to a consensus concerning the main lines of the literary history of the gospels:

1. Jesus revealed God in his life and teaching, death and resurrection.
2. With the guidance of the Holy Spirit his apostles witnessed to his life and teaching, developing their message into a body of apostolic tradition.
3. Inspired evangelists relied upon this body of apostolic tradition to produce the gospels.

Wide acceptance of these three stages has enabled modern scholars to attain a clearer understanding of the *gospel* as a distinct literary form that subordinates historical exactitude to theology and catechesis. The four gospels are considered historical in the sense that they relate the life and message of a truly historical personage. But what makes these books *gospels* is their strict fidelity, not to historical fact or to biographical accuracy, but to the faith of the early Christian church in their presentation of Jesus speaking the message of God, acting with the power of God, dying for our sins and rising from the dead. Their primary intention is not to give us the historical details of Jesus' life and words, but to testify to the truth about the kind of person Jesus was and is, and the kind of relationship that he brings about between God and us.

Acceptance of the three stages has also helped modern scholars to a clearer understanding of inspiration. The Holy Spirit inspired the human author without reducing him to a puppet. Each evangelist wrote in his own personal style, using his own limited resources, yet guided by the Spirit in basing himself upon the inspired apostolic tradition, which was itself derived from the life and teaching of Jesus. Inspiration, then, is not to be understood as God's direct dictation to the evangelists, nor is it to be reduced to merely human inspiration, such as that of the poet or the composer. It was a special grace by which God illuminated the mind and heart of the writer, freeing him from essential error, as he diligently used his human faculties to transmit faithfully the apostolic tradition.

It is also widely perceived that this apostolic tradition served as the norm, not only for the evangelists in writing the gospels, but also for the early Christians in understanding and selecting them. Already instructed in this tradition, they recognized our present four gospels as authentic expressions of their faith, carefully distinguishing them from the many apocryphal gospels that appeared during the first three centuries.

The general acceptance of the use of the historical-literary method by modern scholars has also produced agreement about the meaning of many passages formerly disputed. But there are still important passages that remain ambiguous, even after careful efforts to detect the author's intended meaning, passages given contradictory interpretations by sincere and scholarly Christians. For resolving this difficulty, the following question has become crucial: How did early Christians, who could have consulted the apostles or the evangelists, understand the passage?

Some scholars limit their efforts to answer this question to the scarce historical evidence of how early Christians interpreted disputed passages. These scholars are forced to depend in large part upon educated conjectures from clues within the scripture text itself or in nonscriptural writings of the time. Some have tried to work back to the apostolic traditions upon which the books were based and even to the very words of Jesus. Though their efforts have produced few conclusions upon which they can agree, they have opened up new insights,

22

adding considerably to our understanding of the New Testament.

An increasing number of both Protestant and Catholic scholars supplement this historical effort with a canonical approach, which takes into account the fact that early Christians used in their liturgies only the books they recognized as the authentic expression of their faith and norm of their conduct. These were eventually "canonized" as books of the New Testament.

This canonical approach sharpens the question about how early Christians understood scripture: What in this book or passage did they consider to be the authentic expression of their faith, and how is it therefore normative of our faith? Advocates of this new approach focus squarely upon the faith content of canonical books, subordinating historical and literary considerations to the role of illuminating this content. They see diversity of theological views in these books as evidence of complementary beliefs existing among early Christians. And, because they accept these books as authentic expressions of the faith of early Christians, they reject interpretations that would result in outright contradictions in matters affecting the essence of the Christian faith.

Moreover, they work with the text actually accepted into the canon, even though it may have been edited by others than the original authors. They consider this final form more important for interpretation than reconstructed versions that some historical critics propose. For example, our understanding of the end of Mark's gospel depends in part upon which of several endings found in ancient manuscripts we accept as authentic. There is general agreement that the canonically accepted "longer ending," without which Mark's original version lacks the resurrection appearances of Jesus, was added by someone other than Mark. For this reason some critics deny the authenticity of this longer ending, thereby casting doubt upon the importance that the gospel of Mark assigns to the resurrection. Scholars who adopt the canonical approach accept the longer ending as an integral part of Mark's gospel and therefore as documenting the importance of Jesus' resurrection appearances for understanding this gospel.

These scholars presume that the process by which the community of faith canonized books of the New Testament included the effort to clarify otherwise obscure passages by such editorial work as the addition of the longer ending to Mark's gospel. This concern of early Christians to insure that their books of highest authority accurately expressed their faith bears witness to their consciousness of possessing a body of knowledge by which to judge the accuracy of the writings they selected and edited as the canonical expression of their faith. Obviously, this was the knowledge they had received through the teaching of the apostles.

Interdependence of Apostolic Tradition and Written Word

It is important to distinguish *apostolic* tradition from all other kinds of oral tradition. New Testament books and other early church writings provide evidence of the existence of several different kinds of tradition:

1. Jewish traditional customs, such as washing cups before meals (Mk 7:2-4), often elevated to the level of law.
2. Authorship traditions concerning the evangelists and their sources. These may be erroneous, according to evidence uncovered by modern scholars.
3. Traditional stories such as those concerning the fate of Judas (see Acts 1:16-20 vs. Mt 27:3-10). These have little more value than legends.
4. Apostolic traditions expressing the faith of the apostles based on their life with Jesus (Acts 2:14-40). These are the traditions guaranteed in essence by the guidance of the Holy Spirit (Jn 16:13). Each apostle, as eyewitness of the words and actions of history's most complete personality, could comprehend only partially the meaning of what he saw and heard. In teaching about Jesus and his message, apostles developed traditions often quite distinct from one another, as we see in the diversity of the gospels. Yet early Christians believed that through the guidance of the Holy Spirit traditions of apostolic faith supplemented one another without contradiction.

Luke begins his gospel by testifying to his use of oral apostolic tradition as his source:

> Since many have undertaken to compile a narrative of the events that have been fulfilled among us, *just as those who were eyewitnesses from the beginning and ministers of the word have handed them down to us*, I too have decided, after investigating everything accurately anew, to write it down (Lk 1:1-3; italics mine, as in succeeding quotations, unless otherwise indicated).

24

Evidently Luke expects his readers to come to his gospel with a background formed by listening to the "eyewitnesses . . . and ministers of the word," among whom he certainly considers the apostles as fully authoritative (see Lk 24:47-48). In other words, he invites Christians to judge the truth of his gospel by its faithfulness to the body of apostolic tradition. Conversely, he hopes that his own account will confirm the confidence of his reader in apostolic tradition, for he also professes to write "so that you may realize the certainty of the teachings you have received" (Lk 1:3-4). Luke therefore sees apostolic tradition and written word as existing side by side, mutually sustaining one another. The oral word serves both as the link between Jesus and the written word and as the norm by which Christians interpret it. The written word confirms and preserves the oral tradition.

John's gospel, too, implies a mutual relationship between apostolic tradition and scripture: "There are also many other things that Jesus did, but if these were described individually, I do not think the whole world would contain the books that would be written" (Jn 21:25). Clearly the writer knew an apostolic tradition more extensive than the writings that preserved selected parts of it. Apostolic tradition supplemented the written word.

Apostolic tradition had already supplemented the teaching of Jesus. He had commissioned his apostles to go to all nations, "teaching them to observe *all that I have commanded you*" (Mt 28:20). But the apostles taught more than Jesus' message; they taught also the message *about Jesus*. He had said relatively little about himself; his teaching had centered around the kingdom of his Father. But after his resurrection the apostles realized that Jesus himself was the very embodiment of the kingdom; *he was the message* they were commissioned to convey. From Pentecost on, their message centered upon the person and saving word, action, death, resurrection and exaltation of Jesus himself (Acts 2:22-39). This teaching about Jesus was the most extensive and profound addition to Jesus' original message as transmitted by apostolic tradition and the gospels.

Even before Pentecost, apostolic tradition had begun to make other additions to the teaching of Jesus, not in the sense of changing his teaching but of applying it to new situations. Convinced that Jesus had come for people of all ages the assembled disciples, at the initiative of Peter, selected two candidates and asked their Lord to make known his will about which of them should succeed the fallen Judas: "The lot fell upon Matthias, and he was counted with the eleven apostles" (Acts

1:26). Apostolic tradition now contained the seed of apostolic succession.

The apostles expanded Jesus' good news in a special way during crises. When the problem of whether to admit non-Jews into the new Christian communities without holding them to observance of the Mosaic law arose, a problem with which Jesus had not dealt, the apostles and local church leaders met in Jerusalem to resolve the issue in the light of their knowledge of Jesus' life and teaching. They decided that it was unnecessary to bind Christians to observance of Jewish laws, for as Peter declared, "We believe that we are saved through the grace of the Lord Jesus" (Acts 15:11).

Thus, before it was written into the New Testament, the apostolic tradition was growing through new insights; it was not static but *dynamic*. And it retained its dynamism even after it was incorporated into the New Testament. As the church grew and the apostles died, those whom they had specially formed as their successors continued applying their traditional teaching to new situations. The Letter to Titus attests to the Christian belief that the "bishop as God's steward . . . [is entrusted with] holding fast to the true message as taught so that he will be able both to exhort with sound doctrine and to refute opponents" (Ti 1:7-9).

Hence, when further crises arose it was the bishops as successors of the apostles who held councils to seek answers under the guidance of the Holy Spirit, relying on Jesus' promise that "when he comes, the Spirit of truth, he will guide you to all truth" (Jn 16:13). When Arius denied the divinity of Jesus, the bishops assembled at Nicaea in 325 to defend the traditional faith of the church. In the Nicene Creed they formulated as an authoritative interpretation of the New Testament their belief that the Son is "one in Being with the Father."

Apostolic Tradition Blends Into Church Teaching

At Nicaea we see the continuation of a process by which the apostolic tradition had merged imperceptibly into a post-New Testament church tradition of faith. Christians who accept the Nicene Creed as an authentic interpretation of the New Testament identity of Jesus Christ are at least implicitly accepting the authority of the church through its bishops to interpret scripture within a post-apostolic tradition of faith that develops in the same way that the apostolic tradition developed.

Guided by the Holy Spirit the church grows in her understanding of her faith.

We today receive apostolic tradition not only as written into the New Testament but also in the same way as did the second, third, tenth generations of Christians: through "the church of the living God, the pillar and foundation of truth" (1 Tim 3:15), exercising the teaching authority conferred upon her by Jesus himself in commissioning his apostles. Apostolic tradition survived in the teaching of the church, guardian of her scriptures, which she continued to interpret and supplement, not by inventing new doctrines but by holding to the complete revelation she had received in Jesus and applying it in fresh formulations to new historical situations.

Apostolic tradition, like all oral traditions, had been a fragile thing, subject to the shifting winds of history. But history itself has just suggested to us how it escaped the lot of most oral traditions: First, it was fixed in writing, at least for the most part, in the New Testament; second, it continued to exist in the faith tradition of the church, which preserved and further developed it through her teaching authority, thereby sustaining a constant yet ever fresh interpretation of her scriptures. In this partnership scripture assures continuity, while developing church tradition constantly renews insight into the meaning of scripture as God's revelation.

This dynamic faith tradition enables the church, under the guidance of the Holy Spirit, to adapt herself to changing cultural situations and thus grow in her understanding of her scriptures without altering their essential meaning. As the church passed from a predominantly Jewish background into a world of Greek philosophy, the Fathers of the church utilized in their councils the refined philosophical thought and vocabulary to formulate such doctrines as the Incarnation and the Trinity, doctrines that have clarified and sharpened our understanding of the New Testament. Greek and Latin literature suggested to church Fathers involved allegorical interpretations of scripture hardly suitable for our time but adequate to nourish the piety of ancient peoples. Efforts to convert barbarians led to new insights into the application of scripture in forming value priorities for daily living.

The rediscovery of Aristotle in the Middle Ages enabled Aquinas to construct a powerful synthesis of the secular and Christian knowledge of his time, strengthening the Christian conviction that humanity's knowledge of the world and of God's revelation in scripture complement one another as gifts of the Creator of all. In our time modern science and technology have opened up new insights in our world view, enabling the church to avoid a too literal understanding of the Genesis creation story and concentrate upon its central significance as poetic rapture over the gifts of God. Modern psychology and anthropology open up new insights into the human mind and heart of Jesus and into the moral thrust of his teaching.

Thus, through the centuries the changeless word of scripture and the dynamic tradition of church teaching have worked in a fruitful partnership to remain true both to Christ and to his people of every time and culture.

Some Christians today miss the importance of this partnership. They believe that apostolic tradition has been wholly incorporated into the New Testament and fail to realize that it also survived in church teaching. To interpret scripture they see no need to refer to either tradition or church teaching. They therefore consider the Bible a complete entity within itself and interpret it as a closed system, without a guide beyond itself that rises above the level of scholarship. But no document can interpret itself. Inevitably, those who reject traditional church teaching as a guide to interpretation must rely either upon direct inspiration of the Holy Spirit or upon themselves or some other individual or community as sufficient authority for interpreting scripture. These personal or private interpretations have produced contradictory results dividing Christians into numerous sects, a situation that modern historical-literary study has not been able to remedy.

If the Bible really provided its own interpretation, or if the Holy Spirit directly inspired every sincere and prayerful reader to interpret it correctly, all readers would understand it in essentially the same way, easily unraveling its apparent contradictions. Yet from the very early history of Christianity, readers have been divided even over key questions about Jesus himself. Some today fix their attention on such passages as Colossians 1:15: "He [Christ] is the image of the invisible God, the *firstborn of all creation*," concluding that the writer is saying that Christ is a part of creation and therefore not divine. Others have concentrated on such passages as John 1:1-18:

> In the beginning was the Word . . .
> *and the Word was God. . . .*
> And the Word became flesh, . . .
> Jesus Christ.

They conclude that the Bible does teach the divinity of Jesus. Some Christians would keep these passages "on hold" until they count up texts that point to Jesus' humanity against those that point to his divinity. But most accept the interpretation of church councils that Jesus is *both human and divine*.

As a result of such controversies at least three kinds of scripture readers can be distinguished:

1. Those who accept personal interpretation, their own or another's;
2. Those who accept church interpretation but make no personal effort;
3. Those who supplement their personal effort to interpret scripture with ultimate dependence on authoritative church teaching.

This last group combines personal responsibility with respect for authority in the belief that the Holy Spirit guides the reader to understand scripture, not directly (though often this undoubtedly happens), but indirectly through the church's living and developing tradition of faith expressed in her authoritative teaching. These readers accept the church's traditional interpretation of her scriptures as the continuation of the apostolic tradition from which they were written, growing in precision and clarity through her liturgical prayers and creeds, the continuing reflection of her people, the deliberations of councils and periodic updating of her teaching. Hence, readers who possess adequate preparation for understanding scripture are those who have been well-instructed in the teaching of that church which holds firmly to apostolic tradition and develops it through the ages in exercise of her heritage of apostolic teaching authority.

This position, though with differing emphases, is held both by Catholics and by many Protestants: "It is through scripture, tradition, and teaching authority that the Spirit enables the believing community to settle disputes about the gospel" (*Teaching Authority and Infallibility in the Church: Lutherans and Catholics in Dialogue,* 6, p. 35).

If it is recognized that the apostolic tradition served as source of the New Testament, this same tradition, developed by the church to deal with new situations by recourse to the same authority that established it, should be embraced as the ultimate interpreter of the New Testament. It is therefore not only proper but at times necessary to have recourse to this faith tradition, carefully preserved and developed by the church, to interpret passages that otherwise remain ambiguous or seem contradictory.

Two principal resources, then, are available to those who seek a deeper understanding of the gospels: mastery of the art of biblical reading and reference to the faith tradition expressed in the constant teaching of the church. The first requires that we strive for insight into the biblical writer's intended meaning through analysis of his context, cultural background, literary forms and techniques, major themes, and so forth. The second suggests that when these efforts fail to unlock the meaning of a passage, we refer to the apostolic or post-apostolic faith tradition that clarifies it. But upon which of the differing church traditions of faith shall we rely?

The Problem of Church Traditions of Faith

As the unity of the church was broken, post-apostolic tradition preserved by the teaching authority of the Christian church split into opposing faith traditions. Early deviations from the teaching of the apostles gradually died out, and Arianism and other ancient doctrinal revolts eventually dwindled into insignificance. But in the Middle Ages, after centuries of different and disputed theological understandings, the Eastern Orthodox churches rejected the primacy of the Roman pope and broke with the west. Yet until modern times the Roman Catholic Church remained the only form of Christianity and the sole guardian of the Christian scriptures and faith tradition for nearly all the peoples of Europe.

Then, shortly after the discovery of America, Martin Luther, John Calvin, Henry VIII and others broke away from the Roman Church. The scandal of division followed as Protestants and Catholics accused each other of infidelity to the original Christian faith tradition. Happily most of these mutual recriminations have been set aside in our recent ecumenical efforts to understand, respect and love one another, even to work steadily toward complete reunion, as the Spirit of Jesus Christ urges us.

Yet differences remain, differences not so much of the heart as of the head. Until all Christians accept the same church tradition as authoritative for interpreting scripture, we must unfortunately identify ourselves as Protestant or Catholic, Methodist or Baptist, and so on. And just as the writers of the New Testament did not pretend to give us a neutral portrayal of Jesus but frankly presented the Jesus of their faith, so today it seems only appropriate that those who write about the

New Testament openly profess the faith tradition informing the perspective from which they write.

Hence, courtesy to the reader requires me to state that I write this book as one convinced that he must be true to the Catholic faith tradition, not in a spirit of contention or proselytism, but in the spirit of humility and love that should characterize that tradition. I write for Catholics, but also for all open-minded Christians, for all who seek Jesus in the gospels. In the historical and literary analysis of passages I will use the findings of both Protestant and Catholic scholars. When these efforts result in ambiguity, I will frankly rely upon the faith tradition of the Catholic church to clarify the meaning. But there are relatively few passages that cannot be adequately understood without recourse to an authoritative interpretation by the Catholic church, which has taken an official stand on relatively few biblical passages. Yet even after this recourse to Catholic tradition, some passages will remain obscure, for God's revelation is too rich and vast to be encompassed within the finite grasp of human beings. It is divine mystery beyond the power of the human mind to fathom completely.

Becoming a Scripture-Reading Detective

As the vehicle of divine mystery, scripture invites us to embark upon the great adventure of detecting ever more of its inexhaustible meaning. Reading the gospels can become even more exciting than the work of the detective who follows every clue to penetrate a human mystery. We will look for clues as we begin reading the gospels together. Let us take a preliminary look at the general process of seeking out these clues.

We must begin our search for the meaning of scripture without the preconception that takes every passage on the purely literal level. Nor should we presume that every passage must be symbolic or figurative. As honest seekers we must begin with the simple *common-sense search for the most obvious meaning* conveyed by the very wording of the passage. We must apply all the techniques of good reading: looking up the meaning of unfamiliar words, fitting together words and phrases that build the meaning intended by the author, observing punctuation clues that divide or unite constitutive parts of the overall thought, and so forth. Grasping this *literal sense* will frequently be all that is required to arrive at an adequate understanding. This open-minded and diligent approach to the literal sense—not to be confused with literalism—is our first step.

But many passages refuse to yield up their rich meaning without further effort. A little experience will soon convince us that one of the most important applications of common sense is to read every passage within the context that the author has given it. For instance, John attributes this surprising statement to Jesus: "I came into this world for judgment, so that those who do not see might see, and *those who do see might become blind*" (Jn 9:39). Taken by itself this statement seems to tell us that Jesus has come to do harm as well as good. But as the conclusion of the story in which Jesus heals a man born blind and the Pharisees deliberately blind themselves to the goodness of Jesus' act, the meaning becomes clearer: Jesus tears away the veil that men hide behind; he not only gives sight to the open-minded but also uncovers the blindness of those who refuse to see the light he offers.

If the immediate context—the verses before or after the difficult passage—does not completely clarify the meaning, we must weigh the passage within the context of the whole gospel, confident that an inspired author is consistent with himself. To say that Jesus has come to make people blind is obviously out of tune with the general tenor of John's gospel, which repeatedly tells us that Jesus is the Light of the world who came not to condemn it but to save it (Jn 3:16-17), not to divide men but to unite them in love (Jn 17:20-21). We must conclude that in John 9:39 the writer has used a vigorous literary device to stress the division that already exists between those who seek the light and those who shun it, a division not caused by the coming of Jesus but radically revealed by his coming.

Such apparent contradictions to the author's general theme, especially when deliberately stated with great force, turn out upon closer examination to be paradoxes, so frequent in the gospels that the experienced reader soon sees them as clues to deeper meanings than first suspected. Eventually, perceptive readers will discover that all the gospels are in such basic agreement in their faith in Jesus that a passage left ambiguous by the context of one gospel can be interpreted in the light of another. This procedure presupposes the underlying congruity of the scriptures, possible only if the Holy Spirit has really inspired each separate author.

Not only do New Testament books serve as context for one another, but the Hebrew scriptures are frequently the background context out of which the New Testament authors write. The careful reader must therefore be alert to Old Testament quotations, allusions and echoes in gospel passages. For example, the reader who knows the Old Testament well, or who makes diligent use of footnotes and cross references, will see in the "division" passage cited above, John 9:39, an echo of Isaiah 6:10:

> You are to make the heart of this people sluggish,
>   to dull their ears and *close their eyes*;
> Else their eyes will see, their ears hear,
>   their heart understand,
>   and they will turn and be healed.

If our reading detective makes further use of footnote clues and biblical commentaries, he or she will discover that Isaiah, in his effort to explain the otherwise inexplicable hardness of heart that he encountered in the chosen people, was resorting to an oxymoron, a statement that at first view appears foolish and thereby teases the reader into further thought. By attributing to Yahweh the intention of hardening the heart of his people, Isaiah is so blatantly contradicting his own constant effort to portray God as holy and merciful that he is thereby underlining the monstrous guilt of those who deliberately close their eyes to Yahweh's truth. By echoing Isaiah's language, John's Jesus is identifying himself as the one whom Yahweh sent to give sight to the blind and uncover the blindness of those who claimed to see. Admittedly this kind of research is hard work. To become a scripture-reading detective, even the best reader needs a companion.

Besides contextual clues a reading companion should alert the reader to many other clues by which the author points to his intended meaning: his conceptual priorities (for instance, the extent to which he subordinates facts to meaning), his selection of literary forms for each passage (the parable, the conflict story, the miracle story), his chief literary devices (repetition, parallelism, contrast, figurative language), his major themes, his theological perspective, his implicit use of customs of the times (such as the week-long celebration of marriage feasts underlying the wine problem at Cana). We will try to take these clues into account whenever they help us uncover the deeper meaning of passages that depict some characteristic of Jesus or offer insight into his personality.

Good detectives must maintain objective detachment as they trace the clues that throw light upon the mystery they are investigating. So must good reading detectives. But readers of the gospels, having made every effort to dig out their deepest meaning, will find that the gospels contain mysteries of faith to which they cannot remain purely objective. These are books through which God is calling to each reader in the depths of his or her very life. Readers of scripture must become personally involved in the mystery. Theirs is not only a head-trip but also a heart-trip, a life-trip from here to eternity.

Consequently, a reading companion should do more than help find clues to meaning; such a companion must also stimulate the kind of personal reflection upon the uncovered meaning that helps involve the reader in the mystery of Jesus Christ. To facilitate such reflection I have divided each gospel into convenient daily reading units that correspond, as closely as practicable, to original divisions discoverable in the author's more or less evident outline. And I have concluded each unit with questions and suggestions to encourage reflection on the reader's personal experiences in the light of the passage, meditation on how it might influence personal attitudes and decisions, contemplation of Jesus' words and actions, conversational prayer. In group discussion these same questions may also stimulate lively interchange.

We'll see much more of what it means to be a reading detective as we read. In this whole process we will be indebted to many scholars. Herein lies a further problem. The student of scripture soon finds that scholars frequently disagree. In fact, scholars can be found taking opposite sides on almost every issue. We must therefore do our best to look for consensus, weigh the findings, and finally select what seems most convincing and helpful according to available evidence.

Let's be especially careful to avoid looking for Jesus in our own imagination, making him in our own image or according to our own ideas of who or what he was. Instead, let's look for him in the greatest writings of the early Christians, in those accounts that they held as the authentic expression of their faith formed by the life, death and resurrection of Jesus, in the light of apostolic tradition and subsequent church teaching.

But should we read the gospels separately or combined into one continuous account of the life and teaching of Jesus?

Each Gospel in Its Own Right

From the second century there have been repeated attempts to combine the gospels into a single account. The harmonizer arranges the events of Jesus' life in the ''best'' chronological order and takes each incident from whichever gospel relates it in greatest detail, thereby forming one continuous narrative of the four. Some of these gospel harmonies seem to offer great advantages to the gospel reader: avoidance of repetition, elimination of disturbing differences, unity of approach and perspective.

But these efforts to present a single unified gospel are doomed for several reasons to produce inadequate results: First, because each evangelist writes with distinct objectives. Second, because each sees distinct aspects of the many-faceted splendor of Jesus; scholars speak of Mark's Jesus, Matthew's Jesus, Luke's Jesus, John's Jesus. Third, because the evangelists are often in disagreement about the chronological order of the events of Jesus' life. Fourth, because the effort to combine accounts inevitably loses the distinctive point of view and literary quality of each in a characterless conglomerate that reduces the original inspired authority of each evangelist to whatever scholarly authority the compiler might bring to his impossible task. Sometimes the evangelists give different meanings to the same event by the distinct contexts in which they place it, meanings that are lost or changed by any new arrangement used in combining the gospels.

More basically, those who genuinely respect the New Testament canon reject these gospel harmonies because it was the four gospels—none of the attempts to combine them—that were canonized by early Christians as authentic expressions of their faith. Moreover, modern scholars point out many passages in the gospels that cannot be satisfactorily harmonized. This is not to say that they contradict one another in the essentials of the Christian faith. But it does mean that the only adequate way to study them is to respect their individuality and deal with each as a separate entity, yet also as a part of that more complete revelation of Jesus Christ to be found in the whole New Testament. As an integral part of that whole, each gospel is equally the norm of our faith meriting our full effort of comprehension, appreciation and adherence.

Down through the centuries the four gospels have been recognized as distinct portrayals of Jesus. Modern scholars have made many careful studies of their differences. Comparisons of how the same event is treated in each gospel consistently reveal certain characteristics distinctive to each. The specific problems of each author's community greatly influenced his purpose in writing and therefore his selection of available materials, his sequence of events, his use of literary forms and devices, and so on. Above all, the author's theological vision and human limitations in the face of his inexhaustible subject influenced his Christological perspective:

Matthew sees Jesus above all as the universal Messiah who
fulfills the promises of the Old Testament;
Mark sees him as completely human, yet much more than
man;
Luke sees him as the compassionate, forgiving Savior;
John sees him as the divine Word become man.

The fact that each evangelist sees Jesus from a different perspective makes it imperative that we read each gospel separately as a distinct portrayal of Jesus, yet complementary to the other gospels.

Shall we then start with the gospel of Matthew, traditionally called the first gospel? Until recently, it was thought that Matthew wrote before the other evangelists. This opinion was based upon an early tradition attributed to Papias about 130 and repeated by Eusebius. But most scholars today agree that the evidence points to Mark's gospel as the first to be written, and that Matthew may have made use of Mark in later writing his gospel.

So let's start with Mark, not only because it is probably the first written and the shortest and most easily read, but more profoundly because it gives us the most intimate portrait of the human Jesus. Besides, since nearly all of Mark's gospel is repeated by both Matthew and Luke, the chapter on Mark can serve as our basic study of a large part of the first three gospels. Then, when we read Matthew and Luke, we will be able to concentrate our study on the passages proper to each, except for some observations about the way in which they modified the narration of incidents that they apparently repeated from Mark and about the contexts into which they fitted Jesus' sayings that they both seem to have received from another source, sometimes called Q.

As we read these gospels together, let's remember Paul's warning: "The letter brings death, but the Spirit gives life" (2 Cor 3:6). We must indeed attend to the letter of the text, but only to go beyond it, to read it in the spirit in which it was written. As Vatican II declared, "Holy Scripture must be read and interpreted according to the same Spirit by whom it was written" (*Dogmatic Constitution on Divine Revelation*, No. 12). If we read prayerfully in loving faith, the Spirit will reveal to us the most profound meaning of Jesus, the man-and-God who walked our earth and who still offers himself to us in our daily lives through the church, her community and her sacraments and through our relationships with family members and others. May his Holy Spirit guide us in this noblest search of all.

SUGGESTIONS FOR FURTHER READING OR REFERENCE

Childs, Brevard S. *The New Testament as Canon: An Introduction.* Philadelphia: Fortress Press, 1984. Excellent exposition of the canonical approach to interpretation; an overview of New Testament scholarship.

The Documents of Vatican II. Revised edition. Ed. Walter M. Abbott, S.J. America Press, 1967. Basic modern documents updating Catholic teaching, including *Dogmatic Constitution on Divine Revelation.*

Fitzmyer, Joseph A., S.J. *A Christological Catechism: New Testament Answers.* New York: Paulist Press, 1982. Excellent help for reading the gospels.

Harper's Bible Dictionary. Ed. Paul J. Achtemeier. San Francisco: Harper & Row, 1985. A very complete and informative ecumenical work.

The Jerome Biblical Commentary. Ed. Raymond E. Brown, et al. Englewood Cliffs, NJ: Prentice-Hall, 1968. A thorough and reliable commentary produced by leading Catholic scholars.

Kodell, Jerome, O.S.B. *The Catholic Bible Study Handbook.* Ann Arbor, MI: Servant Books, 1985. Interesting background for reading the Bible.

McKenzie, John L., S.J. *Dictionary of the Bible.* Milwaukee: Bruce, 1965. Valuable reference work on biblical terms and names.

Share the Word. Paulist Catholic Evangelization Center. A bimonthly commentary on Sunday Mass readings.

Teaching Authority and Infallibility in the Church: Lutherans and Catholics in Dialogue, 6. Minneapolis: Augsburg Publishing House, 1980. Joint statement of Lutheran and Catholic scholars and individual presentations.

The Teaching of the Catholic Church. Ed. Karl Rahner, S.J., Staten Island: Alba House, 1967. A selection of the most important church documents through the centuries.

Vatican II: Assessment and Perspectives. Ed. Rene Latourelle. New York: Paulist Press, 1988. Treats *Dogmatic Constitution on Divine Revelation* and other documents.

PART II

Finding the Human Jesus
With Mark

Mark and His Gospel

Of the author of the Gospel According to Mark we know little or nothing. Many scholars consider it probable that he is the John Mark who accompanied Paul and Barnabas on their first missionary journey (Acts 12:25; 13:5). Eusebius quotes Papias' testimony that Mark wrote what he could remember of Peter's teaching about the words and deeds of Jesus. Whether this tradition is true or not, it is interesting to note that at least some early Christians thought that Mark's principal source of knowledge of Jesus was none other than Peter himself. The author of 1 Peter, a letter that may have been written in Peter's name long after his death, reinforces this opinion by calling Mark "my son" (1 Pt 5:13).

It seems likely that Mark wrote his gospel soon after the martyrdom of Peter in Rome about A.D. 64. Perhaps some of the Christians who had read Paul's letter to the Romans or had heard Peter's final instructions and homilies were eager for more details about the events of Jesus' life. The deaths of Peter and Paul would almost certainly have impressed these early Christians with the need to preserve the apostolic teaching in writing.

If Mark really was the first to write a gospel, he must have been a literary genius despite his rough Greek, for he created a new literary genre that came to be known as the *gospel* form and served as model and probably chief source for Matthew and Luke.

Let's read Mark's gospel twice. The first time, just breeze right through it in one sitting. We are so used to hearing short passages from the gospels that it is a great new experience for most people to read an entire gospel from beginning to end without interruption. This is best done with Mark's, the shortest and most dramatically unified.

The cumulative effect is powerful, for Mark has composed his gospel as a drama of two intense acts that successively reveal the identity of Jesus. At the climax of the first act, Jesus himself asks his apostles: "Who do you say that I am?" and Peter says to him in reply, "You are the Messiah" (Mk 8:29). The second act begins with Jesus' prophecy that he must suffer and builds steadily through repetition of this disclosure and the darkening gloom of events to the final revelations on Calvary and at the empty tomb. It is a powerful drama that can be experienced only through continuous reading.

This first reading will prepare us to look more carefully into the details of this gospel in a second, piecemeal reading, for which the following sections are offered as pale substitutes for the companionship help that may have been available to early Christians from an apostle or from a missionary formed by one. Let's read with the intense interest and concentration of those first Christians discovering Jesus in their lives.

Act One: The Mystery of the Messiah
(Mk 1:1—8:30)

The Baptism of Jesus (Mk 1:1-13)

You will probably benefit most by reading the section of Mark indicated in the heading and then the corresponding part of the book. So begin by reading Mark 1:1-13, and then return here.

In his opening line Mark leaves no doubt about where he stands: "The beginning of the gospel of Jesus Christ, [the Son of God]" (Mk 1:1; brackets in *NAB*). Although the bracketed expression, "the Son of God," is missing from some important manuscripts, as part of the canonically accepted version of Mark it expresses the faith of the early Christians. With or without this phrase, it soon becomes obvious that Mark writes from the perspective of his faith in Jesus; he lays no claim to the objectivity of a modern historian.

Yet we should be wary of reading into the phrase "Son of God" the full meaning that theology has subsequently brought to it. Mark's original readers may have understood his opening use of that phrase in the Old Testament sense that was part of their mindset. The prophets spoke of God as the Father of Israel (Jer 31:9; Hos 11:1). In Psalm 89:27 God is called David's Father; in Psalm 2:7, the Lord speaks of Israel's king as his son. Even the ordinary Jew who remained faithful to the will of God could call himself "a child of the Lord" (Wis 2:13).

But, just as we should avoid reading too much into "Son of God," we must also avoid reading too little into it. Mark is obviously saying that Jesus is not just *a* son of God in the same sense as the passages just cited, but *the* son of God in some very special sense. In introducing him as Jesus Christ, Mark points toward a meaning consistent with that of *Christ* as "Messiah," the anointed one, the promised of Israel.

That Mark himself is thinking in Old Testament terms becomes evident when he introduces John the Baptist as Jesus' precursor by combining Malachi's prophecy of a special messenger (Mal 3:1) with Isaiah's prophecy of the voice crying out in the desert (Is 40:3), "Prepare the way of *the Lord*" (Mk 1:3). "The Lord" is the usual Old Testament substitute for "Yahweh," a name that the Jews considered too sacred to pronounce. Mark's application of Isaiah's prophecy to Jesus as "the Lord" for whom John is preparing clearly specifies the full sense of that initial designation of Jesus as "the Son of God": Jesus is "the Lord"! Only gradually, as we continue to read Mark, will the full meaning of these titles become clear to us.

The details that Mark chooses to describe John's dress are reminiscent of Elijah (2 Kgs 1:8), suggesting that John fulfills Malachi's prophecy:

> *Lo, I will send you*
> *Elijah, the prophet,*
> *Before the day of the* LORD *comes,*
> *the great and terrible day* (Mal 3:23).

This new Elijah contrasts his own lowliness to Jesus' power and dignity, his own baptism with water to Jesus' baptism "in the Holy Spirit" (Mk 1:7-8).

It is significant that the very first incident in which Mark's Jesus appears is his baptism in the Jordan by John:

> On coming up out of the water he saw the heavens being torn open and the Spirit, like a dove, descending upon him. And a voice came from the heavens, "You are my beloved Son; with you I am well pleased" (vv. 10-11).

41

Now it is God himself who identifies Jesus as his own Son!

As Moses went to the mountaintop to speak to God, the opening of the sky at Jesus' baptism forecasts a divine revelation by which God breaks into our world of sight and sound. God himself reveals who this Jesus really is! People of the ancient Mediterranean world thought of the dove as a symbol of divine love, a love now expressed in the Father's voice echoing Yahweh's words in Isaiah's ancient prophecy:

> "Here is my servant whom I uphold,
> my chosen one *with whom I am pleased*" (Is 42:1),

the same servant who is to be led "like a lamb . . . to the slaughter" (Is 53:7). But Jesus is much more than God's servant: "You are my *beloved Son*!"

The Spirit takes over the direction of Jesus' life, *driving* him into the desert for 40 days to be put to Satan's test, even as his people were tried during their 40-year sojourn in the desert during their Exodus from Egypt. Though Mark does not give details of the test, he suggests its severity by his reference to "wild beasts" and its victorious outcome by the phrase, "angels ministered to him" (v. 13). Perhaps Mark also wants his community to realize that their martyrs face the "wild beasts" that Jesus has already conquered.

SUGGESTIONS FOR PERSONAL REFLECTION AND PRAYER

General Questions for All Units

> Do I really believe that God is speaking to me in this passage?
>
> How does the passage touch my experience?
>
> How does it light up my life?
>
> To what response in attitude, prayer, action is God calling me?

Come, Holy Spirit, Inspirer of Holy Scripture, inspire me to understand the truth you are here revealing and move me to accept it in faith and to embrace it with love.

Specific Questions for This Unit

> Do I really believe that Jesus Christ is the true and only Son of God?
>
> Do I believe he is yet a man who submitted himself to John's baptism?

Holy Spirit, I know that you are the Spirit who dwelt in Jesus; live also in me. Father, through the Holy Spirit lead me to your beloved Son Jesus.

Jesus Begins His Public Ministry With Power Over Evil (Mk 1:14-45)

John's arrest seems to be the signal for Jesus to begin his public life. He announces the time of fulfillment of Yahweh's promise of his kingdom and therefore calls for faith and reform. "The time of fulfillment" would have evoked anew in the minds of Mark's original readers the prophecy of Malachi that we have already seen him link with John the Baptist:

> Lo, I will send you
> Elijah, the prophet,
> Before *the day of the LORD* comes (Mal 3:23).

Mark's Jesus, then, is telling us that his own day is "the day of the Lord," the "time of fulfillment" of God's promise to bring about his kingdom.

"The kingdom of God is at hand" would bring to his readers the memory of Daniel's prophecy:

> In the lifetime of those kings [of the vision of Nebuchadnezzar] *the God of heaven will set up a kingdom* that shall never be destroyed or delivered up to another people; rather, it shall break in pieces all these kingdoms [of men] and put an end to them, and it shall stand forever (Dn 2:44).

The kingdom of God that Jesus announces as imminent was generally understood by the Jewish leaders of his time to be a state in which God would free his chosen people from all foreign oppression and restore the line of Davidic kings. *Salvation* was seen as a temporal and political good. But, as we shall soon see, Jesus is declaring war on an evil greater than a temporal one. For him, the kingdom of God is the rule of Goodness itself, calling for an all-out struggle against the powers of evil, especially against the spiritual realm of evil, the kingdom of Satan.

As the first words of Jesus reported in Mark, this declaration takes on special significance. It announces the beginning of a new era in the history of the world! It is the beginning "of the gospel of Jesus Christ" (v. 1), the beginning of the message that is Jesus himself, bringer and embodiment of the kingdom of God.

The kingdom or reign of God will become one of the most frequently used expressions in the first three gospels, even their central theme. With the appearance of Jesus, God begins reigning on earth, taking his rightful place in the life of his people. As we proceed through Mark, let us watch how the meaning of *kingdom of God* steadily grows.

God will reign only in the lives of those who "repent, and believe in the gospel" (v. 15). The Greek word *metanoia*, "repent," "reform" or "convert," calls for a definitive change of mind, heart and will—a change of the whole person. Jesus is calling for a change from a life without God or hope of salvation to a life of faith in the God who saves us. Such a change produces a new man or woman, one who not only lets God into his or her life but returns God's loving offer with love. The whole world of such a person changes into the joyful kingdom of God!

According to Mark, Jesus' first act toward bringing the kingdom of God is to choose his closest followers. In relating how he calls them, Mark gives us an initial insight into the dynamic magnetism of Jesus' personality: "Then they left their nets and followed him. . . . left their father . . . and followed him" (vv. 18-20). As he begins teaching in the synagogue at Capernaum his listeners feel this same power: "The people were astonished at his teaching, for he taught them as one having authority" (v. 22).

He gathers followers, he teaches with authority, and he begins to perform mighty works by driving an unclean spirit from a possessed man. We might find ourselves wondering why Mark calls this spirit "unclean," for he seems to be a friendly demon who recognizes Jesus as "the Holy One of God!" (v. 24). But he is one of a group that can expect only destruction at the hands of "the Holy One." In this first healing reported by Mark, Jesus begins his campaign against "the evil one" and all his minions.

Jesus' command that the demon be quiet is the first of his many efforts to keep his identity hidden. Some scholars suggest that this "messianic secret" may have been Jesus' way of gaining time to show what kind of Messiah he really was—one who must suffer—before revealing his identity. The general expectation favored a conquering king in David's line, one who would win independence from the Roman oppressors. From the beginning of his gospel, Mark presents Jesus as a mysterious figure whose real identity will become clear only gradually.

With dramatic power Jesus expels the shrieking demon. The amazed crowd wonders what this action really means. Jesus' reputation spreads "throughout the whole region of Galilee" (v. 28), not so much by what he says as by what he does. In Mark, Jesus is the man of action rather than words.

Now more action: the cure of Peter's mother-in-law. Notice Jesus' delicacy in treating her: "He approached, grasped her hand, and helped her up" (v. 31). She responds with action; she waits on them.

News of the cure travels fast; the people bring all their sick to him and he cures them, again silencing the demons "because they knew him" (v. 34). So ends Mark's presentation of a typical day in Jesus' new public life.

And now, Mark reports another human touch: Jesus rises early to pray apart. He avoids the gathering crowd by moving on to the neighboring villages. But he is not indulging in escapism; he is soon gathering more crowds by continuing his preaching and good works.

This tremendous opening chapter of Mark finally ends with a truly climactic miracle: the cure of leprosy, seen in those days as one of the most dreaded embodiments of evil. For the first of many times Mark points out a human emotion in Jesus: "Moved with *pity*, he stretched out his hand, *touched him*" (v. 41)—touched a leper, an act considered so dangerous that lepers were forced by law to carry a bell to warn people away at their approach! Yet this great wonderworker humbly submits to the law of Moses by sending the cured man to the priest who alone is authorized to verify his cure (Lv 13:16-17). In spite of Jesus' admonition not to tell anyone else (again the messianic secret), the cured man tells everybody and Jesus has no peace from the pressing crowds in the towns or even in the desert.

REFLECTION AND PRAYER

For general questions for all units, see page 42.

> Do I really believe that Jesus can cure all my ills too—the demonic temptations that sometimes obsess me, the leprosy of sin that haunts me, even my physical ills?

Have compassion on me, dear Jesus, and cure me of every evil that shuts off my life even partially from God's reign.

Jesus Opposes Sin, But Not the Sinner (Mk 2:1-17)

Jesus accepts the demands upon him and returns to Capernaum, where Mark says he is "at home" (Mk 2:1), apparently having made Peter's house his headquarters. Mark now relates one of his most descriptive miracles. By carefully pointing out that Jesus is moved to action by the practical faith of the paralyzed man's friends, Mark suggests to his readers the importance of their prayers for one another *as a community*. Jesus sees a deeper paralysis in the man than his physical affliction; otherwise, his first words do not fit the occasion: "Child, your sins are forgiven" (v. 5). The intimacy of that greeting encourages the paralyzed man to believe that Jesus is really forgiving him.

For the first time Mark introduces human adversaries in his drama, the scribes (learned teachers, often Pharisees, v. 16), who now whisperingly accuse Jesus of blasphemy in attributing to himself a power that belongs to God alone. Mark thus introduces the question of the divinity of Jesus.

Jesus reads their grumbling or their minds and, far from retracting, proceeds to prove the invisible healing of the paralytic's spirit by the visible cure of his body, "that you may know that the *Son of Man* has authority to forgive sins on earth" (v. 10). This is the first time in Mark that Jesus refers to himself with that mysterious phrase "Son of Man." At this solemn moment in which he manifests his divine power, Jesus insists on his humanity, his solidarity with his fellow men. "Son of Man" is also a designation of authority and power, as shown by this incident. The crowd is "astounded" by Jesus' power, a power and authority that they instinctively recognize as sacred, for they "glorified God" (v. 12).

This episode clearly shows the function of the miracle story, a gospel form that Mark will continue to use frequently to demonstrate that Jesus acts with the power of God and therefore speaks the message of God.

Jesus continues to choose disciples, this time Levi, one of the despised group of tax collectors. Since Jewish tax collectors were engaged by the Romans to exact from their own people the money that financed the Roman occupation, they were considered traitors—and cheaters, for they could keep as their own whatever they collected above the tax required by the Romans. Not only does Jesus deliberately choose such a man as one of his closest followers, he further violates popular taboos and the oral tradition of the Pharisees by entering the sinner's house, thereby incurring the stigma of becoming ''unclean.'' Still worse, he eats with other known sinners, making himself one of their number. Jesus deliberately ignores the prejudices of the public opinion and religious authority of his time and people, so eager is he to reach the lost sheep of Israel.

For such actions he must eventually pay the price of challenging the leaders of his people, the Pharisees, who consider it their special function to assure the public observance of their law. He is ready with the response: ''I did not come to call the righteous but sinners'' (v. 17). Shocking to the Pharisees, but comforting to us.

REFLECTION AND PRAYER

For general questions for all units, see page 42.

Am I friendly toward those considered the dregs of society?

Do I have the courage to ignore public opinion when I find it running counter to the norms of Jesus?

Lord, I am one of those sinners you have come to save. Just as you cured the inner paralysis of the man lowered from the roof, cure my moral paralysis, too.

Jesus' Controversies With the Pharisees (Mk 2:18—3:6)

Jesus' first brush with the Pharisees seems to remind Mark of other controversies, such as that initiated by the people who question Jesus for not expecting his disciples to fast as do the disciples of the Pharisees and of John the Baptist. Jesus' answer is even more audacious than before: ''Can the wedding guests fast while the *bridegroom* is with them?'' (v. 19). The obvious meaning of this question is that Jesus' presence among his disciples is cause for celebration. But the specific reference to the bridegroom suggests a far deeper meaning to the mind trained in the prophets. Hosea, especially, had spoken poetically of the relationship between God and Israel as that of a groom to his bride (Hos 2:1-18). In biblical language that the Pharisees can hardly miss Jesus is implying that he himself is this groom of Israel, none other than Yahweh!

The obscure passage that follows (vv. 21-22) suggests that with Jesus' coming as Israel's groom—and especially with his death (v. 20)—a new age is dawning, a new relationship of humanity with God through Jesus. God is making a new covenant with his people, not just patching an old garment with new cloth, but forming an entirely new relationship in a new spirit ("wine") that requires a new response by a new people ("skins").

In verse 23 Mark seems to be indicating a time-and-place change between incidents: "As he was passing through a field of grain on the sabbath . . ." Here time and place are so transparently vague as to suggest that Mark uses such references as a literary device to signal the end of one unit (pericope) in his gospel and the beginning of another. In this instance the real relationship between events is similarity of substance. What connects the incidents of this chapter is the difference between the teaching of the Pharisees and that of Jesus concerning the observance of the sabbath. Time and place, then, are often of secondary importance to Mark; frequently he refers to them merely to separate or relate incidents rather than as event markers that he expects us to take as strict "gospel truth."

This time the Pharisees themselves attack Jesus for allowing his disciples to pull off grain from the stalks for a frugal meal. Such taking of grain was not considered stealing, for the Jews were encouraged to be a bit careless in harvesting their crops in order that widows, orphans and the poor might have something to glean (see Dt 24:19-22). These followers of Jesus are not ashamed to be identified with the poor. But according to the tradition of the Pharisees, gleaning is classified as work unbecoming the sabbath observance.

Jesus does not accept the accusation that his disciples have broken the sabbath law by attending to their need for food. In their defense he cites the example of David, who demanded for his hungry followers even the holy bread reserved for priests. According to Mark, Jesus names *Abiathar* as the high priest involved. But 1 Samuel 21:2-7 relates that the high priest in this incident was *Ahimelech*. Both Matthew and Luke, who also report this controversy, seem to be aware of the confusion of names, for they avoid naming the high priest at all.

Was it Jesus or Mark who confused the names? Or is this confusion really due to discrepancies in the traditions reported in the books of Samuel? In 1 Samuel 22:20, Abiathar is the *son* of Ahimelech; in 2 Samuel 8:17, he is the *father* of Ahimelech! Whatever its source, this confusion of names should again make clear to us that insistence on a too literal reading of the Bible can be disastrous. Were we to take this question of Abiathar or Ahimelech as a test of our faith in the word of God, we would have to end up rejecting 1 Samuel, 2 Samuel or Mark—

or all three. But this kind of test is certainly not in accord with what the Catholic church officially holds, as expressed at Vatican II: "The books of scripture must be acknowledged as teaching firmly, faithfully, and without error *that truth which God wanted put into the sacred writings for the sake of our salvation*" (*Dogmatic Constitution on Divine Revelation*, No. 11, italics added). It is hardly necessary for our salvation to know whether it was Ahimelech or Abiathar who gave food to David's men!

But this section in Mark does contain a truth important for our salvation: "The sabbath was made for man, not man for the sabbath" (v. 27). Mark's Jesus would not have us think of God as a maker of marionettes to fulfill his laws; rather he would have us see God as a loving Father who has made all things, including his own day, for our good. Jesus thus defines the Christian attitude toward divine law, not as blind obedience to arbitrary rules, but as grateful acceptance of the loving will of God.

One of the copyists of this passage was apparently so inspired by it that he seems to have added the next sentence: "That is why the Son of Man is lord even of the sabbath" (v. 28). Whether the addition of a copyist, as some scholars believe, or the original saying of Jesus, this little sentence is important for our faith, for it was accepted as a canonical part of Mark's gospel. And it does have something to tell us about Jesus, much more than do the names Abiathar and Ahimelech.

The special emphasis given this point about the spirit of the sabbath identifies this passage as a controversy story, a gospel literary form designed by the writer to utilize a situation as the occasion for an important proclamation—in this case, the loving spirit in which we are to keep the day that God made special for us.

In chapter 3 the running controversy with the Pharisees continues. Does Mark want us to think that the Pharisees deliberately plant the man with the withered hand in front of Jesus in the synagogue? It seems so, for he adds: "They watched him [Jesus] closely to see if he would cure him on the sabbath *so that they might accuse him*" (v. 2). Jesus does not hesitate to take up the challenge, advocating a more humane interpretation of the sabbath obligation. But they respond only with silence. Mark again records strong emotions in Jesus, "looking around at them *with anger* and *grieved* at their hardness of heart" (v. 5). Mark's description seems deliberately worded to remind us of a similar passage in Genesis: "When the Lord saw how great was man's wickedness on earth . . . his heart *was grieved*" (Gn

6:5-6). Even through his description of Jesus' emotions Mark is sometimes able not only to portray the humanity of Jesus, but also to suggest his divinity.

Then the cure. Far from being moved either by the humane appeal of Jesus or by the power of his healing action, Mark's Pharisees now show to what extent their hearts are hardened against Jesus; they join their political enemies, the followers of King Herod (hated because he was put over Judea by the Romans) to plot the death of Jesus. With this sinister development Mark foreshadows the inevitable outcome of the collision course with the Jewish leaders that will be forced upon Jesus if he continues to demand a new understanding of a God who loves men more than these leaders can imagine.

REFLECTION AND PRAYER

> Do I try to see God's laws as the loving directions of a Father who wants the best for me?
>
> Do I try to observe the Lord's Day as Jesus did?

Lord Jesus, give me a share in your great love of the Father!

Jesus Begins Forming His Disciples (Mk 3:7-35)

Jesus does not seek controversy. He withdraws from the cities, but a huge crowd of both Jews and Gentiles crush in upon him to touch him and be cured. Again the unclean spirits call him the "Son of God" (v. 11), and again he orders secrecy.

Retreating up a mountain, he finally achieves enough peace and seclusion to devote himself to his chosen ones. He now brings his struggle against evil to a new dimension by formally naming twelve of his followers to be his special companions and by bestowing upon them his authority over demons. To Simon he gives the new name Peter, reminiscent of God's renaming Abraham to signify his covenant with him and his people (Gn 17:4-5). This special designation of *Peter*, which means "rock," sets him apart as leader of the new people of God. In a less solemn vein Jesus nicknames James and John "sons of thunder," equivalent to "the roaring boys" or "loudmouths." And even at this early point Mark reminds us that one of the Twelve will betray Jesus (v. 19).

Back to headquarters, and sure enough, such a crowd gathers that Jesus can't even eat a meal. Some of his family members come to rescue him from his own fanaticism: "He is out of his mind" (v. 21). Even some of those closest in blood ties to Jesus fail to penetrate the secret of his identity.

Again the scribes attack him, now with the vilest accusation: "'He is possessed by Beelzebul,' and 'By the prince of demons he drives out demons'" (v. 22). They accuse him of submitting to the guidance of a spirit so powerful in evil as to be the "prince of demons," the epitome of evil!

He tries to reason with them: "How can Satan drive out Satan?" (v. 23). But they are now far beyond reason. So he warns them that to call his guiding spirit *Satan* is deliberately to call goodness itself evil, for Jesus' guiding spirit is the *Holy Spirit*, as verse 29 clearly implies. Their attitude is the ultimate closing of the mind to all truth and of the heart to all goodness. As long as they persist in this utter perversity, their sinfulness is unforgivable, for God does not violate the free will that he has given us, even when we turn that will completely against him.

And now comes a passage about which Christians have differed for centuries: "His mother and his brothers arrived" (v. 31). *Brothers?* Did Jesus have blood brothers or sisters? Some Christians emphatically say yes; others just as emphatically say no. The original Greek word *adelphoi* could mean "blood brothers," "half brothers," "cousins," "members of the same clan or tribe," or even "members of the same race or nation." If the "brothers" were really Jesus' cousins, as Jerome and other Fathers of the church thought, Jesus and his disciples would certainly have called them "brothers"; the Aramaic language that they spoke lacked a more precise word for cousins. Such usage would naturally have influenced the evangelists in their choice of words when they later wrote in Greek.

There is some evidence in Mark's gospel that these are not Jesus' blood brothers. In 6:3 Mark names four "brothers" of Jesus: James, Joses, Judas and Simon, and in 15:40 he names three women watching the death of Jesus from afar: "Mary Magdalen, *Mary the mother of the younger James and of Joses*, and Salome." It seems obvious that this second Mary is *not* the mother of Jesus, and probable that she *is* the mother of at least two of the above-named "brothers of Jesus."

But most scholars consider textual analysis inconclusive on this question. In the end, Christians who do not accept the ancient tradition of the church as authoritative in this matter consider themselves free to interpret Mark 3:31 and similar passages as referring to blood brothers of Jesus. Catholics and other Christians who accept that tradition will continue to interpret such passages as referring to Jesus' cousins or relatives, especially in view of another constant tradition of the church: Mary was ever a virgin.

There is still another point of division among Christians at the end of chapter 3. Jesus declares: "Whoever does the will of God is my brother and sister and *mother*" (v. 35). Some readers see this statement as Jesus' own testimony that Mary is no more important to him than any other good Christian. Others see it as an indirect declaration of Mary's importance as the very first model for carrying out God's will. Unfortunately, Mark offers no context by which to resolve this ambiguity. To espouse either of these interpretations without more evidence seems capricious.

In such a case we must look to the broader context of the whole New Testament, of which Mark is an integral part. If God inspired all the parts of the New Testament, they must all somehow fit together, at least in matters of importance for our Christian faith. And it is certainly of great interest to us to know how Jesus thought of his own mother. The answer to that question goes a long way toward identifying the Jesus we believe in, defined by his relationships, especially by his relationship with the human being who was closest to him.

Luke has left no room for doubt about his interpretation of this passage, which he apparently adapted from Mark. When we read Luke's version we shall see how he helps us interpret Mark by suggesting that the Christian who does the will of God is mother to Jesus in the sense of spiritually conceiving him in a heart dedicated to God, as was Mary's heart, an interpretation for which Luke prepares us in his first two chapters.

But Mark is obviously not concerned in this passage with the question of Jesus' relationship with Mary. Rather, he is focusing attention wholly on identifying the true follower of Jesus as the person who does the Father's will and thereby attains *a relationship with Jesus as real and intimate as that of a member of his immediate family*. This is an exciting moment in our search for the inner personality of the Jesus presented in the gospels. In this passage Mark is clearly telling us that Jesus eagerly invites all his followers to the closest possible relationship with him, a spiritual relationship closer than blood ties, and sets a single requirement for attaining this relationship: *Do the will of God*.

REFLECTION AND PRAYER

Do I really believe that if I try to do God's will, Jesus will look upon me as his own brother or sister?

Dear Lord, what a wonderful relationship you are calling me to form with you!

Jesus Teaches in Parables (Mk 4:1-34)

Thus far Mark has reported only a few words of Jesus. Mark's has been the gospel of Jesus-the-great-healer, Jesus-on-the-move. But at last Mark settles down to give us a deeper insight into the message of Jesus in the form of parables. Appropriately, the first parable he relates tells us what to do with a parable: "Whoever has ears to hear ought to hear" (v. 9). The disciples listen but do not really hear him; they ask for an explanation.

In verse 12 Jesus seems to respond that he teaches in parables because he does not really want the crowd to understand him. As we have seen in tracing a similar thought in John 9:39 to Isaiah 6:9-10 (p. 33), this use of Old Testament language by Jesus is really a lament that the people are not hearing him, that they have closed their minds and hearts to him. In verse 33 Mark shows clear awareness that Jesus chose the parable as a simple and intriguing form of presentation precisely because he wanted the simple people to understand his message.

For his disciples, more eager than the crowd to understand him, Jesus meticulously explains the parable point by point to show them the importance not only of listening to the word of God but also of *hearing* it, that is, mulling over it, meditating on it until they penetrate its meaning. Isn't that precisely what we are trying to do in our gospel reading? If the disciples do not really hear Jesus, the kingdom of God can never achieve its full impact upon the world, for "the mystery of the kingdom of God has been granted *to you*" (v. 11). Jesus is back to that opening theme of "the kingdom of God"; they will understand only if they make the effort to hear him, only if they open themselves to the mystery that he is revealing.

That early Christians made this effort to see all the possible meanings of this parable may account for Mark's allegorical explanation in which the seed that symbolized "the word" in the parable is now made to symbolize also the different recipients of the word, "the ones

on the path . . . on rocky ground . . . among thorns . . . on rich soil''
(vv. 15-20).

Jesus follows up this first parable with another. The not-to-be-hidden lamp suggests the role of the true follower of Jesus who, having first understood his message, is called to become a guiding light for others. Notice how often in these verses Mark's Jesus stresses the importance of listening in order to hear.

Another parable, that of the seed that grows without the farmer's knowing how, illustrates the mysterious nature of God's reign, of his silent action among us. Real growth in the kingdom is not our doing, but God's.

The parable of the tiny mustard seed that grows into the largest of shrubs and serves as a nesting place for birds suggests again that the kingdom of God will not really be the work of humanity but primarily of God himself. It also foretells that, although the kingdom begins as a small seed, perhaps like Mark's own community, it will grow rapidly to become a great haven for men and women of all kinds.

Mark's comments in verses 33-34 tell us his own concept of the function of the parable as a literary form: to teach the message in a way the people can understand. Jesus accepts his people as they are and uses the simplest examples from their daily experience, gently coaxing them to open their minds and hearts to him. Through his parables Jesus is preparing the people, so long without a true prophet, to see God and his kingdom in a new way. The parables offer them a vague opening into this new revelation, tease them into listening more intently to the message that Jesus and his disciples will gradually unfold to them.

REFLECTION AND PRAYER

Do I really hear the message of Jesus?

To what extent do I apply it to the details of my own life to open myself to God's reign in me?

Lord Jesus, teach me how to listen to you in my prayers rather than merely fill them with words that you already read in my heart.

New Revelations of Jesus' Power (Mk 4:35—5:20)

Mark now presents Jesus as having so spent himself in these teaching efforts that even a bad squall does not awaken him as he sleeps in the boat. The frightened disciples shake him awake to cope with the situation. Their waking him might seem an act of confidence in his ability to do something about the storm, but he sees it as evidence that they still don't really believe in him. He quiets the storm and then rebukes them. Mark pictures him there in the boat, raising his voice majestically to calm the raging wind and water. Obviously Mark wants us to join the disciples in asking: "Who then is this whom even wind and sea obey?" (v. 41). Mark challenges the depth of our own faith in Jesus.

Aside from the powerful drama of the moment itself, this act of Jesus must have been particularly impressive to the early Christians because of their vivid memories of the Old Testament portrayal of Yahweh, the One who alone could bring order out of chaos as "a mighty wind swept over the waters" (Gn 1:2) or calm the violent storms that frightened the best of sailors (see Ps 107:23-29).

Perhaps as impressive as the picture of the divine power of Jesus in this incident is that of his human frailty. We might wonder whether Mark wants us to think that Jesus was really so deeply asleep that even the violent tossing of the boat on the waves did not awaken him. Is Mark saying that Jesus was testing his disciples? Such an interpretation seems unworthy of Jesus. Can we really imagine Jesus lying there, pretending to sleep, to see what his disciples would do? No, Mark is evidently telling us that Jesus suffered the same human limitations that we do. He needed sleep; he knew exhaustion. And he suffered the same human emotions that we do, the same disappointment with his friends when he saw signs of distrust in them. His surprise at their fright clearly suggests his lack of foreknowledge of how his disciples would react under duress.

The combination of Jesus' divine power and human frailty, which Mark skillfully reveals in this incident, are expressed more explicitly but abstractly by the author of Hebrews: "God spoke . . . to us through a son . . . / who is the refulgence of his glory, / the very imprint of his being, / and who sustains all things by his mighty word" (Heb 1:1-3); and yet, "he had to become like his brothers in every way" (Heb 2:17). "For we do not have a high priest who is unable to sympathize with our weakness, but one who has similarly been tested in every way, yet without sin" (Heb 4:15).

Mark's chapter 5 opens with one of the most curious incidents in the gospels. Mark describes at length the uncontrollable strength (vv. 3-4) and self- destructive actions (v. 5) of the madman dwelling among the tombs, possessed by "an unclean spirit" (v. 2). The man runs to Jesus and falls before him, evidently seeking his help. But the loud voice that comes from him is that of the unclean spirit proclaiming Jesus "Son of the Most High God" (v. 7), an identification far beyond the madman's power. It becomes even clearer whose voice is speaking when he pleads, "Do not torment me!" At Jesus' demand to know his name, he responds, "Legion," that is, enough demons to form a unit of the Roman army! These demons, evidently considering this land as their own "territory" (v. 10), yet realizing that they cannot escape the power of the Son of God, ask for mercy, even if it means exchanging their present habitat for that of swine, animals that the Jews considered unclean. Jesus surprisingly accedes. They further reveal their true identity by self-destructing; they drive the whole herd they now inhabit into the lake—the best thing that could happen to swine, as far as Jews were concerned!

But these Gentiles value their swine more than they do the man now restored to sanity, for they ask Jesus to leave. Jesus does so, but first tells the healed man to proclaim "all that the Lord in his pity has done for you" (v. 19), just the reverse of the messianic secret. The Gentiles needed to know God's mercy through Jesus and would not be confused by any false expectations of the Messiah; they had none to start with.

Perhaps Mark saw a still deeper meaning in this incident. It certainly fits his pattern of urging his readers to have complete confidence in Jesus' power over evil of all kinds. Perhaps today, even more than in Mark's time, we need Jesus' power over the "unclean spirits" of greed, hostility, indifference, destructiveness, despair and suicide.

REFLECTION AND PRAYER

Do I believe that Jesus alone makes life meaningful?

Lord Jesus, save me from the storms that threaten my life.

Jesus Works A Miracles Within a Miracle (Mk 5:21—6:6)

Mark now presents two interrelated miracles, both in favor of members of the historically ill-favored female sex. He occasionally tells one story within another, gaining subtle meaning through juxtaposition.

As Jesus is on his way to attend to the daughter of Jairus, he suddenly becomes "aware . . . that power had gone out from him" (v. 30). The disciples find his question about who touched his clothes rather ridiculous in view of the press of the crowd about him. Trembling, the woman who has been healed by touching him falls at his feet in admission. He comforts and compliments her: *"Daughter*, your *faith* has saved you" (v. 34). Her faith has admitted her into his family in accord with his promise in Mark 3:35!

But the incident leaves us with questions. Is Mark suggesting that Jesus really didn't even know whom he had cured? Is Mark saying that in sharing our human condition, Jesus also suffered our ignorance? Such an interpretation would not be unlikely in view of the surprise, for instance, that Mark has just reported as a possible manifestation of Jesus' lack of foreknowledge of how the disciples would react during the storm on the lake.

However, a much better case can be made here for compassion. This timid woman needed psychological as well as physical help. Surely if Mark's Jesus knew that "power had gone out" from him, and that it was because of her faith, we can conclude that he also knew to whom the cure had been given. His question, "Who touched me?" (v. 31) would then have been the kind of encouragement that this woman needed to calm her fears and bring her forward to witness openly to his compassionate power.

As Jesus is about to continue toward the house of Jairus, he is notified that Jairus' daughter has died. Now he must calm the fears of Jairus. This calming of fear, common to both of these intertwined stories, may be Mark's reason for combining them—if, indeed, he is combining incidents that were originally separate.

To witness this raising from the dead, Jesus selects from the Twelve only Peter, James and John, the three who will later see him in his agony. Though he expels the ridiculing mob with severity, Jesus approaches the dead child with delicate sensitivity: "He *took the child by the hand* and said to her, *'Talitha, koum'"* (v. 41; second set of italics in *NAB*), an expression in the Aramaic language that Jesus actually spoke; it is not understood by those for whom Mark writes, since he proceeds to translate it for them. Then Jesus adds the very human reminder to the parents to give her something to eat (v. 43). Almost casually Mark relates this tremendous miracle of raising the girl back to life.

In this rapid succession of miracles Mark has shown us Jesus' power over evil in many forms: over natural evils by calming the storm, over evil spirits by curing the madman, over chronic sickness by curing the woman with the hemorrhage, and even over death itself by raising the daughter of Jairus.

If he does so much for strangers, what will he do for his own people of Nazareth, to whom he now returns (Mk 6:1)? His sermon astonishes his hometown people in the synagogue—until they remember that he is only one of them, after all. They know him as "the son of Mary" (v. 3), a designation opposite to the Jewish custom of referring to a man as son of his father, even if dead. Is Mark here implying the virginal conception of Jesus? Is he also using "son of Mary" as a more specific equivalent of "Son of Man" in anticipation of the rejection by his own people that Jesus will now suffer?

Jesus knows that "a prophet is not without honor *except in his native place*" (v. 4). Nevertheless their rejection hurts him:

> He was not able to perform any mighty deed there, apart from curing a few sick people by laying his hands on them. He was amazed at their lack of faith (vv. 5-6).

He can work only a few little miracles at Nazareth because he will not violate his people's free will to reject him! Like us, he is vulnerable to the reactions of others; he has human feelings that can be hurt, so badly hurt as to appear to inhibit his power to act. Yet this inhibition is due not to any debilitating resentment on his part but to "their lack of faith." Might not this passage also suggest to us, who have no direct experience of Jesus' presence, that the efficacy of his sacramental presence among us is conditioned by our own response of faith?

REFLECTION AND PRAYER

Do I dare pray for miracles for myself or others?

Is the lack of Jesus' presence in my life due to the weakness of my own faith in him?

Jesus, I know that you suffered the same human condition that sometimes weighs me down. Give me a greater faith in your love for me.

Jesus Continues Educating the Twelve (Mk 6)

Jesus quickly leaves the stifling atmosphere of Nazareth to teach in the neighboring villages. He thus finishes the first phase of the education of his chosen ones, the Twelve, for now he is ready to send them out in pairs. As he does so, he gives them a share in his own "authority over unclean spirits" (v. 7). Jesus' followers are to continue his war on evil, especially moral evil.

The instructions he gives them furnish a model for the simplicity of lifestyle of his missionaries; they are to become increasingly independent of material needs. They are to take neither food nor money.

Mark seems to consider it a concession on Jesus' part to allow them to wear sandals! They are to become dependent on the charity of others for shelter and food. Those who refuse them this elemental charity evidently lack the one disposition required for receiving the gospel message. By following the Jewish custom of shaking "Gentile" dust from their feet, the Twelve are to warn those who will not listen to this message that they are equivalent to pagans.

Off they go, with a good measure of success in expelling demons and working cures. Notice that not all illnesses are attributed to demons. They "anointed with oil many who were sick" (v. 13), the basis for the ritual that eventually came to be known as the sacrament of anointing the sick.

All this missionary activity further enhances the fame of Jesus, so that even Herod hears of him and superstitiously fears that Jesus is really John the Baptist returned to life. Mark here inserts the story of how Herod executed John. Unnecessary as the story may seem—Matthew briefly summarizes it and Luke omits it—by relating it at this point in his gospel, Mark foreshadows the death and burial of Jesus as the inevitable result of his mission against universal evil, the mission in which John had participated by his courageous denunciation of Herod's crime.

In reporting the return of the successful Twelve, Mark significantly speaks of them for the first time as apostles (v. 30), that is, "the sent." Jesus tries to take them to a quiet place for a restful retreat, but they are again so pressed by the crowd that they can't even eat. He tries to escape with them in a boat, but the crowd anticipates his every move. His compassion proves greater than his desire for peace: *"His heart was moved with pity for them*, for they were like sheep without a shepherd" (v. 34). He becomes their shepherd and teaches them. And good shepherd that he is, he feeds them.

Is this, as some scholars contend, a purely symbolic meal to signify that Jesus is feeding their souls by his teaching? Hardly, for Mark has already made the literal statement: "He began to teach them many things" (v. 34). Jesus feeds them a physical meal that symbolizes what is to come: the equally real sacramental meal of his own body and blood (v. 41).

Mark points out how Jesus utilizes the occasion to continue the education of the "disciples" (v. 30)—they are still far from ready to be sent definitively—by involving them in the service of feeding the crowd. And it is no small crowd: "The people took their places in rows by hundreds and fifties" (v. 40). The description sounds like an eyewitness account of a liturgical setting. This impression is confirmed by the ensuing description of Jesus' actions: "Looking up to heaven, he said the blessing, broke the loaves, and gave them to [his] disciples to set before the people" (v. 41). Mark's description may be influenced by the liturgy that has already developed around the Eucharist by the time of his writing.

It has also been suggested that this miracle of feeding the crowd was psychological rather than physical, that some of the people had carried along food, which they selfishly reserved for themselves, but were moved to unselfish sharing with others by the teaching and example of Jesus in sharing the five loaves and two fish carried by the disciples. Such inspired sharing does indeed seem more significant than physical multiplication of food, and perhaps even more miraculous. Nor would it necessarily replace the physical miracle. Whatever the explanation, something marvelous happened on this occasion that gave rise to a strong tradition used by all four evangelists in distinctive ways.

Again Jesus puts the disciples on their own, sending them ahead of him across the lake. Dismissing the crowd, he goes off to the mountain to pray. Mark thereby suggests both Jesus' need for solitude and the elevating effect of his prayer. Mark's Jesus is a human model for Christians.

Jesus does not lose contact with the world of his disciples. As the wind rises over the lake, he sees from his high vantage point the futile efforts of the Twelve to row against the wind; he approaches them, "walking on the sea" (v. 48). They take him for a ghost, and he must reassure them. Not only have they forgotten how he calmed the storm; they have not even understood the multiplication of the loaves on the previous day (v. 52). What a disappointing and lonely moment for Jesus!

And again the crowd presses in upon him, bringing their sick, making ever greater demands upon his energy. He willingly submits to their demands: "As many as touched it [the tassel on his cloak] were healed" (v. 56).

REFLECTION AND PRAYER

Do I consider myself a disciple, a follower, of Jesus?

Even more, do I consider myself an apostle to bring his word of grace to others?

Would I have been one of those who strove to touch Jesus' cloak to be healed?

Lord Jesus, I come much closer to you than that whenever I receive the Eucharist. Heal me even now as I welcome you spiritually into my heart.

Jesus' Mission to the Gentiles (Mk 7:1—8:13)

At the beginning of chapter 7 we learn that Mark is writing for Gentiles, at least as some of his readers; otherwise he would not have to explain such Jewish customs as ritual washing of hands before eating, washing of cups, jugs, kettles, and so forth (vv. 3-4). In their zeal for observance of the law of Moses centered in the ten commandments, the Pharisees had built up an oral tradition of 613 supplementary laws as a kind of fence calculated to keep the people at a distance from breaking the ten. These precautionary laws included dietary rules and hygienic customs, a few of which Mark cites here by way of example. The Pharisees considered the Jew who broke any of these rules "unclean," a state remedied only by ritual washing or sacrifice.

Mark now presents the Pharisees' demand that Jesus account for allowing his disciples to break one of these laws, that of washing before eating.

Jesus uses the occasion to try again to jolt their consciences out of the narrow confines of legalism by openly calling them hypocrites and accusing them of giving God only the lip service that Isaiah had condemned. As an example of their legalistic evasion of God's law, Jesus cites their approval of *qorban* (v. 11). By this law they were encouraging people to will to God for use in the Temple the money that the fourth commandment clearly required them to use in support of aging parents. By declaring the money willed to God, they could continue to use it for themselves during their lifetime, avoiding the obligation to their parents. In verse 15 Jesus goes to the heart of his controversy with the Pharisees by insisting that it isn't what a man eats that makes him immoral (hence the uselessness of the dietary laws), but what he says and does (hence the evil in their approval of *qorban*). Jesus uses the occasion to impress upon his disciples the importance of the inner conscience as the real source of the goodness or evil of a person's actions. Mark's Jesus stands for personal responsibility, inner purpose and freedom of conscience.

After reporting Jesus' private explanation of his proverb-parable to the disciples, Mark adds: "Thus he declared all foods clean" (v. 19), a clue that Mark's community is probably suffering an internal conflict between Christians of Jewish origin and those of Gentile background over the necessity of keeping the dietary laws of the Jews.

Once more Jesus tries to retire from the crowds. He enters the Gentile territory of Tyre and Sidon northwest of Galilee. When a Greek woman begs him for the cure of her daughter, he tells her in figurative language that he is providing first for the children, in other words, the chosen people or Jews. He thus lets the door partially open for the Gentiles to be attended to afterward. But then he seems to close that door by the harshness of the figure of speech that follows: "It is not right to take the food of the children and throw it to the dogs" (v. 27). Inconsiderate as his language sounds to us, he is merely speaking as a true Jew of his time, who commonly referred to the Gentiles as "dogs." The woman humbly breaks through that apparently closed door by accepting the lowly designation of "dog" in asking for the leftovers. Jesus cannot resist such humility and responds with the cure. Mark is assuring his Gentile readers that Jesus reaches out to them, too. And he is telling all of us that humility and faith are two dispositions that Jesus considers worthy of God's approval.

Returning to the Sea of Galilee, Jesus continues southeast into Decapolis ("Ten Cities"), a Gentile region, where he cures a deaf-mute. This cure is one of those passages that we may have hurried over in embarrassment every time we've come upon it, for to the modern reader it may suggest a negative impression of Jesus.

Let's take a closer look at it. Why does Jesus take "him off by himself away from the crowd" (v. 33)? So that they won't see the difficulty of this cure? Apparently exerting strenuous effort, Jesus touches the man in ways that seem indelicate, even vulgar, to us: "He put his *finger into the man's ears* and, *spitting, touched his tongue*" (v. 33). Jesus seems to be having a very hard time with this cure: "He looked up to heaven and *groaned*" (v. 34). Yet when he says "Ephphatha," the man hears immediately, and he begins to speak plainly.

A little background about Jesus' time will help us understand what is really happening here. Spittle was considered to be a healing agent. Don't we instinctively act in similar fashion when we put our burned or cut finger into our mouth? Furthermore, this is not really a slow miracle but an instantaneous one. These considerations make it easier to see that by taking this afflicted man aside Jesus is really treating him with delicate intimacy, and by groaning to heaven Jesus is giving the deaf man a sign that he owes his cure to God's creative power. By the very personal contact of putting his finger into the man's ears and his own spittle on the man's tongue, Jesus signifies to this deprived man that he is giving him a share in his own good hearing and power of speech.

Are not these signs forerunners of the sacramental signs by which Jesus personally touches our deaf and silent souls today? Jesus needed no sacraments; he himself is the supreme sacrament of his Father's presence and power. But by such acts as this Jesus taught his disciples the use of signs as liturgical actions by which his presence and power could be brought to Christians after his ascension, signs eventually understood as sacramental.

And now, having ministered to the Jews first, Jesus feeds the Gentile crowd. Again Mark gives Jesus' motive as a very human emotion: "My heart is moved with pity" (Mk 8:2); and again he involves the disciples in his ministry. He gives thanks—the Greek word *eucharistia* means "thankfulness"—and breaks the loaves. The number seven symbolizes completeness; Mark reports seven baskets of leftovers. The first such miracle, for the Jews, resulted in 12 baskets of leftovers, one for each of the 12 tribes.

The Pharisees renew their attack by asking for a sign—right after the great miracle of multiplication of bread and fish that they must have witnessed! Jesus abruptly refuses and takes off again in the boat.

REFLECTION AND PRAYER

Do I place more importance upon observing the letter of the law than upon keeping the spirit of God's laws?

Do I approach God in prayer with the humility of the Canaanite woman, who so acutely felt her inferiority before Jesus? And with her confidence?

Lord Jesus, I am often too deaf to hear your word and too speechless to relay it to others. Cure me!

Blindness, Yet Insight, of Jesus' Disciples (Mk 8:14-30)

Mark now reveals the extremity of the disciples' ignorance of what is happening. When Jesus warns them against "the leaven [spirit] of the Pharisees and the leaven of Herod" (v. 15)—the Pharisees and the Herodians have united to plot his death—the disciples think he is scolding them for forgetting to bring bread! Exasperated by their literalness, Jesus exclaims: "Do you have eyes and not see, ears and not hear?" (v. 18). This rebuke is also a warning against a too literal reading of the gospels, a reading that sometimes fails to grasp even elemental figures of speech and looks only at the outer surface of language instead of penetrating to its inner meaning. By preceding this incident with the cure of the deaf-mute, Mark has symbolized the spiritual deafness of Jesus' followers. Now he will symbolize their blindness by relating a further cure (Mk 8:22-26).

The cure of this blind man at Bethsaida is another apparently slow miracle. Again Jesus wants to be alone with the afflicted man; he leads the blind man "outside the village" (v. 23) to spare him the confusion of the crowds. Once more Jesus uses spittle, this time on the man's eyes. He begins to see, but not clearly: "I see people looking like trees" (v. 24). Jesus touches him a second time, and then he truly sees. Does Jesus really have to struggle over this cure, or is he rather dealing with this man as an individual? Certainly it has become obvious, by Mark's repeated insistence, that the faith of the recipient is a prerequisite for Jesus' efficacious action upon him. Here, then, Jesus is courteously giving this man time to grow in faith. In this sense it is indeed a gradual miracle. And in this sense, too, the church has deliberately slowed her liturgical life to the leisurely pace necessary to give faith time to grow.

Jesus has also given his disciples time to mature in faith, time to see who he really is. On the way to Caesarea Philippi he prepares them for his big question by a preliminary one: "Who do people say that I am?" (v. 27). After their answer, which gives them time to consider how they themselves might choose among the alternatives they present, Jesus asks the real question: "But who do *you* say that I am?" Impetuous, wholehearted Peter takes the lead: "You are the Messiah" (v. 29), a far deeper and more correct insight than any of the answers of the people. Still in need of time to prepare the people for this revelation, Jesus again orders silence concerning his identity.

We have come to the heart of Mark's gospel and certainly to one of the most important answers to our search for the Jesus of the gospels. Undoubtedly Mark is here challenging each of his readers to propose to himself Jesus' question: "But who do you say that I am?"

REFLECTION AND PRAYER

Who do I say in my own heart that Jesus is?

Who do I tell others that he is?

Has he become the central person of my life, my personal Messiah, my Lord?

Jesus, am I still deaf and blind about who you really are in my life, despite my literally correct answer? Fill my mind and my heart with your human-divine presence.

Act Two: The Mystery of the Son of Man, Son of God (Mk 8:31—16:20)

Jesus' First Prediction of His Passion (Mk 8:31-38)

Immediately after Peter's declaration, "You are the Messiah," Mark relates that Jesus "began to teach them that the *Son of Man* must suffer greatly and be rejected by the elders, the chief priests, and the scribes, and be killed" (v. 31). It is only after Peter's confession of belief in Jesus as Messiah that Mark reports Jesus' consistent and repeated references to himself as Son of Man, and then always in a context of suffering.

This title is especially significant because it is the one by which Jesus most often refers to himself, probably the only one he used, according to many scholars. The evangelists attribute to Jesus the occasional use or acceptance of other titles, such as *Messiah*, *Son of David* and *Son of God*, usually in a loose, non-historical sense that really is an exercise of their own post-Easter faith in him. In applying to himself the title Son of Man, Jesus certainly insists on his truly human identity as Mary's son. But he is also deliberately pointing to Old Testament passages that illuminate his use of this title.

Especially important is that in which Ezekiel described a vision of God's throne, more resplendent than a rainbow, and heard a voice say to him:

> *Son of man*, I am sending you to the Israelites. . . . Hard of face and obstinate of heart are they. . . . But you shall say to them: Thus says the Lord God! And whether they heed or resist . . . they shall know that a prophet has been among them. But as for you, *son of man*, fear neither them nor their words when they contradict you and reject you, and when you sit on scorpions . . . but open your mouth and eat what I shall give you.
> It was then I saw a hand stretched out to me, in which was a written scroll . . . and written on it was: *Lamentation and wailing and woe!*

He said to me: *Son of man . . . eat this scroll*, then go,
speak to the house of Israel. *So I opened my mouth and he
gave me the scroll to eat* (Ez 2:3—3:1).

It doesn't take much imagination to see that Mark has this passage
very much in mind as he writes his gospel. He certainly emphasizes the
obstinate spirit of Israel's leaders just as Ezekiel did. He likewise
stresses the extreme difficulty and danger of Jesus' mission to speak
God's message to them. And he portrays Jesus as being fully aware that
he must eventually accept the consequences of that message: He must
eat his own message as a *scroll of lamentation and woe*, a powerful figure expressing his coming sufferings.

And so, when Jesus appropriates to himself the title Son of Man as
he speaks of his coming sufferings for the first time, Peter understands
enough of what he is saying to be shocked: "Then Peter took him aside
and began to rebuke him" (v. 32), obviously to deter him from such a
terrible path. For his pains Peter receives Jesus' harshest rebuke: "Get
behind me, *Satan*" (v. 33).

It is our turn to be shocked, until we reflect that Jesus is warning
Peter not to be the "adversary" who would block his way toward win-
ning man's salvation, the "tempter" who would have Jesus abandon
the mission that his Father has entrusted to him: "You are thinking
not as God does, but as human beings do."

To reinforce his point about the necessity of suffering, Jesus begins teaching the crowd (v. 34) that all his followers must be ready to
face up to suffering—the cross. Not that they must seek suffering, but
they must be willing to deny their deepest instinct of seeking self first
and thereby lose this life of earthly self-satisfaction to gain the eternal
Life that God gives those who accept his call to follow Jesus the Son of
Man.

Repeatedly now, Mark gives us the impression that he may very
well be writing his gospel to help the Christians of his day face up to
their own trials. There was the family trial that many had to endure; to
embrace Christ was frequently interpreted by the rest of the family as
abandoning either the Jewish faith in the one God Yahweh or the
Gentile faith in the family gods and the gods of Rome. The Romans
were already interpreting faith in Christ as the rejection of the god-
emperor and the goddess Roma. Nero had unleashed the first of the 10
Roman persecutions, depriving the Christians of their two greatest
leaders, Peter and Paul.

This probable background of the writing of Mark's gospel goes a long way toward explaining the somber mood of the first part: Jesus in continuous conflict with the Jewish leaders; Jesus in constant stress from the pressing, ever-demanding crowd; Jesus concerned with the blindness of his own disciples. The second part of Mark, from 8:31 on, will be even darker, enveloped in an ever-deepening cloud.

REFLECTION AND PRAYER

When things go wrong in my life, do I recall that as a Christian I must expect suffering?

Do I try to unite my own sufferings to the cross of Jesus?

Lord Jesus, I offer you all the trials of this day as part of the cross you have called me to bear with you.

Jesus' Promises of Glory (Mk 9:1-29)

Chapter 9 begins with the promise that the cross will lead to glory: "Amen, I say to you, there are some standing here who will not taste death until they see that the kingdom of God has come in power" (v. 1). This sentence taken by itself seems to predict that the second coming of Christ is imminent. But in the context of the first prediction of the passion, it suggests that the kingdom of God, already in existence with the presence of Jesus, will definitively "come *in power*" through the cross of Jesus and the sufferings of his followers. In that case the "kingdom of God" on earth is the Christian church, established in power at the coming of the Holy Spirit and growing steadily in power at the time of Mark's writing, both in her martyrs and in her increasing number of converts.

There follows a spectacular sign of Jesus' future glory, his transfiguration. Jesus selects for this extraordinary mountain experience the same three disciples who had witnessed his raising of Jairus' daughter to life: Peter, James and John. If Jesus' clothes "became dazzling white" (v. 3), how must his face have shown! Moses and Elijah appear with him, evidence that Jesus is not to be considered as either one of them returned to life, but as the fulfillment of what they stood for, the law and the prophets.

Peter is so carried away by the experience that he suggests making tents or shrines to commemorate the event. The climax comes with the voice from the cloud (in Exodus the cloud was the locus of God's presence): "This is my beloved Son" (v. 7). These words of love that the

Father spoke to Jesus at his baptism (Mk 1:11) are here addressed to the disciples with the admonition, "Listen to him." By the transfiguration the three disciples who will be closest to Jesus in his agony are granted a foretaste of the glory prophesied at the beginning of this chapter.

Just as suddenly as it had occurred, the divine manifestation ends; the three see "only Jesus." The mountain experience is over, but it has left its impression; Jesus tells them to keep the secret until he has *"risen from the dead"* (v. 9). They do not understand his meaning, and they are troubled about the appearance of Elijah at the transfiguration. The scribes taught that Elijah would return before "the day of the Lord comes" (Mal 3:23) to purge Israel with fire (Sir 48:1-4). Hence the disciples' question about Elijah coming first (v. 11) implies much more: If Jesus is the Messiah who will bring about "the day of the Lord," presumably by this rising of which he has just spoken, why hasn't Elijah already returned with fire? In his answer Jesus reminds them of other prophecies that as Son of Man he must fulfill (Ez 2:10—3:1); he must suffer and be despised (Is 52:13—53:12). Yet he assures them that Elijah has already come, a veiled reference to John the Baptist as the expected precursor, for Jesus refers to the violent death (v. 13) by which they could know that he was speaking of John.

As they reach the foot of the mountain, they are jarred back to mundane reality by the heated public discussion between the scribes and the disciples over the latter's failure to cure the possessed boy. Jesus vents his disappointment at their lack of faith: "O faithless generation, . . . How long will I endure you?" (v. 19). The glorious glow of transfiguration has suddenly given way to utter frustration. Mark's Jesus experiences the full swing of our own fluctuating emotions.

Mark's description of the possessed boy's reaction to Jesus' presence builds to dramatic intensity. The father pleads: "If you can do anything, have compassion on us and help us" (v. 22). This man knows how to pray to Jesus; he senses that Jesus cannot resist an appeal to his heart. But Jesus finds the man's faith inadequate: "'If you can!' Everything is possible to one who has faith" (v. 23). The father is up to the challenge; he utters the perfect prayer of one who realizes the imperfection of his own faith: "I do believe, help my unbelief!" (v. 24). Jesus' response is one of his most dramatic cures. Mark has frequently insisted on the necessity of faith in Jesus; here he presents the epitome of faith healing.

The disciples want to know why they failed to cure the boy. Jesus' answer, ''This kind can only come out through prayer'' (v. 29), could refer to the prayer of the man seeking the cure for his son as well as to that of the would-be healers.

REFLECTION AND PRAYER

Do I really believe in the glorified Jesus, now permanently trans-figured at his Father's side?

How strong is my own faith in Jesus' power and his willingness to use it for me and mine?

Lord Jesus, I do believe; help my unbelief!

Jesus' Second Prediction of His Passion (Mk 9:30-50)

Again evading the crowd, Jesus predicts his death and resurrec-tion for the second time (v. 31). Once more, his disciples fail to under-stand, as they quickly demonstrate by arguing on the way to Caper-naum about which of them is most important.

Jesus is becoming accustomed to their lack of understanding. He patiently teaches them the futility of rank and the importance of being ''the servant of all'' (v. 35). Then he reinforces his words with an object lesson by hugging a little child in his arms. Mark's portrayal of Jesus certainly includes his gentleness. And note that chain of simple logic: Who welcomes a child ''in my name'' (v. 37) welcomes me; who wel-comes me welcomes the Father—the Christian ideal of hospitality.

But the disciples still haven't learned the lesson. John, one of those ''sons of thunder,'' now gives us an example of why Jesus so named him. He tells Jesus, with intolerant exasperation, about trying to stop an unknown man from expelling demons in Jesus' name. Jesus expresses open-minded acceptance of the man's apparent good will, and then pronounces a principle: ''Whoever is not against us is for us'' (v. 40). There is no neutral ground concerning Jesus; one is either for him or against him. But the one who is not obviously against him must be presumed to be for him.

Jesus uses the occasion to teach the pivotal truth that salvation de-pends upon choosing or rejecting him (vv. 41-48). He promises that even a drink of water given in his name will be rewarded, ''because you belong to *Christ*'' (v. 41). Here Mark's Jesus appropriates a title by which Christians referred to him only after his resurrection. All the evangelists make this premature use of titles when the occasion seems to warrant it.

Jesus warns that those who reject him will be lost, both false teachers and habitual sinners. The teacher who destroys the faith "of these little ones" (v. 42), simple believers in Jesus, deserves a punishment worse than violent death. The sinner who cannot control himself (vv. 43-48), whose sin has become second nature, also risks this punishment.

Three times Jesus employs in verses 43-47 the kind of dramatic hyperbole by which Jews often emphasized the seriousness of a key truth. Literalists must have great difficulty with this passage about cutting off hands and feet and gouging out eyes. But the figurative meaning is clear enough: Whatever the source of your temptation, eliminate it before it condemns you to Gehenna! This figurative meaning clearly throws the stress on the thrice-mentioned Gehenna, "where 'their worm does not die, and the fire is not quenched'" (v. 48). Jesus is here quoting the last verse of Isaiah. Gehenna was a valley near Jerusalem cursed by the prophets as a place where Jews had offered human sacrifices to false gods. In Jesus' time it was still used as the town dump, where burning trash constantly smoked and decaying garbage bred maggots. It therefore served him, as well as Isaiah, as a figure of hell.

It is especially important to understand Jesus' words for our time. Many people today argue that a good God would never create a hell; therefore, hell does not exist. Some point to this figurative passage to deny the existence of hell under the supposition that Jesus is speaking *only* in figures. But it seems obvious that the figures stand for something very real. On the other hand, those who see no symbols here must explain to a modern scientific world how the immaterial spirit of man (before bodily resurrection) can constantly burn and be devoured by worms.

This Markan passage is an example of eschatological language, not meant to describe existing realities but to warn about possible future consequences of evil. Traditional Christian faith has always affirmed the existence of hell, based on such passages as this one, but the few details revealed in such passages are comprehensible only within the cultural level of the time. In the non-scientific Middle Ages, for instance, graphic details of physical fire and pitchfork-bearing devils made morality plays adequate teaching vehicles. But such details were never part of the official teaching of the church and have become repulsive to our scientific age.

Perhaps the most important truth about hell is that it is not the result of God's creative action but of humanity's negation of God's creation. The picture of a God who delights in flicking wicked souls into hell to watch them sizzle is incompatible with the loving Father whom Mark's Jesus has been revealing to us in his compassionate healings. We must conclude that it is really the wicked who create hell for themselves.

Those who love evil choose evil companions and despise the company of the good. Their wicked lives negate the goodness of creation; they reject their very nature. If they are so confirmed in evil that they hate goodness, they must hate above all absolute Goodness, God himself. To live in the presence of this God would become for them the greatest of possible torments. Hence, the God whom Jesus reveals as all-good must allow those who have freely chosen evil to be freely separated from him. Those who waver in their decisions are not fully free, for freedom is the power to make a definitive decision. Those who definitively reject Jesus Christ, God's revelation of his Goodness, permanently separate themselves from God. Thus hell, as this separation, must be thought of as God's mercy permitting the wicked to escape the state that would only increase their torment of self-negation.

Is anybody really in hell? We have no clear revelation on this point. Our prisons attest to our belief that there are evil people in our society, but what do we know of God's judgment of human beings?

Having warned of the unquenchable fire of Gehenna that the wicked will suffer, Jesus now speaks of another fire that he calls upon all to endure: "Everyone will be salted with fire" (v. 49). In Jesus' time salt was used not only to make food savory but sometimes to cauterize wounds; the burning sensation it caused was considered a purifying fire. Jesus therefore uses salt as a twofold figure: It symbolizes the virtues that must flavor the lives of his disciples, making them pleasing to God and peace-giving to "one another" (v. 50); and it symbolizes the purification necessary to acquire these virtues (v.49). The tribulations of life—and persecutions in Mark's time—borne as participation in Jesus' suffering and death (v. 31), purge our sinfulness.

These verses also echo Leviticus 2:13: "Every cereal offering that you present to the Lord shall be *seasoned with salt*. Do not let the *salt of the covenant* of your God be lacking from your cereal offering." In alluding to the "salt of the covenant," Jesus is warning his disciples not to lose the spirit of their covenant with God and with one another, a covenant that will keep its savor only through the endurance of suffering in keeping "peace with one another" (v. 50), the peace that was broken by their argument over rank at the beginning of this chapter.

REFLECTION AND PRAYER

Do I believe in hell?

Do I believe that I may be making my own hell, even on earth, if I fail to be "salted with fire," purified of my sins by suffering, purified by the fire of the Holy Spirit?

Holy Spirit, purge my heart with the fire of Jesus' love burning within me.

Jesus' Teaching About Marriage and Divorce (Mk 10:1-16)

In chapter 10 Jesus leaves Galilee for the last time, moving southeastward. The Pharisees renew their attack with a question about divorce. They seem to be asking Jesus to tell them which of two schools of thought on the question he accepts: the strict rabbis, who follow Shammai in limiting divorce to cases of adultery; or the lenient, who follow Hillel in allowing divorce for nearly any reason, even preference for another woman.

Jesus adheres to neither school. He doesn't even accept Moses' permission for a husband to divorce his wife "because he finds in her something indecent" (Dt 24:1), attributing that stipulation to Moses' attempt to make the best of his people's hardness of heart by allowing them the lesser of two evils, open divorce instead of secret adultery. To confirm his complete denial of divorce Jesus cites the intention of the Creator himself, manifested by his making the human race of two sexes, who need one another for their completion: "The two shall become one flesh" (v. 8, referring to Gn 2:24). Jesus considers the marriage union such an integral part of God's creation that he adds the conclusion: "Therefore *what God has joined together*, no human being must separate" (v. 9). In other words, divorce is unthinkable between two people whose union as a new physical and moral entity has been prepared for and approved by God himself.

His disciples question such strictness. But he does not budge. However, he does clarify his point by telling them, "Whoever divorces his wife *and marries another* commits adultery against her" (v. 11). Jesus here equates divorce to adultery, not when divorce simply separates man and wife, but when it definitively breaks the original marital relationship by forming a new one. The man who "marries another" gravely offends his first wife, his only real wife, by definitively cutting her off after she, by the will of God, has become his own flesh. This concept was all the more surprising to the Jews of Jesus' time because they recognized the marital rights only of the husband. That a husband could offend his wife by divorcing her to marry another was a new and more sensitive application of the law of love.

By the time of Mark's writing Christians had evidently accepted this new teaching of Jesus and perceived its full implications, for Mark is able to add a clause that Jesus would hardly have spoken to Jews: "and if she *divorces her husband* and marries another, she commits adultery" (v. 12). Jewish law did not recognize the right of a woman to divorce her husband.

Scholars point out this clause as an example of the freedom with which the evangelists appear to have added to the words of Jesus. The zeal of scholars to ferret out the exact words that Jesus himself said is certainly laudable, but it has led to little that they can agree upon. Whether we consider verse 12 to be part of Jesus' original statement or Mark's own inspired application of his teaching, it expresses the faith of the early Christians for whom it was written, the real test of the authenticity of New Testament passages.

Mark follows this passage about marriage and divorce with one about children, perhaps to reinforce Jesus' teaching concerning family life. This same Jesus who refuses to accept divorce has a loving heart for little children; when his disciples try to save him from the mothers who would thrust their little ones upon him, he becomes "indignant" (v. 14)—another strong human emotion that he shares with us. Not only does he open his arms to the children, but he also utilizes the occasion to repeat the lesson of childlike humility that the disciples have still not grasped: "The kingdom of God belongs to such as these" (v. 14). This kingdom of God, then, can be defined as the state in which all people are God's children and therefore brothers and sisters of one another. Again, his human touch: "Then he embraced them and blessed them, placing his hands on them" (v. 16). In his loving action Mark's Jesus is the image of the heavenly Father.

REFLECTION AND PRAYER

Do I accept as an integral part of my faith Jesus' teaching on divorce?

If I fail my responsibility to my spouse, can I expect to be faithful to any other commitment?

Lord Jesus, give me your insight into the beauty of marriage and the glory of parenting.

Jesus' Teaching About Riches (Mk 10:17-31)

A man who comes running up to kneel before Jesus seems to receive a rebuff for his enthusiasm and his courteous address, "*Good teacher*" (v. 17). Perhaps his approach is overdone; evidently Jesus is not accustomed to having people kneel before him as to a deity. He challenges the man's motivation: "No one is good but God alone" (v. 18)—only God grants eternal salvation.

Then, to the question of how to inherit this everlasting life, Jesus gives the standard Old Testament answer: Keep the commandments. While Jews generally considered the keeping of the commandments as the way to fulfill God's will, some saw them as a form of ascetic morality by which salvation could be won. At this point, then, Jesus' intention in pointing to the commandments as the way of salvation is not wholly clear.

The man's affirmative response wins Jesus' heart: "Jesus, looking at him, *loved him*" (v. 21). This sincere inquirer is opening his heart to new possibilities; so, to his question about salvation, Jesus gives his New Testament answer: "Go, sell what you have and give to [the] poor and you will have treasure in heaven; then *come, follow me.*" It is now clear that Jesus is not adding one more commandment but pointing out to the rich man that he has until now been keeping only the letter of the original ten. To keep their true spirit requires that he reach out more generously toward the poor by sharing his riches with them, even as Jesus has been doing in his public ministry. Jesus invites him to break the bonds of his own riches and be free at last to love his fellow men and women—and his God.

But Jesus' answer proves too hard, not only for the man who has many possessions, but also for the disciples. And frequently for us Americans, who often have so much more than the wealthy person of Jesus' time and the average third-world citizen of today. Jesus knows how hard his lesson is, but it is also hard for the rich to enter the kingdom of God. He uses a simile that will evoke a ridiculous image in the minds of his listeners, a camel trying to crawl through the eye of a needle (v. 25). The apostles are astounded at this reversal of the Jewish tradition that God rewards with abundance in this life those who are faithful to his will. They are probably thinking of the material blessings promised for obedience to the law in such passages as Deuteronomy 28:1-14.

Great teacher that he is, Jesus has set them up for one of the central lessons of the whole New Testament. To their exasperated question: "Then who can be saved?" (v. 26), he responds: "For human beings it is impossible but not for God. All things are possible for God" (v. 27). His answer is wrapped in mystery, but one thing is crystal clear: Salvation is God's work rather than ours.

Peter throws in what looks like a selfish question: What do we get out of our great sacrifice of giving up everything for you? Jesus does not label Peter's question as we might, but takes him seriously and gives him a magnanimous answer: "a hundred times more now in this present age: houses and brothers and sisters and mothers and children and lands *with persecutions*" (v. 30). That last phrase seems to turn the whole promise into scornful irony—until he adds, "and *eternal life* in the age to come." Christians of Mark's generation needed this message of the incomparable superiority of "the next life" over "this one on earth" because they were suffering persecution; we may need it even more because our present life is so comfortable. Jesus finishes the lesson with that cryptic saying about first and last, probably meaning, at least in this context, that those who put their own interests in this life first will wind up last in the next life.

But how are we to reconcile two apparently contradictory attitudes toward riches expressed by Jesus in this passage? First, he tells the rich man to give up his wealth, to reject riches; he follows up this advice with a solemn warning to his disciples: "How hard it is for those who have wealth to enter the kingdom of God!" (v. 23). Then, within this same conversation, Jesus seems to promise great wealth, even material wealth, to those who have given up anything for him, "*a hundred times more now in this present age*: houses . . . and lands" (v. 30). Those who fix their attention exclusively upon the advice to the rich man advocate a Christianity of severe austerity. On the other hand, there are preachers who cite only the "hundred times more," telling their congregations to expect Christ to reward his faithful ones here and now, even at the expense of unbelievers. True Christianity must hold both sides of this passage in the balance that Mark intended to give them.

A careful rereading of verse 30 in the light of the rest of Mark's gospel shows the major emphasis to be on family ties. More than on houses and lands, the stress falls on "brothers and sisters and mothers and children," climaxed by "eternal life in the age to come." Moreover, the portrayal of the life of the apostles in Acts is far from one of wealth and riches. Their wealth consists rather in the privilege of serving a people so dedicated to one another as to form a new family in Christ: "There was no needy person among them, for those who owned property or houses would sell them, bring the proceeds of the sale, and put them at the feet of the apostles, and they were distributed to each according to need" (Acts 4:34-35).

Ultimately, then, Mark's Jesus is telling us that both attitudes— indifference to worldly wealth and expectation of reward for following him—characterize the true Christian, if held in a balance that neither rejects as evil the goods of this world nor claims right to more of those goods than necessary to fulfill legitimate needs.

REFLECTION AND PRAYER

Do I accept Jesus' teaching about riches?

How serious am I about helping those in greater need than I am?

Lord, help me use my share of the goods of this world for others as well as for myself.

Jesus' Third Prediction of His Passion (Mk 10:32-52)

Now begins the real drama of Calvary: "They were on the way, going up to Jerusalem, *and Jesus went ahead of them*" (v. 32). Mark sometimes suggests things that other evangelists make more explicit; for example, here he insinuates the eagerness of Jesus to pursue his course even though it means *going up*! Mark confirms this first hint of rapidly approaching final action by reference to the disciples' mood of wonder and fear. It is a fitting setting for Jesus' third prediction of his death and resurrection in Jerusalem, detailing sufferings not mentioned before (vv. 33-34).

Enter again the "sons of thunder." James and John, apparently thinking about Jesus' recent answer to Peter's question concerning their reward, seem to picture their situation in terms of the henchmen of an Eastern potentate sitting in state over his newly acquired empire; they formally request to be his right- and left-hand men when he comes into his glory. By now Mark's Jesus is so accustomed to his disciples' failure to understand him that he reacts mildly to their ambitious request. He merely hints at the fallacy of their dream picture by warning of the sufferings to come. He asks whether they can "drink the cup [of agony] I drink or be baptized with the baptism [of pain and death] with which I am baptized?" (v. 38). They boast, "We can," a self-reliance that cannot win those special places at his side, for it is a different kingdom than they imagine (v. 40).

Then all the other disciples get into the act, indignant at the thunderous ones. Jesus again tries to teach them the lesson of humility, this time by appealing to experiences they must all have had of the arrogance of Gentile lords. The reversal of roles in the kingdom of God is especially manifest in the climactic pronouncement:

> "Whoever wishes to be great among you will be your servant; whoever wishes to be first among you will be the slave of all. For *the Son of Man did not come to be served but to serve and to give his life as a ransom for many*" (vv. 44-45).

The kingdom of God is indeed different from the kingdoms that men build on their false values of vanity, greed, power!

That last sentence of Jesus connects two Old Testament titles in the minds of the disciples: *Son of Man* and *servant of all*. In four remarkable passages Second Isaiah described "the servant of the Lord" as a mysterious figure who bears our sins to atone for them:

> We had all gone astray like sheep,
>   each following his own way;
> But the Lord laid upon him [his promised servant]
>   the guilt of us all.
> Though he was harshly treated, he submitted
>   and opened not his mouth;
> Like a lamb led to the slaughter
>   or a sheep before the shearers,
>   he was silent and opened not his mouth.
> Oppressed and condemned, he was taken away,
>   and who would have thought any more of his destiny?
> When he was cut off from the land of the living,
>   *and smitten for the sin of his people*,
> A grave was assigned him among the wicked. . . .
> *Through his suffering, my servant shall justify many,*
>   *and their guilt he shall bear. . . .*
> *And he shall take away the sins of many,*
>   *and win pardon for their offenses* (Is 53:6-12).

Now the New Testament answer to the question, ''Who can be saved?'' (v. 26) has been completed: Whoever aspires to be a true Christian must serve the rest in union with the Son of Man, who has come ''to give his life *as a ransom* for many.'' Here Mark's Jesus is adopting from Isaiah 53:11 the Hebrew use of ''many'' as a universal in the sense of *all* saved by the promised *one*. Jesus' veiled application to himself of Isaiah's servant-of-the-Lord passages (42:1-4; 49:1-7; 50:4-11; 52:13—53:12) gives the reason for his suffering: ransom or salvation from sin and death, salvation from evil in all the forms over which Mark has shown Jesus victorious by casting out evil spirits, calming the raging sea, curing diseases, even raising a child from death.

The moment has come at last for Jesus to reveal fully the kind of Messiah he is. Isaiah's suffering-servant passages had been overshadowed as messianic prophecies by the Davidic prophecies interpreted as predicting a triumphant, political hero who would restore Israel to independence and glory. Now we can see at least one reason for the messianic secret. According to Mark's account, the impression that the Messiah was to be a political liberator forced Jesus to reveal himself gradually enough to give his followers time to realize that the salvation he would bring was not of this world but of the next.

And now, almost as if to say ''At last, we see!'' Mark presents the healing of the blind Bartimaeus. Notice that as the blind man calls out for pity, he identifies Jesus as ''Son of David'' (v. 47). It is the first time that this title appears in Mark's gospel, and to make sure that we don't miss it, Mark's blind man repeats it. Now that Mark's Jesus has identified himself as Isaiah's servant of the Lord, the title Son of David will no longer be misleading. Indeed, the people seem to have grown to know Jesus better, for they reassure the blind man: ''Take courage; get up, he is calling you'' (v. 49). Mark obviously wants us to feel that way about Jesus, too.

With great energy and abandon the blind man ''threw aside his cloak [of fear], sprang up, and came to Jesus'' (v. 50). Jesus assures the blind man that it is his faith that has been essential for the recovery of his sight. The man who *sees* follows Jesus on his way (v. 52).

REFLECTION AND PRAYER

Is my faith strong enough to open my inner sight to Jesus and enable me to follow him on his way?

Even on the way of the cross?

Lord Jesus, I too want to see; give me the grace to follow you up the road of life as one who goes to serve.

Jesus Begins His Jerusalem Ministry (Mk 11:1-26)

The road leads toward Jerusalem, David's city. In chapter 11, with his account of the triumphal entry, Mark begins his only report of Jesus' presence there. He directs the disciples to find a colt "on which no one has ever sat" (v. 2). In light of the law that only an animal never used as a beast of burden was fit for sacrifice (Nm 19:1-5), Jesus' curious command suggests the real meaning of his entry into Jerusalem. It is not the grand entry of an earthly king upon a fiery charger, but the humble coming of the obedient servant of Yahweh, ready to make the supreme sacrifice of his own life for his people. They spread their cloaks before him and shout his praise. No more need for the messianic secret; Jesus has come to establish his new Davidic kingdom: "Blessed is the *kingdom of our father David* that is to come!" (v. 10).

His inspection of the Temple (v. 11) prepares us for the coming incident of its cleansing. And it seems to remind Mark of that strange cursing of the fig tree, which he now relates. He remarks that "it was not the time for figs" (v. 13), yet he quotes Jesus as saying: "May no one ever eat of your fruit again!" (v. 14). Obviously the disciples don't know what to make of this apparent temper tantrum, and at this point neither do we.

Jesus proceeds to drive out of the Temple court those who are "selling and buying there" (v. 15). It is important to note that he drives out not only the sellers, but also the buyers. Yet he is hardest on the moneychangers and the sellers of doves. He won't even let people use the court as a shortcut through which to carry things. Mark wants us to picture the fierce power that this man, so gentle with children, now displays.

Jesus explains his anger by quoting Isaiah 56:7 about the Temple as a house of prayer, and Jeremiah 7:11 about the Jews turning it into a den of thieves. Mark probably counts on the memory of his readers to recall the immediate context of the Jeremiah passage:

> Are you to steal and murder, commit adultery and perjury, burn incense to Baal, go after strange gods that you know not, and yet come to stand before me in this house which bears my name, and say: "We are safe; we can commit all these abominations again"? Has this house which bears my name become in your eyes *a den of thieves*? (Jer 7:8-11).

The context of Jesus' quotation indicates that it isn't just the commerce in the Temple area that disturbs him, but especially the prostitution of Temple worship itself. Temple worship has become a sham.

But instead of listening to him, the priests and scribes of the establishment seek a way "to put him to death" (v. 18).

Now Mark brings us back to the fig tree. It is the next morning when Peter notices that the tree has withered away. Mark's juxtaposition of these events furnishes the key for their interpretation. But we also need to know, as undoubtedly Mark's first readers knew, that the fig tree was used by several prophets as a symbol of Israel. Perhaps these readers would have thought especially of the chapter of Jeremiah just after the one Jesus quoted in the Temple. Still angry at the sinfulness of the chosen people, Jeremiah cried:

I will gather them all in, says the Lord:
no grapes on the vine,
No figs on the fig trees,
foliage withered! (Jer 8:13).

That is why Jesus' action of cursing the fig tree makes sense, even though it is not the season for figs as Mark has expressly stated, evidently to alert us not to take Jesus' action too literally. Jesus is teaching his disciples by means of a parable in action. The barren fig tree is a symbol of sinful Israel, which does not bear fruit even in the Temple worship. By his curse Jesus has shown the fig tree for what it is, a symbol of a barren Israel, which merits only the curse of God.

In the light of this fig tree parable, Jesus' cleansing of the Temple, at first sight a mere display of fury, can now be seen as another action parable, symbolizing the displacement of the Temple by a new kind of worship that Jesus will soon establish.

Jesus makes further use of his fig tree parable as evidence that trust in God can even move a mountain. But just as a parable is not meant to be taken literally, neither are we justified in taking this mountain-moving literally. Is not the mountain a symbol of a spiritual obstacle to our action, such as prejudice? Doesn't it sometimes seem harder to cast our prejudices into the sea than to move physical mountains? And the worst of our prejudices are those that hold back our forgiveness for the grievances we suffer at the hands of others (v. 25). This last verse is as close as Mark comes to transcribing the Lord's Prayer for us.

REFLECTION AND PRAYER

Is my prayer often reduced to the mere empty recitation of formulas?

In my petitions, do I try to change God's mind, or do I ask him to change my will to conform to his?

Do I often praise Jesus as my own Lord?

Lord Jesus, grant me faith to remove my mountainous prejudices.

Jesus' Final Confrontations With Jewish Leaders (Mk 11:27—12:27)

Jesus' cleansing of the Temple has renewed his conflict with the leaders of the people. They challenge his authority for acting as he did, and he replies with a question about the authority of John the Baptist that leaves them on the horns of a dilemma (vv. 31-32); they realize that they are caught no matter which way they answer.

In chapter 12 Jesus continues his attack upon their misguided leadership with the parable of the vineyard, which he adapts from Isaiah: "The vineyard of the Lord of hosts is the house of Israel" (Is 5:7), which, like the fig tree of Jesus' action parable, produces no fruit and therefore deserves the Lord's curse: "I will make it a ruin" (Is 5:6). Jesus changes the focus of Isaiah's parable from the fruitless vineyard (Israel) to the evil tenants (the leaders of Israel), who not only refuse to pay their rent in kind but even abuse and kill the servants (prophets) sent by the owner (God). The climax comes when they kill the owner's son.

To make sure that the leaders do not miss his point—that it is really God's own Son whom they are plotting to kill—Jesus quotes Psalm 118:22-23 about the stone (Jesus) rejected by the builders (leaders) only to become "the keystone of the structure" (new Temple, new worship). It is significant that this quotation stands in the psalm only two verses before the one that the crowd chanted upon his entry into Jerusalem, "Blessed is he who comes in the name of the Lord" (Ps 118:26).

The Jewish leaders get the message and desire all the more to arrest Jesus, but the crowd is with him. So the offended leaders concoct a scheme to discredit him in the eyes of the crowd. The newly allied Pharisees and Herodians are sent to impale Jesus upon the horns of a more dangerous dilemma than the one he has just propounded to the

Jewish leaders. They are indeed a likely coalition to think up a question about paying the tax to the Roman emperor! They're sure they've got him this time: If he says "Pay the tax," the crowd will turn against him in anger; if he says "Don't pay it," the Roman authorities will deal with him as a rebel! But he skillfully turns their trap back against them: "Repay to Caesar what belongs to Caesar and to God what belongs to God" (v. 17). If they have been fulfilling either of these obligations, they have been doing it unwillingly. Jesus misses no opportunity—not even this personal attack upon himself—to emphasize the insignificance of the trials of this life in relation to the importance of our relationship with God.

Now it is another group's turn to attack Jesus. The Sadducees, a group of wealthy and worldly minded priests who traffic with the Romans and often oppose the Pharisees, have united with the Pharisees against Jesus. They quote to him the levirate law by which a brother was to continue his dead brother's lineage by impregnating the dead brother's widow (see Dt 25:5). The Sadducees show their contempt for belief in the resurrection by proposing a ridiculous case involving seven brothers and popping their catch question: "At the resurrection . . . whose wife will she be?" (v. 23).

Jesus goes to the source of their fallacy: "Are you not misled because you do not know the scriptures or the power of God?" (v. 24). These Jewish priests do not understand their own scriptures because their literal legalism—it was usually the Pharisees who were considered guardians of the law—blinds them to the deeper meaning of the scriptures.

Then Jesus confirms the reality of the resurrection and the superiority of life after resurrection to the present life in which marriage is the closest human relationship. He explains that marriage has no place in heaven because the resurrected "are like angels" (v. 25); that is, they enjoy the beatitude of the angels in personal relationship with God and, in him, with one another. Mark's Jesus implies the concept so beautifully expressed in Ephesians 5:32: Marriage is a great mystery symbolizing the relationship between Christ and his church, and hence, between God and the resurrected.

Jesus proceeds to show that if they had read correctly Exodus 3:6, they would have realized it implies at least the eventual resurrection of the patriarchs; for Yahweh, who introduced himself to Moses as the God of Abraham, Isaac and Jacob—long gone from earthly life at the time of Moses—"is not God of the dead but of the living" (v. 27).

REFLECTION AND PRAYER

Do I accept the authority of Jesus as final teacher of morality?

Or do I question his authority as did the Jewish leaders of his day?

Jesus, be the Lord of my moral life.

Jesus Teaches the Supreme Importance of Love (Mk 12:28-44)

A scribe who admires Jesus' answer to the Sadducees proposes a sincere question: "Which is the first of all the commandments?" (v. 28). As we have seen, the oral tradition of the Pharisees comprised 613 laws! The scribe is asking how to bring order and priority out of that chaos.

Unhesitatingly Jesus quotes the beginning of the daily prayer of the Jews from Deuteronomy 6:4-5. To this first commandment he gratuitously adds a second from Leviticus 19:18. The two great commandments are not the invention of Jesus; his originality consists in putting them together from far-removed parts of the Old Testament, thereby showing the intimate interdependence of the two loves involved.

In ratifying the command to "love your neighbor *as yourself*," Jesus clearly implies that we cannot really love our neighbor unless we already love ourselves. But self-love, so natural to our basic psychology, easily degenerates into selfishness. Jesus defines the self-love that he extols by relating it to the commandment to love God above all else. He thereby defines true self-love as esteem for oneself as the creature/child of a Creator/Father, who makes only what is good. This is the kind of self-love that motivates us to grow into the masterpiece that our Father intends us to be, a masterwork so worthy of love that it gives him glory as the creating Father. When we begin to see goodness in ourselves, our vision can open up to perceive goodness in others. Reciprocally, when we begin to see goodness in others, we can see goodness in ourselves. Then we love our neighbor as we love ourselves, as another masterwork of our creative Father.

In experiencing the gratuitous love of parents and spouse we begin to taste the great unmerited love lavished upon us by the Father, who brought us forth from nothingness. Falling in love can become a sacred experience for us when we find in that love a shadow of the freely given love of God. And in finding ourselves lovable, we reach out to love others.

By placing love of God first, Mark's Jesus sets the ultimate priority of our own love; unless we eventually love God above all else, our love remains stunted. And by merging these two commandments Jesus makes it clear that we cannot truly love God with all our heart, soul, mind and strength without at the same time loving our neighbor; nor can we truly love our neighbor without simultaneously loving God. These two loves are really one.

This kind of love is not merely a human, limited love. It is a participation in the limitless love of God. We do not subtract from our love of God to give others more of our love. Both loves grow together. The more we love God, the more we love spouse and friends; the more we love them, the more we love God.

The scribe understands this kind of love. Jesus' compliment to him, "You are not far from the kingdom of God" (v. 34), clarifies the meaning of the kingdom of God in the light of these two great commandments. We are members of God's kingdom if in our vision of the real world God is the Father-Creator of all men and women, and we are all, therefore, brothers and sisters of one another. Hence, true love of God must include love of all men and women as his sons and daughters, and vice versa. The community in which such love reigns is already the kingdom of God. And the person who holds this view of life is "not far from the kingdom of God."

"No one dared to ask him any more questions" (v. 34), so Jesus becomes the questioner. He asks how the scribes can claim that the Messiah is David's son despite Psalm 110:1, attributed by them to David himself: "The Lord [Yahweh] said to *my* lord [David's lord, the Messiah] . . ." (v. 36). How can the Messiah be David's son if David calls him his lord? Mark adds that the crowd is delighted to see Jesus confound their leaders. But does Jesus ask this question just to outwit the scribes? No, he is still trying to open their eyes to the kind of Messiah to expect, not the conquering political hero who will restore the temporal glory of the nation after the manner of David, but one to whom David himself renders a non-political homage as the Lord sitting at God's "right hand."

Jesus fearlessly continues his effort to lead the people away from false leaders by warning them about the scribes' lack of humility, their cruelty to widows and their hypocritical prayers. He finds a sharp contrast to them in the poor widow who gives to the Temple "all she had, her whole livelihood" (v. 44).

REFLECTION AND PRAYER

Do I experience my love for others as bringing me closer to God?

Do I experience my love for God bringing me closer to my spouse and my friends?

If not, what must I do to purify my love for others?

Lord Jesus, give me a more complete participation in your great love.

Jesus' Discourse on the End of the World (Mk 13)

Chapter 13 presents Jesus' famous but difficult discourse about the end of Jerusalem and the end of the world. One of the disciples calls Jesus' attention to the huge blocks of stone forming the great buildings of the Temple, still being worked on since Herod began its rebuilding about 19 B.C. The disciple seems to suggest that such a structure will last forever, but Jesus foretells its complete destruction, a catastrophe actually brought about by the Roman army in A.D 70. However, the western or "wailing" wall and other remnants were left standing, so a strict literalist should have trouble with Jesus' hyperbole, "There will not be one stone left upon another" (v. 2).

To a good Jew of Jesus' day the end of the Temple would seem like the end of the world. Apparently, then, the disciples have in mind both the end of the Temple and the end of the world when they ask, "What sign will there be when *all these things* are about to come to an end?" (v. 4). Jesus' answer seems directed at first to the end of their own lives rather than to the end of the Temple or of the world. He warns them not to follow false messiahs and not to lose their peace over wars, earthquakes, famines, persecutions (vv. 5-8). The special stress upon how to conduct themselves in testifying to their faith and continuing to spread the good news "to all nations" (v. 10) suggests that Mark's community is facing severe trials and needs the special guidance of the Holy Spirit (v. 11), as their families break under the strain (v. 12).

Jesus' warning, "When you see the *desolating abomination* standing where he should not . . . flee to the mountains" (v. 14) would remind his first readers of Daniel 9:27, "On the temple wing shall be the *horrible abomination* until the ruin that is decreed is poured out upon the horror." In Daniel, this "abomination" probably refers to the statue of Zeus placed in the Temple by Antiochus IV, the Syrian king who thereby precipitated the Maccabean revolt. In Jesus' warning the "desolating abomination" seems to refer to the profanation of the

Temple by the Roman army. The ensuing detailed instructions about rapid flight apparently refer to the urgency of fleeing before the destruction of Jerusalem, an event that the Jewish historian Josephus describes as a horror unparalleled in the world's calamities. That this was a true prophecy of Jesus—whether Mark's report of it was written before or after the event—seems verified by the testimony of the early church historian Eusebius that the Christians did escape Jerusalem before its utter destruction by the Romans.

The following part of Jesus' discourse, about the darkening sky and the falling stars (vv. 24-25), is reminiscent of the signs and portents by which Old Testament prophets suggested the cosmic significance, at least to the people of the time, of the fall of Babylon (see Is 13:10). This is apocalyptic language, a literary type used increasingly after 200 B.C. to describe the final cataclysmic struggle between good and evil. Such language is not meant to be taken literally. But the event that Jesus is here foretelling is itself so significant that it merits truly earthshaking figures of speech: It is the second coming of Christ! "Then they will see 'the *Son of Man* coming in the clouds' with great power and glory" (v. 26). This sentence is nearly a direct quotation of Daniel 7:13, where "One like a *son of man*" is seen in prophetic vision coming on clouds to God's throne to receive "dominion, glory, and kingship" over all peoples. The title Son of Man has now taken on a new association with divine power and glory, which can be added to the associations with suffering that we have already seen in Ezekiel's Son of Man who must eat the scroll of lamentation and in Isaiah's servant of the Lord who will endure death for others.

Then Jesus makes a prediction that seems unfulfilled: "This generation will not pass away until all these things have taken place" (v. 30). In the context, the phrase "all these things" apparently refers both to signs presaging the destruction of the Temple and Jerusalem, and to those preceding the second coming of the Son of Man. Many early Christians, Paul among them, were expecting the imminent second coming of Christ (1 Thes 4:13-17). In the whole context of this gospel it seems likely that Mark understands the prediction to refer to his own generation as the last before the second coming, the eschatological generation that must be prepared to carry the cross with Jesus even to the ultimate sacrifice. Yet also consonant with the context of this gospel is the broader interpretation of "this generation" as referring to the Christian people, who will not cease to exist in the world before the second coming.

Jesus has no intention of telling his disciples when to expect his second coming, for he leaves it wrapped in mystery: "But of that day or hour, no one knows, neither the angels in heaven, nor the Son, but only the Father" (v. 32). The succeeding sentences make it evident that Jesus' real point is not the *time* of the second coming, but the fact that it will be the moment of *reckoning*, so "Watch!" (v. 37). After all, death is that moment of reckoning for each of us, "the day of the Lord" that can come at any time, like the return of the master to the servants left in charge (v. 34). The real message, then, is: "Be watchful! Be alert! You do not know when the time [of the end of the world or of your own death] will come" (v. 33).

Much has been made of Jesus' statement here that not even the Son knows the time of the second coming. Some scholars consider it evidence that Jesus shared fully in our human condition of ignorance of the future. Others insist that he was merely using mental reservation to convey the meaning, "I do not know this thing as far as you are concerned; I am not commissioned to reveal it to you." There seems to be no way to resolve the question by analysis of this passage alone. Moreover, the general context of Mark is ambiguous on this point. On the one hand Mark's Jesus formally predicts his passion, death and resurrection three times. On the other hand he reacts with surprise on several occasions in which he discovers his disciples' lack of understanding and faith. It is likely that Mark himself had not resolved in his own mind the mystery of Jesus' knowledge. How could he if it is truly a mystery?

This mystery has intrigued theologians over the years. How could Jesus be the Son of God equal to the Father without knowing what the Father knows? Yet how could he be a real man and know what the Father knows? The church struggled with these apparently contradictory concepts for four centuries before defining the doctrine of Jesus' hypostatic union with the Second Person of the Trinity at the Council of Ephesus (431): He is *one person*, at the same time fully man and fully God. As man he suffers human limitations, including that of knowledge. As God he has no limitations. How these two infinitely different natures with their corresponding modes of knowledge are united and reconciled in the one Jesus of Nazareth is a divine mystery beyond the power of the greatest theologians to explain fully.

Perhaps the best we can do at this point is let this question of the knowledge of Jesus intrigue and tease us as we read further in the gospels, struggling to penetrate deeper into the mystery. But in the end we must allow the mind of Jesus to remain wrapped in mystery, as do the evangelists, as does the church in defining the Incarnation as a mystery. We might feel that it is vital for our relationship with Jesus to enter into his mind and heart, as we do in our most intimate personal relationships. But we must remember that the Jesus who lives in the Christian today is the living Jesus who rose from the dead and ascended to the "right hand of the Father." Whether his knowledge before his exaltation was the same as after it is a part of the mystery that need not concern us unduly, for it is with the risen Jesus that we now have our relationship, yet the very same Jesus walked the roads of Galilee. The mystery of his present knowledge at the right hand of his Father in heaven can be no barrier to the intimate relationship to which he calls us with himself.

After all, Jesus does not call upon us to imitate the *extent* of his knowledge, but rather, its *focus*. Mark's Jesus has made it clear that the great center of his human consciousness is his Father: "Love the Lord your God"; and all men and women: "Love your neighbor as yourself." To enter the kingdom of God in the very mind and heart of Jesus must then mean to keep God so firmly in mind and heart as our Father that we see in all his human creatures our brothers and sisters. It is not the extent of our consciousness that makes us Christians, but its quality of recognizing all human beings as our brothers and sisters, children of our one Father.

This truth, constituting the general context of Mark, supplies the content of what Jesus would have us bear in mind when he commands: "Be watchful! Be alert! You do not know when the time will come" (v. 33), the appointed time for entering into the kingdom of God in its eternal form.

REFLECTION AND PRAYER

Am I ready to die at this moment?

If not, what must I do to become ready, to be able to look calmly upon the moment of my death with confidence in my Lord?

Lord Jesus, I confess my fear of death; it is only my trust in you that calms me when I think of my coming death.

Final Approach to the Passion (Mk 14:1-31)

Jesus' own appointed time is fast approaching! Chapter 14 moves with rapid pace from the plotting of the chief priests and scribes (vv. 1-2) to the woman's anointing Jesus for burial (vv. 3-9), Judas' negotiations with the chief priests (vv. 10-11), the disciples' preparations for the Last Supper (vv. 12-16), the supper itself (vv. 17-31), and the beginning of the passion with the agony in the garden (vv. 34-42).

Significantly, Mark follows his account of the chief priests' decision to execute Jesus with that of the anointing of Jesus by an unnamed woman as he dines in the house of Simon, whom he has apparently cured of leprosy. The disciples, in their new-found zeal for the poor, miss the real meaning of the woman's sacrifice of expensive ointment. But Jesus praises her, pointing out the deep meaning of her act: "She has anticipated anointing my body *for burial*" (v. 8).

In his manner of relating this incident Mark not only foreshadows the death of Jesus, but subtly underlines the identity of Jesus as the Christ, the *anointed one*, David's special heir foretold by Nathan as Yahweh's own son (2 Sm 7:14). Davidic kings were anointed with oil for glorious enthronement in power. Jesus, the *Christ*, is anointed with "perfumed oil" (v. 4) for his ignominious enthronement in helpless agony upon the cross.

Evidently this "waste" so exasperates Judas that he now takes the first step toward betrayal (vv. 10-11).

Mark again sounds the note of impending doom in verse 12: "On the first day of the Feast of Unleavened Bread, when they *sacrificed the Passover lamb* . . ." Jesus, soon to be revealed as the true Passover Lamb, sends two disciples to look for a man carrying a water jar, an unusual sight easily noticed since that was considered women's work. By indicating that Jesus foresees apparently insignificant events leading to his celebration of the paschal meal, Mark is suggesting the importance of this meal, in conjunction with the coming passion and death, for revealing Jesus' true identity.

Mark reports his first words at the Last Supper as foretelling his betrayal by one who is even now celebrating fellowship with him, the one "who dips with me into the dish" (v. 20).

Yet even in this black moment Jesus transforms the ancient Passover meal, which celebrated Israel's liberation from slavery, into the new paschal mystery of salvation from the slavery of sin, salvation epitomized in the Eucharist. Blessing the unleavened Passover bread, he breaks it and mysteriously transforms it into his own body to serve as their food: "Take it; this is my body" (v. 22). Giving thanks (*eucharistesas* in Greek), Jesus transforms the wine: "This is my blood of the covenant, which will be shed for many" (v. 24). Again Jesus uses *many* in the Hebrew sense of "all," as in Mk 10:45. The ancient covenant celebration of Israel's liberation from slavery has been transformed into the new covenant celebration of eternal salvation through the sacrifice of Jesus, now to be accomplished, as he suggests in the final words of Mark's report of the Last Supper: "I shall not drink again the fruit of the vine until the day when I drink it new in the kingdom of God" (v. 25).

Mark does not pause to suggest the thoughts and feelings racing through the minds and hearts of the disciples as they receive for the first time their Lord's body and blood. Why do they need this new form of his presence, since he is already sitting there with them? This new food nourishes them with a share in his own love and courage. He is granting them a new intimate union with his very being dwelling within them and a tangible way to renew that union even after his impending death!

As they sing a hymn and walk to the Mount of Olives, they need that inner life with him as the thought of his death weighs heavily upon them, for Jesus predicts that their faith will be shaken when "the shepherd" is struck. Peter declares that his own faith is unshakable, but Jesus foretells his threefold denial. Rashly, Peter insists on having the last word in the matter (v. 31).

REFLECTION AND PRAYER

When I feel betrayed by others, do I try to remember how Jesus suffered betrayal and unite my hurt with his?

Do I appreciate his gift of the Eucharist enough to accept it often with great gratitude?

Jesus, thank you for offering me your very body and blood to nourish my spirit with a taste of the kingdom of God!

Jesus Suffers Agony and Trial (Mk 14:32—15:20)

Mark reports that Jesus invites Peter, James and John, those he had specially prepared by their presence at his raising of Jairus' daughter and his transfiguration, to witness his agony. Mark stresses Jesus' utter humanity: "He began to be *troubled and distressed*" (v. 34). His poignant words, "My heart is *sorrowful even to death*," draw no response from those he has prepared for this ordeal. He is alone among them. But he still has God as his intimate Father: "Abba, Father, all things are possible to you" (v. 36). Mark is the only evangelist who reports Jesus' use in this solemn moment of the Aramaic word by which a child intimately addresses his father, *Abba*. Then the perfect prayer: "Take this cup away from me, but *not what I will but what you will.*" Jesus is expressing his complete confidence in the prophecy that Isaiah planted in the midst of his suffering-servant songs:

> O afflicted one, drunk, but not with wine,
> > Thus says the Lord, your Master, your God, who defends his people:
> See, I am taking from your hand *the cup of staggering*;
> The bowl of my wrath
> > you shall no longer drink (Is 51:21-22).

Yet even if his Father does not take away that cup, Jesus still accepts it as the expression of the will to which he has always conformed his own, for he knows that "the bowl of my wrath," like "the scroll of lamentation," expresses his Father's disapproval of the sins he has come to expiate.

Even in that renewal of his total commitment to the Father, this very human Jesus still craves the support of his friends. He has to rouse them from sleep. Finding no consolation from them, he returns to his prayer again—and still again.

At last Judas and his mob arrive. Judas identifies Jesus by embracing him! Then the almost equally ironic embrace of arrest: "They laid hands on him" (v. 46). One of the bystanders (Peter, according to John) cuts off the ear of the high priest's slave. Jesus quickly quells the violence by handing himself over without resistance, "that the Scriptures may be fulfilled" (v. 49)—the revealed plan of his Father! All his followers now desert him. One young man even leaves his clothes in the hands of a guard and runs off naked, an insignificant detail omitted by Matthew and Luke, but perhaps a vivid memory for Mark as the man involved.

The Jewish guards lead Jesus to the high priest, who has already assembled the members of the Sanhedrin, the Jewish ruling council. They keep "trying to obtain testimony against Jesus" (v. 55), apparently by bribery, and succeed in getting some witnesses to say that Jesus declared he would destroy the Temple and reconstruct it in three days. But the testimony is marred by such serious discrepancies that the Sanhedrin cannot accept it.

So the high priest changes his strategy and questions Jesus directly: "Are you the Messiah, the son of the Blessed One?" (v. 61).

Mark's Jesus answers directly and unequivocally: "I am." Moreover, he identifies himself as the " '*Son of Man* / seated at the right hand of the Power [God] and coming with the clouds of heaven' " (v. 62, quoting Dn 7:13-14).

To express his utter shock the high priest tears his garments, an act expressly forbidden in Leviticus 21:10. He accuses Jesus of blasphemy, a crime to be punished by stoning (Lv 24:14-16). Jesus is condemned to death, spit upon, taunted, beaten and ridiculed.

Meanwhile, Peter has apparently regained his courage. He follows the arresting party at a distance and even enters the court of the high priest (v. 54). Yet he cannot withstand even the passing challenge of a servant girl without denying any knowledge of Jesus (v. 68). Not once but three times Peter denies Jesus, finally cursing and swearing. Upon hearing the second cockcrow, "he broke down and wept" (v. 72). This is the man that Jesus has been calling the "rock"! Mark carefully details this tragic failure of the leader of the Twelve, his possible source for this account, as a warning to his readers not to depend solely on their own human frailty in the face of persecution.

At daybreak the members of the Sanhedrin decide upon their ultimate course of action. Under the Romans they apparently have the power to execute Jesus by stoning, but in their zeal to disgrace him before his own people they want to see him crucified, a degrading execution reserved to the Roman governor, Pilate. So they drag him to Pilate and level many accusations against him, chief of which, judging by Pilate's question to Jesus, must have been his supposed claim to be king of the Jews—after all, he was always talking about the kingdom he had come to establish. Jesus answers only indirectly, "You say so" (Mk 15:2), giving Pilate no grounds to condemn him. To further accusations he puts up no defense (v. 5).

Pilate is no fool: "He knew that it was out of envy that the chief priests had handed him over" (v. 10). He can see by Jesus' dignified demeanor that he is a better man than they. Perhaps he also knows by report that Jesus has been taking over their religious leadership of the people. In accord with the custom of releasing one Jewish prisoner on their festival, he offers the crowd Jesus, ironically identifying him in this critical moment as "the king of the Jews" (v. 9). To Pilate's surprise the mob, incited by the chief priests, prefer the murderer Barabbas, whose name means "son of the father," obviously a different father from that of Jesus! Then they demand that Jesus be crucified, drowning out Pilate's questions about justice. Many members of this mob are probably the same people who greeted Jesus with loud hosannas less than a week before.

In the end, Mark's Pilate crumbles: "After he had Jesus scourged, he handed him over to be crucified" (v. 15). Scourging by the Romans was indeed a grim torture, an indefinite number of strokes inflicted with leather thongs to which were attached bits of bone or metal that tore the skin mercilessly and could result in death.

The Roman soldiers, experienced in administering torture, decide to have their own fun. They mock Jesus by dressing him in royal purple and pressing upon his head a "crown of thorns" (v. 17), which they repeatedly strike. What a litany of torture: scourging, crowning with thorns, blows, spitting, mock worship! Perhaps Mark is detailing the sufferings not only of Jesus, but also of those who try to follow him.

REFLECTION AND PRAYER

Lord Jesus, suffering Son of Man, I am appalled at your agony. How could your own people bring you to trial? Yet I know that my sins have contributed to bringing you to agony and trial. Forgive me! Unite me to yourself in my times of agony and trial.

Jesus Crucified! (Mk 15:21-47)

Finally, the cross. The soldiers force Simon the Cyrenian to carry the cross of Jesus, a clear indication of the extent to which the previous tortures have weakened him. Simon's sons Alexander and Rufus are evidently known to Mark's original readers, suggesting at least one source of some of the traditions that developed into the Way of the Cross. The details of the events along that way are apparently so well known to Mark's community that he feels no need to mention them here.

As they reach Golgotha, "Place of the Skull" (v. 22), the soldiers show a shred of pity by offering Jesus a drug to deaden his final sufferings. Such drugs were sometimes prepared by compassionate women, perhaps in Jesus' case by those mentioned in verse 40. Jesus refuses even this legitimate alleviation of pain.

"They crucified him" (v. 25), the most concise description of the most excruciating suffering in history! The soldiers who crucify him take as their reward his clothes, for which they gamble. It must have been an ironic pleasure for the winner to be able to sport the garments of the man crucified under the inscription "The King of the Jews" (v. 26)!

We generally think of the final agony of Jesus upon the cross as taking place between noon (following John 19:14) and 3:00 p.m. But Mark tells us that he was crucified at "nine o'clock in the morning" (v. 25), probably meaning sometime between nine and noon by the Roman way of telling time. Later on, Mark says that "at three o'clock" (v. 33) Jesus spoke the only word on the cross that he records, presumably just before dying. The efforts of scholars to explain the discrepancy between Mark and John in the duration of the crucifixion are based upon conjecture. In the end we must remain open to a crucifixion of three to six hours' duration.

Jesus' Aramaic cry, translated by Mark as "My God, my God, why have you forsaken me?" (v. 34), is indeed the cry of a man in the ultimate agony of abandonment. It is his final temptation to give up the mission entrusted to him by this God who seems to forsake him in his greatest need. And it can become a temptation for us: How can Jesus be abandoned by God if he is really divine himself? Mark seems to be telling us that the messianic secret he has stressed so frequently in the first part of his gospel has a much deeper meaning than we at first supposed. The life of Jesus has been so ambiguous, even to his closest followers, that the mystery of his identity as the Messiah remains veiled in the very moment of his saving act on the cross.

Yet Mark has left hints that allow the eyes of faith to penetrate beneath the surface of this apparently despairing cry and perceive a much deeper meaning in it as the first line of Psalm 22, the psalm that centuries before the crucifixion predicted specific sufferings, which Mark—or the transmitter of the apostolic tradition upon which he is relying—perceives as applying to Jesus on the cross. Verses 7-9 of the psalm, in words echoed closely by Mark in verses 29-32, describe the mockery to which Jesus is subjected by the chief priests and scribes. They surely know this important messianic psalm by heart; they can hardly be the ones who think he is calling upon Elijah (v. 35). That first line of the psalm must trigger their memories to run through those opening verses and recognize the direct reference to the very words of scorn that they have just flung at Jesus! In verses 15-16 of the psalm they can recognize the sufferings that they now witness impressed upon his dying body. Verse 19 describes the gambling of the soldiers for his garments. Verses 20-31 proclaim the confidence in God that still lives in Jesus, even within his anguished cry of abandonment, even as he utters "a loud cry" and breathes his last (v. 37).

It must be this holy death-in-the-Lord that moves the centurion

to declare: ''Truly this man was the Son of God!'' (v. 39). This proclamation of Jesus' true identity climaxes the second part of Mark's gospel, in parallel to the declaration of Peter, ''You are the Messiah'' (Mk
8:29), which closes the first part. It was a Jew, the prominent leader of
the Twelve, who uttered the most powerful summary of what is revealed in the ''first act'' of Mark's gospel, but it is an obscure Gentile
who makes that utterance in the ''second act.'' How effective this contrasting parallelism! And how piercing the irony of the almost immediate juxtaposition of ''My God, my God, *why have you forsaken
me?*'' with ''Truly this man was the *Son of God*!''

Note the symbolism of Mark's observation, ''The veil of the sanctuary was torn in two from top to bottom'' (v. 38). The curtain that hid
from the people the sanctuary of God's presence has been rent asunder
to allow free access to him. The old covenant has been fulfilled in Jesus'
death, and its Temple worship replaced by Jesus himself, the sacrifice
most pleasing to God, Father of the new Passover Lamb.

Yet it is still a tragic scene of death. The women mourners are
there (vv. 40-41). Joseph of Arimathea makes hurried burial arrangements; Pilate is assured that Jesus is really dead; and finally Jesus is
buried in a rock-hewn tomb sealed with a great stone. All is finished
before sunset, the beginning of the Jewish sabbath.

REFLECTION AND PRAYER

Do I really believe that Jesus suffered and died?

Do I believe that he died for me in fulfillment of God's eternal
plan of salvation?

When I have something to suffer, do I try to unite my suffering
with that of my crucified Savior?

Lord Jesus, King of Jews and Gentiles, I bow humbly before your cross,
contemplating your sufferings in deep adoration. I accept my coming
death in whatever form God wills, and lovingly unite it to yours.

Jesus' Resurrection Announced (Mk 16:1-8)

It is indeed a sad sabbath for Jesus' followers. During the night
following it, the holy women prepare their perfumed oils so that at
sunrise they may hurry to the tomb and finish the anointing of Jesus'
body (vv. 1-2). Their problem of how to enter the tomb has mysteriously been solved; the stone has already been rolled back from the en-

trance by the time they arrive. But instead of Jesus' body, they see "a young man . . . clothed in a white robe" (v. 5), obviously a heavenly visitor who reports the resurrection of Jesus and instructs them to tell the disciples to go to Galilee to meet him. Frightened, the women flee from the empty tomb and say "nothing to anyone" (v. 8). Thus ends the original version of the gospel of Mark.

Did Mark add a further account of Jesus' appearances, an account that has been lost, or did he deliberately end on this ambiguous note, almost of gloom despite the reported resurrection? At least three later writers tried to remedy what they considered an inadequate ending by adding further details to Mark's gospel.

The Longer Ending (Mk 16:9-20)

"The longer ending," though evidently added in a style quite different from Mark's, has been canonically accepted as an inspired part of the gospel of Mark. Apparently when the four gospels were put together for liturgical and catechetical use, probably toward the end of the first century or the beginning of the second, the editor or editors added these verses to bring Mark into closer harmony with the other gospels. The addition is certainly true to the faith of early Christians, for it adds little more than the details that it culls from these other gospels.

This longer ending is a good example of the editorial work on the gospels that was evidently a part of the canonical process of fitting them together as parts of the larger whole that eventually became known as the New Testament. This ending also gives us clear clues to the original interpretation of the resurrection accounts of the other gospels, from which it was compiled.

Without description, the longer ending reports the resurrection itself, and Jesus' appearances to Mary Magdalene (vv. 9-10; more fully related in John 20:11-18), to the two disciples on the road to "the country" (vv. 12-13; more complete in the Emmaus account of Luke 24:13-35), and finally to the Eleven, whom Jesus commissions to "proclaim the gospel to every creature" (vv. 14-15; following Luke 24:36-47) and baptize those who believe (v. 16; following Matthew 26:16-20).

But the editor departs from the other gospels in a few notable details. Although apparently unmindful of the promise of Mark's "young man" that Jesus will appear in Galilee, he remains loyal to

Mark's severe portrayal of the apostles' lack of faith (vv. 11, 13, 14). He has caught one of Mark's deepest theological ideas, perhaps the one that lies at the root of his use of the messianic secret: close as the disciples were to the fully human Jesus, they could not truly believe in the mystery of his divinity until they had seen him risen from the dead.

In verses 15-18 the longer ending attributes to Jesus a final summary of directives, derived at least in part from the other gospels and from Paul's letters. Jesus explicitly makes faith and baptism the conditions for salvation (v. 16). He promises that "those who believe" (v. 17) will expel demons, speak in tongues, heal the sick and be unharmed by serpents or poison (as in Acts 28:5). Recently two men offered to prove their faith in this passage, one by letting a deadly snake bite him, the other by drinking poison. Within a short time both died. Perhaps these zealous men did prove something about this passage: It is meant to be symbolic, not literal. Jesus is not offering physical immunity to his followers, but protection against the moral poison of the sinful society that he calls them to serve.

After these final promises, apparently still on the day of the resurrection, "Jesus . . . was taken up into heaven and took his seat at the right hand of God" (v. 19), theological expressions derived from the Old Testament (2 Kgs 2:11 ; Ps 110:1) and already used in Romans 8:34 and in Acts 7:55. Yet Jesus is not really absent from Christians; when the Eleven go forth to preach, "the Lord *worked with them* and confirmed the word through accompanying signs" (v. 20).

Comparison of this longer ending with the other resurrection accounts reveals the difficult, if not impossible, task of harmonizing these reports, as the editor apparently attempted to do. Scholars have long considered the resurrection accounts as the most diverse part of the gospels. There seems to be no way of determining the real sequence of events or of reconciling the differing reports of Jesus' appearances. The diversity of the accounts reflects the impossibility of fitting the timeless life of the resurrected Christ within the confines of our time. It also points to the confusion of the witnesses, who were highly excited by the events that they witnessed. The editor of the longer ending obviously opted for a summary in which he could avoid most descriptive details and indicate only vague time references, which would signal his readers that he made no pretense of presenting a strictly chronological order of appearances.

Although this longer ending rounds off the gospel of Mark to fit more neatly into the company of the other gospels, it seems quite possible that Mark deliberately ended his gospel at chapter 16, verse 8. Perhaps those who felt the need to end on a brighter note had lost touch with the circumstances of the community for which Mark wrote, suggested by the somber mood of his gospel as a whole. In the "first act" Mark's readers would see Jesus beset by the crowd at every turn, unable to find a moment's rest even by retreating far from towns, and trying to keep his identity a secret to avoid being completely misunderstood. In the "second act" they would see Jesus repeatedly foretelling the tragedy of the Place of the Skull and finally dying in darkness.

By ending with the negative report that the women fled without relaying the message of the resurrection, "for they were afraid" (Mk 16:8), Mark would be giving his apparently wavering community a powerful warning that, even after Jesus' resurrection, only their faith could penetrate the messianic secret of Jesus' real identity, and only their courage could witness his resurrection to the world.

If Mark wrote this gospel in Rome during the persecution of Nero shortly after Peter's martyrdom, he had good reason to present Christians a somber picture of Jesus' own life and death. Such must be theirs! They could expect, if caught, to be lifted up on crosses, covered with pitch and burned alive to illuminate one of Nero's garden parties or provide "entertainment" at his public shows—and finally to be thrown into an unmarked public grave. Perhaps, then, Mark deliberately refused to brighten his ending with the account of Jesus' marvelous appearances and contented himself with a mere report that Jesus had risen from the dead.

After all, this stark belief was the only foundation upon which his fellow Christians could base their hope. Today it is still the only foundation of our hope.

REFLECTION AND PRAYER

Do I really believe in Jesus' resurrection?

What is its meaning for my life?

How does this belief illumine the meaning of my life, positive experiences as well as negative?

Risen Lord, I renew my pledge of allegiance to you, my part in the new covenant you offer us.

SUGGESTIONS FOR FURTHER READING OR REFERENCE

Achtemeier, Paul J. *Mark*. Philadelphia: Fortress Press, 1975. Analysis of the major themes of the gospel of Mark.

Cranfield, C.E.B. *The Gospel According to Saint Mark*. Cambridge University Press, 1959. A very solid commentary.

Montague, George T., S.M. *Mark: Good News for Hard Times*. Ann Arbor, MI: Servant Books, 1981. Very well-written and interesting commentary.

Van Linden, Philip, C.M. *The Gospel According to Mark*. Collegeville, MN: The Liturgical Press, 1983. Simple, easy-to-read commentary.

PART III

Finding Jesus the Messiah With Matthew

As we read the gospel of Matthew together, we will soon notice that it is quite similar to that of Mark in many ways, yet very different in others. So, too, for Luke's gospel. The remarkable similarity of the first three gospels, in their content, order of events, vocabulary and often in style, has led to many studies placing them in parallel columns to observe this similarity at a glance. From such efforts to construct a satisfactory synopsis, these three gospels are called the synoptic gospels, or simply the synoptics.

Yet often the same event found in two or three of the synoptics is given a distinct focus in each, sometimes even a different meaning. Why are these three gospels so similar, yet so distinct? To what extent did their authors depend on each another or reject one another? What were their basic sources? Such questions gave rise to the "synoptic problem," so complex that scholars have not arrived at a universally accepted solution.

The Synoptic Problem

All three synoptics have in common approximately 360 verses (the threefold tradition), the number depending upon how many minor differences the counter considers equivalent. Besides the basic 360 verses, Mark and Matthew have about 175 further verses in common; Mark and Luke, 50 verses; and Matthew and Luke, 230 verses not found in Mark (twofold traditions). That leaves a unique tradition in

101

Mark of about 70 verses; in Matthew, 330; and in Luke, 520.

From these facts and a minute study of all three synoptics, scholars have advanced toward consensus on the following points:

- From oral apostolic traditions and perhaps from written accounts now lost, Mark was the first to write a canonical gospel.
- Independent of one another, both Matthew and Luke seem to have had access to a copy of Mark that they each used as one of their primary sources.
- Matthew and Luke had another source or sources in common, presumed to be a lost collection of Jesus' sayings called *Q* (from the German *Quelle*, meaning "source").
- Matthew and Luke also had other sources, proper to each.
- All three synoptic evangelists were wholly or largely dependent upon intermediate sources. Theirs were not eyewitness accounts, but rather the third stage in the transmission of Jesus' life and message:

> First stage: Jesus himself
>
> Second stage: eyewitness apostolic traditions
>
> Third stage: the gospels

The two-source hypothesis, considering Mark and *Q* as the two written sources used by both Matthew and Luke, has come under recent attack. But it is still the most widely accepted theory, and those who reject it have not been able to agree on any other theory that would better answer the synoptic problem. The postulating of *Q* seems to be the weakest part of the two-source hypothesis. There is a much stronger consensus that Mark's gospel was the first written, and in our careful reading we will find considerable evidence that both Matthew and Luke made use of it without being wholly dependent upon it.

The similarity of so many of the passages of the synoptics and, despite discrepancies in many details, the overall compatibility of the synoptics with one another, point to the fact that they have a common primary source: the very life and words of Jesus. Their differences are attributable to their distinct sources and their specific purposes in writing. For instance, if we suppose that both Matthew and Luke made use of Mark's gospel, it becomes easily understandable that they would omit parts of Mark that they considered covered more adequately by their other sources or that they thought their communities might find offensive, difficult or unimportant.

Substantial discrepancies resulting in contradictory portraits of Jesus would certainly shake our faith in the truth of one or more of these gospels. But the discrepancies we find in the synoptics, though troublesome, are confined to relatively secondary questions. Moreover, these very discrepancies testify that the evangelists were not slavish copyists; they straightforwardly presented their versions as best they could using their distinct sources and considering the needs of the communities for which they were writing. Hence their agreement on essentials becomes all the more forceful. They certainly reflect the same basic faith in Jesus' identity, action and message.

Authorship of the First Gospel

The theory that Matthew was somewhat dependent upon Mark for much of his material is at first quite disturbing. Wasn't Matthew an apostle, an eyewitness of the events he relates in his gospel? Ancient tradition dating from Papias, about A.D. 130, and quoted by Eusebius, holds that the apostle Matthew wrote down the discourses of Jesus in Hebrew or Aramaic. Some modern scholars suggest that Q may have been this manuscript. Since neither Q nor Aramaic Matthew have ever been found, it is impossible to verify this hypothesis. Moreover, the Greek Matthew contains word plays that would be highly unlikely in a translation from Aramaic, and its Old Testament quotations are taken from the Greek Septuagint—both strong arguments against an original Matthew in Aramaic.

As a test of the tradition that Matthew was written by the apostle, let us compare Mark 2:14-17 with Matthew 9:9-13. Except for the change of the name Levi to Matthew, one account might easily have been copied from the other. If one of these writers were relating his own calling by Jesus wouldn't his gospel contain a more detailed account?

Putting aside the question of whether Levi and Matthew were two persons or two names for the same person, which of these conversion accounts is the original? It is impossible to tell from this comparison; we must try others. Years ago, when people uncritically accepted the ancient tradition that Matthew's was the first gospel written, they presumed that Mark's shorter gospel was a summary of Matthew's. But comparisons between their accounts of the same incident consistently suggest that *Matthew is the summarizer of Mark*, and that Mark's gospel is shorter because it contains fewer of Jesus' sayings. If Matthew wrote first, and Mark then expanded some of his accounts by adding picturesque details, why would he skip so much of Matthew? And why would he transcribe Matthew into a much inferior style?

Let's compare Mark 2:2-12 with Matthew 9:2-8 to see who is doing the summarizing. In this account of the cure of the paralytic, Mark provides many details that are missing in Matthew, such as the lowering of the paralytic from the roof, most of the inner thoughts of the scribes and the statement of the crowd. Apparently Matthew considers these details unnecessary to the story, even distracting from the point that he wants to stress. Matthew's summary of the inner thoughts of the scribes effectively focuses greater attention upon the action and words of Jesus in forgiving sins. To gain concentration upon this forgiveness, Matthew even sacrifices Mark's striking description of the friends' lowering the paralytic from the roof as well as the theological point that Jesus is responding to the faith of the paralytic's friends in forgiving him (Mk 2:5).

As we read Matthew we will see further comparisons of parallel passages in which it will become evident that Matthew is willing to sacrifice many details in order to gain the force of a more concise account and thereby achieve a greater emphasis upon what he considers to be the central issue at hand. In so doing he sometimes omits details that give a greater human touch to the account and to the portrayal of Jesus' action. He thereby seems further removed from the events than Mark. How, then, could he have been an apostle, an eyewitness?

We simply do not know who wrote Matthew's gospel. Use of a pseudonym by an author was a common practice in ancient times, usually without intention to deceive but merely to increase reader interest and acceptance. Of course the evangelist may have been a different Matthew, not the apostle. Or perhaps he was a disciple of the apostle or wrote for a community converted by the apostle Matthew. Whoever he was, the author of the gospel of Matthew usually displays such thorough knowledge of the Old Testament and of the way the rabbis used it in discourse, that some scholars suggest he was a converted Jewish rabbi. Others reject this theory, pointing to instances in which Matthew slips in his mastery of Old Testament trivia; for example, in chapter 23, verse 35 he evidently confuses Zechariah, son of Jehoiada (2 Chr 24:22), with Zechariah, son of Berechiah (Zec 1:1).

He seems to have written the gospel between 80 and 90 in Syria or

Palestine, probably for a community originally of Jewish background to whom his innumerable Old Testament echoes and 41 direct quotations—the most in any gospel—would strongly appeal. His main purpose is to strengthen his community's faith in Jesus as the fulfillment of Old Testament expectations of the Messiah, Son of David, Son of God. But apparently Matthew's community is suffering divisions, presumably caused by the admission of some new members of Gentile origin, for we will perceive in his gospel efforts to deal with such a problem. We will also observe evidence that his community may have recently been excommunicated by a larger Jewish community, and that some members of his community may even be doubting the divinity of Jesus.

So eager is Matthew to portray Jesus as the Messiah expected by the Old Testament prophets that he begins his gospel with two chapters of nativity narratives to establish this point even before his account of the baptism of Jesus.

Prologue: The Nativity Narratives (Mt 1—2)

Genealogy and Birth of Jesus (Mt 1)

By beginning with the genealogy of Jesus, Matthew roots him in the Old Testament as "the son of David, the son of Abraham" (v. 1). Matthew compiles the list of names up to verse 13 from Genesis, Ruth, 1 Chronicles, 2 Samuel and 2 Kings. But where he obtained the rest of his names is unknown. Either he was using family traditions, or simply adding more names to fill in his scheme of three groups of fourteen generations (v. 17)—three times double seven, the biblical seven that stood for completeness. Through this symbolic use of numbers Matthew is implying that Jesus is not only important as a direct descendant of Abraham through David, but that his importance is beyond measure.

Matthew's genealogy includes several women: Tamar, who had tricked her father-in-law Judah into sexual relations with her; Rahab, the "harlot" of Jericho who helped Joshua's spies escape; Ruth, a Gentile so poor that she lived by gleaning the fields of Boaz; and Uriah's wife, with whom David committed adultery and whom he married after murdering Uriah. Jewish lineage was traced through male ancestors; Matthew's inclusion of females deliberately emphasizes the fact that Jesus' lineage includes even sinners and Gentiles. He belongs to the whole human race, male and female, Jew and Gentile, good and bad!

It is significant that in ending with Joseph, Matthew refers to him not as the father of Jesus but as "the husband of Mary" (v. 16). Thus Mary, too, is included in the genealogy; in fact, hers is the thirteenth name after the Babylonian captivity, apparently making that name—unlike those of the other women—necessary to the counting of fourteen generations ending with "Jesus who is called the Messiah."

A further reason for Matthew's strange inclusion in his genealogy of both Joseph and Mary becomes clear in his next passage about the pregnancy of Mary "before they lived together" (v. 18). Although they are still only engaged, the state of betrothal among Galilean Jews was so binding that Joseph could publicly denounce what must appear to him as her infidelity. To expose her could subject her, as a woman suspected of adultery, to trial by ordeal in which she would be forced to drink water mixed with dust to see whether "her belly will swell and her thighs will waste away" (Nm 5:27). Any sign interpreted as failing the ordeal could end in her death by stoning (Dt 22:20-21). Loving her as he obviously does, Joseph is "unwilling to expose her to shame" (v. 19).

Yet Joseph is also unwilling to marry her, for as "a righteous man" he upholds God's law and believes that he must therefore break his union with one who has apparently broken that law by adultery. He decides "to divorce her quietly" by simply writing out a notice of divorce and dismissing her, in accord with Deuteronomy 24:1. But before doing so Joseph has a dream after the manner of Jacob's son Joseph, the great dreamer of the Old Testament. Even more exciting than the dreams of that first Joseph is his dream that, by the power of the Holy Spirit, Mary has conceived a son who is to be named Jesus, "because he will save his people from their sins" (v. 21). The name Jesus, a derivative of Joshua common at that time, had come to mean "Yahweh saves," to which Matthew adds, "his people from their sins" as an integral part of the etymology of the name Jesus.

Matthew makes his own comment to underline, by reference to Isaiah 7:14, one of the main points of this first chapter: The circumstances of Jesus' conception and birth are different from those of all other human beings; he is conceived and born of a virgin! It matters not that the Septuagint, from which Matthew quotes this passage of Isaiah, had translated the Hebrew word for "maiden" by the Greek word for "virgin"; Matthew is expressing the faith of the early church in the virginal conception of Jesus. Nor does it matter that Isaiah was probably thinking only of foretelling the birth of the next king of Israel (Hezekiah); the inspired evangelist sees in Isaiah's words a prophecy about Jesus, the one who above all others would "reject the bad and choose the good" (Is 7:15). By applying to Jesus Isaiah's designation "Emmanuel" and interpreting it to mean "God is with us," Matthew is likewise expressing the faith of the early church that it is Jesus who brings God to men. Just as he has suggested in genealogical terms, Matthew is now announcing in terms of Jesus' conception, birth and naming that he is truly the *Son of God*.

Notice that Matthew introduces his citation from Isaiah with the comment: "All this took place to fulfill what the Lord had said through the prophet" (v. 22). This clause will become a formula that Matthew alone among the evangelists consistently uses to introduce Old Testament citations proper to his gospel.

Matthew insists on Mary's virginal conception of Jesus by declaring that Joseph "had no relations with her until she bore a son" (v. 25). In the original Greek Matthew's use of "until" does not imply that Joseph had relations with her after the birth of Jesus; Matthew is merely emphasizing his point that Joseph was not the real father of Jesus. The strong tradition of the early church that Mary remained a virgin before, during and after the birth of Jesus is not contradicted by any New Testament passage, and is indeed in harmony with the general thrust of this passage, so delicately aware of Jesus' supreme dignity and of its implications for those divinely chosen to be his mother and his legal father.

Matthew ends his opening passage by observing that Joseph obeys the angel of his dream in naming his foster son Jesus, who thereby becomes Joseph's legal son. By reporting that it is Joseph who receives the angelic annunciation and confers Jesus' name, Matthew emphasizes Joseph's role in linking Jesus with the line of David. And Joseph is a worthy legal father of Jesus, for as "a righteous man" he is characterized, just as Jesus will be, by wholehearted obedience to God's word. Matthew presents him as our model in his deep regard for Mary and in his total dedication to God and to Jesus.

REFLECTION AND PRAYER

Has Matthew convinced me that Jesus belongs to the human race, to the same race as I?

Do I imitate Joseph in trying to interpret my dreams and desires in the light of my faith in God?

Do I imitate Mary in letting God direct my life and be my defense before others?

Jesus, Son of Abraham, Son of David, I adore you as God-with-us.

The Magi Story and the Flight Into Egypt (Mt 2)

As Matthew begins the story of the Magi, whom he identifies as astrologers, not kings, he names Bethlehem as the place of Jesus' birth during the reign of Herod. Whether this story is factual or fictitious, as many modern scholars suggest, it illustrates a truth much bigger than its concrete details: Jesus has come not only for Jews, but also for *Gentiles*! He is to be acknowledged as king by all men and women! Matthew is telling his originally Jewish community that Gentiles who follow the star of their own best dreams can find Jesus more surely than could the Jewish King Herod.

Perhaps Matthew composed this story of the Magi after the manner of a midrash, the Jewish rabbis' free use of Old Testament passages to make an important point. He may have imaginatively woven together the following texts:

> The kings of Tarshish and the Isles
> shall offer gifts;
> the kings of Arabia and Seba shall bring tribute.
> All kings shall pay him homage,
> all nations shall serve him (Ps 72:10-11).

> But you, Bethlehem-Ephrathah
> too small to be among the clans of Judah,
> From you shall come forth for me
> one who is to be ruler in Israel;
> Whose origin is from of old,
> from ancient times. . . .
> He shall stand firm and shepherd his flock . . .
> his greatness
> shall reach to the ends of the earth (Mi 5:1-3)

> A star shall advance from Jacob,
> and a staff [scepter] shall rise from Israel
> (Nm 24:17).

> Caravans of camels shall fill you,
> dromedaries from Midian and Ephah;

> All from Sheba shall come
> bearing gold and frankincense,
> and proclaiming the praises of the Lord (Is 60:6).

If we find it easy to think of gold, frankincense and myrrh as gifts symbolizing the veneration of Jesus as king, priest and prophet, why should we find it hard to think of this whole story of the Magi as symbolic? The church has not determined the interpretation of this account as either factual or symbolic. However, the story does acquire a deeper meaning if taken as a symbol of Jesus' significance for Gentiles as well as Jews, indeed, for all humankind. Whether we take this story as factual or symbolic—or both—the statues of the Magi at our Christmas crib scenes should mean more to us than a reminder of a passing incident in the world's history. And significantly, Matthew relates that they "saw the child *with Mary his mother*" (v. 11), as if to tell us where we, too, can best find Jesus.

Now, as had his ancestor, Joseph dreams again. Obediently he takes the child and his mother into Egypt. Throughout the rest of this chapter, Matthew continues to echo the Old Testament. The journey into Egypt echoes that of the Israelites, Jacob's sons (Gn 46). The threat to the child's life is like that to the life of the infant Moses (Ex 2). Matthew uses his formula, "that what the Lord had said through the prophet might be fulfilled" (v. 15), to cite Hosea 11:1, "Out of Egypt I called *my son*" (meaning Israel in Hosea; Jesus in Matthew). By implication, Matthew is saying that Jesus is the new Israel, the very embodiment of the people of God!

The slaughter of the Innocents echoes that of all other males at the time of Moses' birth. Again Matthew uses a variation of his formula, "Then was fulfilled what had been said through Jeremiah the prophet" (v. 17). In Jeremiah 31:15 Rachel, wife of Jacob (Israel), is portrayed weeping for her children, the lost Israelites who were assembled at Ramah centuries after her death there, to begin their long march into Babylonian exile. Matthew now applies the quotation to portray Rachel weeping for her new children, the Holy Innocents who die that Jesus might live, later to die for all.

The dream message by which Joseph is instructed to return "to the land of Israel" (v. 20), recalls the Exodus from Egypt into the land that became Israel. The reason given, "those who sought the child's life are dead," echoes the reason that God gave Moses for returning to Israel: "All the men who sought your life are dead" (Ex 4:19). Jesus is being called back to Israel by Yahweh to become the new founder of his people.

Finally, Matthew reports another dream directing Joseph to settle in Galilee. In accord with the unidentified prophecy, "He shall be called a Nazorean" (v. 23), Joseph takes the holy family to Nazareth. Matthew hints that he is composing this prophecy from Old Testament references, for he attributes it vaguely to "the prophets." Perhaps he intends it as a word play on the similar sounds of the Hebrew words for "Nazareth" and "shoot," to evoke Isaiah's prophecy: "A shoot [Jesus] shall sprout from the stump of Jesse [David's father]" (Is 11:1). Matthew's repeated use of some variation of the formula, "so that what had been spoken through the prophets might be fulfilled" (v. 23), stimulates our reflection upon the meaning of Jesus' life as fulfillment of the plan of God revealed throughout the Jewish scriptures.

All these Old Testament quotations and echoes add up to a prodigious effort on Matthew's part to interpret the life of Jesus as that of the new Moses, and even more significantly, as that of the new Israel. Matthew thereby presents Jesus as the incarnation of the people of God, experiencing their slavery in the flight into Egypt as a foreshadowing of his passion and death, and their Exodus from Egypt into "the land of Israel" as a foretaste of his resurrection and ascension to his Father.

It is pointless to question whether Matthew intended this second chapter to be taken as fact or as symbol. The perceptive reader will see that Matthew is saying in the terms that his own people understood best—Old Testament echoes—who Jesus really is: the man for all times and peoples. We must simply accept Matthew on these terms. He is declaring his own faith in Jesus, and the faith of the early Christians for whom he writes. Whether he is also telling us some of the actual events of Jesus' childhood is secondary to his purpose and impossible for modern scholarship to determine.

REFLECTION AND PRAYER

Do I imitate the Magi in following the guidance of the Spirit (the star) to find Jesus?

Do I find Jesus with Mary and Joseph?

Lord Jesus, I adore you as the very embodiment and life of your people.

Jesus Proclaims the Kingdom and Its Demands Upon Us (Mt 3—7)

Jesus Prepares for His Public Ministry (Mt 3—4)

In chapter 3 Matthew takes up his account of Jesus' life where Mark began, with the appearance of John the Baptist and the baptism of Jesus. If Matthew is writing with a copy of Mark before him, as many scholars suppose, we can see that he follows closely Mark's description of John, but adds to his message a greater demand for reform. In fact, John's opening theme, "Repent, for the kingdom of heaven is at hand!" (Mt 3:2), is identical with that of Jesus (Mt 4:17). And his strong condemnation of the Jewish leaders in verses 7-12 is a prelude to Jesus' even stronger condemnation in chapter 23.

John ends with the promise of one "mightier than I" (v. 11), who will baptize not merely "with water, for repentance," but "with the Holy Spirit and fire." This fire of the Holy Spirit will bring about quite different results when the mightier one, Jesus, separates those who respond to the Spirit from those who do not. Like the Palestinian harvester, Jesus will separate the good wheat from the useless chaff by throwing the grain into the wind (another biblical figure for the action of the Holy Spirit, Acts 2:2) with his "winnowing fan" (v. 12). In Jesus' good "wheat," the Spirit will enkindle the fire of his love; in the wicked "chaff" baptismal fire will become the "unquenchable fire" of squandered grace.

Of the accounts of Jesus' baptism, Matthew's is the only one that reports the intimate conversation in which John says that he should be baptized by Jesus. In his reply Jesus reveals something very significant about himself: "Allow it [my baptism] now, for thus it is fitting for us to fulfill all righteousness [action according to God's will]" (v. 15).

These first words of Jesus in Matthew' gospel identify him as a person wholly dedicated to carrying out the will of God, no matter what the cost. In the new context that Matthew has supplied in verses 11-12, the descent of the Holy Spirit upon Jesus is given greater significance than in Mark. And instead of reporting the Father's words of approval as directed only to Jesus (Mk 1:11), Matthew rephrases these words to direct them publicly to all present at the event: "This is my beloved Son" (v. 17).

In chapter 4 Matthew details the temptations in the desert, temptations that Mark merely reported as having taken place. Since both Matthew and Luke recount the same temptations that Jesus endured *alone*, scholars speculate that both evangelists are utilizing a meditation, current at that time, to illustrate the temptations mentioned by Mark.

As in Mark, it is the Spirit who leads Jesus into the desert. Mark wrote that Jesus "remained . . . for forty days," but Matthew says that he "*fasted* for forty days *and forty nights*" (Mt 4:2), stressing both Jesus' penitential action and its parallel with Israel's forty years in the desert. After such a fast, extreme hunger provides the setting for the first temptation.

Mark reported that in Jesus' first miraculous cure he silenced the possessing demon that had identified him as "the Holy One of God" (Mk 1:24). With this same supernatural knowledge of the identity of Jesus, Matthew's "tempter" addresses Jesus: "If you are the Son of God, command that these stones become loaves of bread" (v. 3). The word "command" suggests that the tempter's knowledge of Jesus is quite imperfect after all, for it identifies him primarily in terms of a power to be used for self-satisfaction. Jesus responds with a quotation from Deuteronomy 8:3 that identifies attachment to God's will, *expressed in his word*, as the real sustenance of life.

So the tempter, now identified as "the devil" (v. 5), cleverly attacks Jesus on his own ground. Trust in God, do you? Then throw yourself off this wall of the Temple trusting that Psalm 91:11-12 will be fulfilled in the angelic catch! The devil shamelessly quotes the book he hates. Jesus counters with another text: "You shall not put the Lord, your God, to the test" (v. 7, quoting Dt 6:16). The unquoted ending of this sentence, "as you did at Massah," would probably occur to Matthew's early readers as a sharp contrast between the rebellious spirit of Israel demanding water in the desert (Nm 20:2-3) and the humble obedience of Jesus.

The devil is persistent. From a mountaintop he offers Jesus all the kingdoms of the world if he will pay him homage. Matthew implies that all these kingdoms are already under the power of Satan. This temptation is a powerful climax, for it offers Jesus the chance to win back the world to his Father without paying the price of Calvary. But Jesus knows that all these kingdoms do not add up to the kingdom of God. With one final quotation from Deuteronomy 6:13, he declares that only God is to be adored and banishes the devil, whom he now identifies as "Satan" (v. 10), supreme agent of evil reigning over the dominion of darkness (see Mt 12:25-26).

By this dramatization of Jesus' temptations Matthew has presented Jesus as God's loyal Son, personified good who overcomes personified evil: "Then the devil left him, and, behold, angels came and ministered to him" (v. 11). Did this series of temptations really take place as Matthew tells it? Whether or not Jesus was tempted in this exact manner, the account certainly illustrates a truth far more profound than the factual level of the incident. Matthew's way of telling this truth must have been much more forceful to his community than was the direct statement of Hebrews: "We do not have a high priest who is unable to sympathize with our weaknesses, but one *who has similarly been tested in every way, yet without sin*" (Heb 4:15).

Following Mark, Matthew reports that Jesus began his public ministry only after the arrest of John the Baptist. But Matthew, again using his citation formula, adds an Old Testament reason for Jesus' selection of the region around the Lake of Galilee as site of his first mission. This was the land of Zebulun and Naphtali, northern Israelite tribes lost in the Assyrian invasion of 721 B.C., and therefore a place where "the people who sit in darkness" under Satan's dominion have special need of the "great light" foretold by Isaiah (Is 8:23—9:1). This passage of Isaiah, freely adapted by Matthew, introduces the famous lines used in our Christmas liturgy:

> For a child is born to us, a son is given us;
> upon his shoulders *dominion* rests (Is 9:5).

Matthew summarizes the message of Jesus to these people in nearly the same words as Mark. But he changes Mark's expression "the kingdom of God" to "the kingdom of *heaven*" (v. 17), a typical Jewish substitution for the name of God, considered too sacred even to write or speak. By placing Jesus' declaration that the kingdom of heaven is at hand almost immediately after the scriptural duel with Satan over the kingdoms of this world, Matthew has given Jesus' words even greater emphasis than did Mark.

Matthew now presents the calling of the first disciples, closely following Mark. But, having already shown Jesus' power over evil spirits by detailing his temptations, Matthew omits Mark's report of the cure of the possessed man and offers instead a general view of Jesus' triumphal tour of Galilee, "proclaiming the gospel of the kingdom, and curing every disease and illness" (v. 23).

REFLECTION AND PRAYER

Do I appreciate my own baptism as the beginning of my union with Jesus?

Do I try to find in this union my strength in time of temptation?

Do I nourish my soul on the word of God as did Jesus?

Jesus, you are the Lord of my life. I deliberately choose you in place of the darkness that sometimes envelops me.

Matthew Presents Jesus' Message in Five Major Discourses

In chapters 5—7 Matthew presents the first of five major discourses or sermons that he attributes to Jesus. They are easy to distinguish from other passages reporting words of Jesus because Matthew ends them by some variation of "when Jesus finished these words" (7:28). Noting Matthew's deep interest in the Old Testament, many scholars think he arranged these words of Jesus in five discourses as a deliberate parallel to the major part of the Old Testament, the first five books the Jews attributed to Moses and called the Torah. This is one of Matthew's many ways of saying that Jesus is the new Moses, the new lawgiver who brings the new covenant to God's people.

These five discourses constitute the major architectural structure of Matthew's gospel. We will therefore divide our reading of this gospel into five sections corresponding to the five discourses and the events or actions leading up to them. Matthew usually succeeds in tying together the discourses and the events to offer keys for the interpretation of both, as suggested in the following outline:

Action	*Discourse*
1. Jesus announces the kingdom of heaven and gathers followers (Mt 4:17-25).	He presents the kingdom law of love in the *Sermon on the Mount* (Mt 5—7).
2. He works 10 miracles showing his power and authority (Mt 8—9).	Then in his *Missionary Sermon* he instructs the Twelve to do likewise (Mt 10).
3. The Jews become hostile to Jesus (Mt 11—12).	He responds by teaching "obscurely" in his *Parables of the Kingdom* (Mt 13:4-52).

4. Further controversies and miracles (Mt 13:53—16:12) lead Peter to confess his faith in Jesus as Son of God. Jesus gives him authority over his future church, which will be endangered by persecution, weakness of faith, political tyranny and ambition (Mt 16:13—18:1).

These divisive forces call forth Jesus' *Sermon on Unity* (Mt 18:2-35).

5. Finally, Jesus moves toward Jerusalem proclaiming his "hardest" sayings (Mt 19—20).

He climaxes his final teaching with his *Sermon on the End of Time and the Last Judgment* (Mt 24—25), prelude to his passion, death and resurrection.

Since these five sermons constitute Matthew's chief claim to originality and strongly influence his handling of his material, they merit special attention in our efforts to understand his gospel. More than other passages, they give us clues to his major intentions, his characteristics as an evangelist and, above all, his distinctive vision of Jesus.

In reading Mark's gospel we discovered that one of his major intentions was to give us an insight into the true identity of Jesus through his actions and reactions. Mark thereby enabled us to enter into the consciousness of Jesus, much as we normally enter into the consciousness of our friends: First, we saw his human emotions through *his reactions* to people and events; second, we read his mind and heart through his *powerful actions* to meet other's needs.

As we listen to Jesus' discourses in Matthew's gospel we will develop a similar awareness of Jesus through use of a different means. Just as we look into the consciousness of a friend through his actions, we can also glimpse the workings of his mind and heart through his words, and in the case of Jesus, especially through *his words of authority*. By arranging these words of authority into five major sermons Matthew enables us to share his own vision into Jesus' consciousness, focused steadily upon our loving Father who provides for us as his children, all brothers and sisters of one another.

The first of these discourses, the famous Sermon on the Mount, is the longest and most powerful New Testament presentation of Jesus' moral teaching, Matthew's insight into Jesus' conscience! Luke reports a great part of this same discourse as being delivered by Jesus ''on a stretch of level ground'' (Lk 6:17). Matthew's setting, ''he went up the mountain'' (Mt 5:1), seems deliberately chosen to parallel God's dramatic presentation of the ten commandments to Moses. As Moses presented the law of the covenant to his people with God's authority, Jesus will now speak with God's authority in presenting the law of the new covenant. In this first solemn discourse Matthew has assembled the sayings of Jesus that serve as explanation of his initial proclamation: ''Repent, for the kingdom of heaven is at hand'' (Mt 4:17). Jesus spells out the reform demanded for entry into the new kingdom.

The Sermon on the Mount: Jesus Challenges Our Values (Mt 5:1-20)

In the Sermon on the Mount, Jesus goes beyond merely forbidding certain actions to present the positive attitudes that he requires of his followers, attitudes that reverse the world's values. The four beatitudes listed by Luke (Lk 6:20-22), apparently from *Q*, are expanded by Matthew to eight—nine, if we distinguish between persecution for the sake of righteousness (v. 10) and persecution for Jesus' sake (v. 11).

The first blessed, ''the poor *in spirit*,'' are members of ''the kingdom of heaven''; they let God rule their lives and therefore already belong to his kingdom. To Luke's version, ''you who are poor,'' Matthew adds ''in spirit,'' avoiding the appearance of promising God's blessing for material poverty. Nor is he promising that blessing for the ''poor spirited,'' or even for detachment from wealth. In the context of Mt 4:16, ''poor in spirit'' refers to those humbly aware of their spiritual poverty and hence their great need for God, Isaiah's *anawim*: ''This is the one whom I approve: the lowly and afflicted man who trembles [in reverence] at my word'' (Is 66:2).

''They who mourn'' seem to be those who grieve enough over the world's injustices enough to try to remedy them; their reward will be God's eternal comfort. ''The meek'' are evidently the non-violent, who do not try to lord it over others or crowd them out in the competition for land or goods; they will inherit their Father's eternal ''land.'' ''They who hunger and thirst for righteousness'' are those who really long for goodness in their lives, especially the supreme goodness, God; he will be theirs. ''The merciful'' are those who surmount their own hurt feelings or prejudices to forgive others; they will receive God's mercy. ''The clean of heart'' must be those simple people who keep God as their true priority; they will indeed see him. ''The peacemakers'' are those willing to commit themselves to that often unrewarded effort to intervene for the peace of others; they are truly children of God. The ''persecuted for the sake of righteousness'' are those who endure censure for their pains in standing up for a just cause; they, too, are members of God's kingdom.

And the last group declared blessed—climactically last, as in Luke—are those who bear insult and injury for their faith in Jesus. They are to rejoice in such treatment, not for love of suffering, but because they are thus classified with the prophets (v. 12) who suffered for uttering God's word, even as will Jesus himself.

In these beatitudes we have the New Testament equivalent of the ten commandments. But whereas the commandments were mostly negative prohibitions of evil action, the beatitudes are positive demands for good action, the demands imposed by love! They are as ''impossible,'' yet necessary and timely, for our own society as for that addressed by Jesus.

In verse 13 the subject seems to change. Perhaps Matthew is patching on other sayings of Jesus found in his sources, first a saying about salt that Luke locates in a different context (Lk 14:34-35), but which the beatitudes suggest to Matthew here. Jesus now addresses his disciples directly: in living his beatitudes they become ''the salt of the earth,'' flavoring the life of others; otherwise they will be useless as ministers. Then there is the figure of the lamp that gives light for others (v. 14). Jesus' disciples are to ''shine before others'' (v. 16), not boastfully, but to lead them to glorify their heavenly Father. Disciples are to surprise others with the unexpected kindness that brings the light of joy into their lives, light that reminds them of the great Giver of all light in our world.

Now the Sermon turns to questions about the old law. The implied transition question may be: Do the beatitudes do away with the commandments? The answer is a resounding *no*: ''Do not think that I have come to abolish the law or the prophets. I have come not to abolish but to fulfill'' (v. 17). Since ''the law and the prophets'' was the ordinary way by which the rabbis referred to the Jewish scriptures, this passage also means that Jesus has come to fulfill scripture—to fulfill the law of the Torah and the promises of the prophets to ''the smallest part of a letter'' (v. 18).

The emphasis on keeping the law fully is so strong that it gives rise to a problem. Does the saying, ''Not the smallest letter or the smallest part of a letter will pass from the law'' (v. 18), include those 613 minute regulations that the Pharisees had added to the commandments in their oral tradition? Evidently not, judging by the rest of this chapter, which uses examples almost exclusively from the ten commandments, and by other passages of Matthew, such as Jesus' denunciation of the Pharisees for sometimes substituting their own oral tradition for the commandments.

REFLECTION AND PRAYER

Do I consider myself blessed when I realize my need for more than money or comfort or land or acceptance by others?

Do I consider myself blessed when I am ridiculed for my belief in Jesus?

Lord, teach me your values!

The Sermon on the Mount: Jesus Reinterprets the Law (Mt 5:21-48)

Beginning with verse 21 Jesus shows how the law must be understood. He uses a most forceful expression of his own authority in introducing each example: "You have heard that it was said to your ancestors . . . *But I say to you . . .* " (vv. 21-22). Far from abolishing the letter of the law, he is demanding also an understanding and fulfillment of its spirit, in accord with the beatitudes. The law against murder, then, must not be restricted to its literal meaning; it also prohibits murdering a person's reputation or even hurting his feelings. Based upon respect for all God's children, this fifth commandment forbids abusive language and even enters the inner court of consciousness to eradicate contempt (v. 22). Sacrifice to God is useless without reconciliation with one's brother or sister (vv. 23-24). The demand to "settle with your opponent quickly while on the way to court with him" (v. 25) may be Matthew's application of Jesus' words to a problem of lawsuits between Christians at the time of writing.

The sixth commandment gets the same treatment: "You have heard . . . But I say to you . . ." (vv. 27-28). Again the basic idea is that sin begins with the attitude at the core of conscience. To dramatize the thought, Matthew adds here that "cutting" passage from Mark (Mk 9:43-48), which he twice summarizes: "It is better for you to lose one of your members than to have your whole body go into Gehenna" (vv. 29-30).

As a further application of the sixth commandment, Matthew abbreviates here Mark's passage in which Jesus prohibits divorce (Mk 10:2-12); but he adds a qualifying clause: "unless the marriage is unlawful" (v. 32). Many scholars think that Matthew inserted this clause to deal with a problem in his own community, probably that of Gentiles asking for baptism who were previously married within the degree of blood relationship prohibited by Leviticus 18:6-18, and were hence living in a union considered unlawful by the Christian community.

The next section, concerning oaths and vows (vv. 33-37), is related to the commandments that forbid taking "the name of the Lord, your God, in vain" (Ex 20:7) and bearing "false witness against your neighbor" (Ex 20:16). To avoid taking the name of God in oaths the Jews had invented many circumlocutions. Rabbis spent much energy speculating about the relative binding power of such oaths, leading to evasions that Jesus here condemns. How can you offer God, or what belongs to God (heaven, earth, Jerusalem, "your head") as surety for your word if you cannot even control the color of your hair? Your trustworthiness should be such that your statements need no oaths at all but only a simple yes or no to attest their truthfulness.

One of the most famous Old Testament punishments for not keeping the commandments was the law of retaliation, here freely quoted from Exodus 21:24: "An eye for an eye and a tooth for a tooth" (v. 38). This was the Jewish revision of the ancient Middle East law of revenge; it limited retaliation to an evil equal to the original one, and it substituted civil authority for the individual or family member as the punishing agent. Nevertheless, this is one part of the Old Testament that Jesus abolishes, not by returning to revenge, but by renouncing even its modified form of retaliation or vindication: "But I say to you, offer *no resistance to one who is evil*. When someone strikes you on [your] right cheek, turn the other one to him as well" (v. 39; brackets in NAB). How strongly we are tempted to reject this teaching of Jesus as impossible! We easily tuck it away into an unvisited corner of our mind.

How literally should we "turn the other" cheek? If scripture is woven by God as a seamless garment in which every part is consistent with every other part, we must interpret one text by its relation to another. And if Jesus' action is consistent with his words, we can interpret his words by his actions. What did Jesus himself do when he was struck on the cheek? John 18:19-23 provides the answer. When the guard struck Jesus, accusing him of arrogance toward the high priest, Jesus did not invite the man to strike him again. But neither did he strike back. Instead, he challenged the man: "If I have spoken wrongly, testify to the wrong; but if I have spoken rightly, why do you strike me?" (v. 23). He challenged the guard to be a human being who reasons instead of reacting like a violent animal. Turning the other cheek, then, means breaking the chain of evil by refusing to answer violence with violence and by rising above one's own hurt to reach out to violent brothers or sisters to save them from their own violence.

The seemingly ridiculous examples of giving your cloak to the person who has already claimed your tunic, going two miles with a person who has pressed you into going one, giving and lending freely—all these concrete examples indicate that Jesus is not only interiorizing the demands of the law but also intensifying them. He is breaking through the excuses we set up for ourselves to avoid involvement in the troubles of others around us. He is insisting that we *are* our brother's keeper.

These examples take on universal extension when we consider them in the context of verses 43-48, in which Jesus reinterprets Leviticus 19:18: "Take no revenge and cherish no grudge against your *fellow countrymen*. You shall love your *neighbor* as yourself." There was a strong tendency to reduce the meaning of "neighbor" in this passage to "fellow countrymen," as the Leviticus context would seem to justify. Jesus uncovers the fallacy of that interpretation by reducing it to unvarnished terms: "You shall love your neighbor and *hate your enemy*" (v. 43). He demands the very opposite: "But I say to you, *love your enemies*." In Jesus' language "neighbor" is not simply "fellow countryman" but "fellow human being."

The inner motivation for all Jesus' reinterpretations of the old law comes in his statement, "that you may be children of your heavenly Father, for he makes his sun rise on the bad and the good, and causes rain to fall on the just and the unjust" (v. 45). This is the core of the new law, New Testament, new covenant: the new fraternal relationship we all have with one another as the result of Jesus' revelation that God is *Father of us all*.

This chapter ends with Jesus' climactic summary: "So be perfect, just as your heavenly Father is perfect" (v. 48), an adaptation of Leviticus 19:2: "Be holy, for I, the Lord, your God, am holy," and an echo of Isaiah 6:3: "Holy, holy, holy is the Lord. . . . All the earth is filled with his glory!" Isaiah is the prophet of God's holiness; Matthew is the evangelist of the holiness of Jesus, who in his vision of the kingdom calls upon us to love God as our Father and all men and women as our brothers and sisters. An impossible ideal? Not according to the Fourth Lateran Council (1215): "Be ye perfect in the perfection of *grace* as your heavenly Father is perfect in the perfection of *nature*" (*The Teaching of the Catholic Church*, p. 99); Matthew's Jesus offers us the grace to imitate the Father's all-embracing love.

REFLECTION AND PRAYER

Do I see God's law as a purely external obligation, or as the expression of his love for me and for all humankind?

Do I turn the other cheek by challenging an offending brother or sister to be a Christian?

Lord Jesus, help me be perfect as my heavenly Father is perfect.

The Sermon on the Mount: Jesus Reinterprets Virtue (Mt 6)

In chapter 6 the Sermon on the Mount continues the theme of heartfelt morality but changes its application from observance of the commandments to the practice of virtue in good works. Religious acts such as giving to the poor, prayer and fasting are to be freed from formalism and external show by the inner orientation of pure love, "so that your almsgiving may be secret. And your Father who sees in secret will repay you" (v. 4). The reward for religious acts must not be the applause of men and women but the approval of God by his grace of motivating love, so beautifully expressed in the heart of this section, the Lord's Prayer (vv. 9-13).

This prayer is perhaps the clearest indication of what Jesus meant in his proclamation: "The kingdom of heaven is at hand." It is at hand when we call upon God as our Father, bless his name above all others, and long for the completion of his kingdom in heaven, but also its achievement on earth through the doing of his will as it is done in heaven.

The kingdom is at hand when we humbly ask the Father for our daily bread, acknowledging his Providence for our bodily needs and especially for our spiritual needs in the *bread of his word*, the symbolic meaning of bread that Matthew's Jesus established in his reply to the first temptation (Mt 4:4). He would also have us think of *the bread that is his own body*, the eucharistic banquet, which Matthew will later report in anticipation of the *eternal banquet* (see Mt 8:11 and 22:1-10). The kingdom is at hand when we are as ready to forgive others as to ask God's forgiveness for ourselves. Finally, the kingdom is at hand when we humbly acknowledge our inability to stand alone in "the final test" against evil, our ultimate dependence on the Father for deliverance through the salvation that this gospel will find achieved in Jesus' sacrifice (see Mt 8:17).

Jesus assures us that by this prayer, sincerely carried into action in forgiving others (v. 14), we begin to bring about the kingdom of God on earth.

In verses 16-18 Jesus calls for the same purity of intention in our fasting as in our almsgiving and prayer. Christians are not to publicize their fasting and other forms of self denial by gloominess; rather, their cheerfulness and cleanliness should hide such practices from all but the Father "who sees what is hidden will repay you" (v. 18).

Now Matthew begins a new section of the Sermon on the Mount. Kingdom-of-God morality requires that love become our inspiration not only to keep the commandments and do good works, but also to determine our priorities (vv. 19-34). Earthly goods must not be treasured above heavenly, "for where your treasure is, there also will your heart be" (v. 21). In both the Old and the New Testament the word *heart* has a more complete meaning than in our modern usage. We tend to confine its figurative meaning to "feelings." But obviously in this passage, as in many others, *heart* is that evaluating center of a person, deep insight that engages the whole mentality, enthralls the emotions, drives the will. *Heart* in biblical language is the whole man or woman inspired by a new vision of faith, set aflame with new love.

The priority of heavenly treasure over earthly is illustrated by a parable based upon the ancient anatomical view that the human eye is the source of the light by which we see our way. A good eye will provide good light for the body (v. 22); a bad eye will leave the whole body in darkness. Jesus' point is that if you have vision for no more than the goods of earth, you are left in utter darkness regarding eternal goods (v. 23).

Jesus is challenging his hearers to examine their true priorities. What should we really love? What should be our fundamental option? What should we spend our lives for—something that will not last or something that will never rot or die? We can't make them both our goal: "You cannot serve God and *mammon* [Aramaic for '*earthly wealth*']" (v. 24).

The point is further illustrated by one of the most poetic passages in Matthew: "Look at the birds in the sky; they do not sow or reap, they

gather nothing into barns, yet your heavenly Father feeds them. . . .''
(vv. 26). Again, the motive is what makes this new priority possible:
God's loving care for us inspires our loving response of absolute trust in
him. Matthew's Jesus speaks the simple language of the heart to his
simple people, the language of their experience in nature—the free
flight of birds, the springing up of wild flowers, the splendor of the
grass. The simple yet gratuitous surprises of life not only bring joy;
they are reminders that ''if God so clothes the grass of the field, which
grows today and is thrown into the oven tomorrow, will he not much
more provide for you, O you of little faith?'' (v. 30). Why worry, then,
about food or clothing? Your worry about the future is a sign of your
''little faith'' that ''your heavenly Father knows'' (v. 32) all your
needs. Matthew will remind his readers again and again that Jesus expects more of us than a *''little* faith.''

REFLECTION AND PRAYER

Do I do good deeds to attract other's attention, or simply to fulfill
the Father's will?

Do I cast all my worries into my Father's arms?

Our Father . . .

The Sermon on the Mount: Jesus Challenges Our Judgments (Mt 7)

In chapter 7 Matthew reports some of Jesus' conclusions concerning Kingdom-of-God morality. Notice the wealth of simple but forceful images in this chapter: the beam in your eye, pearls cast before
swine, knocking at the door, giving a stone for bread or a snake for fish,
the wide gate and broad road to destruction, the narrow gate and constricted road to life, false prophets in sheep's clothing, figs from this-
tles, houses built on sand or rock.

Matthew's Jesus declares that kingdom morality avoids passing
judgment—definitive condemnation of another that fails to take into
account our own frailty (vv. 1-5). Just as God will forgive us according
to our forgiveness of others, so will he judge us in the measure that we
judge others. If we put our trust in him, we will not judge others by
their little faults (splinters); much greater is our own fault of judging, a
beam that blocks our vision. We must stop trying to make others measure up to our standards; we must simply leave them to God's judg-

ment, trusting that he will be more merciful than we are, since he has already proved his mercy in forgiving our far greater faults.

Verse 6 seems to break the progression of thought. Perhaps Matthew is trying to fit into this sermon some of the sayings of Jesus for which he has no other place. The Jews of Jesus' time commonly referred to the Gentiles not only as dogs, but also as the swine that they allowed themselves to eat. The saying would then mean, ''Don't waste time trying to teach kingdom-of-God morality to people who would only misunderstand it and uselessly persecute you.'' The gospel message is too deep to be accepted without the equivalent of Israel's long preparation. Ironically, as Matthew's Jesus will soon suggest in chapter 8, it was often the Jews who trampled the pearls of Jesus and the Gentiles who treasured them.

Verse 7 returns to the theme of trust, applying it to prayer: ''Ask and it will be given to you.'' If you know how to give good things to your children, can't you trust your heavenly Father to answer your prayers with even better things? We have a tendency to think of the radical moral demands of the Sermon on the Mount as applying exclusively to our own efforts. But here we see Matthew' Jesus insisting that we ask our Father for what is good, for our goodness is really his gift ''to those who ask him'' (v. 11).

Verse 12 summarizes kingdom morality in the golden rule: ''Do to others whatever you would have them do to you.'' Of pagan origin, this saying is sometimes interpreted to mean, ''Do good to others in order to receive good from them.'' But in the context that Matthew has provided it must be considered another way of stating the command, ''Love your neighbor as yourself,'' the only sense in which Jesus would use it as the epitome of ''the law and the prophets'' (v. 12).

Verses 13-14 introduce the final part of the Sermon on the Mount with a series of antitheses that repeat the theme of priorities, first in the figures of the wide gate and broad road to destruction rejected for the narrow gate and the constricted road by those who prefer heavenly to earthly values. Then verses 15-23 present a stern warning against following false prophets, probably one of the dangers threatening Matthew's community, judging by the length and intensity of this passage. We will know these false teachers by their evil deeds (''fruits''), which cannot be hidden by crying ''Lord, Lord'' (v. 21). On that day [of judgment], not even prophecies and miracles will cover up their failure to identify with ''the one who does the will of my Father in heaven.''

Final images fix in memory this powerful sermon: "Everyone who listens to these words of mine and acts on them will be like a *wise man who built his house on rock*" (v. 24), unlike the foolish man who, failing to put Jesus' words into practice, built his house (his life) on sand only to see it collapse in the storm (vv. 24-27).

In reporting that "the *crowds* were astonished at his teaching" Matthew hints that this discourse is a compilation of talks to many groups. "He taught them as one having *authority*" (v. 28), the inner authority by which the heart of the listener instinctively recognizes the eternal truth that calls to his or her very depths.

REFLECTION AND PRAYER

Do I allow myself to pass judgment on others?

Do I humbly yet persistently ask, knock, seek good things from my Father?

Father, help me build my life on the rock-solid teaching of Jesus.

The Mission of Jesus and of the Twelve (Mt 8—10)

Jesus' Mighty Missionary Works Respond to Faith (Mt 8)

Between the Sermon on the Mount and the next great sermon Matthew relates a series of 10 miracles that serve to ratify the authority of Jesus' Sermon on the Mount and to prepare for his missionary sermon. These mighty works demonstrate Jesus' will to do good to others and his power over the evils afflicting them: disease, demons, natural phenomena, sin, even death.

The first work is the cure of the leper (Mt 8:1-4). To Mark's account (Mk 1:40-44), Matthew adds a touch that will become characteristic of him: He reports that the leper addresses Jesus as Lord, his clue that the leper really believes in Jesus.

The second cure, that of the centurion's servant (vv. 5-13), lays further stress on faith, the unconditional faith that Jesus finds in the Gentile centurion. This incident is given more ample form in Luke 7:1-10, except for Matthew's addition of Jesus' denunciation of the Jews for lack of faith (vv. 11-12), perhaps to warn his own community, now "the children of the kingdom" (v. 12), against the danger of having too little faith to retain their place at the heavenly banquet. The image of "outer darkness, where there will be wailing and grinding of teeth" (v. 12), will become typical of Matthew's version of final condemnation.

The third miracle is the cure of Peter's mother-in-law (vv. 14-15). To Mark's report (Mk 1:29-34) that in the evening Jesus drove out demons, Matthew adds "by a word" (v. 16), an expression that he will frequently use to suggest that the *word* of Jesus is a healing, creative, authoritative word, like Yahweh's. Matthew also changes Mark's cure of "*many* who were sick," to "*all* the sick" (v. 16), adding the reflection that Jesus thereby fulfills Isaiah's prophecy: "He [Yahweh's servant] took away our infirmities and bore our diseases" (Is 53:4). Matthew thus implies that Jesus can now cure the sufferings of others because he will soon bear the sufferings and "the guilt *of us all*" (Is 53:4-7). Thus Matthew is illuminating Mark's account by applying his own post-resurrection faith. He therefore feels no need to repeat Mark's report that Jesus forbade the demons to reveal his identity (Mk 1:34). He will generally omit Mark's use of the messianic secret.

Matthew now interrupts his chain of miracles to report a pair of incidents in which people ask to follow Jesus. The first is a scribe who addresses Jesus as "teacher," Matthew's signal to his readers that this man lacks the faith to call him "Lord." Jesus answers him with an apparent negative in a statement that underlines his own absolute reliance on Providence: "*The Son of Man* has nowhere to rest his head" (v. 20). This first use of the title Son of Man, occurring immediately after Matthew's quotation from Isaiah, suggests that the sufferings of Jesus in a ministry deprived of life's ordinary necessities are already part of his passion as Yahweh's suffering servant. He who could do so much to alleviate the sufferings of others will do nothing to lessen his own sufferings; indeed, he will take everyone else's suffering upon himself!

Then a believing disciple—he addresses Jesus as "Lord"—is refused permission to bury his father before accompanying Jesus: "Let the dead bury their dead" (v. 22). This apparently harsh denial is forceful Jewish hyperbole meant to stress the priority of Jesus' call over every other claim, even that of parents. Evidently some members of Matthew's community must choose between their belief in Jesus and rejection by their own families. Those who fail to follow Jesus' invitation are the "dead" left to bury their dead; those who follow him will be alive with the new life that he alone gives. Matthew certainly does not intend here to present Jesus as setting aside the commandment to honor parents, for in 15:3-6 he will show Jesus defending this commandment against a Pharisaic tradition.

In verses 23-27 Matthew summarizes Mark's story of the calming of the storm. In Matthew's account the disciples have enough faith to address Jesus as "Lord," but not enough to trust in him completely: "Why are you terrified, O you of *little faith?*" (v. 26). Only then does Matthew's Jesus calm the sea, reversing Mark's order of events. No doubt Matthew would have us join the disciples in marveling at Jesus' power over nature.

Still following Mark, Matthew next summarizes the expulsion of demons (vv. 28-34). However, he changes Mark's Gerasa, a town about 35 miles southeast of the Lake of Galilee, to Gadara, a place much closer to the lake into which the swine were apparently driven. Seemingly Mark's account gave Matthew another difficulty: how can a legion of demons possess one man and speak with one accord? By changing the account to two men possessed, Matthew can speak of demons in the plural without using the name Legion. Nor does he mention Mark's two thousand swine; he is content with "herd." Matthew adds a further touch to the story; the possessed men ask, "Have you come here to torment us *before the appointed time?*" (v. 29). Hence, by driving the demons out of the men, Jesus demonstrates that his ministry fulfills the "appointed time" of the eclipse of Satan's evil power.

The changes that Matthew introduces into Mark's report are very instructive. They show us the freedom Matthew exercises in modifying Mark's account to emphasize his own theological insights and to apply the story to the needs of his community, even though he accepts that account with enough admiration to use it as source. Evidently what Matthew looks for is the larger truth about Jesus rather than the details of events. Illustrative truth, such a truth as the importance of great faith in Jesus' power over evil, is more important to him than factual exactitude.

REFLECTION AND PRAYER

Do I have great faith in Jesus?

Or could he say to me, "O you of little faith"?

Dear Lord, if I had great faith in you, what changes would I make in my life? Give me faith enough to change.

Jesus' Compassion for Sinners (Mt 9)

At the beginning of chapter 9 Matthew summarizes Mark's account of the cure of the paralytic, a story that Mark placed several chapters before the sending of the demons into the swine. It seems obvious that Matthew, like Mark, does not determine his sequence chiefly by the chronology of events; obviously, the sequence of these events has been lost.

In relating this miracle Matthew summarizes so severely that he even omits the most obvious proof of the faith of those carrying the paralytic—their hoisting him up to the roof to let him down before Jesus. At times Matthew is willing to sacrifice even significant details to achieve concentration on what he considers the essential meaning of the incident. He is focusing this event exclusively upon Jesus' compassion for the sinner and his power to forgive him. He wants to fix this power so firmly in our minds that we remember it when Jesus later shares it with his church, a gift Matthew alludes to in closing this account: "The crowds . . . glorified God who had given such authority *to human beings*" (v. 8).

Then follows, as in Mark, Jesus' call of Levi/Matthew, his dining with sinners and tax collectors, and his defense of this act against the attacking Pharisees. In reporting Jesus' conclusion of the argument Matthew characteristically adds an Old Testament reference, this time to Hosea 6:6, "I desire mercy, not sacrifice" (v. 13). If God prefers the practice of mercy to Temple sacrifices, how much more does he prefer Jesus' merciful presence among sinners to the Pharisees' hypocritical avoidance of such contact!

Then Jesus is questioned about not requiring his disciples to fast, but Matthew sharpens the attack by changing the questioners from Mark's "people" to "the disciples of John" (v. 14). Matthew thereby suggests that the severe John may have been having second thoughts about Jesus, perhaps even doubting whether one who consorts with sinners could be the Promised One who would bring about "the day of the Lord," the day that Hosea, whom Jesus has just quoted, had spoken of in fierce warrior terms: "On that day I will break the bow of Israel" (Hos 1:5). Jesus answers that it is unfitting for the disciples to fast while he, Israel's bridegroom, is with them, for his new covenant requires not patchwork but new attitudes (vv. 15-17)—especially the practice of the mercy that he has just extolled by reference to Hosea.

Matthew skips a few chapters of Mark to place here Jesus' cure of the woman with a hemorrhage and his raising the daughter of Jairus. At the beginning of this double episode Matthew reports that the girl is already dead. He severely summarizes the account of Jesus' healing of the woman with a hemorrhage, stressing the importance of faith by following the woman's inward prayer with Jesus' immediate response, "Courage, daughter! Your faith has saved you" (v. 22).

Matthew's summary of the raising of Jairus' daughter sacrifices many details, even the sensitive words Jesus addresses to the little girl and his down-to-earth suggestion to give her something to eat. But by such compression Matthew also gives more force to the only words of Jesus in this brief account: "Go away! The girl is not dead but sleeping" (v. 24). Matthew seems to be telling his community that Christian funerals are not to be characterized by commotion in the expression of sorrow, for one who is touched by Jesus does not die but sleeps in the Lord.

And now even more austere summarizing. In 9:27-31 Matthew apparently compacts Mark's two miracles of giving sight to individual blind men into one of giving sight to two blind men. The cry of the blind men, "Son of David, have pity," seems to identify this miracle with that in favor of Mark's Bartimaeus (Mk 10:46-52), who uses this same unusual title. But the ending command to tell no one points to Mark's account of the cure at Bethsaida (Mk 8:22-26). Matthew loses the intimacy of Mark's first blind-man miracle by omitting the details about the spittle and the gradual leading on of the man's faith. But he regains the emphasis on faith by changing the question in Mark's second miracle from "What do you want me to do for you?" to "Do you believe that I can do this?" (v. 28).

By now it is becoming evident that Matthew's Christology is different from Mark's. We have seen Matthew consistently omit or at least tone down whatever in Mark could give the impression of imperfection or incompleteness in Jesus. It almost seems as if he would transfigure Jesus long before the transfiguration itself. Perhaps there was a tendency in Matthew's community to so stress the humanity of Jesus as to lose sight of his divinity. Such a tendency would explain Matthew's efforts to avoid whatever might encourage it. But in so doing he may be encouraging the opposite tendency, to lose sight of Jesus' humanity. To balance these two tendencies, we need both Matthew and Mark, side by side.

Matthew shares with Luke the last of this series of miracles, the cure of the mute demoniac (vv. 32-34). But unlike Luke, he focuses our attention upon the opposing reactions to the cure. On the one hand the crowds are filled with admiration: "Nothing like this has ever been seen in Israel" (v. 33). On the other the Pharisees try to explain Jesus' power as due to "the prince of demons" (v. 34). Matthew probably intends these opposing views to be taken as typical of reactions to the whole series of mighty works that he here concludes.

REFLECTION AND PRAYER

Do I really believe that Jesus has absolute power over all forms of evil, especially sin?

Jesus, I do believe. I call you Lord! Guard me, Lord, from every evil that could separate me from you.

Second Discourse: The Missionary Sermon (Mt 10)

Toward the end of chapter 9 Matthew finishes his account of Jesus' series of missionary cures and further prepares for his presentation of Jesus' great missionary discourse by a general summary of his ministry, now at the point of attracting crowds so large that he recruits more laborers to gather the harvest.

In chapter 10 Jesus therefore names the twelve apostles (v. 2) and gives them a share in his own "authority over unclean spirits to drive them out and to cure every disease and every illness" (v. 1). For this mission, he gives them instructions, which Matthew apparently combines from sayings that he found in Mark, Q, and his own sources.

This second great discourse is developed in three main parts: first, Jesus instructs his disciples that they are to evangelize by example as well as by word (vv. 5-15); then, he braces them for the persecutions that must follow their efforts (vv. 16-33); finally, he outlines the conditions and rewards for persevering as his disciples (vv. 34-42).

Of the synoptics only Matthew reports Jesus' directive to concentrate evangelizing efforts solely upon "the lost sheep of the house of Israel" (v. 6). This directive must be interpreted as a temporary one, for Matthew will also report that after his resurrection Jesus commissioned his apostles to "make disciples of all nations" (Mt 28:19). In general, the Twelve are to do what Jesus does: Announce the kingdom of God, cure the sick, even raise the dead! Jesus' summary is powerful: "Without cost you have received; without cost you are to give" (v. 8).

The instructions about bringing nothing on the mission are extreme, forbidding even the walking stick and sandals that Mark's Jesus allowed. The fact that Luke concurs in this severity suggests that *Q* offered both him and Matthew a choice between two differing apostolic traditions. Their choice of *Q* over Mark in these details emphasizes again the danger of a too-literal interpretation of the gospels, for the evangelists themselves feel free to choose between such opposite details as "wear sandals" or "do not wear sandals." What is certain in all three gospels is the *spirit* of poverty and utter reliance on Providence that must guide the missionary and indeed every Christian who would share the life of Jesus and therefore his lifestyle of modest use of this world's goods.

This same spirit is to guide the missionary in the choice of a place to stay, humbly accepting the hospitality of anyone who offers it. The curious advice about peace (vv. 12-13) reflects the Old Testament notion that the word of a prophet accomplishes what it says. It can be understood here to mean that whether the disciples' greeting of peace is accepted or not, they must not lose their own peace. They are not to force themselves upon anyone; yet they must warn those who will not listen that their refusal is a serious matter, using the sign by which Jews indicated their separation from unbelievers: "Shake the dust from your feet" (v. 14). The comparison of the fate of "that town" with that of Sodom and Gomorrah underlines the vital importance of the Christian message.

Just as the missionaries are called to share the activity of Jesus, they must also share his sufferings. The next part of this discourse describes these sufferings in such detail as to give the impression that Matthew and his community are actually experiencing these trials themselves. They seem to know firsthand the pain inflicted by the blind refusal of many to accept their message, by floggings in synagogues, by trials before rulers, and by the savage treatment reported in Acts and in Paul's letters. The discourse has now swept into the period after Jesus' resurrection when the disciples give witness to "the pagans" (v. 18) of their belief in Jesus. But they have nothing to worry about, for "the Spirit of your Father" speaks through them (vv. 19-20).

Apparently Matthew's first readers also know the tearing apart of families (v. 21), the hatred of the society in which they live (v. 22), persecutions from town to town (v. 23)—even the same accusations of devil-worship that were hurled against Jesus (v. 25). But these very sufferings should be their joy: "It is enough for the disciple that he become like his teacher" (v. 25).

The deep consolation of the unsuccessful missionary, of even the martyr (v. 28), must be the Providence of the Father who has counted "all the hairs of your head" (v. 30). Whether men accept the message or not, "Everyone who acknowledges me before others I will acknowledge before my heavenly Father" (v. 32).

The final part of the discourse begins with a shocker: "I have come to bring not peace but the sword" (v. 34). Taken out of context, this statement becomes the very opposite of Christianity. It could justify slavery, apartheid, any kind of prejudice, even terrorism! Here it means, "I have come to set a man 'against his father'" in the sense defined by this whole discourse and especially by verses 37-39:

> "Whoever loves father or mother *more than me* is not worthy of me. . . and whoever does not take up his cross and follow after me is not worthy of me. Whoever finds his life [defined by this world's relationships alone] will lose it, and whoever loses his life *for my sake* will find it."

Matthew's Jesus is telling us that such a person no longer suffers any identity crisis. Christianity, usually so logical, can also defy logic. It goes beyond reason. It is our making or breaking. It requires a priority above every other alternative, even above the most important of our human relationships. And even beyond our human relationships it tells us who we are. It gives us an identity to ourselves, to others, and to God. It makes us *Christ's own man or woman*; indeed, so much Christ's own that "whoever receives you receives me" (v. 40). Mysteriously, Jesus is present in the true Christian and acts through the person, whether an apostle (v. 40), a prophet (v. 41), a righteous person (v. 41b), or "one of these little ones" (v. 42). This reward of Jesus' presence is given both to the one who receives or serves the disciple and to the disciple. Matthew is assuring us that even after Jesus' ascension he is not really absent from his people.

This assurance is consoling after all those "hard sayings" in verses 34-39. Matthew climaxes this assurance of Jesus' continued presence by adapting the conclusion of a passage from Mark, which he otherwise skips (a stranger used Jesus' name to expel demons; Mk 9:38-41): "Whoever gives only a cup of cold water to one of these little ones to drink *because he is a disciple* . . . will surely not lose his reward" (v. 42).

Curiously, after finishing this report of Jesus' missionary discourse, Matthew says nothing about the results of the mission of the Twelve, another indication that his major purpose here is not to relate history but to warn and yet encourage his own community, as well as future generations of Christians, including ours.

REFLECTION AND PRAYER

Am I ready to accept the priorities that Jesus requires of me?

What holds me back from becoming a true disciple of Jesus?

Lord Jesus, how little you have asked of me in comparison to your demands upon those first disciples! Help me be faithful at least in that little. Identify me as your own person, as one of your "little ones."

Jesus Counters Jewish Opposition
(Mt 11:1—13:53)

Disbelief of the Jews (Mt 11)

In sending his disciples to Jesus, John the Baptist may be encouraging them to become Jesus' followers. But in the context of their previous question about fasting, their new question, "Are you the one who is to come, or should we look for another?" (Mt 11:3), seems rather to imply that John now has serious doubts about whether Jesus is really bringing about "the day of the Lord," that day of judgment for the wicked foretold by Malachi (Mal 3:23-24). Jesus tells John's inquiring followers to report the good things he has done, in accord with the new day foretold by Isaiah (Is 29:18-19; 35:5-6). Jesus stakes his claim to be the long-awaited Messiah not on the negative but on the positive prophecies.

Jesus uses the occasion to approve of John for his strong convictions; he is not "a reed swayed by the wind" (v. 7) or "someone dressed in fine clothing" (v. 8). He is a prophet, "and more than a prophet" (v. 9). In the words of the Malachi in whom John so trusted, Jesus refers to John as the forerunner of the Messiah (Mal 3:1). Then he calls John one of the greatest men born of woman in pre-kingdom history, but adds that the least of those born into the kingdom of God— evidently by baptism in the Holy Spirit (Mt 3:11)—is greater than John.

Up to this point Matthew seems to be using Q as source, for a similar text is found in Luke 7:18-28. But now Matthew inserts in verses 12-15 a mysterious passage of his own. Perhaps the following interpretation best fits the context. As precursor announcing the kingdom of

God (Mt 3:2), John the Baptist has been treated with violence; and violent persecutors will seem to prevail also against those who try to establish God's kingdom on earth, a shadowy prediction of the extreme violence that both John and Jesus, as well as Jesus' followers, will suffer. John finalizes the line of prophets (v. 13), and is therefore the one thought of as Elijah, who Malachi said would return "before the day of the Lord comes" (Mal 3:23). This means that Jesus has brought that day and, by implication, is the Lord! This is such a veiled yet important revelation that it ends with the attention-getter: "Whoever has ears ought to hear" (v. 15).

Some have heard! They are like obedient children calling to those inconstant childish people who have responded neither to the ascetic "dirge" of John nor to the joyous "flute" of Jesus (v. 17), saying that the austere John was possessed and that Jesus is a glutton and drunkard for eating and drinking with sinners. "But wisdom [personified in Jesus] is vindicated by her works [the mighty deeds of chapters 8-9]" (vv. 18-19). This obscure passage is important evidence that Jesus was seen by his contemporaries as a man of joy rather than as severe and demanding. The towns that witnessed his miraculous signs, yet failed to respond to his teaching, deserve a worse punishment than Sodom (vv. 20-24).

But unlike the self-proclaimed "wise and learned" (v. 25), those who respond like obedient children are open to a great revelation. In a passage that sounds more like John's gospel than Matthew's, Jesus utters his beautiful prayer to his "Father, Lord of heaven and earth" (v. 25), praising him for revealing himself through his Son to "the childlike." Then, addressing his followers, Jesus makes the most explicit statement in the synoptics concerning his own identity: "No one knows the Son except the Father, and no one knows the Father except the Son and anyone to whom the Son wishes to reveal him" (v. 27). Matthew has apparently transposed to this place a post-resurrection saying. We see him increasingly applying his own post-resurrection faith to interpret Jesus' pre-resurrection action and speech.

Then follows that intimate passage: "Come to me" (v. 28). Come to me, my poor burdened people, weighed down with the heavy laws of the Pharisees' tradition. My only law is that you "learn from me," that you become like me, "meek and humble of heart" (v. 29). Then I will give rest to your heart, the rest of a peaceful conscience. In this beautiful echo of Sirach 51:23-27, Jesus is again identified as Wisdom personified.

As in the preceding chapter, Matthew has followed up an especially severe passage with a report of Jesus' consoling promises, this time of peace for those who accept him as the only Son of the Father.

But there is much more to be seen in this passage. Certainly one of the most pressing questions in the minds of the early Christians must have been the presence of Jesus among them after his ascension. Was his life after his death, resurrection and ascension in real continuity with his life among them before these events? Or was he now to be found only at the right hand of his Father? Matthew is here suggesting an answer. Just as Jesus comforted the suffering and burdened before his death, his invitation to approach his gentle heart is still open. He is really the same Jesus at his Father's side as he was when he walked beside his disciples in Galilee, for he is the merciful Father's only Son and still reveals the Father to those who seek him. He is still the champion of the weak, always at hand to lift up the brokenhearted.

REFLECTION AND PRAYER

Do I really believe that Jesus is the only Son of the Father?

With Jesus, I give praise to you, Father, Lord of heaven and earth, for revealing your love for us through your Son Jesus.

The Hostility of the Pharisees (Mt 12)

At the beginning of chapter 12 Matthew presents two controversies with the Pharisees found in Mark 2:23—3:6. To the first, concerning the gleaning of grain on the sabbath, Matthew adds Jesus' argument that since "priests serving in the temple violate the sabbath and are innocent" (v. 5) and "something [Jesus himself] greater than the temple is here" (v. 6), any conflict between keeping the sabbath rest and faithfulness to Jesus must be resolved in favor of service to the cause of Jesus. Matthew's Jesus also adds an Old Testament quotation that he has used previously (Mt 9:13), and that thereby gathers the force of repetition: "I desire mercy, not sacrifice" (Hos 6:6). Thus the dramatic ending of this incident with the claim that the Son of Man is "Lord of the sabbath" (v. 8) identifies Jesus with Yahweh, merciful Lord of creation, who can modify rigid manmade sabbath regulations.

In telling the story of Jesus' sabbath cure of the man with the shriveled hand, Matthew again heightens the note of mercy by adding the image of pulling a sheep out of a pit on the sabbath. When the Pharisees begin plotting his death, Jesus peaceably withdraws and orders the people not to publicize his great deeds (v. 16). Matthew is apparently interpreting Mark's messianic secret as a silence to avoid unnecessarily provoking the Jewish leaders. Yet even in this moment in which Jesus realizes the plot against his life, Matthew changes Mark's "he cured many" (Mk 3:10) to "he cured them *all*" (v. 15).

Matthew's own reflections on Jesus' cures lead him again to identify Jesus with Isaiah's suffering servant, especially in his mercy:

> A bruised reed [weak, hurt person] he will not break,
> a smoldering wick [fainthearted person] he will not quench
> (v. 20).

But the controversy gathers momentum. When Jesus cures a possessed man, both blind and mute (v. 22), the Pharisees accuse him of the ultimate evil of being in league with Beelzebul, prince of demons. To Mark's version of Jesus' self-defense Matthew adds a powerful first conclusion recalling his dominant theme that "the kingdom of God has come upon you" (v. 28).

His second conclusion, "Whoever is not with me is against me" (v. 30), should be taken within this context of controversy with the Pharisees, a situation that allows for no neutral ground. Otherwise it would directly contradict Jesus' more generous principle in Mark 9:40: "Whoever is not against us is for us."

As in Mark, Jesus now calls unforgivable the sin of identifying the Holy Spirit of Jesus as the evil spirit. Then Matthew adds the passage about knowing a tree by its fruit, leading to a third conclusion: The spirit that guides a person may be judged by its external manifestation; that is, speech and words (vv. 33-37). Matthew is apparently using this running controversy as an opportunity to drive home some of Jesus' most important lessons by judicious placement of otherwise unrelated sayings culled from *Q*.

Unmoved, the Pharisees, now joined by the scribes, renew the attack by demanding that Jesus substantiate through signs his claim to work by the Holy Spirit. As though his cures were not signs enough! Jesus refuses to debase his power by using it for show. His resurrection after death and three days "in the heart of the earth" (v. 40) will be the sure sign of his identity. Yet even though this sign will prove Jesus to be greater than their prophets and kings, their generation will never accept him. They are like a man from whom Jesus has ejected an "unclean spirit" (v. 43) but who leaves his house "empty" (by refusing to believe in Jesus and accept his Spirit), and therefore they will end possessed by seven (the complete number) more evil spirits (v. 45).

Matthew returns to Mark's third chapter by concluding the controversy over spirits with the visit of Jesus' family and his powerful statement: "Whoever does the will of my heavenly Father is my brother, and sister, and mother" (v. 50). Those of the family of Jesus share his Spirit by adhering to his Father's will. Obviously Jesus appreciates family ties so highly that he uses these natural relationships to illustrate the kind of intimate spiritual relationship that he wants with us. As the theologians put it: Grace builds upon nature.

REFLECTION AND PRAYER

Judging by my words, what kind of person am I?

Am I one who does the will of the Father whom Jesus reveals?

Lord Jesus, I want to be for you; I want to be your brother, your sister, your true disciple.

Third Discourse: Parables of the Kingdom (Mt 13:1-53)

Jesus' third great sermon is a series of parables that suggest various aspects of the kingdom of God. These parables are seeds of thought planted by Jesus in the minds of his listeners, seeds that will grow only in those whose minds are open to him. In Matthew's context, Jesus has found such opposition that he now has recourse to parables as a way of fulfilling his mission to teach divine truth, yet hide it from his unworthy listeners (vv. 11-15).

The sermon begins with Mark's boat setting for the parable of the seed (the word of God) that falls upon different kinds of ground (hearers). Matthew expands Mark's version of Jesus' explanation of the parable by quoting more fully the passage from Isaiah 6:9-10: "You shall indeed hear but not understand" (v. 14). This is a typically Jewish way of attributing to God's Providence people's inability to understand, even though Isaiah knew and Matthew knows that this inability is due primarily to their own perverse refusal to listen. This manner of expression also serves Matthew's purpose, unlike Mark's, of stressing the difference between the unheeding crowd and the attentive disciples, who must, however, attribute their superior understanding not to their own merit but to God's pure gift of grace: "Blessed are . . . your ears, because they hear" (v. 16). Matthew really knows that Jesus is now telling parables not to hide the truth but to reveal it in greater depth:

"Many prophets . . . longed . . . to hear what you hear" (Mt 13:17).

After repeating Mark's allegorical explanation of the parable, Matthew skips his next parable about the lamp, which he already used in the Sermon on the Mount. Matthew then enhances the parable in which Mark compared the spreading of the kingdom of God to the sowing of good seed (Mk 4:26-29) by adding the picture of an enemy (Satan) sowing weeds among the wheat. This addition gives Matthew the opportunity to draw the more pointed lesson that Christians must be patient with a church that includes bad as well as good members and leave to the Lord the final judgment at harvest, when he will burn the weeds and gather the wheat into his barn (v. 30).

Then, closely following Mark, Matthew presents the parable comparing the kingdom of God to the tiny mustard seed that grows into "the largest of plants" (v. 32). In its proximity to Matthew's coming implication that the church is God's kingdom on earth, Jesus' expression, "the birds of the sky come and dwell in its branches," acquires new significance. A quotation from Daniel (Dn 4:9), it is part of a description of the great tree standing "at the center of the world" (Dn 4:7), symbol of King Nebuchadnezzar, who will know that "the Most High rules over the kingdom of men" (Dn 4:22).

Matthew adds another parable, not in Mark, comparing the kingdom of heaven to the yeast that makes the dough of society rise (v. 33). Again Matthew seems to imply that the church is the kingdom of heaven on earth.

In completing this part of the discourse to the crowds Matthew finds Jesus' justification for teaching in parables about the kingdom in Psalm 78:2:

> I will open my mouth in a parable,
> I will utter mysteries from of old (freely quoted in v. 35).

The continuation of the discourse, now only to the disciples, is a passage proper to Matthew that clearly stresses his chief reason for assembling this discourse. The Sermon on the Mount has spelled out the meaning of kingdom living. The missionary sermon has presented a methodology for spreading the kingdom. This parable sermon now suggests the meaning of the kingdom itself.

This meaning is found especially in the explanation of the parable of the weeds (vv. 36-43). The planter of God's kingdom (v. 38) is Jesus, Son of Man. He plants and cultivates the good seed, "the children of the kingdom," but the devil spreads weeds, "the children of the evil one.'' At the end of the world the judgment will separate for punishment the evil from the good, who will ''shine like the sun in the kingdom of their Father'' (v. 43). In other words the kingdom of God already exists in Jesus and his true followers, but it will only become definitive in heaven at the end of the world. That kingdom is more precious than a buried treasure or a pearl for which a person should be willing to give all he or she has (vv. 44-46).

As fishermen separate from the net the bad fish from the good, so will the angels separate the evil from the good at the end of the world. At last Jesus' chosen disciples, in contrast to Mark's depiction of them, can answer that they understand (v. 51)! Jesus declares that they have become the new scribes or leaders of God's people. They constitute ''the head of the household'' of the church, for they now know how to combine the new teaching of Jesus with the old teaching of the law and the prophets (v. 52).

REFLECTION AND PRAYER

Do I really listen to the word of God in Jesus?

Do I treasure his kingdom as a pearl worth all that I have?

Do I sincerely try to give the church as God's kingdom on earth my total commitment?

Lord Jesus, I cherish your word and rest in your kingdom.

Jesus Prepares for His Church and Calls for Unity (Mt 13:54—18:35)

Events Leading Toward Peter's Confession of Faith (Mt 13:54—15:39)

Following Mark 6:1-6 Matthew now relates Jesus' visit to ''his native place'' (Mt 13:54). Matthew focuses this incident on the person of Jesus himself, whom the Nazarenes think they know to be of lowly origin. They therefore take ''offense'' (v. 57) when he proceeds to teach them. Matthew omits Mark's suggestion that Jesus' distress inhibited his action, but agrees with Mark that ''their lack of faith'' (v. 58) was the real cause of his not working ''mighty deeds'' there.

At his summarizing best, Matthew reduces Mark's story of John the Baptist's death to its major details. He likewise summarizes the consequent effort of Jesus to withdraw, implying that he does so not so much to avoid the constant press of the crowd as to escape Herod's reach. John's death is a shadow across Jesus' future. Yet Matthew's Jesus is "moved with pity" (v. 14) for the people who follow him, and he submits again to the danger of going public by healing the sick and then feeding them all. Matthew stresses the power of this mighty deed by adding to Mark's "five thousand men" the phrase "not counting women and children" (v. 21). And he emphasizes the symbolism of this miracle in prefiguring the Eucharist by referring only to the distribution of the bread.

Still following Mark, Matthew continues with the story of Jesus' walking on the water to rescue his storm-tossed disciples. He obviously interprets Mark's account as allegorical of the storm-tossed church of his own time, for he adds the incident of Peter's unsuccessful effort to emulate Jesus' water-walking. In this first time that Matthew shows us the bold Peter in action, his bravado ends in the pathetic cry "Lord, save me!" (v. 30). This man, whom Jesus will soon call "the Rock" (Mt 16:18), will not owe his firmness to his own inner strength but to his utter dependence upon the power of Jesus. Only Jesus can save Peter now, and as he does so he gently scolds him for his "little faith" (v. 31). The disciples are now able to answer the question they asked after Jesus calmed the sea, "What sort of man is this?" (Mt 8:27): "Truly you are the Son of God" (v. 33). Evidently Matthew is attributing to them an expression that they would have used only after the resurrection; he is preparing us for the coming moment of Peter's profession of faith in Jesus.

Early Christians would see in Jesus' action of saving his disciples from shipwreck a symbol of the loving Savior's continued protection of the travelers in Peter's bark as they encounter crisis after crisis in the stormy world of Roman persecutions. He is the same Jesus whose divine power and compassion healed anyone who merely reached out to touch "the tassel on his cloak" (v. 36).

In chapter 15 Matthew continues to follow Mark's sequence, summarizing the accusation of the Pharisees and scribes that Jesus allows his disciples to "break [much stronger than Mark's "not follow"] the tradition of the elders" (v. 2), and Jesus' counter accusation, "You have nullified the word of God for the sake of your tradition" (v. 6).

In verse 11 Jesus publicly rejects Jewish dietary laws: "It is not what enters one's mouth that defiles that person." Morality, or lack of it, is not a question of diet but of inner attitudes manifested in external words: "What comes out of the mouth is what defiles one." Only Matthew reports that the disciples, alarmed by Jesus' radical rejection of Jewish tradition, warn him of the Pharisees' resentment. In reply Jesus implies that God has not chosen the blind Pharisees to lead his people: "Every plant that my heavenly Father has not planted will be up-rooted" (v. 13). Peter, who will soon be planted as leader with the primary responsibility for deciding such matters as continuing or rejecting the observance of Jewish dietary laws asks for an explanation but is rebuffed for lacking insight.

Jesus explains by using, as in Mark, a bold latrine figure (vv. 17-20). If Jesus so clearly rejects Jewish dietary laws as this figure now suggests, it is difficult to see why the early church had such an agonizing problem with these laws. Perhaps both evangelists here attribute to Jesus a clarification that only gradually occurred in the early church.

At any rate, the latrine figure expands the contrast between the Pharisees' tradition and the true law of morality by including intentions as well as words. Jesus points to the priority of the heart's intention over both word and action. Matthew revises Mark's list of "evil thoughts" to conform more closely to the order of the commandments regarding neighbor. He is obviously telling his readers that in rejecting the Pharisees' tradition Jesus all the more forcefully embraces the ten commandments. And in the context of verse 13, Matthew has given the latrine figure the added meaning that only the Father can plant the roots of right intention and thereby become the true guide of a person's actions.

Having rejected the laws regarding uncleanness, Jesus now enters Gentile territory and engages, over the protest of his disciples (v. 23), in a contact that Jewish law forbade as unclean. In following Mark's account of the request of the Canaanite woman, Matthew again adds an interpretation in another saying of Jesus that he alone reports, "I was sent only to the lost sheep of the house of Israel" (v. 24). This addition was probably meant as an answer to those of Matthew's community who may have been insisting that Jesus directed the church's missionary effort exclusively to the Jews, for the rest of this story illustrates that, although Jesus had sometimes seemed to disapprove of contact with Gentiles, he himself had engaged in it. Some commentators speculate that this saying indicates that it was only through this incident that Jesus became aware that his Father had sent him also to the Gentiles. But Matthew has already presented Jesus' cure of the centurion's servant (Mt 8:5-13) and of the possessed men of Gadara (Mt 8:28-34), both missionary actions for Gentiles. Hence Matthew must here be thinking of Jesus' "house of Israel" saying as a test of the woman's faith, a test that she passes beautifully, as he stresses by changing Mark's report of Jesus' final words from "For saying this, you may go" (Mk 7:29) to "O woman, great is your faith!" (v. 28).

At this point, Matthew substitutes a summary of numerous healings in place of Mark's account of the cure of the deaf-mute. Perhaps Matthew considered this apparently difficult healing incompatible with the reverent impression of Jesus that he intends to give his readers, heightened by the reaction of the crowd: "They glorified the God of Israel" (v. 31).

Returning to Mark' account, Matthew relates Jesus' second miracle of feeding a crowd of four thousand men, to which he again adds, "not counting women and children" (v. 38). Perhaps both evangelists have repeated the multiplication of the loaves to suggest that the Eucharist, symbolized by feeding all with the same bread, is repeatedly offered as the constant nourishment of the lives of Christians.

REFLECTION AND PRAYER

When I find my own life immersed in turbulent waters, do I call upon the Lord and try to walk with him?

Do I reach out to touch "his tassel" for healing?

Lord Jesus, I acknowledge my repeated need of the Eucharist and of communion of desire. Come, at this moment, to live in my heart and renew it with your own life.

Peter Confesses Faith in Jesus as Messiah, Son of God (Mt 16:1-20)

At the beginning of chapter 16 both the Pharisees and the Sadducees once more demand a sign. In the first part of Jesus' reply, omitted in some of the best manuscripts, Jesus reprimands them for their inability to "judge the signs of the times" (v. 3)—the healings and miracles just related. Once more Jesus offers them only the sign of Jonah, his coming resurrection.

As does Mark, Matthew follows this incident with Jesus' warning to his disciples against the leaven of the Jewish leaders. But when they fail to understand his meaning, Matthew's Jesus again chides them for "little faith" (v. 8) and makes his meaning explicit: "How do you not comprehend that I was not speaking to you about bread? Beware of the leaven of the Pharisees and Sadducees'' (v. 11). And Matthew adds that the disciples finally understood that he was talking about the teaching of these Jewish leaders.

Matthew's picture of the disciples is much less harsh than Mark's. Perhaps Matthew is more accurate in his portrayal of the closest followers of Jesus, or perhaps he is deliberately toning down their lack of understanding and faith in view of the authoritative position in the church for which he has been preparing them. Having rejected the teaching of the Pharisees and Sadducees, Jesus is about to confer his own teaching authority upon the Twelve in the person of their leader.

Omitting Mark's account of the ''difficult'' cure of the blind man at Bethsaida, Matthew now proceeds immediately to the incident near Caesarea Philippi. By changing Jesus' initial question from ''Who do people say that I am?'' (Mk 8:27) to ''Who do people say that *the Son of Man* is?'' (v. 13), Matthew heightens the significance of the passage with a note of mystery.

He then expands Mark's account of Peter's profession of faith into a major passage with its own distinct emphasis. To Mark's ''You are the Messiah,'' Matthew's Peter adds: *''the Son of the living God!''* (v. 16). This addition, prepared for in that previous passage in which Jesus, in the presence of his disciples, prayed directly to God as *''my* Father'' (Mt 11:27), suggests that Matthew may be transposing post-resurrection material to a pre-resurrection situation. Perhaps he is using a tradition of Jesus' otherwise undescribed appearance to Peter (see Luke 24:34), a very early tradition, judging by verse 18, in which the play on the words *Peter* and *rock* has clear meaning only in Aramaic (*Kepha*). Peter's reply is powerful testimony not only to his own faith but also to the faith of the early Christians in the divinity of Jesus, a faith that perceives in him an infinitely greater dignity than that which the Old Testament had prophesied of the Messiah.

Peter's confession of faith in Jesus as the Messiah, the Son of the living God, is the high point of Matthew's Christology. This declaration not only defines Jesus for the early Christian reader; it also defines Peter. By his insight into the true significance of Jesus Christ, Peter finds out who he himself really is. Above all, he is a disciple who believes in Jesus as Son of God. Matthew here presents him as spokesmen for all of us who find our true identity by our faith in Jesus Christ as Son of God.

Jesus attributes Peter's new knowledge to a special revelation of the Father. Then, just as Yahweh had declared Abram to be his own by giving him the new name Abraham (Gn 17:5), Jesus claims Simon as his own by conferring upon him the new name Peter, "the Rock." And just as Abraham, in his faith, was "the rock from which you [who seek the Lord] were hewn" (Is 51:1-2), so Jesus now promises to build his church (v. 18) upon Peter. Upon the firmness of Peter's faith, Jesus will build his church as the community that will remain unshakable before "the gates [powers] of the netherworld [of evil and death]," as foretold when Daniel was delivered from the lions' den by "the living God . . . [whose] kingdom shall not be destroyed" (Dn 6:27).

Are we to understand that Jesus is here referring to Peter as merely representative of all true Christians, and therefore that the church will stand upon their faith? Not in view of the immediate context in which Jesus adds the further promise to entrust to Peter—not to all Christians—"the keys to the kingdom of heaven" (v. 19), an echo of Isaiah 22:21-22:

> I [the LORD] will place *the key of the House of David*
>   on his [Eliakim's] shoulder;
>   when he opens, no one shall shut,
>   when he shuts, no one shall open.

By now conferring the keys of the kingdom of heaven (the new church replacing Israel, the House of David) upon Peter, Matthew's Jesus is referring to him as the new Eliakim selected to replace his unworthy predecessor (the present leaders of the Jews) as the servant entrusted with the keys that give the new people of God access to their Lord. Evidently Jesus is giving Peter a share in his power not only to admit members into his church or exclude them, but also to exercise his authority over this new church, the doctrinal and disciplinary authority to bind or loose. According to some scholars, this is a refinement and extension of the kind of authority attributed to the rabbis of Jesus' time to interpret (unlock) the Hebrew scriptures for the faith and life of their people.

Despite his own weaknesses as a man, so vividly manifested by his failure to walk on water (Mt 14:31) and his future triple denial of Jesus (Mt 26:69-75), Peter in his commissioned power as keeper of the keys will eventually be the solid rock confirming his brothers and sisters in their faith in Jesus (Lk 22:32) and feeding their love for him (Jn 21:15-19).

Historically these passages have served as the principal scriptural bases for the doctrine in the ancient Christian church of the primacy of the bishop of Rome as legitimate successor of Peter, a primacy unanimously recognized at the Council of Ephesus in 431 and formally decreed by the First Vatican Council (see *The Teaching of the Catholic Church*, p. 201).

Matthew 16:18-19 places "my church" and "the kingdom of heaven" in such close association as to identify them in some way. Evidently Jesus is bringing the kingdom to earth, giving it temporal form in his church, and naming Peter as its highest authority, again the expression of the post-resurrection faith of the early Christians. By now it hardly surprises us that Matthew would take the liberty of attributing to Jesus a saying that he is confident expresses the faith of the first Christians. The fact that this belief could be so stated and accepted by the time of Matthew's writing, manifests the firmness and universality with which it was held among the early Christians; its acceptance substantiates the claim of the church to be founded by Christ.

Further, the close association of "my church" with "the kingdom of heaven" makes this passage a significant key to the interpretation of one of Matthew's major themes: "The kingdom of heaven," "kingdom of God," "reign of God," are equivalent expressions for the supra-terrestrial reality to which Jesus gives concrete earthly embodiment in "my church." It is, then, for humankind in general and for this church in particular that the Sermon on the Mount has spelled out a new moral code, the missionary sermon has outlined a program of growth, and the parables of the kingdom have suggested descriptive detail.

REFLECTION AND PRAYER

Do I really believe that Jesus is my Messiah, the Son of the living God?

Do I define my own identity before others as one who believes this?

Can others so identify me by my actions, by my way of relating to them?

Jesus, I believe that you are the Son of God!

Suffering Son of Man, Yet Glorious Son of God (Mt 16:21—17:27)

As in Mark, Matthew's Jesus immediately begins to teach his disciples the kind of Messiah he is: not the glorious conquering king that the Jewish leaders of the time expected from their almost exclusive reliance on the Davidic prophecies, but the suffering servant so prominent in Isaiah's prophecies. Matthew alone reports Peter's words of protest: "God forbid, Lord! No such thing shall ever happen to you!" (v. 22). To Mark's report that Jesus called Peter "Satan!" Matthew's Jesus adds, "You are an obstacle to me" (v. 23), a word play signifying that the Rock that should sustain the church is here becoming a stumbling block to Jesus himself by repeating the most severe of Satan's temptations, that is, to be a Messiah without a cross of suffering (Mt 4:8-10). As on that occasion, Jesus sets behind him both the temptation and the tempter.

Matthew continues to follow Mark in presenting here Jesus' teaching on the key requirement for true discipleship: self-denial in carrying the cross of suffering "for my sake" (v. 25). In an allusion to the last judgment, soon to be described in detail, Matthew's Jesus adds, "The Son of Man . . . will repay everyone according to his conduct" (v. 27). And he changes the last part of Mark 9:1 from "There are some standing here who will not taste death until they see that *the kingdom of God has come in power,*" which could refer to the church's rapid growth, to "until they see *the Son of Man coming in his kingdom*" (v. 28). Although this change may express the expectation of the imminent second coming of Christ so widespread among the early Christians, "coming in his kingdom" probably refers to Jesus' resurrection when the full meaning of the title "Son of Man" could be understood in terms of his definitive establishment of God's kingdom on earth. This interpretation conforms to the context of Jesus' promise to give the keys of the kingdom to Peter (v. 19) and his first prediction of his passion and resurrection (v. 21).

Immediately after foretelling his sufferings, Jesus gives the three disciples who will witness his agony a foretaste of his glory in his transfiguration before them. Although closely following Mark, Matthew's account of the transfiguration takes on the added function of confirming Peter's recent confession of faith in Jesus as Son of God.

To Mark's description of the brilliance of Jesus' clothing, Matthew adds an image of Jesus' face shining "like the sun" (Mt 17:2). Matthew emphasizes Peter's overconfidence by portraying him as saying "*I* will make three tents" (v. 4), reminiscent of the Lord's tent carried by the Israelites through the desert during the Exodus. Evidently Peter wants to make this religious experience permanent with a shrine, a new Temple, in which the Lord can be consulted, together with

Moses and Elijah, spokesmen of the law and the prophets. Immediately, from the "bright cloud" (v. 5), the Father speaks in favor of his "beloved Son" (v. 5). It is he to whom they are now to listen as to a new Moses, a new Elijah, the new embodiment of the law and the prophets, the new Temple. Only Matthew reports that the disciples fall prostrate in adoration and that Jesus touches them with the encouraging words, "Rise, and do not be afraid" (v. 7).

In rewriting Mark's account of the ensuing conversation, Matthew reports that Jesus calls the transfiguration a "vision" (v. 9), evidently of his coming state after the resurrection, until which time he enjoins them to silence. Is Matthew saying that the transfiguration was not a real event? He probably never speculated about the matter. He finds events in the life of Jesus so meaningful that the dichotomy that we often posit between fact and symbol never seems to occur to him. For him fact and symbol run together so that the transfiguration, whether fact or symbol or both, probably expresses the fleeting moments of visionary insight experienced by at least some of Jesus' disciples even before his resurrection.

Matthew also explicitly adds that in saying Elijah has already come, Jesus is "speaking to them of John the Baptist" (v. 13), whom the literal-minded Jewish leaders failed to recognize (v. 12). Jesus uses the occasion to foretell that the Son of God, whom they have just seen in glory, is also the Son of Man who must suffer the same violent death as has John.

Matthew drastically shortens Mark's account of the cure of the demented boy. To Mark's version of Jesus' reproach ("O faithless generation"; Mk 9:19), Matthew adds "and perverse" (v. 17), making it doubly clear that Jesus is directing this severe reproach to the Jews who deliberately refuse to hear him rather than to his disciples to whom he has been consistently attributing at least a "*little* faith," too little to effect this cure (v. 20). To bring home to them how little faith they have, Matthew's Jesus adds that if their faith were even the size of a mustard seed, "the smallest of all the seeds" (Mt 13:32), they would be able to move mountains. In the context of the parable in which the church as kingdom of heaven on earth is compared to the plant that grows from the mustard seed (Mt 13:31-32), Matthew may also be suggesting that the faith of the diminutive new church is already moving the religious center of the Roman Empire from paganism to Christianity.

There follows, as in Mark, Jesus' second prediction of his passion, death and resurrection. In Mark the disciples "did not understand" (Mk 9:32), but in Matthew they are "overwhelmed with grief" (v. 23).

Then Matthew inserts a curious passage found nowhere else. Peter is apparently so well-known by now as Jesus' "right-hand man" that the collectors of the Temple tax ask him whether Jesus pays the tax. Jesus uses the occasion to reinforce Peter's faith in him as Son of God who makes others "sons" (the meaning of the Greek word translated as "subjects" in *NAB*, v. 25) of the true king of the people who worship him in his Temple. As sons, Jesus' disciples can claim exemption from the tax, for in him they now have their new Temple. Yet, to avoid scandal, Jesus orders Peter to pay the tax anyway by means of that strange little miracle of the coin in the mouth of the fish that Peter, the professional fisherman, is to catch.

This curious little fish story is so different from the rest of Jesus' miracles that it seems to be a symbolic story intended to stress the Christian believe that Jesus is the new Temple replacing the old and that Christians were no longer morally obliged to support the Jewish Temple, destroyed in 70, considerably before the time of Matthew's writing. The story could also be used to illustrate the point that, although Christians had no moral obligation to accede to the Roman demand for taxes to maintain pagan temples, they should do so to avoid unnecessary problems. The fact that Peter is to pay with a coin earned by his trade suggests how Matthew's community might be expected to pay.

REFLECTION AND PRAYER

> Do I really believe that Jesus is at the same time glorious Son of God and suffering Son of Man?
>
> Do I look to his church to strengthen my faith in him and guide me in being true to him?

Lord Jesus, I adore you as Son of God and confidently approach you as Son of Man.

Fourth Discourse: Jesus Calls for Unity in His Church (Mt 18)

In chapter 18 Matthew assembles into Jesus' fourth discourse sayings from Mark 9:33-50 and other sources, using as setting the disciples' divisive question about who is the greatest in the kingdom of heaven. Since Matthew has already suggested that the kingdom of heaven begins on earth with the church, the answer to that question can be interpreted as a well-organized sermon on order and unity within the church. Although the word *unity* is not used, it is the key concept that holds the sermon together:

1. Unity requires humility;
    Illustration: Jesus places a little child in their midst (vv. 1-4).
2. Unity is broken by scandal that leads little ones astray;
    avoid it at all costs, for it will be punished in hell (vv. 5-9).
3. Unity requires great care to save the straying one;
    Illustration: Parable of the lost sheep (vv. 10-14).
4. Unity must be preserved by a process of fraternal correction;
    a. The wronged one privately points out the wrong doer's offense;
    b. He calls in witnesses;
    c. He refers the case to the church;
    d. The church "binds," that is, it punishes or excommunicates; or it "looses," forgives or readmits (vv. 15-18).
5. Unity in Jesus is pleasing to the Father;
    to those so joined, he will grant "anything whatever" (vv. 19-20).
6. Unity requires constant forgiveness.
    Illustration: Parable of the merciless official (vv. 21-35).

Now let's look at this sermon in some detail. Jesus begins with an action parable. Placing a child among his disciples, he lets them observe the humble obedience of the typical child of his time and calls upon them to imitate the child's unpretentious dependence upon the Father (vv. 3-5).

Anyone who leads those who have become these "little ones" (v. 6) into such a sin as ambition to become "the greatest" (v. 1), deserves the greatest of punishments. Though scandal is inevitable, it is not excusable; even extreme measures must be taken to avoid it, illustrated here by physical maiming (vv. 8-9), the powerful hyperbole used by Mark (9:42-48) in a similar context of scandal.

Far from despising such "little ones," whom Jesus' Father so dearly loves as to assign guardian angels to protect them (v. 11), a true leader of the church must become their good shepherd. This beautiful parable of the shepherd who so cares for each sheep that he leaves the 99 that are safe to seek out the stray is found also in Luke (15:4-7). Its vivid portrayal of the sensitive Providence of God is one of Matthew's recurring themes. By placing the parable in the context of this sermon, Matthew is insisting that those who exercise authority in the church must be good shepherds of the flock in imitation of God's loving Providence and the absolute dedication of his Son, Jesus.

The sermon now turns to the elimination of scandal by a process of fraternal correction proper to Matthew's gospel. Although the final part of the process (vv. 17-18) makes no reference to any authority within the church, it is part of the discourse addressed to the disciples and therefore implies their role in convoking the assembly of the local community in order to take up the case envisioned here. Moreover, the repetition of the same expression about *binding and loosing* that had been used in reference to Peter (Mt 16:19) suggests an authority on the local level that is to participate in Peter's general authority. Such an interpretation of these two texts is implicit in the historical development of authority within the early church, the power explicitly formulated at Vatican I in defining the jurisdictional authority of the bishops (*First Dogmatic Constitution on the Church of Christ*, No. 380) and at Vatican II in defining their collegial authority (*Dogmatic Constitution on the Church*, No. 22).

Not only in binding and loosing is the church to act in unity, but especially in praying (vv. 19-20), a passage also proper to Matthew. So pleasing to the Father is unity in prayer that he will grant "anything" to such prayer. But notice that this "anything" is made dependent in the next verse upon unity "in my name" (v. 20); in other words, unity in Jesus is so pleasing to the Father that it calls forth his boundless graciousness. This presence of Jesus in his church is becoming another of Matthew's most important themes: "Where two or three are gathered together in my name, *there am I in the midst of them*" (v. 20). This theme will reach its climax at the very end of Matthew's gospel. In the present passage it seems especially applicable to couples who wed in Jesus' name and bear witness to their faith in him in the presence of their children.

Having listened to Jesus' directives about handling the case of the recalcitrant brother and the demand for unity in prayer, Peter interrupts the sermon with a question by which he suggests that he now understands Jesus well enough to anticipate what he will say about forgiving the brother who is not recalcitrant. But Jesus' answer, "not seven times but seventy-seven times" (v. 22, which may also be translated "seventy times seven"), makes it clear that Peter has hardly begun to understand! Lamech, descendant of Cain, had demanded to be avenged "seventy-sevenfold" (Gn 4:24). In reversing this demand Jesus calls for unlimited forgiveness.

Jesus proceeds to illustrate his point in the parable of the merciless official, found only in Matthew (vv. 23-35). This parable clearly underlines the responsibility of authorities— "servants" in the kingdom, such as Peter and his fellow disciples are becoming. They are to be as forgiving toward one another and toward those under their care as they hope God will be toward them.

The dominant theme of unity running through this discourse suggests that disunity may have become one of the major problems of Matthew's community. The homily clearly stresses that Matthew's Jesus demands humility, avoidance of scandal, charity, acceptance of church authority, family and community prayer, and untiring forgiveness as the binding forces to achieve unity in him.

REFLECTION AND PRAYER

Do I strive for unity with my fellow Christians?

Do I strive for unity especially by childlike humility, by steadfastly avoiding scandal, by reaching out toward the stray, by fraternal correction, by prayer, by forgiveness?

Lord Jesus, help me forgive seventy-seven times.

Jesus Approaches His Final Sacrifice (Mt 19—25)

Attitudes Required for Entering the Kingdom (Mt 19)

At the beginning of chapter 19 Matthew formally closes Jesus' fourth great discourse and his Galilean ministry. These transition verses suggest that the following incidents take place on the way to Jerusalem, a journey in which Jesus is followed by great crowds (v. 2).

Returning to Mark's sequence, Matthew takes up the question of divorce. To the Pharisees' question about the lawfulness of divorce Matthew's version adds, "for any cause whatever?" (v. 3). Matthew thereby prepares his readers to see Jesus' negative reply as a complete rejection of divorce. The sharpness of Jesus' reply manifests his firmness in this matter: "Have you not read . . . ?" (v. 4). Matthew rearranges Mark's account to present first Jesus' appeal to God's will in creating male and female; according to the Genesis account husband and wife are "joined together" as "one flesh" in the closest of unions, not humanly breakable. This new arrangement gives Matthew's Pharisees the opportunity to imply that Jesus rejects the law of Moses granting "a bill of divorce" (v. 7). Jesus' response goes beyond the letter of Moses' law to the reason behind it, "the hardness of your hearts" (v. 8)—the hardness of the Israelites' hearts in constantly opposing God's will expressed by Moses in the desert, and the same hardness of the Pharisees' hearts in constantly opposing God's will expressed by Jesus.

Matthew's Jesus rejects all reasons for divorce "unless the marriage is unlawful" (v. 9), in which case the attempted union would not have been a marriage and there would be no need for divorce but only for a declaration of annulment. The church has consistently interpreted all the synoptics as prohibiting divorce (separation with the right to remarry) for any reason, but allowing annulment (declaration that a union was never a true marriage) for a sufficient reason, such as the one Matthew may be alluding to here: marriage of pagans within a degree of blood relationship prohibited by Leviticus 18:6-18 before their entry into the church.

In his report of the resultant conversation of Jesus with his disciples, Matthew adds the passage about deliberate renunciation of marriage "for the sake of the kingdom of heaven" (v. 12). Traditionally this text has been understood, in conjunction with Matthew 22:30, as the basis for the vow of chastity voluntarily taken by Catholic religious as a sign of the kingdom of heaven: "At the resurrection they neither marry nor are given in marriage but are like the angels in heaven." Not everyone is called to this special vocation: "Whoever can accept this ought to accept it" (v. 12). The lives of those who do so become a sign of the final form of the kingdom of God, in which God's true children will be totally dedicated to all.

This passage makes it clear that marriage and celibacy are not rival vocations but complementary callings that should mutually sustain each other in the church. To widen their love for each other until it embraces the whole body of Christ, married couples need the example of dedicated celibates. To deepen their love for the members of the body, celibates need the example of married couples totally devoted to each other. Faithful marriage is a great good; it is also a great good to give up marriage "for the sake of the kingdom."

Still following Mark, Matthew next relates Jesus' blessing of the children, compacting the last part of Jesus' comment into that memorable saying: "The kingdom of heaven belongs to such as these" (v. 14).

In telling the story of the rich man Matthew clarifies a possible misreading of Mark by changing his version of the man's question from "*Good teacher*, what must I do to inherit eternal life?" (Mk 10:17) to "Teacher, *what good must I do* to gain eternal life?" (v. 16). This change allows Matthew to avoid Mark's ambiguous version of Jesus' answer: "Why do you call me good? No one is good but God alone." Only Matthew speaks of the man as *young* (v. 20). Only Matthew's Jesus ends his recital of the commandments with the general precept that shows the spirit in which they are to be kept: "You shall love your neighbor as yourself" (v. 19). And only Matthew's Jesus challenges the young man: "*If you wish to be perfect*, go, sell what you have and give to [the] poor. . . . Then come, follow me" (v. 21; brackets in *NAB*). But in the Sermon on the Mount Jesus demanded that all "*Be perfect*, just as your heavenly Father is perfect" (Mt 5:48). How can the *demand* that everyone be perfect be reconciled with the *invitation* to the rich young man to be perfect?

One traditional but non-official effort to reconcile these passages holds that they point out two levels of following Christ: the minimal imperfect level of keeping the commandments demanded of all for salvation, and the higher level of perfection to which only the few are invited through the practice of the evangelical counsels of chastity, poverty and obedience. Both levels involve *doing something* to win a lower or higher level of happiness in the kingdom. Hence, this interpretation seems to be incompatible with the belief that salvation is not won by our doing but is a pure gift of God, as expressed in the ensuing conversation of Jesus with the disciples: "For human beings this [being saved] is impossible, but for God all things are possible" (v. 26).

The invitation to the rich young man does not therefore distinguish between two levels of following Jesus, but rather clarifies what it really means to keep the commandments, to be perfect, to follow Jesus. What prevents this young man from becoming a true disciple is evidently his attachment to his wealth. In advising him to give it up, Jesus is pointing out to him that his understanding of the commandments has been too literal. He thinks he has observed them, but he has not grasped the true spirit of loving neighbor as self; he has kept his wealth for himself instead of sharing it with others. Jesus' prescription to "sell what you have and give" is not, then, a general directive to all his followers, but only to those for whom, like this young man, possessions prove an obstacle. "Follow me by surmounting with my help whatever obstacles prevent you from doing so" becomes the general directive to all, the determinant of being or not being a true Christian. Vatican II declared that all persons are called to the same perfection of holiness but in different ways, according to the special disposition and state of life of each (*Dogmatic Constitution on the Church*, No. 41).

Lest his readers complacently conclude that Jesus' directive about riches applies only to the young man of the story, Matthew adds Jesus' warning to his disciples about wealth as an obstacle to entering the kingdom of heaven (vv. 23-25). Riches cannot save anyone, but neither can poverty; Jesus' good news is that God is the one who saves us (v. 27).

In the ensuing question about rewards (vv. 27-30) Matthew's Jesus adds a sentence to Mark's account that offers a reason why Jesus chose *12* apostles: "You who have followed me, in the new age, when the Son of Man is seated on his throne of glory, will yourselves sit *on twelve thrones, judging the twelve tribes of Israel*" (v. 28). Careful reading of this passage will reveal something more profound than the reason for the number 12. Notice that the new age begins with the enthronement of Jesus in his glory; that is, after his resurrection and ascension. It is then that the Twelve will take their places as judges (rulers in Jewish usage) of the new Israel, the church. The picture of "the Son of Man . . . seated on his throne of glory" also evokes the scene of the last judgment, suggesting the further meaning that the Twelve will share with Jesus in passing judgment upon the nation now rejecting him and soon to pass judgment upon him and his disciples.

Jesus then promises, as in Mark, abundant rewards to anyone who gives up anything "for the sake of my name" (v. 29). Matthew's omission of Mark's "in this present age" suggests that he considers all these rewards as equivalent to inheriting "eternal life" (v. 29). Hence, the paradox: "Many who are first [in the estimation of this world] will be last, and the last [in human estimation] will be first [in the definitive kingdom of God]" (v. 30).

REFLECTION AND PRAYER

Do I try to adopt the attitudes required for belonging to the kingdom of God: faithfulness in marriage, childlike dependence upon God, indifference to wealth, willingness to share what I have with others?

Lord Jesus, teach me to be willing to be last for your sake.

"The Last Shall Be First" (Mt 20)

Matthew's Jesus illustrates the paradox of first and last with a parable that emphasizes the gratuity of the Father's gift of salvation and his complete freedom in giving it (vv. 1-16). In the kingdom of heaven the accepted human values are upset by the landowner (God) who pays the last workers first and pays all workers equally. Since we cannot really deserve anything from God, his rewards are gratuitous, and he freely gives them to whom and when he pleases. Hence, he will first reward the last (the followers of Jesus in the eyes of Jewish leaders). And all the workers in the Lord's vineyard will receive the same wage: eternal life. Who could ask for more?

There is another possible meaning, which Matthew may have intended for his community, perhaps predominantly converts from Judaism: The first who entered the church (Jews) may not lay claim to a higher reward than the last (Gentiles). In Matthew's mixed community this problem of prior claim could very well have been severe, judging by the many times he returns to the quarrel about who shall be first in the kingdom.

Modern readers, sensitive to the claims of economic justice, still find difficulty with this parable. But we also find difficulty reconciling the two apparently opposed concepts of *reward* and *gift*. How can Jesus say in Matthew 19:26 that salvation is not a reward for our merit and in Matthew 19:29 that it is a reward for following him? Only if following him is also a gift of the Father. And this is precisely what the parable of the laborers in the vineyard suggests, if we remember that Matthew's Jesus has already used harvesting as the symbol of apostolic work (Mt 9:36-38).

As Jesus goes up to Jerusalem (v. 17) he foretells for the third time his coming passion (vv. 17-19), in much more detail than before. To Mark's account Matthew's version adds the significant detail ''to be . . . *crucified*'' (v. 19). According to Matthew Jesus foresees even the manner of his death.

Following Mark, Matthew then presents the episode in which James and John lay claim to the highest places in the kingdom. If they were present for the parable of the laborers, they certainly didn't hear what Jesus was saying! But Matthew presents them as more subtle than does Mark: They enlist their mother to do the asking. Jesus promises that they will drink of the same cup of suffering that will be his, but leaves the determination of places to the Father. He further uses the incident to teach the indignant disciples that authority in the kingdom—and therefore in the church—means service rather than honor. Jesus holds up the servant as their model of greatness; and the slave as their model of leadership. They must even participate in the sacrifice of the Son of Man who has come "to give his life as a ransom for many" (v. 28).

Still following Mark, Matthew here presents the cure of blindness at Jericho. But as he now seems accustomed to do, he enlarges the miracle by making it a cure of two blind men instead of one, perhaps as contrast with the spiritually blind James and John. Matthew repeats some of the same elements that he used in the similar miracle recounted in chapter 9. But this time the cured men become Jesus' followers, even on the road to Jerusalem.

REFLECTION AND PRAYER

Do I believe that many of those whom the world considers last may be among the first in the kingdom of God, here and in eternity?

Jesus, Son of David, cure my spiritual blindness!

Jesus' Stormy Ministry in Jerusalem (Mt 21:1—23:14)

Matthew cuts many of the details of Mark's account of the triumphal entry into Jerusalem. Characteristically he adds his own free combination of Isaiah 62:11 and Zechariah 9:9. Perhaps from a desire to show literal fulfillment of Zechariah's prophecy, Matthew slips into a literary lapse, depicting Jesus simultaneously mounting two animals: "They brought *the ass and the colt* and laid their cloaks over them, and *he sat upon them*" (v. 7)! It is consoling to find that the inspiration of the Holy Spirit is not an overly fastidious protection against literary error. The important point still emerges clearly: "Your king comes to you, *meek*" (v. 5), riding not as a great man of this world but as a lowly one. Yet the crowd hails Jesus as "Son of David . . . who comes in the name of the Lord" (v. 9), and Matthew's distinctive ending stresses the dignity and power of Jesus: "The whole city was shaken" (v. 10) as by an earthquake, and the crowd proclaims Jesus "the prophet from Nazareth in Galilee" (v. 11).

Matthew now presents a series of incidents and parables that depict Jesus as God's authorized teacher of Israel, replacing "the scribes and the Pharisees," Matthew's ordinary designation for the Jewish leaders. He follows Mark in reporting Jesus' cleansing of the Temple, but again presents a distinctive aftermath in which Jesus heals the blind and lame inside the Temple area, thereby symbolizing the true use of the Temple as God's place of healing souls. Significantly, even children recognize Jesus within the Temple as "Son of David" (v. 15), but the chief priests and scribes do not. Furious, they object, but Jesus defends the children with a quotation from Psalm 8:3. Jesus himself is supplanting the Temple; he is the new focal point of true worship.

In verses 18-22 Matthew combines the two parts of Mark's story of the fig tree; in Matthew's version the tree withers instantly. He thereby dramatizes the condemnation that Israel, symbolized by the barren fig tree, will suffer for its failure to recognize its Messiah, and he gains concentration on the lesson of the power of faith in prayer.

Matthew follows Mark very closely in his account of the challenge of the chief priests and elders to the authority of Jesus and his counter question about the origin of John's baptism (vv. 23-27). Then Matthew inserts a parable found nowhere else, that of the two sons (vv. 28-32). It is admirably tied to the preceding question about John's baptism. Jesus implicitly likens the sinners who accepted John's call for repentance to the apparently disobedient son who fulfilled the father's will. The son who said yes but acted otherwise obviously represents the "chief priests and the elders" (v. 23), probably equivalent here to the "Pharisees and Sadducees" whom John had refused to baptize because of their insincerity.

In relating Mark's parable of the tenants (vv. 33-44) Matthew enhances its allegorical element by dividing the servants sent by the landowner into two groups that represent the prophets sent by God before the Exile and the "more numerous" (v. 36) after the Exile. At the end of the parable the Jews answer Jesus' question about action to be taken by the landowner, unwittingly condemning themselves. Matthew's Jesus explains the parable's meaning: "The kingdom of God will be taken away from you [Jews] and given to a people [Christians] that will produce its fruit" (v. 43).

The references in this parable to the production of fruit (vv. 34, 41, 43) point back to the fig tree that produced no fruit (v. 19). In Matthew, then, the parable of the tenants not only condemns the Jewish leaders (v. 45), but also throws light upon Jesus' act of cursing the unfruitful fig tree, showing it to be an action parable that parallels this parable of the vineyard in condemning the failure of the Jews to produce the fruit of faith in Jesus. The vineyard symbolism has been expanded to represent the kingdom of God, already existing at least partially in the people of Israel (v. 43), but soon to be transferred to the Christian church.

In chapter 22 Jesus continues with the parable of a wedding banquet, in some details like Luke's parable of a great dinner (Lk 14:16-24). Matthew's parable, as the king's "wedding feast for his son [Jesus]" (v. 2), is more evocative of the Eucharist and of the eternal banquet. The invited guests (Jews) have other priorities and end by killing the servants sent to invite them (apostles). The king destroys the murderers and burns their city (v. 7), an early Christian interpretation of the destruction of Jerusalem in A.D. 70 as God's judgment upon the Jews, who had rejected his Son. He then invites others (Gentiles) to the feast. The king's entry suggests the initiation of the eternal banquet with the final judgment, for he orders that the man improperly dressed (one who has not responded with the appropriate change of heart) "be cast into the darkness outside" (v. 13).

The conclusion, "Many are invited, but few are chosen" (v. 14), has sometimes been thought to mean that the invitation offered by God's revelation is available to all, but that only a few are given the grace of election or salvation. This extremely narrow view seems unwarranted by the context, which obviously stresses the rejection of Jesus by the Jews, the broadening of the invitation to "whomever you find" (v. 9), and the mention of only one man improperly dressed. The conclusion can therefore hardly refer to numbers, but must rather mean that to be invited is not enough; one must also respond appropriately to the invitation to be admitted to the heavenly banquet. Matthew is warning his community that external membership in the church does not guarantee salvation.

REFLECTION AND PRAYER

Do I really believe in Jesus' authority as the great Teacher of how to live?

Do I deliberately try to pattern my life according to his teaching?

Lord Jesus, help me respond gratefully and wholeheartedly to your invitation to the final wedding feast with you and to the Eucharist as preparation for that feast.

Jesus' Final Clashes With the Jewish Leaders
(Mt 22:15—23:39)

Matthew climaxes his presentation of Jesus' ministry in Jerusalem with a series of controversies in which Jesus demonstrates his authoritative superiority over the leaders of the Jews, who cunningly set out to discredit him publicly.

In 22:15 Matthew returns to Mark's account, presenting the effort of the Pharisees and Herodians to trick Jesus into taking a public stand for or against paying taxes to Caesar. Jesus' answer silences them, for it not only justifies repaying Caesar for providing the coinage and peaceful climate of daily business, but it also renews the demand that Jesus has been making since his cleansing of the Temple: Give God the true worship that is his due.

The Sadducees continue the questioning with their attack on the resurrection, which Jesus has recently taught by implication in his parable of the heavenly banquet. Jesus reasons that since the Jewish tradition has always believed Yahweh to be the God of the living and scripture has identified him as the God of the patriarchs (Ex 3:6), these great believers must still be living. Thus, by using the Torah, the only part of the Jewish scriptures accepted by the Sadducees, Jesus establishes the revelation of immortality and, because the Jews of Jesus' day thought of immortality as somehow involving the body, he implies the truth of the resurrection.

The Pharisees return to the attack. Matthew changes Mark's introduction to the question about the greatest commandment by attributing it to a hostile lawyer instead of Mark's admiring scribe. Matthew's Jesus goes straight to the commandment to love God "with all your heart . . . soul . . . mind" (v. 37), adding to Mark's account the precise, "This is the greatest and the first commandment" (v. 38). Having underlined this priority, Jesus immediately adds the second command of love of neighbor. Matthew's version ends the controversy with another addition: "The whole law and the prophets *depend* on these two commandments" (v. 40), powerfully symbolizing love of God and neighbor as the great peg that anchors all laws and scriptures. Love inspires the observance of every law and interprets every scripture text to avoid such casuistry as that which the Pharisees and the Sadducees have been using in these attacks.

Matthew concludes all these controversial questions, as does

Mark, with Jesus' counter questions about the identity of the Messiah. But he gains dramatic force by transforming Mark's account from an instruction of the crowd to a dialogue with the Pharisees. When they identify the Messiah as David's son (v. 42), Jesus quotes David's Psalm 110:1 and asks: "If David calls him 'lord,' how can he be his son?" (v. 45). In the whole context of Matthew's gospel, including the infancy narratives, this key question, far from denying that the Messiah is David's son, implies that he is much more. It leaves the Pharisees speechless. Not only has Jesus reduced his attackers to silence, he has also given them and the people a conundrum to shake them into a new view of the Messiah. And the quotation, "Sit at my right hand" (v. 44), has evoked a scene of future glory leading toward Matthew's account of Jesus' passion, death and resurrection.

In chapter 23 Matthew continues to follow Mark in presenting Jesus' warning to the crowd against the spirit of the scribes and Pharisees, but he greatly expands Mark's passage, partly from Q (see Luke 11:39-52) and partly from his own sources.

Surprisingly Matthew now presents Jesus as acknowledging the teaching authority of the scribes and Pharisees (vv. 2-3), in contradiction to his rejection of their authority in the controversies just presented. Some scholars suggest that Matthew may be including here a tradition from an earlier period of his community before its definitive break from the synagogue. Perhaps he includes such a tradition to heighten the contrast between the Pharisees' preaching and their practice. In particular, Jesus condemns their legalistic burdening of people's consciences (v. 4), their vanity in reducing religious practices to outward show (v. 5), and their pride of place and title at banquets, at prayer and in business (v. 6).

Taken too literally or out of context Jesus' command, "Call no one on earth your father" (v. 9), might seem to condemn the practice of Catholics in regard to their priests. But the context makes it clear that Jesus is condemning the use of titles out of pride; that is, in any way that would blur God's unique claim to the title Father, or Christ's unique claim to the title Master or Teacher, as emphasized so strongly in the Sermon on the Mount: "You have heard that it was said to your ancestors . . . But I say to you . . . " (Mt 5:21). Jesus alone is *the* teacher who interprets God's law; his disciples are commissioned to teach, not their own interpretations, but only what "I have commanded you." Leadership among Christians must be a service, a humble service in obedience to Jesus Christ. Matthew is warning the leaders of his community to avoid the pitfall of pride into which the Pharisees have fallen.

In now pronouncing a series of "woes" upon the scribes and Pharisees (vv. 13-36) Jesus is following the usage of Old Testament prophets (Is 10:1; Jer 22:13). A "woe" was a sorrowful warning to another of the gravity of his state before God. It was often used in Jewish apocalyptic passages of dire predictions about the end of the world and the terrible punishment awaiting the wicked. Matthew's present passage has made the word *Pharisee* synonymous with "hypocrite," the epithet used repeatedly here for those who fail to practice what they preach.

Modern scholars point out that the Pharisees were often sincerely austere rabbis who insisted on a multitude of laws as a means of impressing upon the Jews the holiness required of them as God's chosen people, a nation set apart from the Gentiles. These laws became the means by which the Jews could identify themselves, especially after their dispersal at the fall of Jerusalem in A.D. 70. Christians increasingly rejected Judaism as the majority of the Jews continued to refuse to recognize in Jesus their Messiah and excommunicated from the synagogue those who did, even persecuting and killing them. Many scholars suggest that in this environment of mutual hostility New Testament writers tended to exaggerate Jesus' opposition to the Pharisees and their oral tradition of laws. Scholars speculate that the original words of Jesus may have been considerably less severe than those that Matthew attributes to him in this concentrated attack, reflecting perhaps the bitter feelings between Christians and Jews resulting from years of growing estrangement after the stoning of Stephen (Acts 7:54-60).

Specifically, Jesus accuses the scribes and Pharisees of blocking entry to the kingdom of God by opposing Jesus himself who opens its doors (v. 14); of perverting their own converts by confusing their priorities through a false hierarchy of oaths (vv. 15-22); of exaggerated fidelity to their own trivial laws while neglecting God's essential laws of justice and mercy (vv. 23-24); of confusing outer appearances for inner substance (vv. 25-26); of giving a holy exterior to a state of inner evil (vv. 27-28); of pretending to honor the prophets while harboring murder in their hearts (vv. 29-36).

It is Jesus himself whom they are already planning to murder: "You are the children of those who murdered the prophets; now fill up what your ancestors measured out!" (vv. 31-32). Masterful irony, this, justifying the harsh denunciation: "You serpents, you brood of vipers, how can you flee from the judgment of Gehenna?" Nor will they stop their violence with Jesus' death; they will continue persecuting his followers, the new prophets whom he will send (vv. 34-35).

Matthew climaxes this passage with a lamentation that Luke places in a different setting (Lk 13:34-35): "Jerusalem, Jerusalem, you who kill the prophets and stone those sent to you!" (v. 37). Recalling the ancient lamentations over the ruined city of Jerusalem, Jesus sees the real ruin to be within the hearts of her people, especially her leaders. In its tragic beauty this passage in which Jesus expresses his yearning "to gather your children together, as a hen gathers her young under her wings," echoes such Old Testament passages as, "Hide me in the shadow of your wings" (Ps 17:8). Jesus is the new figure of Yahweh protecting his people as a mother bird protects her young. "But you were unwilling!"

"Behold, your house [Jerusalem and the Temple] will be abandoned" (v. 38), evidently by God. But it is also Jesus who will desert it until he returns as judge at the end of time (v. 39). Clearly the implication is that God's presence is in Jesus as the new Temple, the new center of worship. Significantly, Matthew adds, "Jesus left the temple area" (Mt 24:1) and gives no further report of any return.

REFLECTION AND PRAYER

To what extent am I hypocritical in failing to practice my own advice to others?

Dear Lord Jesus, I do believe in you. Help me carry out my faith in action.

Fifth Discourse: The Last Events (Mt 24—25)

End of the Temple and of the World (Mt 24:1-44)

Upon his final leave-taking from his Father's house Jesus begins his last discourse, appropriately about the end of the Temple and the end of the world. Matthew changes Mark's version of the disciples' question, distinguishing the end of the Temple from Jesus' second coming at "the end of the age" (v. 3); he thus clarifies Jesus' ensuing predictions as referring to the time between the two endings. Jesus warns his disciples not to believe the promises of false messiahs, even in times of war and natural calamities, which are only "the *beginning* of the labor pains" leading to the second coming of the Messiah (vv. 4-8).

To Mark's account of coming persecution Matthew's Jesus adds: "And then many will be led into sin; they will betray and hate one another" (v. 10). A little later he stresses a similar thought: "Because of the increase of evildoing, *the love of many will grow cold*" (v. 12). Apparently Matthew is inserting into Mark's original account details that to some extent reflect the experience of his own community under the stress of the persecution foretold by Jesus. Yet Jesus' promises remain: "The one who perseveres to the end will be saved" (v. 13), and "this gospel of the kingdom will be preached throughout the world as a witness to all nations, and [only] then *the end* [of the age] will come" (v. 14).

In verses 15-25, following Mark almost verbatim, Matthew reports Jesus' predictions and warnings concerning the destruction of Jerusalem. In Matthew's context the sufferings of that time can be seen as a foreshadowing of those preceding the end of the world. Verses 27-28, expanding Mark from *Q*, connect this passage with the glorious second coming of the Son of Man like lightning, a coming that will strike fear into the wicked, as suggested by the ominous picture of vultures gathering over the dead (v. 28).

Verse 29, which in Mark 13:24 seems to refer only to the tribulation at the fall of Jerusalem and therefore implies that the end of the world will soon follow, in Matthew clearly refers to the end of the world when "the sign of the Son of Man will appear in heaven" (v. 30). That sign is probably the cross that "all the tribes of the earth will mourn" (see Zec 12:10), the sign of the victory of the Son of Man, who will come "upon the clouds of heaven" to gather "his elect from the four winds" (v. 31).

Verses 32-36 follow Mark closely to make the point that although the tribulations referred to above will indicate the nearness of the end, only the Father knows the "day and hour" (v. 36). Despite his conviction that the gospel must first be preached to all the nations (v. 14), Matthew retains Mark's stress on the imminence of the second coming ("this generation will not pass away until all these things have taken place," v. 34), perhaps to bring greater emphasis to the next part of the discourse urging fervent preparation for the endtime.

Verses 38-44 constitute another expansion, corresponding at least in part to Luke 17:26-35 and 12:39-40. In three parables Jesus stresses the need to be ready at all times for his second coming. The first parable is a simple comparison: Just as in Noah's time people neglected to prepare for the flood, so many will fail to prepare for the end of the world (vv. 37-39). The second parable points out that of two men and two women who seem indistinguishable in this life "one will be taken [into the kingdom], and one will be left [out]" (vv. 40-41). The third parable likens the unannounced coming of the Son of Man to that of a thief in the night (vv. 43-44), stressing our uncertainty of the time of his coming. All three parables lead to the moral, "Stay awake! . . . Be prepared" (vv. 42, 44). Of course an end-time comes for each of us at the moment of our death, to which the advice about watchfulness equally applies. Here ends the first part of this final discourse.

REFLECTION AND PRAYER

Am I ready for death?

What specific changes in my way of life will improve my readiness?

Dear Lord, the prospect of death frightens me. Give me a share of your courage, your love.

Preparing for Judgment (Mt 24:45—25:46)

The second part of Jesus' final discourse stresses through three longer parables the good use to be made of the delay until the end comes; then it pictures that end as final judgment.

The first of these parables, paralleled in Luke 12:42-46, is addressed to church officials who, because of the delay in the Master's return, may be tempted to abuse their authority or live in careless abandon (v. 49). The good servant will be blessed, but the wicked one will be punished severely—literally "cut in two"—and condemned "with the hypocrites" (vv. 50-51), the scribes and Pharisees with whom he is equivalent.

The second parable of wakeful diligence is that of 10 bridesmaids (Mt 25:1-13), a parable proper to Matthew. The meaning reinforces the point already made at the end of the preceding chapter: Be ready always for the return of the bridegroom. In comparing the groom to Jesus, whose return will be his second coming, this parable implies his identity with Yahweh, Israel's bridegroom according to the prophets.

During the delay before his coming the wise virgins have provided enough oil of good works to greet him with burning lamps—hearts aglow with love. But the foolish virgins, caught unprepared, are locked outside, and their cry, "Lord, Lord" (v. 11), is not enough, as Jesus warned in the Sermon on the Mount (Mt 7:21).

The point of making good use of the interim time is further emphasized in the parable of the talents (coins of high value), which Luke 19:11-27 tells in a modified form. Matthew's version (vv. 14-30) is a simple story that forcefully tells us to prepare for the master's return by diligent use of his gifts. On his return "after a long time" (v. 19), the master rewards the two faithful servants with greater responsibilities and the beautiful, "Come, share your master's joy" (v. 21). The master gives to each the same reward to show that what he expects of each is faithfulness "according to his ability" (v. 15). The stern characterization of the master by the inactive servant, corroborated by the master himself (vv. 24-26), underlines Matthew's purpose of stressing the seriousness of this life as preparation for the parousia. The stark ending in which the negligent servant is punished by being thrown "into the darkness outside, where there will be wailing and grinding of teeth" (v. 30), echoes the conclusion of the preceding chapter.

This discourse about the end of time reaches its climax in the depiction of the last judgment (vv. 31-46). The Son of Man upon returning in his glory will majestically judge "all the nations . . . assembled before him" (v. 32). As shepherd (v. 32), Lord (v. 37) and king (v. 41), he will separate the good (sheep) from the evil (goats) on the basis of a single criterion: "Whatever you did for one of these least brothers of mine, you did for me" (v. 40). It is obvious that the examples of good works for those in need could be multiplied to cover all the physical, spiritual and psychological needs that men and women experience. Matthew's Jesus powerfully stresses the seriousness of the final judgment by contrasting each positive point with its negative counterpoint up to the damning summary: "What you did not do for one of these least ones, you did not do for me" (v. 45). And the final state of all human beings is clearly represented by the complete contrast between "eternal punishment" and "eternal life" (v. 46). This "eternal life" is defined in verse 34 as inheritance of "the kingdom prepared for you [by my Father] from the foundation of the world."

Found only in Matthew, this passage powerfully identifies those in need with Jesus himself. Matthew clearly hopes to inspire us to help anyone in need and to console us when we are the ones in need, the persons in whom Jesus can be served. Once more Matthew is assuring us that Jesus does not remain aloof from us after his ascension. He is still present in our suffering, so truly present that all we have to do to touch him is reach out to him in our suffering brother or sister in need, and when we are ourselves in need let others minister to him in our own suffering.

This passage is one of the chief sources of the church's teaching about the last things: the second coming of Christ, the last judgment, heaven and hell. The ending stresses the reality of eternity: ''These [who failed to serve their brother in need] will go off to *eternal* punishment and the righteous to *eternal* life.''

REFLECTION AND PRAYER

Do I believe that in helping my brother or sister in need I am serving Jesus?

Dear Lord, help me to see you renewing your passion in the sufferings of those around me. Help me to reach out to you in them. And when I am suffering, assure me of your presence in the ministrations of others.

Climax: The Passion, Death, and Resurrection of Jesus (Mt 26—28)

Jesus' Anointing, Last Supper, Agony, Arrest (Mt 26)

The great climax of all the gospels and their most uniform part is the account of Jesus' passion and death. Evidently Mark had already incorporated most of the basic apostolic traditions in his account, for both Matthew and Luke follow him closely. The differences that Matthew introduces may sometimes be due to his preference for a somewhat varying tradition, but often they seem rather to be his own omissions or additions, intended to bring out more clearly the meaning he sees in these events. We will therefore understand his inspired vision of the passion more clearly if we fix our attention on the changes that he introduces into Mark's account. This approach will also avoid repetition of much of what was said in the chapter on Mark. But it disturbs the cumulative power of Matthew's passion when read for itself. Hence, after noting the differences between the two accounts indicated in the following pages, you will probably want to reread Matthew's passion to experience this cumulative effect.

After identifying Jesus with suffering humanity in the last of the five great discourses, Matthew reports a fourth time in which Jesus prophesies his own coming passion, specifying crucifixion "in two days' time" (Mt 26:2). Matthew's Jesus clearly knows the future and is therefore in control of events. By contrast, the Jewish leaders, though resolved to "put him to death" (v. 4), are indecisive for fear of "a riot among the people" (v. 5).

Matthew continues the motif of Jesus' impending death by shortening Mark's account of the anointing at Bethany to focus upon Jesus' words, "In pouring this perfumed oil upon my body, she did it to prepare me *for burial*" (v. 12).

In reporting Judas' visit to the chief priests Matthew adds his own touch in Judas' haggling to betray Jesus for *30 pieces of silver* (v. 15), the wages paid contemptuously by the sheep merchants to the Lord's chosen shepherd in Zechariah's allegorical prophecy (Zec 11:10-13) and the legal compensation for a gored slave (Ex 21:32). Yet the price for Jesus is higher than that for Joseph, sold by his brothers into slavery for *20* silver pieces (Gn 37:28). As savior of his people from famine, Joseph prefigured Jesus, whose pitiful betrayal price will save from eternal death all who accept him.

Matthew abbreviates Mark's account of the preparations for the Passover to highlight Jesus' prophetic words, "My appointed time draws near" (v. 18).

In reporting the scene during the Last Supper in which Jesus speaks of his betrayer, Matthew makes two significant additions to Mark's account. The disciples ask, "Surely it is not I, *Lord*?" (v. 22). Obviously these are the ones who believe in him strongly enough to address him by the title that really came into use only after his resurrection. Judas' question, "Surely it is not I, *Rabbi*?" (v. 25) betrays his lack of faith by the title he uses, thereby suggesting the source of his hypocrisy.

Note two further additions to Mark in Matthew's account of the first Eucharist. At the consecration Matthew's Jesus says: "This is my blood of the covenant, which will be shed on behalf of many *for the forgiveness of sins*" (v. 28), thus emphasizing the reason for his coming death and its close relationship to the Eucharist. Just as Moses signified the ancient covenant as a blood relationship between God and his people by sprinkling the blood of sacrificed bulls upon the altar representing Yahweh and the people (Ex 24:6-8), Jesus opens the new covenant by giving his new people his own body and blood, his very life, to be sacrificed the next day for the forgiveness of their sins. And to the statement in Mark 14:25, ''I shall not drink again the fruit of the vine until the day when I drink it new in the kingdom of God,'' Matthew adds, *''with you''* (v. 29), thereby stressing the dimension of the Eucharist as a foretaste of the eternal banquet with Christ ''in the kingdom of *my Father.''*

In his account of Jesus' prediction of Peter's threefold denial, Matthew omits the word ''twice'' in Mark's phrase, ''before the cock crows *twice''* (14:30), again summarizing to fix attention on the central meaning: This very night Peter will repeatedly deny that he knows Jesus.

At the beginning of Jesus' agony in the garden Matthew changes Mark's statement, ''He . . . began to be *troubled* and distressed,'' to ''feel *sorrow* and distress'' (v. 37), avoiding the possible impression that Jesus is not in control. To Mark's report that Jesus admonished the three of his inner circle to *watch*, Matthew adds ''with me'' (v. 38), stressing Jesus' need for human companionship in his sorrow ''even to death.'' Matthew's description of Jesus' prayer intensifies the bodily expression of Jesus' sorrow by the addition of the word ''prostrate'' (v.39). His omission of Mark's ''Abba'' loses intimacy at the expense of formality, but his change of Mark's ''take this cup away from me'' to ''let this cup pass from me'' (v. 39) highlights the reverence of Jesus' prayer.

Matthew's addition to Jesus' reprimand to Peter, ''So you could not keep watch *with me* for one hour?'' (v. 40), softens its sting with intimacy. Jesus' admonition, ''Watch and pray that you may not undergo the test'' (v. 41), gathers more meaning in Matthew than in Mark, for it harks back to the penultimate petition of Matthew's Our Father (Mt 6:13) and defines ''the test'' as the final death-struggle against the evil of opposing the Father's will or of slothful indifference to his will. To stress the importance of watchful prayer Matthew is not content with simply following Mark's ''he prayed, saying the same thing''; he reports the words themselves: ''My Father, if it is not possible that this cup pass without my drinking it, your will be done!'' (v. 42). Notice the change from ''My Father, if it is possible'' in verse 39 to ''My Father, if it is *not* possible'' in verse 42. In his second prayer Jesus no longer pleads for the removal of the cup; instead, he expresses his total acceptance of it: ''Your will be done,'' the exact words of the third petition of the Our Father. Jesus is practicing what he preached.

Matthew changes considerably Mark's account of the arrest of Jesus. He adds Jesus' response to Judas' greeting, "Friend, do what you have come for" (v. 50). In verses 52-54 he adds Jesus' reprimand to the disciple who drew a sword, ending with the powerful statement that expresses the faith of the early Christians: "But then [if my Father should send a legion of angels in place of each of the Twelve] how would the scriptures be fulfilled which say that it must come to pass in this way?" (v. 54). All must take place in accord with his Father's eternal plan, as verse 56 repeats. Matthew's Jesus will have it no other way, no matter what it costs him.

In relating the efforts of the Sanhedrin to "obtain false testimony against Jesus" (v. 59) Matthew implies, contrary to Mark, that two witnesses agreed Jesus had declared he could destroy the Temple (v. 61). Matthew adds to the high priest's direct question to Jesus the solemn adjuration: "*I order you to tell us under oath before the living God* whether you are the Messiah, the Son of God" (v. 63). Matthew changes Jesus' answer from the direct "I am" of Mark to the more Jewish indirect equivalent: "You have said so." He leaves no doubt that this is an affirmative answer, for he reports that Jesus adds the picture of his coming in glory, quoted from Daniel 7:13. Condemnation and initial punishment follow immediately.

Matthew condenses and slightly alters Mark's account of Peter's threefold denial of Jesus, bringing out more clearly the progression from a simple denial (v. 70) to a denial "with an oath" (v. 72) to a denial with a curse (v. 74). As the cock crows, Peter remembers and repents.

REFLECTION AND PRAYER

Father, if it is possible, let my present suffering and anxiety pass from me; yet, not as I will, but as you will. My Father, even if this is not possible, your will be done.

Jesus' Trial, Crucifixion, Death (Mt 27)

Matthew continues to follow Mark, but spells out the intention of the Sanhedrin "to put him to death" (v. 1) as they proceed to hand him over to Pilate.

Then Matthew inserts an account of the final actions of Judas. Implying that he has not expected Jesus to be condemned, Matthew states that he "deeply regretted what he had done" (v. 3). Declaring his sin

169

of betrayal, he flings the 30 pieces of silver into the Temple. In contrast, the elders display crass indifference and piously observe the law about "blood money" by using it "to buy the potter's field as a burial place for foreigners" (v. 7). Matthew sees in this ironic act the fulfillment of a prophecy of Jeremiah, who illustrated how God will smash his people by breaking a potter's flask in the valley that "shall be a burial place" (Jer 19:11). With this passage Matthew combines Zechariah 11:12-13, applicable to Judas' act of throwing the 30 pieces into the treasury of the Temple.

Matthew's report that Judas "hanged himself" (v. 5) implies that his regret was rooted in despair rather than in the contrition of faith and hope. Acts 1:18-19 attributes the purchase of the field to Judas and his death to a headlong fall upon it. These discrepancies suggest that both Matthew and Luke based their differing versions on some vague tradition, partially lost.

Matthew condenses Mark's account of the trial before Pilate, but adds some interesting details. Amazed by Jesus' silence, Pilate reminds the crowd of the custom by which he offers to release either "[Jesus] Barabbas, or Jesus called Messiah" (v. 17; brackets in NAB indicate the inclosed name is not in some of the best manuscripts and may therefore be an addition of a copyist to heighten the contrast between the two prisoners). Matthew inserts the intervention of Pilate's wife on behalf of Jesus, "that righteous man" (v. 19) about whom she has dreamed. Her attitude contrasts sharply with that of the chief priests and elders, who stir up the crowd against Jesus.

Another addition is Pilate's attempt to escape guilt for condemning a man he deems innocent by washing his hands before the crowd. Their reply, "His blood be upon us and upon our children" (v. 25), may be Matthew's way of attributing to the Jews the major responsibility for Jesus' death. To his Christian readers it is also a reminder of the blood that washes away our sinfulness.

In his account of the crowning with thorns Matthew rearranges Mark's account to emphasize that the soldiers "mocked him" (v. 29, repeated in v. 31); he thereby heightens the irony of their unwitting recognition of Jesus as "King of the Jews." Matthew adds a reed as scepter and, instead of Mark's royal purple, reports that they "threw a scarlet military cloak about him" (v. 28), a more appropriate color to suggest his suffering.

Matthew summarizes Mark's account of the way of the cross and the crucifixion, which, as in his report of the scourging and crowning with thorns, he mentions only in passing, too excruciating to describe. As the bitter-tasting addition to the wine offered to Jesus, Matthew changes Mark's *myrrh* to *gall*, obviously to suggest the fulfillment of Psalm 69:22, "They put *gall* in my food, and in my thirst they gave me vinegar to drink." Matthew adds "This is Jesus" (v. 37) to Mark's inscription, "The King of the Jews," highlighting the ironic truth of Jesus' title, even as he hangs there dying the most ignominious death that ancient "culture" could devise.

To the insults of the Jewish people Matthew adds: "Save yourself, *if you are the Son of God*, [and] come down from the cross!" (v. 40; brackets in *NAB*). To the taunts of their leaders he adds: "He trusted in God; let him deliver him now if he wants him. For he said, '*I am the Son of God*'" (v. 43). Matthew's repetition of "Son of God" clearly stresses the point that he considers this claim of Jesus as the central issue of the passion and the major reason for his condemnation by the Jewish leaders.

In recounting the cry of Jesus on the cross and his death, Matthew follows Mark very closely. He does, however, change Mark's "breathed his last" to "gave up his spirit" (v. 50), thereby expressing Jesus' final complete submission to his Father.

To the apocalyptic tearing of the Temple veil Matthew adds the account of the earthquake, the opening of tombs and the raising up of "bodies of many saints" (v. 52). This last sign of the meaning of Jesus' death is evidently reported here in anticipation of Jesus' resurrection, mentioned in the next verse: "And coming forth from their tombs *after his resurrection*, they entered the holy city and appeared to many." Apparently Matthew presents these signs to motivate the declaration of "the centurion and his men . . . 'Truly, this was the Son of God!'" (v. 54). By attributing this statement to the soldiers as well as to Mark's centurion, Matthew suggests its symbolic meaning as the confession of faith of the sinful Gentiles, who would replace the unbelieving Jews as God's people.

With some slight changes Matthew follows Mark's description of the women, faithful to Jesus even in the absence of the men who had followed him. Although he condenses Mark's description of the burial of Jesus, Matthew adds the details that Jesus' body was wrapped in "*clean* linen" and buried in Joseph's own "*new* tomb" (v. 60), suggesting the reverence already paid to Jesus' body. Matthew ends this passage in profound contemplation: "Mary Magdalene and the other Mary remained sitting there, facing the tomb" (v. 61).

Here Matthew adds his own exclusive account of the Jewish leaders' visit to Pilate to request surveillance over Jesus' tomb lest his disciples steal the body to pretend that he rose from death. This passage strongly suggests that the Jewish leaders actually made such a claim to explain away the resurrection, and that therefore they were aware that the tomb was empty "after three days" (v. 63).

REFLECTION AND PRAYER

Do I really believe that Jesus, Son of Man and Son of God, suffered and died on a cross?

Do I believe that he deliberately submitted to such a death to atone for my own sins?

Dear suffering Savior, I believe that you live on in the suffering people around me. I want to do all I can to relieve those sufferings. I accept my own sufferings in union with yours.

Jesus' Resurrection Appearances (Mt 28)

In his short account of the resurrection events Matthew follows Mark in reporting the empty tomb, though he alters many details. He mentions only two of Mark's three women witnesses, the same two who witnessed the burial (Mt 27:61) and who now come "to see the tomb" (Mt 28:1).

At this point Matthew introduces apocalyptic fireworks to highlight the significance of what is happening. The great earthquake implies Jesus' indescribable resurrection and ties it to the earthquake at his death to signal Jesus' death-resurrection as the earthshaking event that brings about the new age of God's kingdom on earth. The "angel of the Lord"—who had predicted to Joseph the coming virginal birth of Jesus through the power of the Holy Spirit—now appears "like lightning" (v. 3) to roll back the stone, striking such fear into the guards that they become "like dead men" (v. 4). The angel speaks not to these dead in faith but to the believing women. His message is basically the same as that of Mark's young man: The crucified Jesus is now the risen Jesus! Tell his disciples that they will see him again in Galilee, as he predicted at the Last Supper (Mt 26:32). This reference to Galilee, the place where the disciples had learned to follow Jesus, suggests that now they will see him in a new light and will teach others to follow him.

Matthew radically changes the reaction of the women. According to the original ending of Mark the women "fled from the tomb, seized with trembling and bewilderment. They said nothing to anyone, for they were afraid" (Mk 16:8). In Matthew they "went away quickly from the tomb fearful yet *overjoyed*, and ran to announce this to his disciples" (v. 8). Matthew then continues the account that Mark had ended here.

Matthew's Jesus appears to the two Marys and lets them embrace his feet in reverent worship. His risen body is real! But he allows them little time for adoration, for there is work to do. Jesus repeats the angel's message for the disciples, referring to them as "my brothers" (v. 10). By his death-resurrection he has released them from sin, forgiving them for abandoning him in his moment of greatest need.

Matthew interrupts his account to finish the matter of the guards. He pictures them reporting the marvelous events to the chief priests, who bribe them to say that his disciples "stole him while we were asleep" (v. 13)! That Matthew's account is here influenced by the Christian-Jewish polemic of his time is suggested by his statement that "this story has circulated among the Jews to the present [day]" (v. 15; brackets in *NAB*).

The climax of Matthew's gospel is Jesus' appearance to the eleven disciples on a mountain in Galilee, in accord with the angel's and with Jesus' own predictions. Like the Sermon on the Mount where he began, Matthew's Jesus will end his teaching on a mountain in Galilee.

Upon *seeing* him the disciples express their repentance in the worship that they now realize is his due (v. 17). Yet, like Christians of Matthew's community and like Christians today, "they doubted." Even now their faith is fragile; after Jesus' mighty works and teaching, after the proof of his love in crucifixion, after his resurrection evidenced in this very appearance, they are still men of "little faith." They still need his reassuring presence: "Then Jesus approached" (v. 18).

Before his resurrection Jesus' power was awe-inspiring; now it is absolute: "*All power in heaven and on earth* has been give to me [by my Father]" (v. 18). When Jesus first sent them out, he restricted their mission to the Jews (Mt 10:5-6); now, by his supreme authority, he solemnly commissions them as apostles who are to make his new disciples "*of all nations*" (v. 19). Matthew clearly implies that the Jews are no longer the chosen nation of God; they have forfeited their privileged status and must be evangelized, even as other nations. Nor is circumcision any longer the initiation into the chosen people of God;

now the new apostles are to bring people into the kingdom of God on earth by "baptizing them in the name of the Father, and of the Son, and of the Holy Spirit." Evidently this trinitarian formula was already in use at the time of Matthew's writing, for there is nothing in his gospel to prepare his readers for its sudden appearance here. And the apostles are to teach these new Christians to observe not the law of Moses but "*all that I have commanded you*": the kingdom vision and morality developed in the Sermon on the Mount and in the other four major discourses related by Matthew.

Matthew ends his gospel with Jesus' magnificent promise: "And behold, I am with you always, until the end of the age [of the church just beginning]" (v. 20). Matthew's gospel has repeatedly assured us that the same Jesus whom the angel had called Emmanuel, "God is with us" (Mt 1:23), and who walked with his disciples in Galilee, still walks with those who have accepted him as their Lord—will always walk with them till the end of time!

More than any other element, that which distinguishes Matthew's gospel from the others is its stress upon the words and actions of Jesus in founding the church as the new people of God, the kingdom of God on earth, and in giving it his own authority and his own mission to reach out toward all people to bring them to the kingdom of God in heaven. This purpose leads Matthew to incorporate in his gospel passages found nowhere else and becomes one of his chief norms for interpreting the life, death and resurrection of Jesus. Hence Matthew's gospel is often called the gospel of the church.

Clear and explicit, Matthew's gospel has been used by the church throughout the centuries as its standard catechetical instrument. Before the recent revision of the liturgy mandated by Vatican II, most of the gospel readings selected for Mass were taken from Matthew. The present effort to include all the gospels more completely over a three-year cycle is a broader educational approach, but also requires greater effort to understand the differences between the gospels and deal intelligently with them. Hence the increased need for the kind of study we have been engaged in here.

REFLECTION AND PRAYER

Do I really believe that Jesus has been raised from the dead?

Do I react as did the women, overjoyed?

Lord Jesus, I worship you! I resolve to live true to my baptism in observing all that you have commanded. I embrace your authority as Lord of heaven and earth!

SUGGESTIONS FOR FURTHER READING OR REFERENCE

Brown, Raymond E. *The Virginal Conception and Bodily Resurrection of Jesus*. New York: Paulist Press, 1973. A scholarly treatment.

Harrington, Daniel, J., S.J. *The Gospel According to Matthew*. Collegeville, MN: The Liturgical Press, 1983. Good short commentary.

Kingsbury, Jack Dean. *Matthew*. Philadelphia: Fortress Press, 1977. Easy-to-read discussion of the major themes of the gospel.

Meier, John P. *Matthew*. Wilmington, DE: Michael Glazier, Inc., 1980. Technical but very readable and full of insight.

PART IV

Finding the Compassionate Savior With Luke

Let's try an experiment. First read Exodus 19:16-25. Be sure you *read* it. Hear the peals of thunder, the crash of lightning, the loud trumpet blast. See Mount Sinai wrapped in a heavy cloud of smoke and fire. Feel the violent trembling of the earthquake. Hear the awesome voice of God in dire threats to strike down the people who get too close. Get the whole picture of the dread-inspiring majesty of God.

Then read Luke 15:11-32. Take careful note of the callous younger son who lacks even the courtesy of waiting for his father to die before demanding his share of the family estate. And note the lavish father, who bountifully responds to his son's desire. Imagine the son's careless squandering of the father's gift on dissolute living, his fall to the level of pigboy (remember that Jews despised swine!), his extreme hunger, and finally his decision to return to his father, if only to ask to be a hired hand. Watch the father catch sight of him up the road and rush out to meet him with open arms, embraces, kisses—before the son can express his repentance! See the father call for the finest robe, ring, shoes, feast—his ecstatic joy at his prodigal son's return! And consider his patient, wise handling of the older son's jealousy.

Two pictures of God, so completely different—the Sinai God of fire and thunder, and the loving Father of unloving sons! How can these two pictures fit into the same book? And how can we say that both are *inspired* images? The growth of revelation is strikingly exem-

177

plified in these two passages of scripture from the awe-inspiring God of Moses to the loving Father of Luke's Jesus.

Yet, don't we really need both concepts of God? Like the Israelites in the desert, we easily stray from goodness, truth, beauty; we need to be reminded that God is our Creator and we are his creatures, utterly distinct from him, completely subject to him, owing him reverence, fearful of offending him. But like the spiritually poor of Jesus' time, we are in even greater need of participating in Jesus' refreshingly familiar relationship with God as Father, the Father whose intimate love, utter goodness and sensitive gentleness Luke portrays in the life and words of Jesus himself.

Who is this Luke? Almost the only thing that scholars agree on concerning his identity is that he is the same person as the author of Acts. Although some modern scholars are of the opinion that Luke never knew Paul, many others think that he must have been one of Paul's closest associates as suggested in Acts, the same Luke referred to in some of Paul's letters and called the "beloved physician" in Colossians 4:14. He seems to have been of Gentile background, for he wrote in excellent Greek, apparently addressing himself to Greek-speaking Christians between A.D. 80 and 90.

After reading Mark and Matthew we may find ourselves tiring of repetition of much of the same material in Luke, one of the synoptic gospels precisely because it does repeat these incidents and sayings. Yet Luke is frequently quite original in his use of them and in the subtle changes he makes in ordering and reporting them. He also makes even more use of his own sources than he does of either Mark or Q. And we will find the general tone of his gospel much more joyful than that of Mark or Matthew.

In these parallel notes I will try to avoid repetition by passing rapidly over passages already studied to concentrate on those proper to Luke; but some repetition will be inevitable and beneficial, especially to see Luke's modifications of passages that he apparently takes from Mark and the different contexts in which he places those that he shares with Matthew from Q.

Prologue: Infancy and Boyhood Narratives
(Lk 1—2)

Luke begins his gospel with an introduction (vv. 1-4) much like that of Acts. Rather surprisingly he says that "*many* have undertaken to compile a narrative of the events'' (v. 1). The fact that only four gospels eventually became part of the New Testament canon suggests a highly critical selection on the part of the early Christians. Moreover, Luke invites his readers to use critical judgment in testing his work against the background of what has been handed down by ''those who were eyewitnesses from the beginning and ministers of the word'' (v. 2) and ends with the hope that Theophilus (either a patron or any ''beloved of God'' reader, the literal meaning of the name Theophilus) ''may realize the certainty of the [traditional] teachings you have received'' (v. 4). According to Luke, interdependence between sacred tradition and sacred scripture (see pp. 24-26) is the norm of Christian faith; this concept was strongly upheld at Vatican II in *The Dogmatic Constitution on Divine Revelation*, No. 9.

Like Matthew, Luke dedicates his first two chapters to the infancy of Jesus. Yet the two writers present completely different narratives! Apparently writing about the same time, unaware of one another's efforts, they both feel the same need to fill the blank in Mark's gospel, but they present accounts distinct in nearly every detail except the following: an angel *announces the coming birth of Jesus* (to Joseph in Matthew's gospel; to Mary in Luke's), both *Joseph* and *Mary* are told *to fear not*, there is *no prior marital relation* between Joseph and Mary, the child is *conceived virginally through the Holy Spirit*, his name is to be *Jesus*, he is born in *Bethlehem* and reared in *Nazareth*. The probability that these concurring points are based on firm apostolic traditions is enhanced by the fact that they are conveyed by such different stories as those of Matthew and Luke.

Annunciations of the Births of John and Jesus (Lk 1:5-38)

We have seen that there are good reasons to consider at least some of Matthew's infancy narratives as his own compositions intended to illustrate truths about Jesus rather than relate facts. Somewhat in contrast, most of Luke's narratives have the ring of family traditions that suggest traits of character, first of Mary, then of Jesus. Yet Luke's conscious use of parallel structure also points to the probability that he composed at least some of these infancy narratives or parts of them.

Observe, for example, the parallelism between the annunciation of the birth of John the Baptist and that of Jesus. Both annunciations are unexpected, the annunciation of John's birth because of the advanced age of his parents and the sterility of Elizabeth, that of Jesus' birth because Mary is a virgin and evidently intends to remain a virgin. The angel Gabriel is the messenger in both cases. He arouses fear; then is questioned.

But there are contrasts too. Gabriel announces John's birth to his *father*-to-be; he announces Jesus' birth to his *mother*-to-be. Zechariah not only questions Gabriel but also doubts his answer and is struck dumb; Mary not only believes Gabriel but wholeheartedly accepts his answer and is blessed for her trust. This deliberate combination of parallelism and contrast points to Luke's intention of stressing the complete dedication of Mary's final answer as well as the incomparable superiority of Jesus over John. Some scholars suggest that Luke composed his story of Gabriel's visit to Zechariah as a foil for the more momentous annunciation to Mary.

Let's take a closer look at Luke's account of Gabriel's annunciation to Mary. Does Luke really want us to believe that Mary was visited by an angel, or is he simply following the Old Testament pattern of angelic announcements of the coming births of great personages, such as those of Isaac (Gn 17) and Samson (Jgs 13)? Luke sometimes seems to represent interior religious experiences by angelic visitations. Perhaps he is now using for his purpose the angelic messenger he found in Daniel 8—10, striking the prophet speechless with awe by his formidable appearance and prophecy:

> "*Seventy weeks* are decreed
>   for your people and for your holy city:
> Then . . . *a most holy will be anointed*" (Dn 9:24).

Gabriel's report that Elizabeth is now in her sixth month of pregnancy (v. 36) indicates a period of approximately "seventy weeks" between Gabriel's annunciation to Zechariah and the presentation of Jesus in the Temple, the event that Luke may very well be interpreting as the anointing of the "most holy." Hence, by introducing Gabriel into these prophecies of John's and Jesus' birth, Luke is also alluding to this "seventy weeks" prophecy.

No doubt Luke personally believed in the existence of angels; Jewish literature of his time speaks much of angels. In any case it is doubtful that Luke is really concerned as to whether we take his Gabriel story literally, as long as we catch his main point: Mary believes in her heart that she is being asked to consent to become the mother of God's only Son. As we shall see, Luke is much more interested in the greater truth than in the supporting incidents, and that is how he evidently intends his readers to understand him here, real angel or angel as literary device.

Christian tradition has consistently considered Gabriel's address to Mary, "Hail, favored one! The Lord is with you" (v. 28), as more than a mere greeting; it is also a statement of the fact that God has already prepared her with special graces for the astounding mission to which he is now calling her. Chief among these graces, according to ancient traditional interpretation, refined by Aquinas during the Middle Ages and formally defined in 1854 by Pope Pius IX, was Mary's immaculate conception, by which God made her his privileged daughter from the first moment of her existence, exempting her from original sin and its effects in anticipation of her redemption by his only Son and in preparation for his plan to call upon her to mother that Son. How could God invite anyone ever touched by sin, inherited or personal, to become the mother of his Son? And if "the power of the Most High" overshadowed Mary to grant her the ineffable blessing of becoming the mother of his only Son, would that same power have failed to grant her the lesser blessing of her immaculate conception?

Mary's troubled reaction to Gabriel's reverent salutation identifies her as one of those poor of the loyal remnant spoken of by the prophets, one of those humble few who most acutely realize their need of God—one of those poor whom her Son will declare to be the first to enter the kingdom of his Father (Lk 6:20).

Gabriel assures her that her lowliness has "found favor with God" (v. 30). He uses Old Testament prophecies to tell her about this son whom she has been chosen to conceive. He is that long-awaited promised heir of David; Gabriel's words echo Nathan's report of God's message to David:

> "I will raise up your heir after you. . . . And I will make his royal throne firm forever. I will be a father to him, and he shall be a son to me" (2 Sm 7:12-14).

But Mary, already "betrothed [engaged in the solemn manner of the Galilean Jews of the time] to a man named Joseph" (v. 27), asks a key question: "How can this be, since I have no relations with a man?" (v. 34). Although many scholars today do not consider this question as evidence that Mary had taken a vow of virginity, the question obviously reveals that she has been a virgin up to this moment. And it seems equally obvious that her question is pointless if she intends to consummate her coming marriage to Joseph. She must therefore be manifesting a decision to remain a virgin, strange as this may seem in view of the tradition by which her people considered childlessness to be "a disgrace" that God inflicts or takes away (v. 25). Luke is telling us that we have here no ordinary woman, but one who is completely responsive to an extraordinary grace of God to be wholly at his disposition in soul and body.

Gabriel reveals the mystery:

> "The holy Spirit will come upon you, and the power of the Most High will overshadow you. Therefore the child to be born will be called holy, the Son of God" (v. 35).

Matthew reported the same prediction to a different person in a different setting—"the angel of the Lord" said to Joseph in his dream:

> "Joseph, son of David, do not be afraid to take Mary your wife into your home. For it is through the Holy Spirit that this child has been conceived in her" (1:20).

These two quite different stories strongly testify to the faith of the early Christians in the virginal conception of Jesus by the intervention of the Holy Spirit, and therefore in the divine origin of Jesus. This intervention of the Holy *Spirit* must, of course, be understood as purely spiritual, in no way similar to the sexual relationship between a god and a human woman in Greek and Roman mythology.

The phrase, "the power of the Most High will overshadow you," recalls the cloud that covered the tent in which the ark of the covenant was kept, the cloud that signified the presence of Yahweh (Ex 40:34-38; 19:16). Mary is being asked to become the new ark of the covenant bearing the new pledge of the Most High to humanity, the "holy" one (v. 35)—the very "Son of God" (vv. 32, 35). God himself, represented by Gabriel, awaits her answer! Such is his sensitive respect for his beloved daughter's free response.

Gabriel offers a test of the truth of his message by adding that Elizabeth is pregnant. But Mary needs no confirmation of Gabriel's word before declaring her readiness for any plan of God:

> "Behold, I am the handmaid of the Lord. May it be done to me according to your word" (v. 38).

We can be confident that Luke's abrupt ending of the annunciation with these climactic words of Mary clearly implies that the mysterious overshadowing of the Holy Spirit brings about in her the most marvelous conception of history. In this short scene Luke has presented

Mary as the privileged daughter of the Father, spouse of the Holy Spirit and mother of Jesus "Son of God" (v. 35).

To Luke, Mary is immensely important as a model for all those who would be followers of her Son Jesus Christ. We will see him characterizing her again and again, especially in his opening chapters, as the model follower of Christ. Within this context his annunciation account implies that Christians are to imitate her by embracing, as did Mary, the Father's plan to bring forth in their own lives, through the power of the Holy Spirit, the very life of his only Son, Jesus Christ. Like Mary, every Christian is called to become a special child of the Father by espousing the Holy Spirit to bring forth Christ to the world.

Those who would interpret Luke's annunciation scene as purely symbolic sometimes hold that Mary conceived Jesus by sexual intercourse with Joseph. Their problem is how to reconcile such an interpretation with the doctrine of the pre-existence of Jesus as Son of God, a doctrine expressed by both Paul (Gal 4:4; Phil 2:6-7) and John (1:1-18; 17:5). The fetus begotten by a human father and mother is a new human person. How then, if Jesus were so begotten, could he be the same person as the pre-existent Son of God? What happens to the key Christian doctrine of the Incarnation? The apparent impossibility of reconciling the truth of Jesus' pre-existence as Son of God with his conception by the union of a human father and mother may be one of the reasons for the traditional Christian heritage of belief in the virginal conception of Jesus. But the basic reason for that belief is the concurrence of Matthew and Luke in revealing the virginal conception of Jesus through their infancy narratives.

In its deepest meaning the annunciation is a climactic moment in the relations between God and his people. When a person acts arrogantly, we sometimes ask, "Does he think he's God?" But the God revealed at the annunciation is the complete opposite of arrogance; he humbly respects the freedom in which he created us. Through Gabriel he asks the human race in the person of Mary: "Will you accept me? May I become one of you?" Mary responds for all of us: "Yes!" And God becomes human!

REFLECTION AND PRAYER

*Has Luke convinced me that Mary is my true model as a Christian
wholly dedicated to the accomplishment of God's will?*

Do I try to imitate her lowliness, her complete dependence upon God for her personal fulfillment?

Heavenly Father, I am overwhelmed by your loving kindness in sending your Son to us, conceived of a woman into our very race!

Mary's Visit to Elizabeth (Lk 1:39-56)

Shortly after the annunciation Mary sets out to help the aging Elizabeth in the final months of her pregnancy. A striking biblical argument against abortion might be derived from the scene of the visitation: "When Elizabeth heard Mary's greeting, the infant leaped in her womb" (v. 41), strong testimony to the biblical faith that not only human life but even human emotion is experienced in the womb. More important, in what follows it immediately becomes evident that the two fetuses already possess their identity as persons. Mary's fetus is the "Lord," (v. 43) who so blesses Elizabeth's fetus that the "infant in my womb leaped for joy" (v. 44). This scene, like that of Gabriel's annunciation to Mary, presupposes the early Christian faith that human life begins with conception.

Some scholars hold that this scene is not meant to be read as a factual event, but rather as a Lukan composition to illustrate the truth that John became the Baptist by the grace of Jesus Christ. Even if this symbolic interpretation is correct, Luke is still relying upon the belief of early Christians that in some real sense human life begins with conception, which clearly implies that this life may not be aborted without violation of the commandment, "You shall not kill" (Ex 20:13).

Of course Luke is not thinking of countering abortion; he is expressing the faith of the early Christians in the efficacy of Mary's presence, or more precisely in the power of Jesus' presence in Mary. The unborn John leaps for joy and Elizabeth is "filled with the holy Spirit" (v. 41). I s Luke suggesting that Jesus' presence here is equivalent to baptism of the Spirit for John *the Baptist* and his mother, in fulfillment of Gabriel's prophecy in verses 15-16? It will later be through baptism "in the name of Jesus Christ" (Acts 2:38) that his apostles bring men and women into his Spirit-giving presence.

The inspired—inSpirited—Elizabeth expresses the faith of the early Christians that Mary is "most blessed . . . among women" (v. 42), the *new ark of the covenant* bearing God himself in her womb; for Elizabeth's question, "How does this happen to me, that the mother of my Lord should come to me?" (v. 43), clearly echoes David's question, "How can the ark of the Lord come to me?" (2 Sm 6:9). Elizabeth continues with her act of faith that Mary has been chosen by God to be the mother of his Son because of her complete trust in God: "Blessed are you who believed that what was spoken to you by the Lord would be fulfilled" (v. 45).

In a beautiful song of praise, Mary gives voice to this trust:

"My soul proclaims the greatness of the Lord;
    my spirit rejoices in God my savior.
For he has looked upon his handmaid's lowliness;
    behold, from now on will all ages call me blessed" (vv. 46-47).

Her lowliness sets off in higher relief the greatness of her Creator and Savior, source of her joy and blessings. All will call her blessed, not because of her own greatness, but because of the great thing God is even now accomplishing in her. In his mercy he has always put down the proud and raised up the lowly; now, in Mary's lowliness, he is fulfilling his promises to Abraham and his descendants (vv. 49-55).

In 1 Samuel 2:1-10 Hannah, mother of Samuel, sings a similar hymn:

"My heart exults in the Lord,
    my horn is exalted in my God."
But in what a different spirit:
"I have swallowed up my enemies;
    I rejoice in my victory" (1 Sm 2:1)!

Because of her childlessness Hannah had been ridiculed by her husband's other wife. But finally God favored her with a child, and her hymn expresses not only her joyful gratitude, but also her triumph over her tormentor. Considering the close resemblance between many of the thoughts in both hymns, yet the strong contrast between the triumphant Hannah and the humble Mary, it is easy to suppose that Luke composed this hymn and attributed it to Mary to make his point. Of course it also seems quite possible that Mary was well enough acquainted with the story of Hannah to utter her own joy in the idiom of Hannah, changing the spirit to her own.

Whether Mary composed and sang this beautiful hymn on the spot or whether it was carefully composed from Old Testament models by Luke, the Magnificat is a glorious expression of what Luke and the Christians of his time thought of Mary. Either way it serves to characterize her in a most striking manner as a woman of deep love and poetic feeling.

REFLECTION AND PRAYER

Do I try to find Jesus in Mary's presence as did Elizabeth and John the Baptist?

Do I try to imitate Mary's faith in God, her humility, her dedication to the poor?

Sweet Virgin Mary, lead me to your Son, Jesus.

Births of John and Jesus (Lk 1:57—2:20)

At the birth of John, there is great rejoicing (v. 58)! At his circumcision and naming, Zechariah's speech is restored! "Fear," in the sense of awe, fills the neighborhood. "All who heard these things took them to heart, saying 'What, then, will this child be?'" (v. 66). Here again we see Luke preparing for parallels that he will show us at Jesus' birth.

Zechariah's canticle parallels Mary's, or rather continues it. For Zechariah begins where Mary ended, with God's fulfillment of his covenant promises to visit and ransom his people in Mary's unborn son, "a horn for our salvation" (the bull's horn symbolized great strength), in the line of David (vv. 68-72)—promises that God had made all the way back to Abraham (vv. 73-75). Zechariah's thought turns naturally to his own son, "prophet of the Most High," who will prepare the way for the Lord by his message of "salvation through the forgiveness of their sins" (vv. 76-77). Finally, he attributes the work of his son to "the tender mercy of our God," who will give us "the daybreak from on high" in the person of Jesus, "to shine on those who sit in darkness and death's shadow" (vv. 78-79; see Is 42:7). Zechariah's hymn, like Mary's, is filled with Old Testament echoes. Whether composed by Zechariah or by Luke, it expresses the faith of the early Christians that Jesus is the Messiah sent by God, is even the Lord himself in person (v. 76), and that John is his precursor.

Luke reports that John "became strong in spirit" (v. 80), in the Holy Spirit that he has received from Jesus. And he goes into the desert, as Jesus will do. Great as John the Baptist has been shown to be, Luke's consistent use of contrasting parallelism in this first chapter is clearly calculated to present Jesus as infinitely greater.

In chapter 2 Luke places the birth of Jesus during the rule of Augustus Caesar, which was from 27 B.C. to A.D. 14, and Quirinius, whom Luke calls "governor of Syria" (v. 2). Historians have found no records of a census "of the whole world" (v. 1), but the Jewish historian Josephus mentions a provincial census taken at the time Quirinius was legate of Syria, about A.D. 6-7. Scholars have not been able to explain satisfactorily this discrepancy between Luke's data and that of Josephus. Perhaps Luke, vaguely recalling such a census, connects it with the birth of Jesus to prepare for his coming point that Jesus is the Savior of the whole world.

Luke presents the census as the reason for Jesus' birth in Bethlehem, "the city of David" (v. 4). Luke's simple account of that birth contains an expression that might easily be misunderstood: "her firstborn son" (v. 7). But his original readers would not have seen here any implication that Mary later had other sons, for "firstborn son" was a legal term among the Jews to designate the principal family heir.

Our nativity scenes of Jesus' birth in a stable or cave-shelter for animals, inspired by St. Francis of Assisi, accurately represent Luke's report that Mary "laid him in a *manger*, because there was no room for them in the inn" (v. 7). Luke is saying that Jesus chose poverty even at his birth.

Matthew's visitors to the infant Jesus were the knowledgeable astrologers from the East; Luke's are the poor unlettered shepherds of the locality. Matthew's point is the universality of Jesus' mission. Luke's point is Jesus' preferential mission to the lowly, as already stressed in Mary's hymn and Zechariah's.

The angelic message to the shepherds reveals three of Jesus' most important titles: Savior, Messiah and Lord (v. 11). This is the first time in the gospels that we have seen the title Savior applied to Jesus. Although Luke uses it sparingly (in chapter 1 he quoted Mary as rejoicing "in God my *savior*"), it proclaims one of his major themes: Salvation is through Jesus alone. Among Greek-speaking peoples the word *soter*—savior—was used of a benevolent ruler, especially Caesar Augustus, who saved his people from their enemies and brought them peace. Addressing himself primarily to people of Greek background, Luke probably considers the word more meaningful to them than the Jewish term *Messiah* or the more general title *Lord*. Luke is saying that Jesus is really the one who brings peace to the world.

This angelic hymn of joy expresses not only the reaction of heaven to the birth of Jesus, but also Luke's own joyous faith in Jesus and that of the early Christians for whom he writes, a faith that can now look back after the events of Jesus' life to interpret them in the light of the resurrection. It is a life that brings "glory to God in the highest" (v.

14) by revealing who God really is, a life that brings "on earth peace to those on whom his [God's] favor rests" by revealing himself in his Son. As Luke's gospel will clearly demonstrate, the peace that Jesus brings is a far more profound and all-embracing peace than that of Augustus or any other earthly savior.

Much as the angelic hymn sounds like a Lukan composition, the visit of the shepherds to "the infant lying in the manger" (v. 16) seems real enough. It is quite plausible that the simple core of the story was one of those family memories kept alive by Mary, who "kept all these things, reflecting on them in her heart" (v. 19).

REFLECTION AND PRAYER

Does my belief that Jesus was born of Mary in poverty have any influence on my choice of living conditions?

Do I hasten to find Jesus with Mary as the shepherds did?

Do I try to keep everything that I can learn about Jesus in my heart as his mother did?

Sweet Virgin Mary, lead me to your Son, Jesus.

The Child and Boy Jesus in the Temple (Lk 2:21-52)

Jesus' circumcision, naming and presentation in the Temple are events that Luke could take for granted as involving "every male that opens the womb" (v. 23) among Jews observant of the Mosaic law. His story of the events that occurred on the visit of the holy family to the Temple stresses obedience to the law and has the ring of family memories, perhaps embellished by his own literary touch to bring out more clearly the full significance of these religious events in the life of Jesus.

There were two legal reasons for their visit to the Temple: to con-secrate to God the "firstborn" Jesus in thanksgiving for God's sparing the firstborn Jews from the tenth plague against the Egyptians (Ex 13:2), and to make an offering to fulfill the law requiring that the mother be "purified" after childbirth (Lv 12:6). Luke's omission of any ransom payment to "buy back" the firstborn Jesus, according to the prescription of Leviticus 18:16, seems to imply that Jesus' parents think of him as belonging wholly to God (see 1 Sm 1:11-28). Their offering of two young pigeons for Mary's purification, instead of a lamb and a pigeon, identifies Jesus' family as poor (Lv 12:8). Is Luke also implying that Jesus himself is the Lamb of God being offered to his Father? Though Luke never uses the expression, he is certainly familiar with Isaiah 53:7, "He submitted . . . like a lamb led to the slaughter," in the suffering-servant songs that lie at the root of Simeon's prediction: "This child is . . . a sign that will be contradicted (and you yourself [Mary] a sword will pierce)" (vv. 34-35).

Simeon's prophetic intervention serves to highlight the significance of the consecration of Jesus to his Father in the arms of a patriarchal figure. Simeon calls Jesus God's "salvation, / which you [Lord] prepared in sight of all the peoples, / a light for revelation to the Gentiles, / and glory for your people Israel" (vv. 30-32). "In sight of all the peoples" suggests the final public self-consecration of Jesus to his Father on the cross.

That Luke really wants us to see this consecration in the Temple as a foreshadowing of the crucifixion is confirmed by Simeon's prediction that "this child is destined for the fall [of those who refuse to accept him as Savior] and rise of many in Israel" (v. 34). The word *many* is used here in the Hebrew sense of "all people," similar to the use of *many* that we have seen in both Matthew and Mark. Jesus will be "a sign [of God's saving mercy] that will be contradicted [by those who put him to death or nullify the efficacy of his death in their lives] . . . so that the thoughts of many hearts may be revealed" (vv. 34-35); that is, he will uncover the hidden motives by which every man and woman will be united with him or separated from him in his agony for all. Mary will be given a special share in Jesus' suffering: "You yourself a sword will pierce" (v. 35), above all at the foot of the cross.

Luke's gospel of the poor, the lowly, the forgotten, is also the gospel of women, lowly and forgotten at his time. Here in the Temple he introduces the first of many women not mentioned by the other evangelists. Anna, the prophetess, predicts that the child Jesus is given for "all who were awaiting the redemption of Jerusalem" (v. 38), the salvation of Israel.

Then the holy family returns to Nazareth and the child grows, "filled with wisdom; and the favor of God was upon him" (v. 40). At 12 he is initiated into religious duty and responsibility by accompanying his parents in their Passover visit to the Temple.

How seriously he takes his entry upon his religious duties! He remains in the Temple for days, even forgetting his human family in his absorption with the worship of his Father. Luke would no doubt have us imagine the boy's fascination with the sacrifices and prayers as well as with the daily public meeting of the rabbis to discuss the meaning of the scriptures.

He probably begins on the outer circle, listening to the learned search for deeper meanings, then ventures a question of his own. By the third day he is a full participant, even a leader in the discussion: "All who heard him were astounded at his understanding and his answers" (v. 47).

His parents too are astonished, but for a different reason; as a most considerate son, he has never before given them cause for alarm. To their further surprise, he wonders why they have not known where to find him: "Did you not know I *must be in my Father's house?*" (v. 49). He is impatient to grow up and take on his lifework. These first words of Jesus reported by Luke are a deep revelation to his parents—and to us. By the time he is 12 years old and perhaps long before that, Luke is telling us, Jesus' unique filial relationship with God has occupied the very center of his consciousness. And that relationship will remain his centering force throughout his life; Luke will report his last words on the cross as "*Father*, into your hands I commend my spirit" (Lk 23:46), in fulfillment of the commitment already in progress at the age of 12.

Luke is careful to tell us that Jesus returns to Nazareth "*obedient to them*" (v. 51). Then he hints at a possible source for his knowledge of this incident: "His mother kept all these things in her heart." This is the second time that Luke has referred to Mary's reflective treasuring of memories of Jesus' infancy and childhood. Obviously he wants his readers to cherish and imitate one of her chief characteristics: her loving, prayerful contemplation of Jesus. In these first two chapters Luke has clearly presented her as a model whose lead he would have his readers follow in their search for Jesus.

Luke ends his presentation of Jesus' early life by repeating his favorite thought about his boyhood: "Jesus advanced [in] wisdom and age and favor *before God and man*" (v. 52; brackets in *NAB*). His life is an open book, not only to be read by God, but even by men and women. A book of wisdom and grace, growing steadily in himself, but also upon his "readers."

REFLECTION AND PRAYER

Do I believe Jesus to be my personal Savior, as Simeon and Anna did?

Do I search as diligently for Jesus as Mary and Joseph did?

Jesus, my Lord and Savior, give me a share of your eagerness to fulfill the Father's will in my life.

Jesus Prepares for His Public Ministry
(Lk 3:1—4:13)

More than any other New Testament writer Luke manifests a sense of history. He has already placed Jesus' birth within its historical context. Now he pinpoints the time of Jesus' preparations for his public ministry by mentioning seven prominent men at the moment of John the Baptist's public appearance. Obviously it is important for Luke to show his readers that Jesus is not an invention of his followers but as real a human being as Tiberius Caesar, Pontius Pilate, Herod, Philip, Lysanias, Annas and Caiaphas—an impressive array, allowing modern scholars to calculate that the beginning of John the Baptist's mission took place between A.D. 27 and 29.

Luke's account of John's ministry seems to follow Mark's and shares some source in common with Matthew, presumably Q. Even more freely than did Matthew, Luke quotes Isaiah 40:3-5 about the herald's voice in the desert, extending his quotation to include the promise to the Gentiles: "And *all* flesh shall see the salvation of God" (v. 6). To describe the fulfillment of this universal plan of God in Jesus, Luke added Acts to his gospel.

John the Baptist demands sincere reform. In verses 10-14, found only in Luke, John requires generosity of all, honesty of tax collectors, fairness of soldiers. The people think that John might be the Messiah, but he disillusions them by contrasting the baptism in water that he confers with that which Jesus will administer with the Holy Spirit and fire, a baptism that will ultimately separate the good wheat (the responsive Christians) from the useless chaff (the unresponsive). In reporting that Jesus will baptize with the Holy Spirit and fire, Luke may be thinking also of the Pentecost event that he will report in Acts, the coming of the Holy Spirit upon the apostles as "tongues as of fire" (Acts 2:3).

Luke summarizes the mission of John in the words, "He preached good news to the people" (v. 18), thereby characterizing him as the model evangelizer whose role it is to prepare minds and hearts for Jesus' entry.

191

Like Matthew, Luke apparently finds parts of Mark too diffuse, for at this point he merely mentions John's censuring of Herod and consequent imprisonment, reducing Mark's longer report and even skipping entirely his story of John's execution, to which he later refers only in passing (Lk 9:9).

Luke also skips the description of the baptism of Jesus. He reports the descent of the Holy Spirit upon Jesus and the approving voice of the Father as occurring while he "was praying," *after* being baptized (v. 21). Luke thereby emphasizes the prayer of Jesus even more than his baptism, implying that he does not need John's baptism to receive anointing with the Spirit and approval of the Father. In Luke's context the presence of the Father and the Spirit confirm the identity of Jesus as Mary's son conceived by the overshadowing of the Holy Spirit, very much aware, even as a boy, of his unique filial relationship with the Father. Luke sees this descent of the Spirit upon Jesus as his anointing for ministry, a point that he will imply in the next chapter when he presents Jesus' opening words of ministry as applying to himself the prophecy of Isaiah: "The Spirit of the Lord is upon me, because he has anointed me" (Lk 4:18 quoting Is 61:1).

After telling us that Jesus began his public ministry at "about thirty years of age" (v. 23), Luke presents Jesus' credentials for this all-important mission. He works out Jesus' genealogy in the opposite direction from Matthew's, that is, from Jesus up the family tree to his supposed father Joseph (again the male line, even though Joseph is only the legal father of Jesus), to Heli, and so forth. But even at this early point Luke disagrees with Matthew about the name of Joseph's father! This disagreement continues all the way back to David. Scholars conjecture that Matthew, eager to trace Jesus' lineage through the Davidic line of kings, took the route of the royal line, while Luke selected a humbler lineage consistent with his presentation of Jesus as one of the poor, or perhaps had at hand a list of names from Joseph's family traditions.

Some scholars speculate that, in order to link Jesus with the prophetic tradition, Luke traces Jesus' lineage from David through his third son, Nathan (2 Sm 5:14), confusing this Nathan with the prophet who foretold that an heir of David would rule forever as God's son (2 Sm 7:13-14). This view is reinforced by Luke's decision to place Jesus' genealogy immediately after his anointing for ministry, just as Exodus 6:14-25 presents the genealogy of Moses, traditionally considered the first prophet, after his call to lead his people out of Egypt.

Moreover, in the incident at Nazareth related shortly after this genealogy, Jesus identifies himself as a prophet (Lk 4:24-27). If Luke is really using his genealogy to tell us that Jesus is in the line of the prophets, he is giving it a much greater function than the mere presentation of a list of names.

From Abraham to David the genealogies of Luke and Matthew are in close agreement, in accord with Old Testament genealogies available to both writers. But Luke, using lists from Genesis, continues Jesus' lineage all the way back to ''Adam, the son of God'' (v. 38). Matthew's genealogy begins with Abraham, evidently because of his interest in establishing Jesus' Jewish origin as the one who fulfills God's covenant with the chosen people. But Luke, by tracing Jesus' lineage to Adam, emphasizes Jesus' status as universal Savior of the human race. And in calling Adam ''son of God,'' he suggests that our creation in the image of God bestows on us the possibility of a filial relationship with God, a possibility that Jesus, just proclaimed to be the unique Son of God (v. 22), will bring to fulfillment.

Accepting Mark's chronology Luke now tells us that *''filled with the holy Spirit*, Jesus . . . was *led by the Spirit* into the desert for forty days, to be tempted by the devil'' (Lk 4:1). Luke is assuring us that Jesus is under the guidance of the Holy Spirit during his endurance of temptation. Like Matthew, Luke presents the three temptations in detail. But though the devil begins with the same expression in both accounts, ''If you are the *Son of God*,'' Luke's context, in which Adam is also called the ''son of God,'' suggests that Jesus is to be seen here as the second Adam, the new and now complete representative of the human race.

Supposing that both Matthew and Luke are working from *Q*, it seems to be Luke who changes the order of the last two temptations, losing perhaps the original climax, but gaining a new climax of his own by ending the temptation in Jerusalem, the place of Jesus' final triumph over the devil.

REFLECTION AND PRAYER

Do I believe that Jesus is the true and only Son of God, yet also a man tempted even as I am?

When I am tempted, do I call upon him for help?

Lord Jesus, give me a share in your absolute faithfulness to your Father and mine.

Jesus' Ministry in Galilee (Lk 4:14—9:50)

Jesus Formally Opens His Ministry in Nazareth (Lk 4:14-44)

As does Mark, Luke indicates that Jesus began his public ministry in Galilee, but adds, "in the power of the Spirit" (v. 14). Frequently and forcefully Luke calls his readers' attention to the fact that Jesus does not act on his own but by the Spirit. In presenting Jesus' Galilean ministry Luke's emphasis will be upon the power of that ministry as Jesus teaches and works "in the Spirit." In Acts Luke will emphasize the power of the apostles' ministry as they likewise teach and work under the guidance of the Spirit given them at Pentecost. Luke's message is clear: The Christian who would reach Jesus and help others to him will be able to do so only "in the power of the Spirit."

Luke temporarily skips several chapters of Mark's account to focus on Jesus' visit to Nazareth as an impressive first picture of his public ministry. From his own sources or inspired imagination Luke greatly expands Mark's account.

Jesus volunteers to read at the synagogue service, deliberately choosing Isaiah 61:1-2:

> The spirit of the Lord is upon me;
>> therefore he has anointed me.
> He has sent me to bring glad tidings to the poor.

Luke captures the drama of the moment: "The eyes of all in the synagogue looked intently at him" (v. 20). Quietly and indirectly Jesus states that he himself is the one of whom Isaiah spoke. He continues with "gracious words" (v. 22), to which they react favorably. In reminding one another that he is Joseph's son, a hometown boy, they raise the expectation that he himself expresses: "Do here in your own native place the things that we heard were done in Capernaum" (v. 23).

But he also reminds them by Old Testament references that prophets are neither accepted among their own people (v. 24) nor called to a ministry of miracles for them (vv. 25-27). Implicitly Jesus has identified himself as a prophet in the line of Elijah and Elisha, called to a ministry beyond their own people.

In anger they turn against him, even try to throw him over a cliff. But he calmly walks "through the midst of them" (v. 30). In this very first scene of Jesus' public ministry Luke foreshadows the ultimate fate

194

that awaits him as the inevitable result of his faithfulness to his mission to all humankind, not just to his own town or race.

Now Luke returns to Mark's first description of Jesus' ministry (Mk 1:23-39), the typical day in Capernaum that begins with the cure of the man possessed by "an unclean demon" (v. 33). Following Mark very closely Luke continues with the cure of Simon's mother-in-law. But instead of taking her hand, as in Mark, Luke's Jesus "rebuked the fever" (v. 39), a curious change for a possible physician to introduce into the account. Luke seems to be saying that just as Jesus can address evil in the form of an unclean demon, so can he address it in the form of sickness and human weakness. In Luke's gospel Jesus has not yet called Simon Peter to follow him; Peter is being prepared by this miracle in his own house to make a thoughtful decision.

To Mark's account of Jesus' curing the sick of the town at sunset, Luke adds that before Jesus silences the demons, they call him "the Son of God" (v. 41), again drawing our attention to his central title.

Jesus resists the urging of the people to stay. He must continue to other towns. Here again Luke departs from Mark's account. Instead of reporting that Jesus preached and worked miracles throughout *Galilee*, Luke substitutes *Judea*, apparently in the generic sense of Palestine, thus broadening the scope of Jesus' mission and perhaps suggesting that the center of his saving work will be Jerusalem, capital of Judea.

REFLECTION AND PRAYER

Do I try to imitate Jesus in his dedication to the poor, the sick, the neglected?

Do I try to imitate his constancy in prayer, his union with his Father and mine?

Dear Jesus, I wish to be your true disciple; help me follow you more closely in the way I think and live.

Jesus Calls and Prepares His Disciples (Lk 5:1—6:16)

Luke's chapter 5 begins with an incident proper to his gospel; pressed by the crowd, Jesus asks Simon to assist him in his ministry by furnishing his boat as a pulpit. Then Simon, evidently impressed by Jesus' preaching as well as by the miracles he has already witnessed, follows Jesus' advice about fishing, against his own professional judgment. Overwhelmed by the miraculous catch, Simon is suddenly struck with fear of Jesus' power. For the first time Luke refers to him as *Peter* as he falls at Jesus' knees and exclaims: "Depart from me, Lord, for I am a sinful man" (v. 8). Luke is evidently suggesting that in this moment of conversion, Simon is already on his way toward becoming Peter the "Rock," ready now to understand the meaning that Jesus gives the incident: "Do not be afraid; from now on you will be catching men" (v. 10). According to Luke, this was the manner of the call of Simon and his fishing partners James and John.

The miraculous catch that motivates their readiness to follow Jesus' call to discipleship, and eventual commissioning as apostles, serves also to symbolize that while they cannot "catch men" by their own unaided efforts, they can produce undreamed-of results through Jesus' power. They now witness that power in a series of further miracles, preparing them for their formal naming as apostles.

Returning to Mark 1:40-45, Luke relates the cure of the leper and the resultant popular demand for more miracles. At the end of the account Luke adds a significant sentence to give us insight into the source of Jesus' power: "He would withdraw to deserted places *to pray*" (v. 16).

Again referring to Jesus' power (v. 17), Luke follows Mark 2:1-22 very closely in relating the cure of the paralyzed man, the call of Levi, the subsequent question about fasting and the figurative expressions of the radical superiority of Jesus' new covenant over the old. But Luke's Jesus adds the thought about finding the old wine better (v. 39), perhaps an ironic reference to the ultraconservative attitude of the Jews that helps explain why so many of them eventually rejected Christianity. However, there is no hint of irony in Luke's manner of expression. It therefore seems more likely that in adding this saying, Luke has here inadvertently shifted the meaning of "old" from "inferior" in the preceding verses to "superior." His meaning then becomes: The Christian who has tasted the superior (aged) wine that Jesus brings can no longer prefer the inferior wine of the Pharisees.

In chapter 6 Luke follows Mark 2:23—3:6 in relating two disputes about the sabbath observance. Luke now precedes Mark's summary (Mk 3:7-12) with the formal selection of the Twelve. But first he inserts a significant detail that adds solemnity to the occasion: "He departed to the mountain *to pray, and he spent the night in prayer to God*" (v. 12), before making his choice of the Twelve. In naming the Twelve Luke slightly alters Mark's order and changes *Thaddaeus* to *Judas the son of James*. He considers the Twelve to be distinct from Jesus' other disciples; they are now "apostles" (v. 13), selected to be the special witnesses of his acts and words from the beginning of his public ministry to his resurrection (Acts 1:22).

REFLECTION AND PRAYER

Do I try to follow the will of Jesus as humbly and unquestioningly as did Peter?

Lord, I, too, am sinful. Just as you gave Peter the strength to overcome his fears, give me the courage to surpass mine.

Jesus' Sermon on the Plain (Lk 6:17-49)

Having selected his closest followers, Jesus now instructs them, together with a large crowd. The newly named apostles are on the scene to provide the testimony that Luke and the church will later consider official. Luke's introduction to this Sermon on the Plain, very much like Matthew's Sermon on the Mount, is reminiscent of Moses' descent from the mountain to address his people (v. 17). And like the Sermon on the Mount, this sermon presents a summary of moral attitudes based on a Christian value system in stark contrast to that of the society of Jesus' time—and of ours.

Luke's Jesus begins with four beatitudes addressed directly to "his disciples" (v. 20), not just to the Twelve but in the larger sense of the people who "came to hear him" (v. 18). His heart goes out in blessing to those among them who are poor, hungry, weeping, hated (vv. 20-23). But he issues dire warnings to their opposites: the rich, the full, the laughing (heedless), and those accepted as were "the false prophets" (v. 26) who spoke what men wanted to hear rather than what God wanted to tell them.

Luke's version of the beatitudes is much simpler than Matthew's, more like a description of the real physical state of his followers. Yet it is also obvious from Luke's context of such passages as the Magnificat (especially 1:51-53) that he, too, is congratulating the spiritually poor who recognize their need for God in contrast to the proud and mighty rich; those who hunger for God in contrast to those whose material plenty has emptied them spiritually; those who weep for the coming of God's kingdom in contrast to those fully satisfied with the kingdom of this world. In Acts Luke will give examples of those who, like Stephen, were persecuted and even killed "on account of the Son of Man" (v. 22).

Luke's next section, on love even of enemies (vv. 27-38), presents the same basic teaching as Matthew's Sermon on the Mount and many of the same sayings. Although Matthew's version attains greater force by its powerful series of contrasts between the old teaching and Jesus' new interpretation of the commandments (Mt 5:17-48), Luke's version has its own power in a series of compact examples that force the reader to reflect seriously upon the implications of true Christian love. Such a specific precept as "from the person who takes your cloak, do not withhold even your tunic" (v. 29) is so extreme in its demand that it bursts beyond its literal meaning to the general attitude of willingness to share whatever we have, even with those who offend us. Christians who see in Jesus' example the merciful compassion of the Father shining through (v. 36) can then think of dozens of ways in their own life of breaking the chain of enmity in relations with others by a deliberate return of good.

Significantly, instead of Matthew's summary, "Be perfect, just as your heavenly Father is perfect" (Mt 5:48), Luke's version has: "Be *merciful*, just as [also] your Father is merciful" (v. 36, brackets in *NAB*). This difference again points up the added emphasis that Luke's gospel gives to compassion, forgiveness and outreach to the poor and forgotten.

Verses 37-42 present a series of rather loosely connected and highly figurative sayings on refraining from judging and condemning others, pardoning and giving generously, being a teacher with vision, imitating such a teacher and avoiding criticism. It is typical of Luke's Jesus that when he speaks of giving and its reward he insists upon generosity, picturing the "good measure, packed together, shaken down, and overflowing" (v. 38).

In verses 43-45 Luke brings together sayings of *Q* that Matthew uses in different contexts. Luke thereby makes an explicit comparison between the fruit by which a tree is known to be good or bad and the deeds and words that reveal a person as good or evil. But words alone are not enough, even the verbal acknowledgment that Jesus is "Lord" (v. 47). Words must be verified by acts that carry out the words of Jesus (v. 48).

Luke ends this great sermon as does Matthew, with Jesus' promise that if we really hear his words and put them into practice we will be building our lives on a foundation of rock.

REFLECTION AND PRAYER

Do I consider myself blessed by God, even when I am poor in material or spiritual possessions?

Do I consider myself blessed especially when I am poor?

Do I try to do something good, even for those who seem hostile to me?

Do I struggle to avoid judging others harshly?

Dear Jesus, give me a deeper understanding of what you want of me, and a more generous and compassionate heart in trying to carry out the Father's will.

Jesus Shows His Compassion in Word and Deed (Lk 7:1—8:3)

In chapter 7 Luke reports Jesus' cure of the centurion's servant, an account he shares with Matthew 8:5-13, but to which he adds the interesting detail that the centurion had favored the Jews by building their synagogue. We are reminded of that later centurion in Acts 10, Cornelius, "who was religious and God-fearing," the first Gentile to be admitted to the church by Peter. Luke seems to be presenting the centurion of his gospel as a model for his Gentile readers. The cooperation of this model Gentile with the Jews evidently meets with Jesus' approval, for he sets out for his house. This consideration on Jesus' part moves the centurion to a deep personal conversion: "I am not worthy to have you enter under my roof" (v. 6), similar to Peter's recent exclamation, "Depart from me, Lord, for I am a sinful man" (Lk 5:8). Both Jew and Gentile need Jesus; both are purified by faith in him and moved to imitate his compassion for others. Luke's insertion of the episode about the centurion's cooperation with the Jews brings into sharper focus for his own community the ensuing praise of the centurion's faith and the cure on his behalf.

Now follows one of the most touching stories found in the gospels, presented only by Luke. Entering Nain, Jesus is "moved with pity" (v. 13) upon seeing the widow in the funeral procession of her "only son" (v. 12). Unable to resist her tears he restores her son to her *alive*, his first raising from the dead recorded by Luke. The miracle is so reminiscent of a similar miracle by Elijah (see 1 Kgs 17:17-24), yet so superior to it, that the crowd cries out, "'A great prophet has arisen in our midst,' and 'God has visited his people'" (v. 16).

199

Luke 7:18-35 is nearly the same as Matthew 11:2-19. Both relate the incident in which John the Baptist sends disciples to question Jesus, his answer to them and praise of John, and his lament that the people have rejected both John's austere warnings and Jesus' joyful friendliness even toward sinners.

How can Luke's statement "the least in the kingdom of God is greater than he [John the Baptist]" (v. 28) be reconciled with his report that John leaped for joy in Elizabeth's womb at the presence of Jesus in Mary (Lk 1:41)? Wasn't that the moment Jesus prepared him for his mission as precursor by admitting him into the kingdom through the equivalent of baptism in the Spirit? Perhaps Luke did not intend to convey that meaning, or does he simply present two apparently opposing traditions without choosing between them? He is probably willing to risk appearing to contradict himself in order to make the point that Jesus prepared John for his special mission and at the same time stress the importance of belonging to the kingdom of God.

Matthew's account implied that the people in general rejected both John and Jesus. But Luke's insertion of verses 29-30 suggests that the ordinary people, "including the tax collectors," were open to Jesus because they had submitted to John's baptism and had therefore repented, while the Pharisees and lawyers were closed to Jesus because they had refused this preparation, which was part of God's plan.

In verses 36-50 Luke illustrates this difference between the humble and the proud in their reaction to Jesus. His account of the anointing of Jesus by the penitent woman in Simon's house is very different from Matthew's (Mt 26:6-13) and Mark's (Mk 14:3-9). According to them, the unnamed woman anointed Jesus' head at the house of "Simon the leper" in Bethany near Jerusalem, thus preparing Jesus' body "for burial." But in Luke's account Simon is an unrepentant Pharisee of the type to which Jesus has just referred (v. 30); his house is in Galilee; the woman is a known sinner, perhaps one of those who had been present at Levi's reception for Jesus (Lk 5:29); she anoints Jesus' feet, wipes them with her hair and kisses them. The central point of Luke's story is the contrast between her loving repentance, manifested in her touching services to Jesus, and Simon's impenitent neglect of even customary hospitality: "You did not give me water for my feet, but she has bathed them with her tears and wiped them with her hair" (v. 44).

Except for superficial similarities, the two versions could very well be based on distinct incidents. Apparently Luke has recast the story as an illustration of Jesus' power as the prophet who sees into hearts to distinguish the humble from the proud, his power as Savior to attract the love of those humbly open to him, and his readiness and power as Son of God to forgive their sins. This power is highlighted by his consoling final word to the unnamed woman, "Your *faith* has *saved* you; go in *peace*" (v. 50). Luke is obviously presenting this woman to his readers as an example of those who respond to Jesus in faith and love.

In chapter 8 Luke continues the related theme of Jesus' regard for women and their dedication to him. It is easy to surmise that the woman who wiped Jesus' feet with her tears may have joined this group of women as the "Mary, called Magdalene, from whom seven demons had gone out" (v. 2). Luke is the only evangelist who tells us that women accompanied Jesus and the Twelve on their journeys and "provided for them out of their resources" (v. 3). It was not unusual for rabbis to allow women to assist them, but in letting women accompany him on the road, Jesus is ignoring a taboo of his time and risking the accusation of giving scandal. And Luke, by associating these women (v. 2) with the Twelve (v. 1) as those who accompany Jesus, is implying that the women share the privilege and responsibility of testifying to Jesus' words and deeds along the way.

REFLECTION AND PRAYER

Do I have a humble faith in the power of Jesus like that of the centurion?

Do I believe that Jesus can even raise me from death as he did the son of the widow of Nain?

Do I humbly repent of my sins as did the woman who wiped his feet with her tears?

My compassionate Lord, have compassion upon me for all my sins and lack of faith!

On Hearing the Word of God and Keeping It (Lk 8:4-21)

Luke 8:4-18 closely follows Mark 4:1-25, relating the parables of the sower and of the lamp. But by directly quoting the passage from Isaiah (Is 6:9), Luke softens the impression possibly left by Mark that Jesus is purposely hiding his meaning from the crowds. Luke also alters the ending of the parable of the sower to stress that the right response to the word of Jesus—and to the testimony of the Twelve and of the women—is to "embrace it with a generous and good heart, and bear fruit through perseverance" (v. 15).

By giving the parable of the lamp (vv. 16-17) a new context, Luke directs it more clearly to the Twelve, the women, all Jesus' followers. They have an obligation to light the entry into the church (the lamp stand was usually in the vestibule of the Jewish house) for "those who enter."

The way to listen to the word of Jesus (v. 15) and light it up for others by active response to it (v. 16) has now become Luke's context for the incident of Mary's visit to Jesus (vv. 19-21). As we discovered in our reading of Mark (Mk 3:31-35), Jesus' comment, "Whoever does the will of God is my brother and sister and mother," seems open to the interpretation that Mary's maternal relationship to Jesus means no more to him than the relationship of any person who truly carries out the will of God. But when Luke relates the same incident he has already provided a context in this chapter and especially in his first two chapters for a much different interpretation. We noted also that his slight alteration in the wording of Jesus' comment deliberately recalls that context: "My mother and my brothers are those who *hear the word of God and act on it*" (v. 21). This change still conveys the same basic idea of "doing the will of God," but it also propels the reader's memory back to Mary, who heard the word of God given her by Gabriel and immediately acted upon it: "Behold, I am the handmaid of the Lord. May it be done to me *according to your word*" (Lk 1:38).

Furthermore, in chapter 2 Luke has repeatedly characterized Mary as the one person who, above all others, "kept all these things [about Jesus], reflecting on them in her heart" (v. 19). In chapter 8, then, when Jesus says, "My mother and my brothers are those who hear the word of God and act on it," he is holding her up as the model for every Christian in listening for God's will and carrying it out. And in the very next chapter, at the transfiguration, the Father will express his will: "This is my chosen Son; *listen to him*" (Lk 9:35). More than anyone else, Mary has listened to him; when Jesus said, "Did you not know that I must be in my Father's house?" (Lk 2:49), "his mother kept all these things in her heart" (Lk 2:51).

If we read Luke's gospel carefully, putting it together as he would obviously have us do, we must hear Jesus tell us that he would have us form with him the same relationship that his mother did in carrying out God's will by listening to the Father's words and his. Then we will be conceiving him in our heart, in imitation of our model and spiritual

202

mother, the Virgin Mary, who "received the Word of God in her heart and in her body, and gave Life [Jesus] to the world" (*Dogmatic Constitution on the Church*, No. 53).

REFLECTION AND PRAYER

Do I hear the word of Jesus in a spirit of openness?

Do I retain it and bear fruit through perseverance?

Do I imitate Mary by trying to hear the word of God and act upon it?

Dear Jesus, let me be one of your true brothers or sisters by listening carefully enough to your word to cherish it as guide to my actions.

Jesus' Power and His Gift of Power to the Twelve (Lk 8:22—9:6)

Luke 8:22-56 corresponds to Mark 4:35—5:43 in recounting Jesus' calming of the storm, his cures of the Gerasene demoniac and of the woman with the hemorrhage, and his raising of the daughter of Jairus.

In relating the calming of the storm Luke softens Mark's portrayal of Jesus' emotions by reducing his rebuke to his disciples after the storm to the question: "Where is your faith?" (v. 25).

Luke's account of the cure of the Geresene man possessed by demons introduces many literary changes to improve the flow of the story while preserving Mark's basic content. Luke adds the interesting touch that the demons ask Jesus "not to order them to depart to the abyss" (v. 31), the prison of demons from which rises the apocalyptic beast (Rv 11:7). This unearthly reference motivates the great fear of the Geresenes (vv. 35-37).

To Jairus' request for his daughter Luke adds to Mark's account the touching note that is sure to win Jesus' compassion: She was his "*only* daughter" (v. 42). In relating the cure of the woman with the hemorrhage, Luke (the physician?) omits Mark's comment about exhausting her savings in useless treatment by doctors. In his account of the raising of Jairus' daughter Luke adds a remark worthy of a physician to verify the real nature of the miracle: "Her breath returned" (v. 55).

Luke now omits Mark's account of Jesus' visit to Nazareth, which he has already placed at the beginning of the public ministry, and in 9:1-17 follows Mark 6:7-44 in relating the mission of the Twelve, the curiosity of Herod about Jesus and the multiplication of loaves. By this alteration of Mark's sequence Luke brings added emphasis to Jesus' gift to the Twelve of the "power and authority" (9:1) that he has just exercised over the natural elements, evil spirits, diseases and even death.

In his account of sending the Twelve on their experimental mission, Luke distinguishes between two kinds of cures. Whereas Mark says that Jesus gave them "authority over unclean spirits" (Mk 6:7), Luke specifies "power and authority over all demons *and to cure diseases*" (v. 1). Though he distinguishes between ordinary diseases and diabolical possession, he still retains this reference to demons. Ancient peoples generally presumed that madness depriving a person of psychic control of his or her own body must have been due to some demon who displaced the person's spirit as possessor of the body. Even if Luke was a physician, in his time he could distinguish between mental and bodily cures only in the way suggested by his above phrase.

At first it may surprise us to find Jesus working within this confused cultural background. But a little reflection convinces us that it would have been far from his real mission to introduce notions of modern psychology or physiology utterly foreign to the concepts of his people. In our own more sophisticated way of explaining such phenomena we should not lose sight of evidence that at least some of Jesus' mighty works consisted in exorcising evil spirits.

Luke summarizes these first efforts of the apostles in terms of two activities: "proclaiming the good news and curing diseases everywhere" (v. 6). Acts will relate such activities in detail, giving repeated examples of the kerygmatic preaching of the apostles and even paralleling the four preceding miracles of Jesus: Paul will save his shipwrecked companions from a storm (Acts 27:33-44); he will release a girl from the domination of an evil spirit (Acts 16:16-18); Peter will cure many sick people (Acts 5:15-16) as will Paul (Acts 19:12); Peter will raise Tabitha from the dead (Acts 9:36-45) and Paul will restore Eutychus to life (Acts 20:7-12). Luke is convinced that the sole source of the apostles' extraordinary power of word and deed is the very power of Jesus working through them.

REFLECTION AND PRAYER

Do I believe in the power of Jesus over the forces of nature?

Do I believe in his power over illnesses of every kind, mental as well as physical? Over even death itself?

Do I believe that he gave these powers over evil, especially spiritual evil, to his apostles and their successors—to his church?

Lord Jesus, heal me of my weakness and sinfulness.

Answers to Two Key Questions (Lk 9:7-27)

Chapter 9 is central to Luke's theology. He here provides answers to two key questions: Who is Jesus? and Who are his true disciples?

In telling of Herod's curiosity (vv. 7-9), aroused by Jesus' expansion of his ministry by sending out the Twelve, Luke introduces a subtle change in his obvious source. According to Mark 6:16, Herod concluded that Jesus was John the Baptist raised from the dead. Luke apparently supposes it unlikely that the irreligious Herod would think of resurrection as an explanation. His Herod merely ends his ruminations with a question that Luke evidently presents as a challenge to his readers as well: ''Who then is this about whom I hear such things?'' (v. 9). It is significant that Luke now proceeds to close Jesus' Galilean ministry with implied and expressed answers to that basic question, the very question of our own reading search.

Skipping Mark's detailed story about the death of John the Baptist, Luke immediately offers two implicit answers to Herod's question: Jesus is the one who ''healed those who needed to be cured'' (v. 11), and Jesus is the one who nourishes his people (vv. 12-17). In relating how Jesus feeds his people by the multiplication of the five loaves and two fish, Luke summarizes Mark's account (Mk 6:34-44). Luke apparently suspects that Mark's second account of such a miracle (Mk 8:1-9) is another version of the same event, for he omits it.

In fact, Luke now skips a considerable part of Mark's gospel (Mk 6:45—8:26). Since most of the events of this ''great omission'' occur in Gentile territory, some scholars suggest that Luke's intention may have been to restrict his account of Jesus' ministry to the Jews and reserve for the apostles the ministry to the Gentiles in Acts. Whatever his reason, this omission enables Luke to present Peter's confession in such close proximity to Herod's question about Jesus' identity that it allows an almost immediate explicit answer to that question.

Luke 9:18-50 follows Mark 8:27—9:40 rather freely: Peter's profession of faith, Jesus' first prediction of the passion, his transfiguration, cure of the possessed boy, second prediction of his passion, and warning against ambition.

Although by omitting Mark's buildup to Peter's profession of faith (Mk 8:14-26) Luke seems to lose some of Mark's dramatic power, he brings special solemnity to the occasion by changing Mark's immediate introduction from the journey to Caesarea Philippi to "once when Jesus was *praying in solitude*" (v. 18). At every turning point in his life, Luke's Jesus prays.

When Jesus asks, "But who do you say that I am?" Peter replies, as in Mark, "The Messiah"; but Luke's version adds "*of God*" (v. 20). Herod's question about the identity of Jesus is here given an adequate answer. Notice that Luke's version, the Christ of God, sets up a paradoxical contrast with the title by which Jesus immediately refers to himself, "the Son of Man" (v. 22). Luke's version thereby stresses Jesus' role as mediator between God, whose Messiah he is, and humanity, with whom he claims solidarity as a human being who must suffer. As the Son of Man, Jesus claims special title to suffering; he must suffer rejection and death before he can enter into the glory of his resurrection.

And so must his disciples (vv. 23-27). Following Mark, Luke begins his delineation of what constitutes a true follower of Christ. He brings special emphasis to his answer by omitting Mark's account of Peter's objection and Jesus' reply, "Get behind me, Satan" (Mk 8:33), an outburst that obviously does not fit well with Luke's conception of a gentler Jesus and nobler disciples than Mark's. However, Luke's Jesus is not "soft," for in his teaching about self-denial he demands that his faithful follower "take up his cross *daily*" (v. 23). When Jesus says, "Follow me," Luke understands him to refer to the ordinary circumstances of daily living. It is in our day-to-day decisions and actions taken in the footsteps of Jesus that we lose our life of selfishness to gain "the whole world" (v. 25) of eternal life. Many of those standing there with Jesus will "see the kingdom of God" (v. 27) in the glory of his resurrection and ascension to his Father and in the glorious beginnings of the church. Three of them will soon see it in the glory of Jesus' transfiguration.

REFLECTION AND PRAYER

Do I believe that Jesus is both the suffering Son of Man and the chosen Son of God?

Do I accept my daily frustrations and pains as my cross to bear with him?

Lord Jesus, I wish to follow in your footsteps, even though I know it will cost me dearly.

Climax of Jesus' Galilean Ministry (Lk 9:28-50)

No sooner does Jesus predict his death than he shows Peter, John and James a foretaste of his coming glory in his transfiguration. Luke's change in Mark's order of naming these three, associates John with Peter, as in the early chapters of Acts. Following Mark, Luke relates that Jesus went "up the mountain," but he adds "*to pray*" (v. 28). This repeated prayer of Jesus is not only becoming one of Luke's favorite ways of characterizing Jesus, but also his signal that he is about to relate a very solemn event. He is convinced that it is by prayer, and especially by Jesus' prayer, that God's plan of revelation is fulfilled.

In relating the transfiguration Luke makes several significant additions to Mark's account. For instance, he notes that while Jesus was praying, "his face changed in appearance" (v. 29); he thus prepares us for the subsequent incident in which two disciples will fail to recognize the risen Jesus on the road to Emmaus (Lk 24:13-35).

Luke also adds that Moses and Elijah "appeared in glory and spoke of his [Jesus'] *exodus* that he was going to accomplish in Jerusalem" (v. 31). Luke thereby gives us his own insight as to why it was especially appropriate that these two should have been the representatives chosen from the Old Testament: to show that Jesus' coming passion and resurrection would fulfill the old covenant. Moses was not only the great lawgiver; he had also led the Israelites through their Exodus to the Promised Land. Elijah was not only regarded as the great prophet; according to the traditional rabbinical interpretation of 2 Kings 2:11-12, he had passed without death "up to heaven" in a fiery chariot. Luke sees Jesus' coming passage through death to resurrection as superior to Elijah's passage and Moses' Passover. Both are symbols of Jesus' coming resurrection.

Another of Luke's additions, "Peter and his companions had been overcome by sleep" (v. 32), prepares us for their sleep in the garden as Jesus' "passage" begins. A further addition, "becoming fully awake, they saw his glory," foreshadows their awakening from their slumbering faith to the glory of Jesus' resurrection. Still another addition, "they became frightened when they entered the cloud" (v. 34), echoes the Old Testament fear of entering into the inexpressible presence of God, symbolized by the cloud over the ark of the covenant (Ex 40:34-38).

In the message of the voice from the cloud, Luke's change of Mark's "my beloved Son" to "my *chosen* Son" (v. 35) recalls Psalm 89:4, "I have made a covenant with *my chosen one*," again emphasizing the theme of the new covenant through God's Son, Jesus. This is the definitive answer to Herod's question, the high point of Christology in Luke's gospel. Only the Father can reveal the complete identity of Jesus. By all the additions and changes noted above, Luke has sharpened the meaning of the transfiguration as a foreshadowing of Jesus' passion and resurrection.

The Father's command, "Listen to him," is the first thing that one must do to become a follower of Jesus. The aftermath of the transfiguration will give Luke the opportunity to return to his theme of discipleship.

Luke skips Mark's account of the discussion about Elijah (Mk 9:9-13), for he has just shown us in his version of the transfiguration that Elijah's mission is being fulfilled by Jesus rather than by John the Baptist (as suggested in Mark 9:13). Luke, then, brings us abruptly down from the mountain to the stark reality of the disciples' failure to exorcise the possessed boy. He cuts through Mark's details, emphasizing the rapidity and power of the cure but losing some of Mark's stress on faith. However, by adding to the man's plea for help, "he is my *only* child" (v. 38), Luke again introduces a circumstance that has unfailingly won the compassion of Jesus (Lk 7:12; 8:42). Luke ties this event to the transfiguration by adding after the cure, "And all were astonished by the *majesty of God*" (v. 43) shining through the power of Jesus.

Skipping the conversation with the disciples about their inability to cure the boy, Luke immediately presents in abbreviated form Jesus' second prediction of his passion. By adding to Jesus' words the admonition, "Pay attention to what I am telling you" (v. 44), Luke reminds us that the Father has just commanded us to listen to Jesus. And by omitting the prediction of the resurrection in Mark's version, he concentrates our attention upon the passion, implying that the true disciple must likewise "be handed over to men." To explain why the disciples fail to understand, Luke adds the strange expression, "Its meaning was hidden from them [evidently, by God] so that they should not understand it" (v. 45). God's plan is so different from the plans of his people, who still expect a triumphant Messiah instead of a suffering one, that only Jesus' death and resurrection can awaken their understanding.

In verses 46-50 Luke admirably summarizes Mark's report (Mk 9:33-37) of Jesus' instruction on childlike humility and acceptance of others in Jesus' name. In Mark, Jesus sums up this point with the statement, "If anyone wishes to be first, he shall be the last of all and the servant of all" (Mk 9:35). Luke's version is even more forceful: "The one who is least among all of you is the one who is the greatest" (v. 48). And in reporting the incident of the unknown exorcist (Mk 9:38-41), Luke brings home the message to his reader by changing *us* to *you* in the summary: "Whoever is not against you is for you" (v. 50).

Thus by many subtle alterations of his source, Luke has presented in this chapter a remarkable summary of his theology: Jesus is the Messiah of God; the Son of Man who must suffer rejection; the Father's chosen Son who speaks with his authority. The true disciple listens to him, suffers what he suffers, humbly accepts and serves others as he does.

REFLECTION AND PRAYER

Do I really listen to Jesus?

In hope of the resurrection that he forecasts in his transfiguration, do I find courage to carry his cross daily?

Lord Jesus, Son of Man, Son of God, heal me as you healed the boy who so needed your compassionate help.

Jesus' Journey Toward Jerusalem
(Lk 9:51—19:27)

Luke now presents the longest journey in the gospels. The events of Jesus' walk from Galilee to Jerusalem take up only one chapter in Mark, two in Matthew, but 10 in Luke. Obviously Luke is converting this journey into a major structural element as a literary device by which to fit into his gospel the events and sayings that he does not find in Mark and for which he has no chronological clues. Some of these sayings are also found in Matthew, but a large portion of these 10 chapters are Luke's own contribution to our knowledge of Jesus. This unique material, along with his first two chapters, become our focal point for grasping the special character of Luke's portrayal of Jesus.

Much of Luke's new material seems to have come to him in disjointed pieces. In his effort to fit it all together he uses association, often of ideas, but sometimes of key words, lost at times in translation. Some of these chapters will therefore seem to be rather unsuccessful patchwork, with little or no appearance of unity. Yet Luke is a skillful author; we can be confident that he really perceives connections, even where they are no longer obvious to us. We must therefore make the effort to discover those connections, even at the expense of remaining uncertain as to whether they always correspond completely with the relationship of parts that Luke intended.

On Following Jesus and Participating in His Mission (Lk 9:51—10:24)

Luke sets an almost tragic tone at the very start of this journey: "When the days for his being *taken up* were fulfilled, he resolutely determined to journey to Jerusalem" (v. 51). A glance at the map will show that the shortest line from Galilee to Jerusalem runs through Samaria. Mark and Matthew report that Jesus went the roundabout way through Perea, east of the Jordan River. Luke's Jesus sends messengers ahead into Samaria, hostile territory for Jews. When they return rejected by the Samaritans (v. 53), James and John, whom Jesus calls "sons of thunder" (Mk 3:17), offer to call down fire to destroy the enemy! But that is not Jesus' way.

Luke 9:57-60 corresponds closely to Matthew 8:19-22 in relating Jesus' demand that any follower of his consider the kingdom of God worth the sacrifice of every comfort, and even of family ties. Luke adds a third would-be follower (v. 61), reminiscent of Elisha, who was granted permission by Elijah to kiss mother and father good-by (1 Kgs 19:19-20). But Jesus requires more than Elijah! Evidently Luke is presenting this passage as a symbol of the wholehearted attitude required of a true disciple, not as a rule of action to be followed literally, for early Christian practice demanded love of one's own: "Whoever does not provide for relatives and especially family members has denied the faith" (1 Tim 5:8).

In chapter 10 Luke reports Jesus' sending of 70 or 72 disciples (both numbers are found in important manuscripts) in pairs to towns he wanted to visit. Luke is the only evangelist to mention these 72, perhaps a symbolic number to correspond to the 72 nations listed in Genesis 10, thus signifying the universality of Jesus' mission. His instructions expand the brief advice he has recently given the Twelve (Lk 9:3-6). Many of these stipulations are also found in Matthew's missionary sermon (Mt 10:5-42).

The return of the disciples (v. 16) strikes the note of joy characteristic of Luke's unique passages. Jesus rejoices to see their triumph over evil, symbolized by Satan's fall (v. 18) and by the disciples' power to tread upon serpents and scorpions (v. 19). But even more important than these triumphs is the fact that their "names are written in heaven" (v. 20): God is saving them!

Jesus rejoices in the Holy Spirit (v. 21), Luke's way of introducing a most important revelation, also found in Matthew 11:25-27: God is a Father who loves especially his humblest children, a Father whom only Jesus knows as Son, and those to whom Jesus reveals him (vv. 21-22). Jesus declares his disciples blessed for seeing and hearing his intimate prayer to his Father, the revelation of his unique filial relationship with God.

REFLECTION AND PRAYER

Do I think of my life as a journey with Jesus?

When have I most intimately experienced Jesus' presence in my life's journey?

Is my highest priority on this journey obedience to his words: "Come after me"?

My Jesus, lead me to the Father, whom you alone truly know.

On Love of God and Neighbor (Lk 10:25—11:13)

Luke 10:25-27 parallels Mark 12:28-31 and Matthew 22:35-38, but introduces significant changes. In Mark and Matthew this pronouncement about the great commandments is introduced by a scribe's question about the greatest commandment, in Luke by the question that the rich man will also ask (Lk 18:18): "What must I do to inherit eternal life" (v. 25). In Mark and Matthew, Jesus pronounces the two great commandments; in Luke, he elicits the answer from the questioner, who combines them into one commandment (v. 27), a much more forceful way of showing the interdependence between love of God and love of neighbor. Luke's version, then, strongly emphasizes the point that there is no real love of God without love of neighbor, and vice versa. In fact, his version makes love of neighbor an integral part of loving God, as integral as loving God with heart, soul, strength and mind.

The lawyer's attempt to justify his apparently simple question by further asking, "And who is my neighbor?" (v. 29), gives Jesus the cue for that marvelous parable of the Good Samaritan. That a Jew would tell a story in which a Jewish priest and a Levite do less for a fellow Jew than a despised Samaritan must have been extremely shocking to his obviously Jewish audience. Yet this is exactly what many of Jesus' parables were calculated to do—shock the audience out of old prejudices into the new kingdom vision in which every person is neighbor, child of the same Father, God. Only such a vision could inspire the otherwise excessive solicitude of the Samaritan who administers first aid to the fallen Jew, lifts him up on his animal, takes him to an inn and pays lavishly for his care. Luke's placement of this parable shortly after the inhospitality of the Samaritans (Lk 9:53) gives special emphasis to Jesus' own forgiving attitude in choosing a Samaritan as his model of loving service.

Luke follows up with another model of love in an incident proper to his gospel: Martha's solicitous service of Jesus, and Mary's absorbed attention to his words. Jesus' brotherly familiarity with women must have been another shocker to the Jews of his time. Martha's complaint sounds petulant. But instead of scolding her, he first consoles her and then delicately points out that her priorities are nevertheless inferior to those of Mary. By placing this incident immediately after the parable of the Good Samaritan, Luke reminds his readers that true love of God and neighbor in active service to others can only proceed from the contemplation that gives it deep meaning. Love of neighbor must be motivated by the love of God that comes from sitting as a disciple "beside the Lord at his feet listening to him speak" (v. 39). Luke underlines this thought by referring to Jesus three times in this incident as "the Lord."

And what should be the content of this prayerful contemplation? In chapter 11, after seeing Jesus himself at prayer, one of his disciples asks him how to pray (v. 1). Jesus responds with the Lord's Prayer in a shorter version than that of Matthew 6:9-13, who perhaps added clarifying phrases to the original version upon which both evangelists drew. Luke's version is basically equivalent to Matthew's; even "your will be done" is implicitly contained in "your kingdom come." Yet the absence of "your will be done on earth as it is in heaven" sharpens the petition for the rapid realization of God's kingdom, a petition that requires the courage to hold as priority Mary's way rather than Martha's. The true disciple of Jesus must long for the consummation of Jesus' mission, plead that the Father accelerate the coming of his kingdom when his name will be universally recognized as holy and all men love him as Father and one another as his children.

The proximity of the Martha-Mary story also suggests that "give us each day our daily bread" is to be understood to refer to the spiritual nourishment received by listening each day "at his feet." The longest petition, about forgiveness, is slightly different in meaning from the phraseology in Matthew, but even more forceful in its implication that we cannot expect God's forgiveness unless we are already forgiving those who have wronged us. And finally, in recognition of our own weakness we ask the Father to guard us from temptations that might prove too strong for us. To Luke's first readers "the final test" could very well have meant the trial of faith preceding torture or death during Roman persecution. To all Christians it can obviously refer to the ultimate trial of facing death. In placing the Lord's Prayer so close to the great commandment of love of God and neighbor, Luke has presented it as the fulfillment of that commandment in the prayerful longing that should precede meaningful action.

Even though Luke still uses the literary device of placing events in some locale, this device has become so routine that even "a certain place" (v. 1) will do. It is becoming increasingly obvious that the real link between each passage in this part of Luke's gospel is whatever association of ideas or words he finds suitable to his purposes. We can therefore expect Luke to follow the Lord's Prayer with other sayings about prayer. And so he does.

First he presents Jesus' little parable about a man who disturbs his friend in the middle of the night to ask urgently for bread (vv. 5-8). In the typical situation of Jesus' time the friend would have had to climb over his children asleep on the floor to accommodate the petitioner. The image is therefore calculated to convince his listeners that they must be persistent in their petition. But in the immediate context of the Lord's Prayer, the bread that they are to ask for so insistently is that "daily bread" available only "at the Lord's feet."

The first image is reinforced by the rapid-fire images of asking, seeking, knocking (vv. 9-10), and those of a father who won't deceive his son by substituting a snake for a fish or a scorpion for an egg. But we are to ask our Father for more than fish or eggs; we are to ask for the

Father's greatest gift, the Holy Spirit (v. 13)! Presented in the shadow of the Lord's Prayer, this petition for the Holy Spirit becomes the equivalent of its key petition "your kingdom come." Luke's gospel is deservedly called the gospel of the Holy Spirit, who will eventually bring about the realization of the kingdom of God.

REFLECTION AND PRAYER

Do I believe that I love God by loving my neighbor and that I love my neighbor by loving God?

To foster that dual love, do I place myself at Jesus' feet like Mary to listen?

Father, hallowed be your name, your kingdom come. . . . Send us your Holy Spirit!

Jesus Condemns Pharisaic Lack of Love (Lk 11:14—12:12)

Having presented Jesus' teaching on love and its application in prayer, Luke now turns to Jesus' energetic condemnation of its opposite. Perhaps the very mention of the Holy Spirit triggers Luke's mind to that incident of Mark 3:22-30 in which Jesus is accused of expelling demons by an evil spirit, Beelzebul. Luke has at hand another source to supplement Mark's account, a source he shares with Matthew 12:22-30. But where Matthew reports Jesus' words as "if it is *by the Spirit of God* that I drive out demons, then the kingdom of God has come upon you," Luke has "*by the finger of God*" (v. 20), a truly graphic image of the power of the Holy Spirit working in Jesus as his guiding Spirit.

In verses 21-26 Luke's Jesus adds the further image of the strong man (Beelzebul) being disarmed by the stronger (Jesus), whose weapon is the "finger of God." But the person who does not remain with Jesus soon turns against him (v. 23) upon being revisited by the unclean spirit and many more (vv. 24-26).

Luke ends the passage with the woman's cry of admiration, declaring Jesus' mother blessed to have such a son (v. 27), and Jesus' reply: "Rather, blessed are those who hear the word of God and observe it" (v. 28). By this gentle correction Jesus declares that even greater than giving him physical birth is bringing his Spirit to birth in our lives by keeping his word as that of God. In the context of Luke's gospel we already know that Mary was the first to hear God's word and keep it, and that she is therefore the model of all who would bring Jesus' Spirit to birth in their lives. Jesus' answer also makes clear that the source of his power is neither the evil spirit Beelzebul nor even the gentle spirit of his mother, but rather the "word of God" that guides him, the word revealed by the Holy Spirit (v. 13).

When Jesus cast out the mute demon (v. 14), besides those who accused him of doing it by Beelzebul there were those who were demanding of him "a sign from heaven" (v. 16) that he had done it by God's power. Having answered the accusation about Beelzebul, Jesus now addresses himself to the demand for a sign (vv. 29-32). He will give no sign but that of Jonah: "Just as Jonah became a sign to the Ninevites, so will the Son of Man be to this generation" (v. 30).

How was Jonah a sign that convinced the Ninevites to reform their lives? By merely preaching? They would hardly have listened to a Jew. In Jesus' interpretation of the story the Ninevites must have seen Jonah emerge *alive* from the belly of the whale (which doesn't mean that Jesus would have us take the story literally). Only at his resurrection will Jesus, the Son of Man, *become the sign* that he is the true bearer of the word of God, of the very Spirit of God. Those who still reject him will be denounced by the Ninevites and by "the queen of the South," the Queen of Sheba, who listened with admiration to Solomon (1 Kgs 10:1-10). Both the Ninevites and the queen were Gentiles who accepted lesser signs than the person of Jesus.

The passage ends with Jesus' warning: Open your eyes to see the sign! He uses a parable comparing the guiding light of a lamp to the guiding light of one's eyes: "Take care, then, that the light in you not become darkness" (v. 35). He thereby warns his hearers to be aware of the spirit that guides them in judging him as a sign of Beelzebul's presence or of God's.

In verses 37-54 the scene changes to a meal at a Pharisee's house. Jesus accepts the Pharisee's invitation; he has not given up his efforts to convert these Jewish leaders, who have been consistently rejecting him. By neglecting to wash his hands and cup, Jesus deliberately violates one of the demands of the Pharisaic tradition (see Mk 7:2-4), thereby challenging his host to look more deeply into the futility of that tradition. With the solemn introduction, "The *Lord* said to him" (v. 39), Luke presents Jesus' denunciation of their raising to the level of law a merely hygienic practice. Jesus severely reprimands the Pharisees for their hypocrisy in attending to outward but not inward cleanliness (vv. 40-41), in insisting upon such trifling customs as paying tithes on certain plants but ignoring "love for God" (v. 42), and in demanding marks of outward respect though they are inwardly dead (vv. 43-44).

Then the lawyers (Luke's occasional substitution for "scribes" as a term more intelligible to his readers of Greek background) line up on the side of the Pharisees. Jesus does not hesitate to condemn them for their minute laws that burden people's consciences and their pretense of honoring the prophets by building great tombs for them.

In verses 47-54 Jesus excoriates not only the scribes but the Jewish leaders in general. He uses biting irony: "You build the memorials of the prophets whom your ancestors killed" (v. 47), pretending to honor the prophets but really consenting to their death. Luke's Jesus predicts that along with the prophets some of his apostles will be persecuted and killed by the Jewish leaders (v. 49). With his own death in mind, soon to come at their hands (he is on his way to Jerusalem to die there), Jesus declares that this generation will be "charged with the blood of all the prophets shed since the foundation of the world" (v. 50), for this is the generation that will kill the One whom these prophets awaited with greatest expectation. "From the blood of Abel to the blood of Zechariah who died between the altar and the temple building" (v. 51) stirs the memory of the dying words of Zechariah: "May the Lord see and avenge" (2 Chr 24:22). How subtly Luke is preparing his alert reader to see Jesus' incomparable superiority to Zechariah as God's prophet; it is only Luke who will report Jesus' words on the cross: "Father, forgive them; they know not what they do" (Lk 23:34)!

After such a powerful attack Luke's conclusion sounds like an understatement: "The scribes and Pharisees began to act with hostility toward him" (v. 53).

In chapter 12 Jesus continues his attack on the Pharisees by warning, first his disciples and then the crowd, so dense "that they were trampling one another underfoot" (v. 1), to avoid hypocrisy and concealment. Jesus advises his "friends" (v. 4), the only time in the synoptics that he uses this address, not to fear the Pharisees who can kill only the body (as they will soon arrange for him!), but to fear God who can inflict eternal punishment for unfaithfulness in the time of trial. The inner contrast is between two kinds of death: temporal and eternal. Hence the fear of God referred to here is really the fear of eternal death, not a slavish fear of God as a hard master but rather the reverential fear of offending One who has counted "the hairs of your head" (v. 7) and whose loving Providence reaches even to sparrows.

Jesus assures his friends that in the time of their trial they will have nothing to fear if they profess their faith in him (v. 8). Yet, even if out of weakness they should disown him, they can still repent and be forgiven (v. 10). But there is no hope of forgiveness for the person who "blasphemes against the holy Spirit," that is, who perversely considers good to be evil by calling the Holy Spirit of Jesus "Beelzebul" (Lk 11:18). God will not violate the freedom he has given us to follow our own will even when it is turned against God himself! But those who really believe in Jesus will let his Holy Spirit teach them what to say in time of trial (v. 12). For this function of the Holy Spirit, John's gospel will call him the "Paraclete," a lawyer or advocate who defends the accused in a trial (Jn 15:26-27).

REFLECTION AND PRAYER

Do I really want Jesus' Spirit, the Holy Spirit, to rule my life?

Do I let the Spirit fill me with total trust in the Father who counts the hairs of my head?

Do I acknowledge Jesus before others as Son of Man and Son of God?

My Jesus, I acknowledge you as Lord of my heart.

Jesus Urges Reliance on God's Providence (Lk 12:13—12:59)

A man in the crowd interrupts Jesus (v. 13) to present his case against his brother. Although he acknowledges the authority of Jesus as an accepted rabbi to resolve such cases, Jesus refuses to be sidetracked. His refusal is significant as a lesson that authority in his church is not to become secularized. The power of the Holy Spirit to which he has just alluded (Lk 12:12) will guide his true followers to resolve their own family problems amicably instead of having recourse to an outside authority.

Jesus uses the occasion for a lesson against greed in the parable of the man who stored up grain for a future he never enjoyed (vv. 16-21). Taken out of context this parable could be understood to condemn making provision for the future. But in the context Luke has given it the parable merely points out the true priority of the spiritual riches of grace over material wealth (v. 21). To reverse the order is to worship wealth instead of God—idolatry.

This point leads into Jesus' warning (vv.22-34) about too much concern for food and clothing, the beautiful passage of total reliance on God's Providence that he shares with Matthew 6:25-33. How great is our need today of Jesus' admonition: *"Do not worry any more.* . . . Instead, seek his kingdom, and these other things will be given you besides" (vv. 29-31)!

Luke's portrayal of Jesus, more than that of any other evangelist, reveals Jesus' radical indifference to possessions: "Sell your belongings and give alms" (v. 33). Yet, lest we understand him too literally, we must take into account the context that places this statement as part of the larger ideal of living in total reliance on the Father, trusting implicitly in "an inexhaustible treasure in heaven" (v. 33). Jesus is not praising utter poverty, but demanding that we share what we have with those who have less. He is calling upon us to participate in God's Providence by considering the goods of this world, even the things we possess, as his gifts to *all of us.* What we cherish most highly lays claim to our love (v. 34); we must not let *things* lay this claim upon us. Only God and our neighbor can claim our love.

Like servants waiting for their master's return, we must remain spiritually prepared for our Lord's second coming on Judgment Day (vv. 35- 37). Jesus' picture of himself gathering in his tunic to wait on his faithful servants at table (v. 37) is striking, but it is not surprising when we remember John's description of Jesus girding himself with a towel to wash his disciples' feet during the Last Supper (Jn 13:4-20).

Peter's question about the reference of this parable leads Jesus to apply it in greater detail to the "steward" (v. 42) or leader of the church, like Peter. The "faithful and prudent steward" will be greatly rewarded (v. 44). The willfully self-serving steward will be cast out "with the unfaithful" (vv. 45-46). The knowingly negligent steward will be "beaten severely" (v. 47). The ignorant steward will get off more lightly (v. 48). We are all stewards of God's gifts in some degree, but "more will be demanded of the person entrusted with more" (v. 48).

In verse 49 Jesus bursts out with an ardent desire to complete his mission to set the earth afire with the Holy Spirit, even though it demands his submission to the baptism of suffering that he ardently longs to complete (v. 50). Luke's Jesus has retained his burning enthusiasm to fulfill the mission confided to him by his Father, the enthusiasm that he manifested even at the age of 12. He warns his followers that they, too, will participate in his suffering by experiencing the tearing of their dearest family relationships between those who will follow him and those who will not. Evidently the community for which Luke writes has suffered such heartrending divisions.

Jesus declares that the signs of the true meaning of his mission (v. 57) should be as clear to his listeners as weather signs (vv. 54-56). And he warns them that if they do not straighten out their relationships in this life (v. 58), they will have to suffer the consequences in the next (v. 59). This is one of the passages that led later theologians toward the doctrine of a purgatory after death for the temporal ''settlement of accounts'' left unsettled during life on earth.

REFLECTION AND PRAYER

Do I firmly believe in God's Providence as my loving Father who cares for me?

Where is my treasure—in worldly goods or in my Father's goods?

Am I always ready for my Lord's coming?

Lord Jesus, give me a share in your love of the Father's will, even when it means suffering.

Jesus Calls for Reform of Life (Lk 13)

In chapter 13, when asked about the Galileans killed by order of Pilate as they were offering sacrifices (v. 1), Jesus corrects the tendency of his people to consider violent death as God's punishment for secret sins and turns the incident into an occasion to urge reform of life. He underlines this lesson by referring to others who have been accidentally killed, clearly implying that such natural events are not to be attributed to God's Providence except insofar as they can be considered reminders of the importance of being ready for death always. The Father's Providence works only for good, never for evil, even when it might seem otherwise.

To stress further the need for reform, Luke inserts here the fig tree incident (Mk 12:12-27), which he converts into a parable about an unfruitful tree (vv. 6-9). Luke has thereby not only avoided the difficulty that Mark's version of the cursing of the fig tree might cause some readers, but has also introduced a note of mercy in the gardener's offer to give the tree another chance. Evidently the fig tree may represent the reader; the merciful gardener, Jesus; and his care of the tree, his offer of further grace.

The scene changes to the synagogue in which Jesus cures the stooped woman, only in Luke (vv. 10-13). As usual, the Jewish leader sees no good in Jesus' action, only the appearance of his breaking the sabbath. But the simple people "rejoiced at all the splendid deeds done by him" (v. 17). They, at least, see Jesus' miracle as a sign that he is bringing about the kingdom of God (Lk 12:56).

There follow two parables about the kingdom that we have already seen in Matthew (Mt 13:31-33), the mustard seed and the yeast. Then Luke reminds us that Jesus is on his way "to Jerusalem" (v. 22). This context of the impending passion suggests an application of these parables quite different from that of Matthew. Luke seems to be saying that Jesus himself, who brings the kingdom of God, is the mustard seed, which has to be planted—has to die—to become the haven of birds, the "tree of life" (Gn 3:22) lost long ago by Adam and Eve. Jesus is the yeast that, buried in the mass, will raise up the whole people. The freedom with which the evangelists suggest new applications of the parables should encourage us to do likewise, always of course within the general context of the gospels. Evidently this personal exploration of meaning is the basic reason why Jesus left most of his parables open-ended, without offering any specific application of his own.

To the question, "Lord, will only a few people be saved?" (v. 23), Jesus gives an ambiguous answer in the parable of the narrow door: "Many, I tell you, will attempt to enter but will not be strong enough" (v. 24)—no one will be able to save himself. But there is more. Those who do not enter while the master leaves the door open (offers the grace of salvation) will find it locked to them forever (v. 27). He will reject even those who ate and drank with him and heard him teach in their streets but did not really know and follow him. Others (the Gentiles) will take their places in the kingdom (vv. 28-30).

Some apparently friendly Pharisees warn Jesus to leave Galilee, for Herod is trying to kill him. Or are they simply anxious to see him get on to Jerusalem where his danger will be even greater? Jesus' mention of the "third day" (v. 32) is a hidden reference to his resurrection, when he will accomplish his purpose. His reference to Herod as "that fox" suggests that by threatening him, Herod is simply hurrying him on his way toward Jerusalem, outside of which "it is impossible that a prophet should die" (v. 33). And as if to prove that Jesus is a prophet, Luke appends here the beautiful prophetic lament over Jerusalem that we have seen in Matthew 23:37-39. In Luke's context of rejection this lament has a special poignancy.

REFLECTION AND PRAYER

Do I reject the temptation to blame God or his Providence for the evils of life?

Do I think of God as merciful and loving, revealing himself in Jesus who yearns to gather us together "as a hen gathers her brood under her wings"?

Merciful Lord, I lovingly adore you.

Jesus Invites All to the Eternal Banquet (Lk 14)

In chapter 14 Luke changes the setting to a sabbath meal at which the Pharisees deliberately set up a "temptation" to entice Jesus to break their law. Knowing his great heart, they seat him "in front of . . . a man suffering from dropsy" (v. 2). Jesus obliges them by curing the man, but they gain nothing, for his reference to their own practice of saving a man or animal that falls into a pit on the sabbath silences them.

Jesus tries again to reach their hardened hearts by a parable ending in the advice to sit in the lowest place at a feast and thereby be invited to take a higher place: "Then you will enjoy the esteem of your companions" (v. 10). Not the usual altruistic motivation that we have come to expect of Jesus, but the kind of self-serving reasoning that he knows the Pharisees can understand. This is masterful irony calculated to move the pharisaic mentality to at least a first positive step toward reform. The truly Christian principle illustrated by the parable shines clear in the final sentence: "Everyone who exalts himself will be humbled, but the one who humbles himself will be exalted" (v. 11)—by God, of course.

Then follows a shocker: the advice to invite to dinner not friends or relatives, but beggars and cripples who cannot repay you, "for you will be repaid at the resurrection of the righteous" (v. 14). Again the context guides us away from a too-literal interpretation by which we might think that Jesus is telling us to replace friends and relatives with strangers. Rather, instead of indulging in the servile attitude of looking for temporal reward for service to others, we are called upon to serve the needy and leave the recompense to God in eternal life.

The admiring exclamation of one of the listeners about the happiness of the eternal feast sets up Jesus' parable of the banquet spurned by the invited guests who are selfishly absorbed in their own interests.

New acquisitions of land or oxen (today, a home or a car), new relation-ships, even marriage, can become obstacles in our way to the eternal banquet. If we allow our temporal affairs to block out the true priority of God's claim upon our love, our places at the eternal feast will be filled by others (vv. 21-24). When the exasperated host finally tells his servant to "make people come in" (v. 23), he is taking into account the psychology of his time; a guest often turned down a first invitation to elicit a second more insistent one. The parable is a warning to the Jews that their places at the banquet will be taken by Gentiles. Luke is also warning his readers to take very seriously God's invitation to the eternal feast.

It is noteworthy that the happiness of heaven is often represented in the gospels by the great banquet at God's table. In our day, when the abundance of modern conveniences tempts us to forget the eternal joys of heaven, Luke would no doubt continue to stress Jesus' simple way of illustrating everlasting happiness in terms of community cele-bration.

In verse 25 Luke leaves the dinner scene that has served him so well as context for assembling some of Jesus' sayings and parables on the need for reform, humility and response to God's call. But he con-tinues to emphasize the priority of God's claim upon us over all others: "If anyone comes to me without hating his father and mother, wife and children, brothers and sisters, and even his own life, he cannot be my disciple" (v. 26).

Taken literally, "*hating* . . . father and mother" stands in direct contradiction to the commandment that Luke will soon quote on Je-sus' lips: "Honor your father and your mother" (Lk 18:20). But taken in the context of the next verse, "Whoever does not carry his own cross and come after me cannot be my disciple" (v. 27), this "hating" is simply a most forceful way of stating the priority of God's claim to our love over family claims. Luke's Jesus is using a Jewish literary device of expressing a comparison (love God more than parents) in terms of stark contrast (love God, hate parents). In Luke's time, following Jesus often meant being cast out by one's own family. Enduring even the rupture of family ties for the kingdom was therefore seen as an application of carrying the cross. Following Jesus can still demand heroic sacrifice to-day.

Hence, like one who wishes "to construct a tower" (v. 28), we must foresee the cost before we start the serious project of following Jesus. Like the king about to commit his forces against his enemy (v.

31), we must calculate the risk before taking up Jesus' cross. In this context "every one of you who does not renounce all his possessions cannot be my disciple" (v. 33) means that if it comes to a choice between everything else and Jesus, we must choose Jesus.

And if Christians are called to be the salt of society—that which seasons it, gives it value—the Christian who is unfaithful to this call to be ready to renounce everything else for Christ is no longer "worth his salt." So might Luke have concluded for our day the meaning of Jesus' salt metaphor (vv. 34-35).

REFLECTION AND PRAYER

Do I consistently think of God as my loving Father who wants me to help others, even on his holy day, and invites me to his eternal banquet?

Do I give up everything and everyone that interferes with that invitation?

My Lord Jesus, help me be ready to give up every obstacle in my life to accept my Father's invitation to eternal life.

Jesus Presents Parables of the Father's Merciful Love (Lk 15)

In chapter 15 Luke combines three parables to illustrate that Jesus' true followers must above all have compassion. They must be like the shepherd who risks all for his lost sheep, like the woman who never gives up looking for her lost coin, like the father who is always ready to celebrate the return of his lost son.

The objection of the Pharisees and scribes to Jesus' association with sinners provides the setting for the parable of the lost sheep in which the shepherd leaves 99 safe sheep to seek the one that is lost. Luke reinforces the picture of heavenly rejoicing over the repentance of one sinner by adding a similar parable not found elsewhere, that of the woman who searches anxiously until she finds the lost coin. Like the shepherd, she calls in her friends to celebrate with her the finding of that which was lost. These are two very simple experiences that Jesus' listeners can relate to their own daily lives for a better understanding of the profound truth of God's love for the lost sinner! Jesus also seems to be implying that the Pharisees and scribes should join him in his own joy upon recovering even one sinner among those with whom he associates.

Then the greatest parable of them all! Only Luke relates Jesus' parable of the Good Father, often known as the parable of the Prodigal Son. Although we began our study of Luke with the contrast between the Sinai picture of the unapproachably majestic God of thunder and this unbelievably good God of never-failing love, this parable merits further consideration. Luke has placed it after that difficult passage about leaving everything, even family, to follow Jesus (Lk 14:26). This is the Father to whom Jesus leads us! He is like no earthly father of our experience. By human standards he would be considered a doting fool to divide up his property in order to give his adolescent son his share of the inheritance, and then, after he squanders it sinfully, to welcome him back even before an expression of regret and shower gift after gift upon him in celebration. Our picture of the real father—forced upon us to some extent by the brokenness of our times and not unlike the real father of Jesus' time—is perhaps typified by the man who tells his son: "You are free to leave my house at any time; but if you do, never come back." Hence, in this parable Jesus is saying: "Your heavenly Father is so much more loving than your earthly fathers that you can't even imagine how good he is!"

Again Jesus is confronting the Pharisees and scribes with the implied question: If your heavenly Father so rejoices in the return of what you would consider a worthless son, why can't you rejoice in my efforts to reform sinners? In this context the older son, who sulks at his Father's generous reinstatement of the younger son, becomes a figure of these sulking Pharisees, so intolerant of Jesus' own outgoing love toward sinners.

REFLECTION AND PRAYER

Am I like the prodigal son? Or like the elder son?

Do I really believe that God is my loving Father, so loving that he is ready to forgive me even before I ask him?

Do I respond to his inconceivable goodness with all my heart?

O Father, I thank you for your love, and I love you in return!

Priority of Kingdom Values Over Worldly Ones
(Lk 16:1—17:10)

Chapter 16 begins with another switch in time and topic. Now it is to his disciples that Jesus speaks. The parable of the clever manager who knows how to win friends by offering reductions when his master gives notice that his service is ending, concludes in biting irony: "The children of this world are more prudent in dealing with their own generation than are the children of light" (v. 8). Of course Jesus is not advising his "children of light" to be devious; he is merely chiding them for their lack of enterprise and initiative, their lack of enthusiasm in advancing the kingdom of God. Luke's Jesus also challenges us to refuse to surrender the initiative to the "children of this world" in the formation of the society in which we live.

The advice that follows in verse 9 at first appears to be an ironic suggestion to follow the example of the wily manager. But on closer reading we discover that Jesus is really telling us to use this world's wealth—"dishonest" because it tempts us toward dishonesty—to make friends, not with the dishonest, but with those (presumably the poor in need of our generosity) who can ask for us a welcome "into eternal dwellings" when worldly goods can no longer be of use to us. Another application of the parable: "If, therefore, you are not trustworthy with dishonest wealth [of this passing world], who will trust you with true wealth [of eternity]?" (v. 11). A third application: "If you are not trustworthy with what belongs to another [in stewardship of church services, for example], who will give you what is yours?" (v. 12), the reward that would have been given to the good steward.

Nor, continues Jesus, can you compromise between God and money. You can't serve both (v. 13). At this, the Pharisees, who according to Luke "love money" (v. 14), sneer in derision, implying that Jesus is thereby setting aside the law. Taken literally, Deuteronomy 28 promises great material blessings for carrying out the law. Jesus assures the Pharisees that although they can fool men by their interpretation of the law and their resultant "virtue," they cannot deceive God, who reads their hearts.

Jesus agrees that until John the Baptist came, God's norms were known through "the law and the prophets" (v. 16), that is, the Jewish scriptures. But with John a new era has begun, a new way of knowing God's will: the good news of the kingdom of God proclaimed by Jesus himself, inviting everyone, even sinners, to enter the kingdom "with violence," that is, against the will of the Pharisees, by following Jesus in his radical dedication to the Father and to neighbor. Hence, far from casting aside the law, Jesus is giving it its full inner meaning so that not "the smallest part of a letter" (v. 17) is lost. Thus the law of marriage, in Jesus' interpretation (v. 18) contrary to that of the Pharisees, admits of no exception, thereby protecting the woman from the caprices of her husband to whom alone the Pharisees would grant the divorce and re-marriage that definitively destroy the dearest human relationship recognized by the law.

To clinch the main point of this instruction on kingdom values, Jesus adds the parable of the beggar and the rich man, reversing the values of people like the Pharisees. The despised Lazarus is "carried away by angels to the bosom of Abraham" (v. 22), symbolic of the abode of the just awaiting the redemption that Jesus will bring. But the rich man suffers torment in "the netherworld" (v. 23), abode of the dead, awaiting the final judgment for having neglected Lazarus' human needs and rated him with the dogs that licked his sores—recall that the Jews called the Gentiles "unclean dogs." This parable is an apt exemplification of the first beatitude and the first woe presented in Luke 6:20,24. The climactic line is aimed directly at the Pharisees and their kind: "If they will not listen to Moses and the prophets, neither will they be persuaded if someone should rise from the dead" (v. 31)—which Jesus will soon do!

In chapter 17 Luke assembles sayings of Jesus still addressed primarily to his disciples to continue their education in his kingdom-of-God value system. First, Jesus warns them against the grave evil of scandal. Following his condemnation of the Pharisees' teaching concerning riches, this warning seems especially directed against such false teaching.

In verses 3-4 Jesus demands fraternal correction of the sinner, yet if he repents, unending forgiveness, "seven times in one day." Troubled by such demands, the apostles make that model prayer to the Lord, "Increase our faith" (v. 5). Jesus replies that even a little faith, "the size of a mustard seed" (v. 6), can uproot a tree from its soil and transplant it in the sea, a change in the face of the earth symbolizing the change that faith can make in our moral ecology. As our response to God's untiring forgiveness toward us, faith inspires in us the unending forgiveness that Jesus demands.

Yet we must not allow our achievements as God's servants to turn our heads, the point illustrated by the parable of the servant who, after plowing his master's field or tending his sheep, is also expected to wait on him at table: "We are unprofitable servants; we have done [only] what we were obliged to do" (v. 10).

REFLECTION AND PRAYER

Do I try to compromise between temporal and eternal values?

Am I too much involved in getting money and things to attend to the needs of others?

Do I try to forgive unendingly, even as God has forgiven me?

Lord Jesus, your way is hard for me; make it easier by sharing with me your love for the Father and his children, my brothers and sisters.

On Preparation for the Coming of the Kingdom
(Lk 17:11—18:30)

In verse 11 Luke again reminds us that Jesus is on his way to Jerusalem, the place where he will firmly establish the kingdom of God on earth. Along the way he cures the 10 lepers who cry for pity, a multiple cure told by Luke alone. Only one recipient of the cure returns to thank Jesus, and that one is a Samaritan. Jesus complains about the lack of gratitude of the nine Jews and blesses the Samaritan: "Your faith has saved you" (v. 19)—not only physically, but also spiritually for entry into the kingdom of God. Of the 10 cured, only the Samaritan has also received inner conversion in recognizing the gift that God has bestowed on him through Jesus and in responding to it. The point of the story is that grateful faith is the sole appropriate response to Jesus' ministry—the saving response. A secondary point: In granting the cure Jesus does not distinguish between Jew and Samaritan, as the Pharisees would have demanded; in fact, it is the Samaritan who is saved, even as, by implication, the Jews are not.

The Pharisees ask Jesus when the kingdom of God will come. He answers that it is useless to try to calculate the time; yet he adds, "the kingdom of God is among you" (v. 21), implying that in some sense the kingdom already exists here in their midst.

It is significant that "kingdom of God" has two meanings in this short passage: In verse 20 it refers to the definitive coming of the kingdom, "the day of the Lord" used by the prophets in the sense of the day of final judgment (Mal 3:23-24), the realization of God's reign in the eternal kingdom that will exist at the end of time as the new world order. In verse 21 it means the concept, the vision, the ideal expressed in the parable of the Good Father of all, and in the parable of the Good Samaritan, who sees even his supposed enemy as his brother, a child of the same good Father. In this sense the kingdom of God already exists on earth: "For behold, *the kingdom of God is among you*." It has begun in Jesus himself, who brings forth the kingdom in the disciples he has won over to follow his lead. It will be formally established through the death and resurrection of Jesus and his sending of the Holy Spirit. And it must grow until the end of time when the kingdom of God will come definitively on "the day of the Lord." Luke would have his readers grasp the all-important truth that the kingdom of God is within each of us who regularly pray "your kingdom come" (Lk 11:2).

That Luke understands "the kingdom of God" in both these senses of "already here" and "not yet" becomes more evident from the interplay of these two meanings in the next passage, much of which Matthew includes as part of the eschatological discourse (Mt 24:23-41). Here Jesus speaks of his disciples' longing to see "one of the days of the Son of Man" (v. 22), a day in which the Son of Man really reigns in people's hearts. He foretells confusion as people follow many different leaders who claim to be their savior (v. 23). Were he writing today, Luke would no doubt refer to the confusion of voices in our highly commercialized world, offering us salvation from every worry and pain, from economic want, even from moral obligation.

But before the real Son of Man comes in glory (v. 24), "he must suffer greatly and be rejected by this generation" (v. 25). Yet just as the people ignored the warnings of Noah (vv. 26-27) and those of the angels who led Lot out of Sodom (vv. 28-29), so will many remain un-prepared for the second coming of the Son of Man (v. 30). Like death, the final reckoning will come suddenly, unexpectedly, catching one person on a rooftop and another in the field (v. 31). "Whoever seeks to preserve his life will lose it, but whoever loses it [in serving the Lord] will save it [in eternal life]" (v. 33).

Since Jesus won't tell them when all these things will take place, they ask him "Where, Lord?" (v. 37). His reply is again enigmatic; there is no more need to ask that question than to ask where a dead body lies when you see vultures circling in the sky. Yet Jesus' message is clear: Don't bother about when the end will come or where it will find you; be prepared always and everywhere for it.

In 18:1-8 Luke reports a parable, which he relates to the second coming of the Son of Man (v. 8). Jesus has just warned his disciples not to confuse the coming of the kingdom of God in their hearts with the coming of the Son of Man at the end of time to establish the definitive kingdom. Now he urges them not to tire in their longing for the king-dom in both senses: "Pray always without becoming weary" (v. 1). He illustrates this admonition by the parable of the unjust judge who finally gives the widow her due, if only to be free of her insistent petitions. Who but Jesus would dare to compare God to such a judge? It would seem that in the original context of this parable Jesus addresses a people whose idea of God is still very primitive; he accepts them as they are, speaks a language they understand, and tries thereby to bring them a step further toward a more complete understanding. The last sentence in this passage, "When the Son of Man comes, will he find faith on earth?" (v. 8), points back to the passage about the coming of the Son of Man and thereby suggests that even when God seems to delay his justice, we must continue to pray "without becoming weary" (v. 1). God will do all of us justice on the "day of the Son of Man."

Another parable found only in Luke, that of the Pharisee and the tax collector, illustrates a further quality of our prayer: humility before God and one another. At the introduction of the story Jesus' listeners would expect the Pharisee to be the one whom God would hear, not the despised tax collector. The Pharisee relies upon his good works to win God's favor, as though God must reward him for them. The tax collector, standing "off at a distance," simply admits his sinfulness and asks for mercy. He is the one who "went home justified" (v. 14). Again Jesus has reversed worldly values in a powerful lesson for any time, but especially in Luke's context of awaiting the parousia—and for our time of superficial stress on status and status symbols.

"People were bringing even infants to him that he might touch them" (v. 15). Jesus uses the occasion not only to bless the children, but also to reinforce the lesson of the parable of the Pharisee and the tax collector: To become a true member of the kingdom requires childlike humility.

Having dipped back into Mark (Mk 10:13-16) for this picture of childlike humility, Luke continues following him with the account of the rich man, whom Luke makes "an official," perhaps to fit better into his context of value reversal in view of the parousia. This official, who seeks eternal life, may be presumed to have become wealthy at the expense of the people he is supposed to serve and is not ready to share this wealth with others. Evidently he is not ready either "to enter into the kingdom of God" (v. 24).

The ensuing conversation about the danger of wealth is especially appropriate to Luke's gospel, oriented as it is toward the poor and the deprived. Luke adds his own touch to Mark's account. In Mark, Jesus promises Peter, "There is no one who has given up house or brothers or sisters . . . for my sake and for the sake of the gospel who will not receive a hundred times more'' (Mk 10:29-30). Luke makes two significant changes: ''There is no one who has given up house or *wife* or brothers . . . *for the sake of the kingdom of God*'' (v. 29). Luke's addition of ''wife'' is consistent with his recurring theme of the importance of women in the nascent church. And his rephrasing of the motive, ''for the sake of the kingdom of God,'' ties this promise into his context of preparing for the definitive coming of the kingdom (Lk 17:20-37) and praying for it ''without becoming weary'' (Lk 18:1-8).

REFLECTION AND PRAYER

Am I trying to further the growth of the kingdom of God on earth?

Is my way of life a preparation for the definitive kingdom in heaven?

Do I keep praying, even when God seems not to hear?

Father, with the tax collector I pray: ''Be merciful to me a sinner.''

Jesus' Final Approach to Jerusalem (Lk 18:31—19:27)

Jesus now formally announces to the Twelve that they are ''going up to Jerusalem and everything written by the prophets about the Son of Man will be fulfilled'' (v. 31). This urgency to fulfill all the prophecies will become one of Luke's major themes. Again following Mark he presents Jesus' third prediction of his suffering, death and resurrection. Luke seems to excuse the disciples for not understanding: ''The word remained hidden from them'' (v. 34). Perhaps Luke's intention is to present the disciples in a better light than does Mark, for he now skips the ambitious request of James and John to sit at Jesus' right hand in the kingdom and continues directly with the cure of the blind man near Jericho.

Luke summarizes Mark's account but adds a characteristic touch in relating the reaction to the cure. The blind man follows Jesus, ''giving glory to God,'' and the people also ''gave praise to God'' (v. 43). As before, Luke's additions highlight his conviction that what really saves the blind man, not just from physical blindness but also from spiritual, what saves for the kingdom both him and the witnesses is their recognition that God is working their salvation in Jesus and their faith response of praise.

In chapter 19, before ending this long journey to Jerusalem, Luke has a few more of his own stories to tell us. The comical picture of the diminutive Zacchaeus climbing a tree, to watch the now-celebrated Jesus pass by, fittingly preludes his joyous conversion: "Behold, half of my possessions, Lord, I shall give to the poor" (v. 8). Jesus' initiative in offering to stay at his house calls forth this enthusiastic response and his generous promise of fourfold restitution, even though the law required only full restitution plus a fifth of its value (Lv 5:16). Jesus acclaims this response as evidence of a conversion that brings salvation to Zacchaeus as a true descendant of Abraham. And Luke's Jesus now clearly formulates the primacy of the claim of the poor and the lost upon him: "The Son of Man has come to seek and to save what was lost" (v. 10). The rich Zacchaeus, so poor and lost in heart, needs Jesus even more than do those he has impoverished.

Zacchaeus' newfound generosity seems to suggest to Luke a parable (vv. 12-27) that is also related to Jesus' approach to Jerusalem, where "they thought that the kingdom of God would appear . . . immediately" (v. 11). We have seen this same question about the time of the coming of the kingdom in Luke 17:20-37, wherein Jesus distinguished two moments in that coming: the death-resurrection by which the Son of Man formally established the kingdom on earth, and the second coming or parousia at which he will judge the nations, definitively establishing the kingdom of God at the end of time. Luke's return to the question suggests that some members of his community have been confusing these two moments, probably like those "who have deviated from the truth by saying that [the] resurrection has already taken place and are upsetting the faith of some" (2 Tim 2:18; brackets in *NAB*). Believing that the kingdom has already been definitively established by Jesus' resurrection, they conclude that their own resurrection has already taken place in a symbolic sense and therefore deny the future resurrection of the body. Luke's answer is this allegorical parable in which the two moments of Jesus' death-resurrection and his second coming are clearly distinguished and the age between them is designated as the time for his followers to prepare diligently for that second coming. Matthew 25:14-30 presents a similar parable but in a simpler form.

In Luke's version this parable throws light upon the events about to take place in Jerusalem as prelude to the formal establishment of the kingdom of God on earth: "A nobleman [Jesus] went off [after his death and resurrection] to a distant country [by his ascension into heaven] to obtain the kingship for himself [or from the Father] and then return [at the parousia for the final judgment]'' (v. 12). Before leaving he entrusts gold coins (spiritual gifts) to his servants (followers). But he is rejected by his ''fellow citizens'' (the Jews), led by a delegation (the scribes and Pharisees): ''We do not want this man to be our king'' (v. 14). When he returns as king (at the last judgment) demanding an account, he rewards those who have used his gifts well and punishes the man who has merely buried them: ''To everyone who has [used the king's gifts], more will be given'' (v. 26). But those who have deliberately opposed his kingship will receive the most severe punishment, eternal death (v. 27).

Inconsistency in this parable betrays Luke's hand in combining from different sources the two themes of the rejected king and the good/bad servants. In verse 13 the king ''called *10* servants.'' But in the course of the story only three servants render account. The moral, however, rings out loud and clear: Work with the Lord's gifts during the interim before he requires an account.

Luke has now completed his major additions to Mark; he therefore brings to an abrupt close Jesus' long journey from Galilee to Jerusalem.

REFLECTION AND PRAYER

Do I make good use of the gifts God has given me?

By what specific decision can I make better use of them?

Lord Jesus, give me the gratitude and generosity of the reformed Zacchaeus.

Jesus' Jerusalem Ministry (Lk 19:28—21:38)

Jesus Clashes With the Leaders of the Jews (Lk 19:28—21:4)

Luke 19:28 states that Jesus ''proceeded on his journey *up to Jerusalem.*'' Indeed, the road from Jericho does lead steeply up to Jerusalem, but Luke also wants us to think of Jesus' climb toward the cross. In Jerusalem Luke will now present Jesus' public disputes with the Jewish leaders, disputes that bring him directly to that cross.

In relating the triumphal entry into Jerusalem, Luke follows Mark 11:1-11, omitting some details and adding a few touches of his own. One of these additions is the statement that ''his disciples began to

232

praise God aloud with joy for all the mighty deeds they had seen'' (v. 37). It has become one of Luke's distinguishing characteristics to point out that Jesus leads his followers to praise God. And in Luke it is ''the whole multitude of his disciples'' (v. 37), not the crowd, who proclaim Jesus ''king'' (v. 38), a word not in Mark's account. Luke thus ties this event to the parable preceding it (Lk 19:11-27) and gives that parable the function of preparing the reader for this apostolic proclamation. Perhaps out of deference to his Gentile readers, Luke omits Mark's Jewish ''Hosannas.'' He also skips Mark's reference to the reign of David, which risks suggesting a vision of Jesus as a conquering king. To make the contrary point that Jesus is the king of peace, Luke adds a sentence reminiscent of the angels' hymn at Jesus' birth (Lk 2:14): ''Peace in heaven and glory in the highest.'' That early promise is about to be fulfilled here in Jerusalem.

When the Pharisees object to the acclamation of the disciples, Jesus declares that it is not a moment for silence, that even the stones would cry out at his coming, thereby underlining the importance of this key moment in his ministry.

But the mood dramatically changes as Luke's Jesus gets his first sight of the city since his youth. He weeps (v. 41), the only time that a synoptic gospel pictures his tears. This second lament reported by Luke is quite different from the first (Lk 13:34-35). This time the city's eventual refusal to accept him is seen as the cause of her downfall, soon to come at the hands of the Roman army. Whether this passage reflects Jesus' prophetic judgment or the hindsight interpretation of events by early Christians, it certainly expresses their faith that the man now visiting Jerusalem deeply loves the city and is thoroughly capable of saving it from such a tragedy, even though he will not save himself from ignominious death on a Roman cross.

Luke skips Mark's account of the cursing of the fig tree and downplays Jesus' ejection of the traders from the Temple, probably to stress his daily teaching in the Temple with ''all the people . . . hanging on his words'' (v. 48) as the deeper reason for the plotting of the Jewish leaders ''to put him to death'' (v. 47).

In chapter 20 Luke continues to follow Mark. In his account of Jesus' confrontation with the leaders over the question of authority, Luke adds a bit of drama by representing the inner thoughts of the leaders in an anxious conference over the baptism of John. Instead of looking for an answer that will reflect their real opinion, they seek one that will discredit Jesus without displeasing the people. Their failure to take a public stand either for or against the authenticity of John's voice as a prophet discredits them as authoritative teachers of the people. And it forces them into the same appearance of neutrality about the authority of Jesus, for whom John was merely precursor.

But they are not really neutral; they are completely hostile toward Jesus, as he immediately discloses in his allegorical parable of the tenant farmers who kill the son of the vineyard owner. Besides improving on Mark's style in telling this parable, Luke adds that the tenants throw the owner's son "out of the vineyard" before killing him, bringing the story into closer parallel with the crucifixion of Jesus outside Jerusalem. To make sure that the Jews who are rejecting him understand that he is applying the parable to them, Luke's Jesus looks directly at them (v. 17). He likewise adds the warning in verse 18, powerfully describing the punishment of those who reject the cornerstone of Israel, Jesus himself.

Unable to arrest him for fear of the crowd, the leaders try sending "agents pretending to be righteous" (v. 20) to trap him in a question that would justify their handing him over "to the authority and power of the governor [Pontius Pilate]" (v. 20). What better question than that concerning the authority of Caesar to tax the Jews? Jesus' answer, distinguishing clearly between Caesar's authority and God's, reduces them to silence. Luke's Jesus is consistent with this answer by respecting civil authorities in their rightful jurisdiction without submissiveness in matters beyond that jurisdiction, as we shall soon see in his conduct before Herod. On the other hand, he openly opposes the religious leaders of his people in fearless non-violent confrontation. In Acts Luke will portray these same attitudes in Jesus' followers.

Forward the Sadducees, who have probably watched the fate of the chief priests and Pharisees at the hands of Jesus without much regret. They ridicule the concept of resurrection by their story of seven brothers trying to fulfill the levirate law of Moses by continuing the line of the dead brother through his wife (Dt 25:5-10). Although they ask only the question about whose wife she will be at the resurrection, they are really questioning the resurrection itself: In view of the levirate law, how could there be a resurrection that in this case would require the unthinkable situation in which a wife has several husbands?

Luke deftly adds a few touches to Mark's account to clarify Jesus' answer as a revelation that after death "the ones who will rise" (v. 36) have no need of marriage because heaven itself fulfills superabundantly both ends of marriage: to give love and to give life. They have no need of marriage as an expression of intense love, for in heaven their full awareness that "they are the children of God" (v. 36) intensifies their love for him and for all their brothers and sisters in him. And since, like angels "they can no longer die," they have no need of children to continue their lineage, the only kind of immortality that those who reject the resurrection can hope for.

Then Jesus addresses their hidden question by showing that if God is the Lord of the patriarchs, they must still be alive, since Yahweh is the God of the living; either they have already risen from death or will rise in the future.

The scribes who believe in the resurrection congratulate Jesus for his answer. Nobody dares ask any more questions (v. 40). Jesus then proposes his own: "How do they claim that the Messiah is the Son of David?" (v. 41) if David sings of him as "my lord"? Still following Mark, Luke continues with Jesus' unmasking of the scribes. In public they put on a pious appearance, but inwardly they are among the worst of sinners, for "they devour the houses of widows" (v. 47), claiming their homes in payment of debt and hiding their greed behind "lengthy prayers."

By inserting this reference to the exploitation of widows, Luke has prepared his reader for the next scene, in which Jesus calls attention to the otherwise unnoticed generosity of a poor widow who, in contrast to the exploiting scribes, contributes to the Temple "her whole livelihood" (Lk 21:4).

REFLECTION AND PRAYER

Do I accept the authority of Jesus in my life?

Do I trust completely in him for my own resurrection?

Lord Jesus, I listen to you to find the Father's will for me, to give myself for others with the generosity of the poor widow.

Jesus Predicts Persecution and Calls for Perseverance (Lk 21:5-38)

As does Mark, Luke completes his presentation of Jesus' Jerusalem ministry with the "eschatological" discourse, introducing changes to achieve his own purposes more fully. For instance, instead of addressing four disciples on the Mount of Olives, Luke's Jesus addresses the people in the Temple, evidently to give this discourse greater solemnity as his final public teaching.

Jesus begins by foretelling the destruction of the Temple. His listeners want to know when this will happen and a sign before it does. But, as in Mark, Jesus merely warns them to be constantly ready, not to listen to those who pretend to be able to foretell the end of time (v. 8), separated here, more clearly than in Mark, from the end of the Temple. Wars and calamities will continue, but they will not be clear signs of the end.

Writing considerably later than Mark, Luke no longer expects the end of the world to follow closely upon the end of the Temple. Between these cataclysmic events he foresees a period of time in which Christians will suffer the persecutions that Jesus now foretells in more detail than in Mark. But Jesus promises to sustain their courage and inspire them with "wisdom in speaking" (v. 15). Yet even family members will betray Jesus' faithful followers, handing them over "to death" (v. 16). This dire prediction seems strangely contradicted in verse 18: "But not a hair on your head will be destroyed." Verse 19, however, "by your perseverance you will secure your lives," makes it clear that Jesus is referring to their eternal lives. Some of them will lose their mortal lives for Jesus, but the Father will note their perseverance to the end and save their every hair in raising them to eternal life.

With his knowledge of the fall of Jerusalem, Luke interprets Mark's vague clause, "When you see the desolating abomination standing where he should not" (Mk 13:14), by his own clear description: "When you see Jerusalem *surrounded by armies*, know that its desolation is at hand" (v. 20). Luke summarizes Mark's passage about fleeing, yet sharpens his picture of the catastrophe: "Jerusalem will be trampled underfoot by the Gentiles until the times of the Gentiles are fulfilled" (v. 24). Just as the Jews have had their time to receive God's revelation, so now will the Gentiles, until the Christian message has reached the ends of the earth. Luke will record the beginning of these new times of the Gentiles in Acts.

Jesus' sentence about the fulfillment of the times of the Gentiles serves as transition from the end of the Temple to the end of the world, when cataclysmic events are to take place preceding the coming of the Son of Man "in a cloud with power and great glory" (v. 27). Then Luke's version adds another strong sentence: "When these signs begin to happen, stand erect and *raise your heads because your redemption is at hand''* (v. 28). At the final judgment followers of Jesus have nothing to fear and everything to hope for.

As surely as one can tell the coming of summer by the budding of the trees, so can the coming of ''the kingdom of God'' be foreseen (vv. 29-31). Indeed, the present generation has already seen its beginning (v. 32) in the growth of the church. The difficulty in the sentence, ''This generation will not pass away until all these things have taken place'' (v. 32), is resolved by recalling that Luke speaks of the reign of God in the two senses that we saw in 17:20-21. Luke obviously knew that the generation to which Jesus spoke had already passed away without seeing the cataclysmic signs of the end of the world when the reign of God is to be definitively fulfilled. He must therefore be thinking of Jesus as saying that his generation would not die before the kingdom of God was established in Jesus' followers, the church.

Luke's Jesus ends this discourse about the last things with the warning: ''Beware that your hearts do not become drowsy from carousing and drunkenness and the anxieties of daily life, and that day catch you by surprise like a trap'' (v. 34). He is referring not only to the day of this world's end but also, for each of us, to the day of our death, as the next sentence suggests: ''For that day will assault *everyone who lives on the face of the earth''* (v. 35). We are to live each day, then, as if it is our last.

REFLECTION AND PRAYER

Do I live each day as if it were my last?

Do I believe in the resurrection of the dead? In my resurrection?

Dear Lord, give me a firmer faith in your love for me and the marvelous future the Father has planned for me.

Climax: The Passion, Death, and Resurrection of Jesus (Lk 22—24)

The Paschal Meal (Lk 22:1-38)

Following Mark, but with greater freedom than Matthew in the handling of details, Luke begins his account of the passion with the plot of Jewish leaders ''to put him to death'' (v. 2). Skipping the anointing at Bethany, which he has already presented in a much different version (Lk 7:36-50), Luke immediately relates the betrayal of Judas as playing into the hands of the plotting Jewish leaders. In an expression similar to John's (13:2, 27), Luke says that "Satan entered into Judas" (v. 3). Both evangelists see Judas' willingness to hand over Jesus to the Jewish leaders as nothing less than satanic.

In relating the preparation for the Passover supper, Luke closely parallels Mark, adding the names of Peter and John, so prominent in the early chapters of Acts, as those designated by Jesus to make the arrangements.

Luke begins his account of the Last Supper with greater solemnity than does Mark: "When the hour came, he took his place at table with the apostles" (v. 14). Note that Luke refers to the Twelve here with the word *apostles* instead of the usual *disciples*. He evidently has in mind the ordination that they are about to receive during this meal, the decisive step in that special commissioning by which they are transformed from followers into leaders in the kingdom of God.

Luke's Last Supper account resembles some aspects of John's. Luke refers to "the hour" (v. 14) that John explains: "His hour had come to pass from this world to the Father" (Jn 13:1). In Luke, Jesus' opening statement, "I have eagerly desired to eat this Passover with you before I suffer" (v. 15), is close in thought to John's reflection in opening his account of the Last Supper (Jn 13:1). And after the Eucharist Luke's Jesus gives a short discourse, similar in part to the much longer discourse in John.

After reporting the eucharistic words of Jesus, Mark quoted his prediction: "I shall not drink again the fruit of the vine until the day when I drink it new in the kingdom of God" (Mk 14:24). In addition to this picture of Jesus celebrating in heaven, Luke suggests another meaning by expanding this statement in verses 16-18. Jesus' prediction now implies that he will again eat and drink with his disciples when "the kingdom of God comes," that is, when the church is established through his own death and resurrection. He is about to do something of profound significance, symbolized by the cup of wine that he passes to his disciples (v. 17), one of the ceremonial actions of the Jewish Passover meal, in which all drink from the same cup to symbolize their solidarity in their covenant with Yahweh. By speaking of this drink as his last before establishing the kingdom (v. 18), Luke's Jesus links this Passover meal, in which he and his apostles celebrate Israel's Exodus from slavery, to his own impending exodus, referred to in Luke's account of the transfiguration (Lk 9:31). It now becomes clear that Jesus' exodus will be the true Passover bringing about the fulfillment of the kingdom, not of Israel but of God, and that the eucharistic banquet will become the Passover celebration of God's new covenant in Jesus (v. 20). His death, resurrection and sending of the Holy Spirit will definitively establish the church in which the Eucharist will relive his Last Supper, his communion with his own.

The eucharistic consecration takes place in verses 19-20. To Mark's account Luke adds Jesus' significant command, "Do this in memory of me," thus authorizing (ordaining) his apostles to renew this sacramental meal down through the ages so that all his followers may participate in the banquet in which he nourishes them with his very being.

To the words of consecration over the cup, Luke's Jesus adds the word *new* before *covenant*, stressing its contrast with the old covenant. The former union between God and his people had been *symbolized* by Moses' act of sprinkling the blood of bulls on God's altar and his people; the new, more perfect union between God and his people will be *effected* by Jesus' shedding of his precious blood on Calvary (see Heb 9:11-28).

Luke's version of the words of consecration further make clear that the body of Jesus "given for you" (v. 19) on the cross and the blood of Jesus "shed for you" (v. 20) are the same body and blood given in the Eucharist, the same Jesus who died for us all and now lives exalted at the Father's side, yet comes sacramentally to unite us to himself and the Father in the Spirit. The old covenant brought about Israel's juridical relationship with God through Israel's acceptance of God's externally dictated commandments. The new covenant brings Christians into a filial relationship with God through their embrace of his gift of a new inner spirit (see Jer 31:33), the Holy Spirit (Lk 24:49). And this relationship is nourished by sacramental communion with the very person—body and blood, soul and divinity—of Jesus Christ, the Father's unique Son.

Unlike Mark and Matthew, Luke places Jesus' reference to the betrayer after the Eucharist instead of before it. Perhaps he has transposed the order of these events as a warning to his readers that the Eucharist can be received unworthily. He probably has the same reason for presenting here the dispute among the disciples that both Mark and Matthew placed before the triumphal entry into Jerusalem. Participation in the Lord's Supper is no automatic guarantee against betrayal and dissension. The church must guard constantly against these abuses, evidently experienced in several of the earliest Christian communities, as attested by the concern expressed in New Testament passages (1 Cor 3:1-9; 11:17-34; Jn 13:12-20; Mt 23:1-11).

Jesus' words about betrayal give rise to disputes among the new apostles, first about "who among them would do such a deed" (v. 23), then "about which of them should be regarded as the greatest" (v. 24). Jesus defines leadership among them as *service*: "I am among you as the one who serves" (v. 27). This is the kind of leadership required in the "kingdom my Father has conferred . . . on me" (v. 29), the kind of leadership that Jesus now confers on his apostles (v. 30).

Jesus' declaration, "It is you who have stood by me in my trials" (v. 28), leads into his warning to one who would fail to stand by him in his coming trial: "Simon, Simon, behold Satan has demanded to sift all of you like wheat, but I have prayed that your own faith may not fail; and once you have turned back [in repentance], you must strengthen your brothers" (v. 32). Only after Peter has learned his own weakness in his bitter experience of denying Jesus will he at last replace his brash self-confidence with complete trust in Jesus and thereby be able to strengthen the others. Only then will he become the "rock" upon which Jesus will build his church.

To dramatize the coming separation Jesus suddenly reverses his previous advice to take along nothing for their missionary journey (Lk 10:4). Now they must provide everything for themselves (v. 36), for he will no longer be with them; he is about to leave them. They must even provide for their own self-defense by buying swords!

They take him too literally, showing him their two swords (v. 38), a pitiful arsenal against the opposing forces already at work. His laconic reply, "It is enough," clearly indicates that he has been speaking figuratively. Indeed, they must make provision to defend themselves in the future, but not as soldiers or conquerors in the physical sense. It is God's plan, written in scripture, that Jesus, God's suffering servant, be "counted among the wicked" (v. 37, quoting Is 53:12). They must arm themselves spiritually in readiness to become suffering servants in their turn!

REFLECTION AND PRAYER

Am I ready to be "counted among the wicked," to be ridiculed for my faith?

Instead of relying upon myself, do I place all my confidence in Jesus?

Do I believe that Jesus gives me his own body and blood in the Eucharist as his new covenant with me?

Dear Jesus, take over my life, even though it means that I must share in your suffering for others.

Jesus' Agony, Arrest and Trial (Lk 22:39—23:25)

Although Luke follows Mark in relating most of the events of Jesus' passion, he introduces many subtle changes to achieve his own purposes. He gives us a hint of one of these purposes by inserting the phrase "the disciples followed him" (v. 39) as Jesus goes out to the Mount of Olives. Luke thereby begins his account of the passion of Jesus by reminding his readers that to be true disciples they must follow Jesus as supreme model even in his sufferings. That this is Luke's intention is confirmed by a second change: He presents Jesus' agony in the garden as taking place not only in the presence of Peter, James and John (as in Mark) but before all the disciples; all Jesus' true followers are called to participate in his agony.

Twice Jesus tells his apostles to "pray that you may not undergo the test" (vv. 40.46), a clear reference to the last part of the Lord's Prayer (Lk 11:4), now directly applicable to their situation. Then he gives the example of how they are to pray. His agonized prayer is basically the same as that reported in Mark, but rephrased to stress the Father's will: "Father, *if you are willing* [instead of "all things are possible to you"], take this cup away from me; still, *not my will but yours be done*" (v. 42). In Luke the religious significance of the moment is heightened by the immediate answer to Jesus' prayer in the form of an angel strengthening him (v. 43), perhaps a scribe's addition, but in harmony with Luke's frequent mention of a heavenly visitation in answer to prayer (Lk 3:21-22; 9:28-31; Acts 4:31; 7:55; 10:1-16). The perseverance and fervor of Jesus' prayer match the duration and intensity of his psychological agony, dramatized physically: "His sweat became like drops of blood falling on the ground" (v. 44)—perhaps another addition, again in harmony with Luke's use of exterior phenomena to dramatize inner experiences (Acts 2:1-4; 9:1-9; 10:44-48).

Luke omits Mark's preliminaries to the arrest of Jesus, probably to focus attention on the irony of Judas' greeting: "Judas, are you betraying the Son of Man *with a kiss?*" (v. 48). The disciples have not understood Jesus' correction of their literalness (v. 38), for now they ask,

"Lord, shall we strike with a sword?" (v. 49). Without awaiting authorization one of them cuts off the right ear of the high priest's servant. Jesus calls for a stop to violent action and returns the assault upon himself with his healing touch; only Luke reports that Jesus heals the man's ear (v. 51). Even in this chaotic moment Luke's Jesus remains sensitive to the suffering of others. And he is strong in the face of his own suffering; he stands up to those who have come against him with weapons, and he answers only with reason (vv. 52-53). In the end he knows what to expect: "But this is your hour, the time for the power of darkness" (v. 53). There is more evil here than meets the eye; the passion of Jesus is brought about by satanic forces.

Luke does not mention the mock trial during the night but simply reports that Jesus' captors "took him into the house of the high priest" (v. 54). Then Luke recounts Peter's triple denial of Jesus, omitting Mark's "he began to curse and to swear" (Mk 14:71) and adding a climactic moment: "The Lord turned and looked at Peter" (v. 61) to trigger his memory of Jesus' prediction and motivate his remorse. Even in his own time of anguish, awaiting trial, Luke's Jesus touches the heart of his failing disciple to bring about repentance and conversion.

In contrast to his weak disciple, Jesus now endures the ridicule and beating of the guards, who blindfold and taunt him while he awaits his morning trial (vv. 63-65). In relating the trial Luke omits Mark's false witnesses to focus upon the real issue, the identity of Jesus. Questioned by them all as to whether he is the Messiah, he gives no direct answer, for they have closed off access to faith (vv. 67-68). His answer does not evoke a picture of the final judgment, as in Mark, but fixes squarely upon the key image: "The Son of Man will be seated at the right hand of the power of God" (v. 69). This answer arouses their final question: "Are you then the Son of God?" (v. 70). Luke's Jesus answers obliquely; he does not deliberately seek the condemnation that a direct affirmative would bring upon him. Yet neither does he resort to evasion, as his reply, "You say that I am," might seem to the modern reader. Jews used this indirect form of speech to imply an affirmative answer, as attested by the conclusion: "What further need have we for testimony?" (v. 71).

In reporting the trial before Pilate, Luke expands Mark by spelling out the fundamental accusation of the Jewish leaders against Jesus: "We found this man misleading our people" (Lk 23:2). In their eyes Jesus has been a false religious teacher, drawing the people away from their leadership by his new revelation of God. But religious quarrels would mean nothing to Pilate, so for him they reinterpret "misleading the people" as two political offenses: "He opposes the payment of taxes to Caesar and maintains that he is the Messiah, a king" (v. 2). Pilate focuses upon the last accusation. Perhaps Jesus' public answer to the provocative question about taxes has been reported to him; if so, he probably suspects that their second accusation is also a lie. When Jesus calmly responds to his question about being king of the Jews, "You say so" (v. 3), Pilate evidently understands his indirect answer as a denial. Luke's version again indicates that Jesus did not actively seek martyrdom. Pilate is satisfied that there is no case against him and ends the trial by declaring Jesus not guilty (v. 4).

Excitedly the Jewish leaders insist that Jesus stirs up the people, beginning in Galilee, seedbed of rebellions (see Acts 5:37). Pilate seizes upon the word *Galilee* as his way out of this difficult case and sends Jesus off to Herod, puppet king of Galilee. Only Luke reports this mock trial. Herod's questions elicit not a word from Jesus, partly because they are frivolous—Herod "had been hoping to see him perform some sign" (v. 8)—and partly because Jesus does not recognize Herod's jurisdiction in the case. Frustrated, Herod mocks Jesus but does not condemn him (v. 15), sending him back to Pilate with whom he now ironically becomes a friend. Luke seems to be placing them both on the side of darkness, against Jesus, the light.

Pilate, again confronted with the case, announces in a somewhat pompous summation speech: "I . . . have not found this man guilty of the charges you have brought against him" (v. 14). Yet he concludes that he will release Jesus only after having him flogged (v. 16), a punishment obviously calculated to appease the Jewish leaders.

But the crowd will not be appeased. They demand the release of Barabbas and the crucifixion of Jesus. In their unreasoning fury they have forgotten that Barabbas has been imprisoned for the same crime of which they have accused Jesus, misleading the people, and worse, for murder (v. 19). For the third time Pilate declares that Jesus is not guilty. Luke is repeatedly emphasizing Jesus' innocence, warning his readers that they, too, while not seeking suffering or martyrdom, must be ready to accept both, despite their innocence. Pilate tries again to let Jesus off with a mere flogging, at the hands of Roman soldiers an excruciating torture. At last, for fear of the threatened violence of the mob, Pilate ironically decrees the greatest violence—crucifixion!

REFLECTION AND PRAYER

Do I pray regularly?

Do I pray with greater constancy and intensity when I am troubled, upset, suffering?

Do I make a conscious effort to unite my sufferings to those of Jesus?

My Lord, give me the courage to bear ridicule and rejection for love of you.

The Death and Burial of Jesus (Lk 23:26-56)

Though he omits the crowning with thorns, Luke follows Mark in reporting that the Romans make Simon of Cyrene carry Jesus' cross (v. 26) and adds the phrase "behind Jesus," another reminder that the Christian is called to follow Jesus, even on the way of the cross.

To make sure his point is not missed Luke immediately expands his account with an incident proper to his gospel. He reports that "a large crowd of people *followed Jesus*" (v. 27) on his way of the cross, obviously sympathizing with his sufferings, for the crowd includes "many women who mourned and lamented him." Far from withdrawing into himself in his extreme suffering, Jesus is sensitive to the future awaiting them. He comforts them and warns them to prepare for their own coming sufferings. His address to the women as "daughters of Jerusalem" (v. 28), and his predictions (vv. 29-30), similar to some of those in the eschatological discourse (especially Lk 21:20-25), suggest that Jesus is referring to the tribulations at the fall of Jerusalem or the end of the world, in which the innocent will have to suffer along with the guilty. Verse 31 would then mean that if the green wood (the innocent Jesus) is so burned (with suffering), how much more will the dry wood (guilty Jerusalem) burn!

But, taking into account Luke's reminders that Christians are called to follow Jesus on his way of the cross and the evident sympathy of the women Jesus addresses, the sufferings that he predicts in verses 29-30 would rather seem to refer to the persecutions that followers of Jesus must expect, an interpretation that is also in harmony with parts of the eschatological discourse (especially Lk 21:12-19). In this interpretation verse 31 would mean that if Jesus, the new green wood of the tree that symbolizes the kingdom of God (Luke 13:19 has already used a large bush as a symbol of the kingdom), must suffer the way of the cross, so must Jesus' followers as the dry wood of the mature church expect to suffer the way of the cross—the only way of Christ's true followers.

Whichever interpretation is preferred, Luke's main point about Jesus is clear: For the third time during his passion Jesus rises above his own sufferings to reach out to the needs of others. So must the true follower of Jesus do.

Luke alone reports as the first word of Jesus upon the cross, "Father, forgive them, they know not what they do" (v. 34). Although this saying is not found in some ancient manuscripts, it is certainly typical of the Jesus that Luke has been portraying for us, a person characterized by a love for his Father that embraces his love for others as he again reaches out to those in need, even in forgiveness to those who cause him racking pain.

Three times Jesus is tempted to save himself from this agonizing death, first by the Jewish rulers (v. 35), then by the Roman soldiers (v. 36), and finally by the unrepentant criminal (v. 39). No doubt Luke would have us sense that Jesus' last temptations to abandon the mission of his life are much more severe than the three temptations he reported before the beginning of Jesus' public life (Lk 4:1-13). But Jesus remains nailed to his cross in steadfast obedience to his Father's mission.

Luke alone reports the dispute between the crucified criminals concerning Jesus, "destined for the fall and rise of many in Israel" (Lk 2:34). The unrepentant criminal rejects Jesus, but the one who repents by admitting his own guilt recognizes the innocence of Jesus and appeals to him as Lord of salvation: "Jesus, remember me when you come into your kingdom" (v. 42). This man, criminal that he has been, has evidently listened to Jesus and understood the kind of king that he is. Jesus' magnanimous answer, "Today you will be with me in Paradise" (v. 43), grounds the faith of the early Christians in the power of Jesus' saving death, the death by which he opens heaven to the souls awaiting his redeeming action (see 1 Pt 3:18-20). For the fifth time Luke's Jesus has risen above his own suffering to reach out to the one in need.

Although Luke says nothing about the presence of Mary, the mother of Jesus, at the foot of the cross, the controversy between the two criminals over Jesus reminds us of Simeon's prediction cited above. Part of that same prophecy included Simeon's word to Mary: "You yourself a sword will pierce" (Lk 2:35), which seems to imply that Mary is there at the cross, sharing the sword of Jesus' passion and death. For confirmation we will have to wait for John's gospel (Jn 19:25-27).

As does Mark, Luke reports the afternoon darkness, which he attributes to an eclipse, a phenomenon used in ancient literature as a portent of a great man's death. Luke omits Jesus' mysterious cry of abandonment (Mk 15:34), perhaps thinking that some of his readers would find it inappropriate or incomprehensible. Instead, he reports: "Jesus cried out in a loud voice, 'Father, into your hands I commend my spirit'" (v. 46), a quotation from Psalm 31:6, except for the addition of the word "Father." Jesus' dying moment of consciousness points in the same direction as his first recorded word in the Temple at the age of 12 (Lk 2:49)—to the Father whose will has been his whole life's orientation.

By putting the synoptic gospels together, the church has attained a more complete understanding of Jesus' death. Mark and Matthew report the mysterious cry of Jesus as he is dying, "My God, my God, why have you forsaken me?" That cry not only refers to the circumstances of Jesus' death as fulfillment of the prophecies in Psalm 22, but it also emphasizes the stark reality of his death. It is a death as real as ours, a death in which everything slips away from the dying person: consciousness of the outer world and gradually of the inner world of thoughts and convictions. Even the ground of our consciousness, the God who sustains our life, slips away from us as we sink into the abyss we call death.

It is this same death into which Jesus now sinks. Yet even at the moment of slipping into what seems utter nothingness, Jesus uses his last breath in the loud cry, "Father, into your hands I commend my spirit" (v. 46), his final declaration of loving obedience to his Father. This is what makes his death characteristic of his life from his first words of loving obedience toward his Father (Lk 2:49), a death that fulfills all his living moments, likewise committed to his Father. Luke is telling us that this is what makes Jesus' death the model of every Christian death—that complete faith, that final hoping and loving trust with which he hands over his life to the Father who initially gave it to him. Only the Christian who has also tried to live as Jesus did, in loving orientation to the Father and to all the other children of the Father, will be able to die as Jesus did in utter abandonment of his life into his Father's loving hands. Luke obviously believes that such a death would be impossible for us poor men and women, especially in the confusion of dying consciousness, were it not for the gracious help of this loving Father, who showers upon us in our moment of extreme need the grace won for us by his dying only-begotten Son, Jesus.

In Luke's account Jesus' dying cry attests his divine Sonship. Luke can therefore reduce the declaration of Mark's centurion from ''truly this man was the Son of God!'' (Mk 15:39) to ''this man was innocent beyond doubt'' (v. 47), a declaration that again highlights one of Luke's key points: Jesus suffered and died despite his innocence. The Book of Job had wrestled with the question, Why must the innocent suffer? Job rejected the easy answer that his sufferings were a punishment for his secret sins, but could find no better answer than the inscrutability of God's ways. Luke presents a much more satisfying answer: Though suffering is still a mystery to us, Jesus, the supreme Innocent One, suffered and died for our sins; every true Christian is called to follow him in suffering and dying, not only for his or her own sins but also for those of others.

Besides the centurion other people too are impressed by the death of Jesus: ''They returned home beating their breasts'' (v. 48), obviously repentant for their part in the previous taunting of Jesus. Luke adds, ''All his acquaintances stood at a distance, including the women who had followed him from Galilee and saw these events'' (v. 49). Although in Acts Luke will consider the apostles as the official witnesses of these events, he delicately gives special mention in this moment of grief to the women.

Similarly to Mark, Luke reports the burial of Jesus, adding the reverent touch that he is laid in a tomb ''in which no one had yet been buried'' (v. 53). Luke also explicitly states that the women see ''the tomb and the way in which his body was laid in it'' (v. 55). He thereby stresses two facts: Jesus was really dead, and there would be no mistake about which tomb they found empty on Easter morning. Luke adds a final touch to this account. In spite of their grief the women prepare the materials required for a more decent burial before the sabbath so that they can observe the sabbath rest ''according to the commandment'' (v. 56). They are already following Jesus in rising above their hurt to be true to the Father's will in the details of daily life.

REFLECTION AND PRAYER

Lord Jesus, King of the Jews and my King, I am overwhelmed by your suffering and death to save us. Your death convinces me of your absolute love for me. Help me endure all my sufferings, in union with you, out of love for the Father and for my brothers and sisters.

The Resurrection Appearances of Jesus (Lk 24)

In recounting the visit of the women to the tomb "at daybreak" that Sunday, Luke resembles Mark, but with some notable differences. For instance, when the women enter the tomb Luke pointedly adds, "they did not find the body of the Lord Jesus" (v. 3). The two heavenly visitors (one in Mark) ask, "Why do you seek the living one among the dead?" (v. 5), emphasizing the truth that the resurrection is unto life. And instead of saying that Jesus will appear to his disciples in Galilee, they remind the women that Jesus foretold his resurrection "while he was still in Galilee" (vv. 6-7). Instead of saying "nothing to anyone" (Mk 16:8), Luke's women "announced all these things to the eleven and to all the others" (v. 9). Only at this point does Luke name three of these women (v. 10), as if to give them official status as witnesses to the resurrection pronouncement.

Although the "apostles . . . did not believe them" (vv. 10-12), Peter runs to the tomb, as in John 20:3-7, where he sees "the burial cloths alone" (v. 12). Notice the care with which Luke makes the point that far from expecting the resurrection, their leader was "amazed at what had happened." Peter's witness to the empty tomb confirms that of the women; having "turned back" (Lk 22:32) to the Lord, he begins to strengthen the others.

From here on Luke seems to rely solely on his own sources, compressing all the events that he now relates into the one glorious day of the resurrection.

First, he presents one of the most engaging additions of his gospel, the Emmaus story. Cleopas and his unnamed walking companion are "*prevented* from recognizing" Jesus (v. 16), an indirect way of suggesting that he is somehow changed. Jesus' resurrection is entirely different from mere resuscitation. Good teacher that he is, Jesus accepts his former followers in their ignorance and through his probing questions stirs their dying faith into the beginnings of hope (vv. 17-19). But when they disbelievingly report the testimony of the women and others concerning the empty tomb (vv. 19-24), Jesus explodes:

> "Oh, how foolish you are! How slow of heart to believe all that the prophets spoke!". . . Then beginning with Moses and *all* the prophets, *he interpreted to them* what referred to him in *all* the scriptures" (v. 25-27).

Here is Luke's insight into the real source of the many Old Testament references in the gospels: Jesus himself is the interpreter of the Jewish scriptures for the early Christians.

Jesus so strongly impresses the two that they entreat him to stay with them; he graciously obliges. When he "took bread, said the blessing, broke it, and gave it to them . . . their eyes were opened and they recognized him" (vv. 30-31). It is in the Eucharist that they find him again; Luke is telling us that in the Eucharist we too find Jesus.

Just as we saw Matthew give a strong affirmative answer to the question of whether Jesus is still present to his followers, we now see Luke answering that same question just as affirmatively, though somewhat differently. The early church has evidently been struggling with this problem and has found several solutions. Mark merely implied that somehow the risen Jesus is still with his people (Mk 16:6-8). But how? Matthew suggested at least two ways in which Jesus is still present to Christians: through their prayer, both personal ("Come to me," Mt 11:28) and communal ("Where two or three . . . ," Mt 18:20); and through the commissioned authority of the apostles ("Go, therefore, . . . I am with you always," Mt 28:19-20). Luke's Emmaus story adds that Jesus still walks with us, even as he walked with his disciples, though we do not recognize his presence clearly except in the Eucharist.

Only after Jesus breaks the bread do his companions recognize him and realize at his disappearance how lovable they have found him to be: "Were not our hearts *burning* [within us] while he spoke to us on the way and *opened the scriptures* to us?" (v. 32; brackets in *NAB*). Luke is clearly implying that through the scriptures, too, we can find the risen Jesus. That is exactly what we have been trying to do!

The two walking companions hurry back to Jerusalem to tell the Eleven. But even before they can relate their adventure, they must listen to the excited account of Jesus' appearance to Simon Peter.

As they share their joy, Jesus himself stands "in their midst" (v. 36). To assure them that he is not a ghost, he invites them to recognize him by the wounds of his hands and feet and to touch his real flesh and bones (v. 39). He even sits down with them to eat a piece of fish. Good choice—the fish bones will be a relic that they can gaze upon afterward when their emotions subside enough to allow reason to return and bolster faith. Luke's account clearly stresses the truth that Jesus' new life includes the resurrection of his body. If Christians are to follow Jesus on his way of the cross, so are they to hope for a bodily resurrection like that of Jesus.

Jesus' predictions about his passion, death and resurrection have come true, according to "my words that I spoke to you while I was still with you" (v. 44). Then Jesus tells again why he had to suffer: "Everything written about me in the law of Moses and in the prophets and psalms must be fulfilled" (v. 44). The Father's will was expressed in the Old Testament; Jesus perceived it there and carried it out as the mission of which he was conscious, even from his earliest years (Lk 2:49). Luke adds another key sentence: "Then he *opened their minds to understand the scriptures*" (v. 45). The church of Luke's time believes that Jesus is the real and only interpreter of the Old Testament, for the central function of the Old Testament was to prepare for his coming. An important implication seems clear: Just as Jesus alone received the mission to interpret for his people the meaning of the Old Testament, so the church alone, to which he is about to entrust the continuation of his mission (vv. 47-49), is empowered (Acts 2:1-41) to interpret the fulfillment of the Old Testament in the life, ministry, suffering, death and resurrection of Jesus (v. 46), as expressed in its apostolic tradition and its New Testament.

Jesus commissions his apostles to preach "repentance, for the forgiveness of sins . . . to all the nations, beginning from Jerusalem" (v. 47), and to be his appointed witnesses (v. 48). He promises them the Holy Spirit: "I am sending the promise of my Father upon you" (v. 49)—the promise through the prophet Joel (Acts 2:16-21)—and instructs them to wait in Jerusalem until that empowering event.

That same night, according to Luke, obviously telescoping time, Jesus leads the apostles to a place near Bethany, probably the Mount of Olives, where he blesses them and is "taken up to heaven" (v. 51). They immediately adore him as divine: "They did him homage" (v. 52). They are filled "with great joy," the predominant tone of Luke's gospel, and are henceforth to be found "*continually in the temple praising God*" (v. 53), who has worked such wonders for them in his only Son, Jesus!

In the opening verses of his sequel, the Acts of the Apostles, Luke gives a much different version of the time of Jesus' ascension: "He presented himself alive to them by many proofs after he had suffered, *appearing to them during forty days*" (Acts 1:3). This discrepancy clearly illustrates how Luke subordinates chronological exactitude to the theological meaning that he perceives in the events he relates. Evidently he telescopes time in his gospel account of Jesus' appearances and ascension in order to dramatize and unite the glorious events of the resurrection and ascension. But in Acts, because his intention is to relate the work of Jesus' apostles as reliable and authoritative witnesses, he stresses the "many proofs" that Jesus presented them over an extended period of time. With Jesus' ascent into heaven the new era of the church begins.

Luke ends his gospel as he began it, in the Temple of Jerusalem, the place that he associates with all the paschal events. But his story is not finished; his good news continues in the sequel, the Acts of the Apostles. As the most consciously historical writer of the New Testament, Luke perceives three distinct phases in the history of God's plan of salvation: Jesus is the centerpiece of that history; all that happens before his coming is in preparation for him; all that follows his ascension is the unfolding of his work of redemption under the guidance of the Holy Spirit.

Luke gave us a clue to this division of history when he reported Jesus' saying: "The law and the prophets lasted until John; but from then on the kingdom of God is proclaimed" (Lk 16:16). This and other passages in Luke present the time of the old covenant, "the law and the prophets," as the preparation period of salvation history. John the Baptist introduces the central period of history as the precursor of the central person of history, Jesus himself, who proclaims and is in person "the kingdom of God." The coming of the Holy Spirit inaugurates the final period of salvation history, the period of the Holy Spirit's work in the church and the church's work among men, as indicated by Jesus himself:

> He enjoined them not to depart from Jerusalem, but to wait for "the promise of the Father about which you have heard me speak; for John baptized with water, but in a few days you will be baptized with the Holy Spirit. . . . You will receive power when the holy Spirit comes upon you, and you will be my witnesses in Jerusalem, throughout Judea and Samaria, and to the ends of the earth" (Acts 1:4-8).

To get the full impact of Luke's grand concept, you might want to read Acts at this point as Luke's sequel to his gospel, or at least page through it to see how Luke develops his outline of history.

REFLECTION AND PRAYER

My risen Savior, I believe firmly in your Resurrection, the model that also offers me the promise of resurrection. And I believe in your presence among us today. Walk with me along my path of life. Send your Holy Spirit upon me, upon us all.

SUGGESTIONS FOR FURTHER READING AND REFERENCE

Brown, Raymond E., S.S. *The Birth of the Messiah*. Garden City: Doubleday, 1977. A thorough treatment of the first chapters of Matthew and Luke.

Fitzmyer, Joseph A. *The Gospel According to Luke*, 2 vols. Garden City, NY: Doubleday, 1985. Anchor Bible Series. A solid, very detailed commentary.

Kodell, Jerome, O.S.B. *The Gospel According to Luke*. Collegeville, MN: The Liturgical Press, 1983. A short, readable commentary.

O'Toole, Robert F., S.J. *The Unity of Luke's Theology*. Wilmington, DE: Michael Glazier, Inc., 1984. An excellent analysis of Luke-Acts.

Talbert, Charles H. *Reading Luke: A Literary and Theological Commentary on the Third Gospel*. New York: Crossroad, 1984. Technical, but easy to read and full of fine insights.

Van Linden, Philip, C.M. *The Gospel of Luke and Acts*. Wilmington, DE: Michael Glazier, Inc., 1986. A good, popular commentary.

PART V

Finding the Divine Jesus
With John

Fittingly, we reach the climax of our reading with the gospel of
John. It will stretch our intellectual and imaginative capabilities beyond their ordinary limits and challenge us to the fullest use of all the
resources that we have been acquiring for penetrating to the inner
meaning of biblical passages. Almost certainly the last of the canonical
gospels to be written, John's gospel is a profound reflection on the
deepest meaning of the life of Jesus, thereby recapitulating all the previous gospels, yet without repeating most of their material.

Whether the author had access to any of the synoptic gospels is a
matter of conjecture. If, as many scholars suppose, the gospel of John
was written during the last decade of the first century, it would seem
likely that the writer had some knowledge of the other gospels. But if
he did know any of them he seems deliberately to have avoided repeating them. He records only a few of the same incidents of Jesus' public
life and relatively few of the synoptics' details of his passion and resurrection appearances.

Moreover, John's tone and perspective are far different from those
of the synoptic authors. His faith is basically the same as theirs, but he
is much more explicit in expressing the divinity of Jesus and much freer
in molding his material to express that faith. Who, then, was this author?

Modern scholars are not sure, but most agree that he was not one
of the Twelve, not the apostle John, even though Irenaeus, a disciple of

Polycarp who was himself a disciple of John, reported about A.D. 180 that John, a disciple of the Lord, *published* the gospel in Ephesus. As suggested by Irenaeus, the person most responsible for the production of a book is not necessarily the writer. A widely accepted theory is that the apostle John formed a group of special disciples, later led by John the Elder, who wrote the gospel *based upon the reflections and reminiscences of John the apostle.* Some scholars question whether "the beloved disciple," who figures prominently in the latter part of the gospel, is the same person as the apostle John, but none of their alternative theories has gained wide acceptance.

There is a strong suggestion in the gospel itself that the apostle John, presumably "the beloved disciple," was already dead when the gospel was written. Jesus' question to Peter, "What if I want him [the beloved disciple] to remain until I come?" (Jn 21:22), had evidently been interpreted to mean that John would not die until Jesus' second coming. His death must have caused the consternation that the writer of the gospel apparently addresses in his remark: "But Jesus had not told him [Peter] that he [John] would not die, just 'What if I want him to remain until I come?'" (Jn 21:23).

This "beloved disciple" is the eyewitness upon whose authority the gospel is based: "It is this disciple who testifies to these things and has written them [perhaps in his own notes or the jottings of a secretary], and we know that his testimony is true" (Jn 21:24). It is not hard, then, to imagine the apostle John, now grown old, instructing his select "school" in the life of Jesus and in his own inspired insights into its deepest meaning, the fruit of his long meditations over the years. Nor is it difficult to picture the best writer or writers of this group editing their notes or memories into the fabric of the gospel "that you may [come to] believe that Jesus is the Messiah, the Son of God, and that through this belief you may have life in his name" (Jn 20:31; brackets in *NAB*).

The readers that the author of this gospel has in mind are no longer the first-generation Christians, but rather those "who have not seen and have believed" (Jn 20:29). Evidently as the eyewitnesses died, the problem of faith-without-seeing and of faith without the direct testimony of an eyewitness was becoming more acute. In reading this gospel, we will see many conscious efforts on the author's part to help readers with this problem, an even graver problem in an age of accelerating secularization such as ours.

By the time the gospel of John was written, Christian reflection, guided by the Holy Spirit, had gradually developed clearer expressions of the Christian mystery since the advent of the earliest New Testament writings. Yet the very first of these, 1 Thessalonians as far as scholars have been able to determine, gives evidence of the faith of the first Christians in the divinity of Jesus: "The *Lord* [Jesus] himself . . . will come down from heaven, and the dead in Christ will rise first" (1 Thes 4:16). Some of Paul's readers might have inferred that he believed Jesus was made Lord at his resurrection, "established as Son of God in power . . . through resurrection from the dead, Jesus Christ our Lord" (Rom 1:4). At the writing of Mark's gospel it was clear that Jesus was divine at least by the time of his baptism: "You are my beloved Son" (Mk 1:11). Matthew and Luke both speak of the virginal conception through the power of the Holy Spirit, thus making it evident that inspired reflection had by then clarified the Christian faith that Jesus was divine from the moment of his conception in the womb of Mary.

Yet some of Paul's letters state that as Son of God Christ pre-existed his birth as a man: "When the fullness of time had come, *God sent his Son*, born of a woman, born under the law, to ransom those under the law, so that we might receive adoption" (Gal 4:4-5). Paul can therefore urge, "Have among yourselves the same attitude that is also yours in [regard to] Christ Jesus,

> Who, though he was in the form of God,
>> did not regard equality with God something to be grasped.
> Rather, he emptied himself,
>> taking the form of a slave,
>> coming in human likeness" (Phil 2:5-7).

Later Pauline letters are even more explicit: "God . . . chose us in him [Christ] before the foundation of the world" (Eph 1:3-4). "In him [the Son] were created all things in heaven and on earth" (Col 1:16).

Yet these statements do not clearly break through the web of time into eternity. It is John's gospel that finally brings this question to its logical conclusion in completely unambiguous terms: If Jesus Christ is truly divine, he never *became* divine—*he has always been divine!*

Prologue: "The Word Became Flesh" (Jn 1:1-18)

How could Jesus exist before his human conception? To express this thought, so far beyond our human experience, John speaks of God's "Word" already existing in his presence before "the beginning" of our world. To the Greek mind, "Word" (Logos) would have deep philosophical meanings. Stoics thought of the Logos as the spiritual principle holding the world together in a coherent pattern, a kind of world soul. Gnostics believed that salvation from the bonds of material existence was attainable only through secret knowledge (gnosis) revealed by Logos. In speaking, then, of the Logos of God, John may be addressing the Greek thinkers of his day in their own terms.

But it is much more likely that he is making use of a trend of thought already begun in the Greek Septuagint translation of the Old Testament in which *logos* was used to translate the creative "word" of God at creation. Further, the Book of Proverbs had personified the knowledge or wisdom of God as his companion in the work of creation:

"The Lord begot me [Wisdom], the firstborn of his ways,
   the forerunner of his prodigies of long ago. . . .
When he established the heavens I was there,
   when he marked out the vault over the face of the deep . . .
Then was I beside him as his craftsman,
   and I was his delight day by day, . . .
   and I found delight in the sons of men" (Prv 8:22-31).

To this remarkable interpretation of the Genesis creation story, John gives a still more striking meaning:

In the beginning was the Word [God's creative Word of Wisdom],
   and the Word was *with God,*
   and the *Word was God* (Jn 1:1).

This very first sentence of John's gospel defies logical analysis. If the Word was with God, he was not God himself; yet John immediately declares that the Word *was* God. Human logic and language will not bear the weight of John's insight! They break under the strain.

Yet this insight is obviously the fruit of Christian reflection on the deepest meaning of Jesus' life and words as already found in the synoptics and in the Pauline letters; Paul had already called Christ "the wisdom of God" (1 Cor 1:24). Not only does John's opening sentence echo that of Genesis, "In the beginning," it also implies that God's Wisdom, expressed in the Word, never had a beginning, that the Word of God is coexistent with the eternal God himself. In some way the one God is both Father and Word—the Word who becomes Jesus (v. 14). We already see an effort to express the belief that will eventually be developed into the doctrine that the Father and the Son are one in being.

Great theologians have struggled with John's concept. Augustine, applying his faith that "God created man in his image" (Gn 1:27), used an analogy from human psychology to explain that by generating his "Word" God perfectly expresses himself, and therefore "the Word" is *Person*, like the Father himself and equal to him from all eternity. God is eternally Father by spiritual generation; yet his Son is not another God, a new pure spirit, but the same God as the Father, the One God himself. This is indeed mystery! No wonder it took Christians three centuries to refine and re-refine their expression of this mystery until the creed elaborated at the First General Council of Nicaea in 325! No wonder it is still as incomprehensible today as it was then! And yet the Nicene expression "consubstantial [one in Being] with the Father" is only a more philosophical expression for John's "the Word was God," which itself is only another way of saying that Jesus is divine, Jesus is the Lord!

John continues, "All things came to be through him" (v. 3), an echo of the Proverbs passage quoted above. The Word, as God's firstborn, is matrix of all God's creative activity, especially in regard to human beings:

> What came to be through him was life,
>   and this life was the light of the human race (v. 4).

But John is also saying that the life that Jesus gives us is new life, a new creation under a new sun. Jesus himself is the real light of our lives. His life in us is a new creation, a new light that dispels our darkness, gives meaning to our lives and is not overcome by the evils symbolized here as "darkness" (v. 5).

Many scholars think that up to this point John may be quoting an early liturgical hymn into which he now introduces his own comment in verses 6-9 about John the Baptist, who testified "to the light" but was not himself "the true light [the Christ] . . . coming into the world" (v. 9). But that real light of which created light is but a shadow was not recognized by the very world made through him (v. 10). Though really a man among us, "his own people did not accept him" (v. 11).

Another interruption in the poem explains that to those few who did accept him "he gave power to become children of God" (v. 12), through faith "in his *name*," a name already interpreted in Matthew

1:21 to mean the one who "will save his people from their sins." These few have become children of God not by physical means, "nor by a man's decision but of God" (v. 13), by his gracious gift.

Verse 14 constitutes the heart of the poem, implicitly identifying the Word as Jesus:

> And the Word became flesh [a human being like us]
>> and made his dwelling [literally, "pitched his tent"] among us,
>
> and we saw his glory [after his resurrection],
> the glory as of the Father's only Son,
> full of grace and truth.

To the Jews, the word *flesh* referred to the whole person, soul as well as body. Here it emphasizes the fact that the Word really did become fully human, as earthly as we are. "The Word became flesh"! The heart of Christianity is its belief that its God is different from the gods of all other religions because, though infinitely above us, *he himself became a man*! Christianity reveals a God who is not only the Almighty One, the majestic Creator of all else that exists, but also a human being like us in all things except sin. Christian theology treats of a God who will forever be also a man, the very Son of God mediating before his Father for all other men and women and sharing his power of mediation with us so that we, as one body with him, may all mediate for one another as one great human family! John introduces us to an inconceivably loving God, who became one of us to lift us up into everlasting communion with himself!

The hymn ends here, according to the revised *NAB* version, but John adds some further reflections. He recalls the testimony of John the Baptist (v. 30) that the one (Jesus) who follows him in time precedes him in rank "because he [as the Word] existed before me" (v. 15). Moreover, from Jesus' fullness of grace (v. 16), "we have all received grace [of the new covenant of life in Jesus] in place of grace [the old covenant of law] . . . given through Moses" (v. 17). At last John names the Word as "Jesus Christ"! The Word of Wisdom is not merely a personification as in Proverbs; he is a real divine Person, the Word who became the real man Jesus.

The Prologue ends as it began, with a solemn declaration of faith in the divinity of Jesus: "The only Son, God, who is at the Father's side, has revealed him [the Father]" (v. 18). In seeing Jesus, we see God himself. Jesus is the complete revelation of God, for he is the only one who has "ever seen God"; indeed, he is "the only Son, God."

Although John's Prologue is only the reflective expression of the faith already implicit in the synoptics, it must have looked to many of its first readers like a daring new interpretation of the true significance of Jesus. Some probably thought that John's "Christology from above" (a modern designation to emphasize the belief that the Son of God descended from "on high" to become the Son of Man) really contradicted the synoptics' "Christology from below," which stressed the rising of the Son of Man to his place as Son of God at the right hand of the Father. But extant writings of early Christian leaders show that the gospel of John was generally accepted and quoted in the same fashion as were the synoptic gospels. John and the synoptics were seen by the early Christian church, not as contradictory views of Jesus, but as complementary.

Today, too, we need both. Since the early councils John's gospel has so dominated Christian theology as to give rise to the tendency to emphasize the divinity of Christ and allow his humanity to recede into the background. However, with the rise of modern biblical studies, especially since the 1940s, there has been a tendency on the part of some theologians to insist so exclusively on the synoptic view as to obscure Jesus' divine origin. It is the ancient mystery of the "hypostatic union" of the divine and the human nature in the Incarnation, the problem of how to hold in unified balance the divinity and the humanity of the one Person, Jesus Christ. We still need both John and the synoptics to complement each other.

The literary function of John's Prologue is to establish the perspective from which we are to read the rest of his gospel. Obviously John wants us to see the Jesus whose life he is about to present as both divine and human, yet utterly one. The Jesus who rose from the dead and ascended to his Father is the same Jesus who called his disciples and walked with them in Galilee and Judea. John can think of the earthly Jesus as already the glorified Christ because he is really the divine Person, "the Word," sharing the Father's glory.

REFLECTION AND PRAYER

Has John convinced me that Jesus is the only Son of God, really divine from eternity, become true man as Son of Mary?

Do I accept his testimony as fully as did the early Christians?

Jesus, my Lord, I believe that you are the Word become flesh!

Jesus Gives Signs of His Identity (Jn 1:19—12:50)

Many scholars agree with a twofold major division of John's gospel: John 1:19—12:50 is frequently called the Book of Signs, signs by which Jesus testifies to his identity as Son of God; chapters 13-21 are called the Book of Glory, glory foreshadowed at the Last Supper, even during Jesus' passion, and shining through the resurrection events.

As we read we will increasingly notice that John's basic theme is unity, the unity of the earthly Jesus with the glorified Christ, his unity with his heavenly Father, his unity with us through love, the loving unity with one another to which he calls us—the unity so powerfully epitomized in 1 John 4:16, "God is love." In his gospel John expresses this theme through the *signs* that Jesus works and the meaning that Jesus himself gives to these signs, and even more forcefully in the *anticipated glory* of Jesus' Last Supper, passion and death, and in the *achieved glory* of his resurrection. But first John will present the preparations for Jesus' public life.

Jesus Prepares for His Public Ministry (Jn 1:19-51)

Like the synoptics, the fourth gospel presents the ministry of John the Baptist as prelude to Jesus' own preparation for his public ministry. But unlike the synoptics, it gives no account of the origin or character of the Baptist. Obviously presupposing his readers' previous knowledge of the Baptist either from the synoptics or apostolic traditions, this gospel plunges into the Baptist's testimony concerning himself (vv. 19-27) with no more preparation than to tell us that he was "sent from God" (v. 6).

In verse 19 "*the Jews* from Jerusalem" are obviously the Jewish leaders who send a delegation to inquire into the Baptist's identity. We will find the fourth gospel consistently using "the Jews" in this sense, ordinarily with connotations of hostility, as in this passage. Scholars see in this usage a reflection of the antagonism between the Christians and the Jews at the time this gospel was written.

Much more explicitly than in the synoptics John's Baptist openly declares that he is not the Messiah, perhaps to counteract an early heresy that John the Baptist, not Jesus, was the real Messiah. Nor is he Elijah, nor "the Prophet" (v. 21), the "prophet like me" who Moses foretold would be raised up by the Lord "from among your own kinsmen" (Dt 18:15).

Further, instead of quoting Isaiah directly to characterize the Baptist, as do the synoptics, John emphasizes the central role of the Baptist by attributing to him the quotation adapted from Isaiah 40:3:

I am "*the voice* of one crying out in the desert,
'Make straight the way of the Lord' " (v. 23).

John agrees with Mark in quoting the Baptist as admitting that he baptizes only with water; but instead of completing the contrast with Jesus' baptism, John contrasts the dignity of the Baptist with that of Jesus, "whose sandal strap I am not worthy to untie" (v. 27). And instead of describing the baptism of Jesus, John reports the Baptist's testimony that Jesus is "the Lamb of God, who takes away the sin of the world" (v. 29), who comes "*after* me," yet "existed *before* me" (v. 30). With this reference to Jesus' pre-existing the Baptist, John lifts this passage from the ordinary time sequence of history into the realm of theology. The fourth gospel is functioning here, as in other places, as a theological interpretation of the synoptic gospels with which the canon unites it.

John is the only evangelist who attributes to the Baptist this characterization of Jesus as the Lamb of God, identifying him with Isaiah's suffering servant by echoing his passage about the "lamb led to the slaughter" (Is 53:7) who "gives his life for the sin of his people" (Is 53:10). This unique characterization of Jesus as the Lamb of God is frequently repeated in that other Johannine book, Revelation.

In John's gospel the Baptist is much more explicit about his mission than in the synoptics: "The reason why I came baptizing with water was that he [Jesus] might be made known to Israel" (v. 31). And unlike the synoptics, the fourth gospel presents a Baptist who admits not having recognized Jesus until he saw the Spirit descend from the sky like a dove to "remain upon him" (v. 32) and heard God testify that "he is the one who will baptize with the holy Spirit" (v. 33).

The episode ends with the Baptist's solemn statement: "Now I have seen and testified that he is *the Son of God*" (v. 34). This gospel will frequently use the words *testify* or *testimony* concerning the identity of Jesus as the Son of God.

And now, for the first time, John lets us see Jesus himself, introduced to the two followers of the Baptist as "the Lamb of God" (v. 36). Jesus' first words recorded by John formulate the simple question, "What are you looking for?" (v. 38). Yet what a significant start! Evidently, in our first encounter with Jesus in this gospel, John would have us see him challenging us to ponder what we, too, are looking for in life. John is telling us the only reason for reading his gospel should be to find Jesus.

To their question about where to find him, he goes right to the heart of the matter: "Come, and you will see" (v. 39), a clear invitation to follow him, to live with him. John's Jesus is a man of most attractive personality for anyone truly looking for something more in life!

Only one of these first two disciples is named, Andrew. We are left with the supposition that the unnamed disciple is the one testifying to the account, "the beloved disciple" who will be so referred to only much later (Jn 13:23). The few words of the Baptist's introduction and of Jesus' ensuing conversation are enough to convince Andrew that Jesus is the Messiah, for so he tells his brother Simon (v. 41). Jesus immediately lays personal claim to this Simon by renaming him *Kephas*, the Aramaic name translated into Greek by *Petros* (Peter) and into English by *Rock*.

John continues with Jesus' call of Philip, who then recruits Nathanael in words that incidentally show John's knowledge of traditions that name Nazareth as Jesus' hometown and Joseph as his father—obviously "legal father" to an evangelist who has already presented him as the Incarnate Word. Nathanael is not listed among the Twelve in the synoptics; perhaps he is the same as Bartholomew or the Matthias later chosen to take the place of Judas Iscariot (Acts 1:26). At any rate he doesn't seem to be one to believe easily, at least not in a man who hails from Nazareth (v. 46) only a few miles from his native Cana (Jn 21:2). His declaration of faith in Jesus as "the Son of God . . . the king of Israel" (v. 49) therefore suggests that Jesus' simple statement, "I saw you under the fig tree" (v. 48), must have more meaning for him than we can see in it.

The event closes with Jesus' prediction: "Amen, amen [an expression of special solemnity in John's gospel], I say to you, you will see the sky opened and the angels of God ascending and descending on the *Son of Man*" (v. 51). In this first use of *Son of Man*, John's Jesus significantly stresses the reality of his human nature in the context in which for his new disciples he opens the sky to the world of God himself, even as Yahweh had long ago opened the sky for Israel's vision (see Gn 28:12 on Jacob's ladder). As we shall increasingly discover, the title Son of Man is given in John a much different connotation from that in which we have ordinarily seen it used in the synoptics. Rather than connect it with Isaiah's suffering servant, John's Jesus already applies it to himself as the Lord of glory.

How different from the synoptics we are finding John's account, even in relatively important matters! How are we to deal with such great differences from the synoptics as we find in John's version of the Baptist's presentation of Jesus and his recruitment of his disciples?

First, we must note that the real divergence between the accounts is not in the essential faith about who Jesus is, but in the order and circumstances of events. Next, we must listen to what these differences really tell us about these gospels: the events are secondary. All the evangelists agree that Jesus was prepared for by the Baptist and that Jesus did recruit special followers who eventually believed in him as the Messiah. But when they disagree about whether Jesus recruited his disciples along the lake of Galilee or along the Jordan River, whether these men immediately believed in him as Messiah or only gradually came to such a belief, the evangelists are honestly admitting to a degree of uncertainty or even ignorance concerning the details of these matters. By canonizing all four gospels as the norm of Christian belief about Jesus, the early church clearly tells us that timing, order of events and even many of the circumstances of these events are secondary to their inner meaning.

It is of great importance for our biblical reading that we perceive that the writers are using these events, in whatever version each one offers, to convey that deeper meaning of who Jesus really was for them and should be for us. We can speculate—as scholars have been speculating since the gospels were written—about which account is more historically accurate. But we must not miss the point of the writers themselves, which was not primarily historical accuracy but the meaning of these events for our faith life.

REFLECTION AND PRAYER

My Jesus, I revere you as "the Lamb of God, who takes away the sin of the world." To your question, "What are you looking for?" I heartily respond: "Only for you, Son of God, my Lord!"

Jesus Begins His Ministry of Signs at Mary's Request
(Jn 2:1-11)

John tells us nothing about the early life of Jesus, yet he relates an incident that characterizes Jesus' mother as clearly as do those events of Jesus' infancy and boyhood told by Luke. At the wedding feast at Cana, probably lasting about a week in accordance with the Jewish custom of the time, Mary is not only an invited guest; she also seems to be helping behind the scene, for she discovers that the wine is giving out. Although she has never seen Jesus work a miracle (v. 11), she knows where to go for help. Instead of making a request, Mary simply states: "They have no wine" (v. 3).

At first Jesus' answer seems about as inconsiderate as that of a spoiled adolescent whose mother has asked him to provide refreshment for guests: "*Woman*, how does your concern affect me? My hour has not yet come" (v. 4). The reply seems less hostile if we know that the word *woman* was a dignified and courteous form of address among the Jews of this time. When we come to Jesus' second use of this address to Mary, as he hung upon the cross, we will look further into its significance. But Jesus still seems to be excusing himself from any responsibility—almost as though Mary had been accusing him of causing the shortage by bringing along so many thirsty friends. That mysterious sentence about his "hour" not yet coming also leaves us wondering. Later Jesus will again speak of his hour: "The hour has come for the Son of Man to be glorified" (Jn 12:23). At Cana, then, he is implying that the hour in which he begins the signs of his identity is an integral part of the hour of his glorious triumph over evil.

There is more to the story than literary analysis reveals. Either John is not telling the story very well or he is teasing us into wondering what kind of extraverbal communication is going on between mother and son. For, contrary to what John has led us to expect, Mary says to the waiters, "Do whatever he tells you" (v. 5), boldly confident that he is going to tell them something significant. John is telling his story in such a mysterious way as to arouse his reader to thought, evidently to the thought: "I, too, am being instructed by Mary to do whatever her Son tells me."

And he does tell them to do something; apparently he has seen in Mary's word to the waiters the signal that his hour for revealing himself publicly has come. He tells them to fill the jars with water. But how will water help the situation? Isn't that the way it is in our lives, too? How will the little things that the Lord tells us to do contribute to such a disproportionate result as eternal salvation? Although the waiters don't understand what is going on, they obey Jesus' strange order, and then that even stranger command, "Draw some [water] out [of the jars] now and take it to the headwaiter" (v. 8). Do they think that Jesus is mad or engaging in some farce? In spite of their doubts, they obey.

To their amazement the headwaiter calls it wine, the very best wine, and what an abundance! John leaves the rest of the story to our imagination, telling us only that this was the way Jesus began his *signs*, thus revealing his glory—''and his disciples began to believe in him'' (v. 11). It is significant that John sees this event as a *sign* rather than as a miracle; evidently he considers the real value of Jesus' astonishing deed to consist in its function as a sign of his true identity.

Notice that John's Jesus first reveals his glorious power in celebration of marriage. Jesus' presence at this marriage, and especially his evident blessing of the marriage by the first of his signs, gave form to Christian celebration of marriage as a religious rite eventually included within the sacramental system of liturgical signs of Jesus' living contact with his people. Christian marriage has therefore been distinguished from other forms of marriage by reason of this special blessing of Christ, a blessing that extends beyond the ceremony to guarantee his continued presence in the loving relationship of the married couple, gracing their daily services to one another. By combining Matthew's, ''Where two or three are gathered in my name, there am I in the midst of them'' (Mt 18:20) and ''As often as you did it for one of my least brothers, you did it for me'' (Mt 25:40), with John's Cana story, the early church found her theology of marriage, which was perhaps best epitomized by Paul: ''This [Christian marriage] is a great mystery, but I speak in reference to [the union of] Christ and the church'' (Eph 5:32). In their love for one another, spouses love Jesus Christ and provide for others an image of his love for his church.

It is also significant that this first miracle of changing water into wine foreshadows the sacrament Jesus will institute by changing wine into his own blood; this Cana miracle becomes a sign of the divine power capable of instituting such a sacrament. Because of this association of marriage and the Eucharist in John's gospel, many Christians deem it most suitable to celebrate marriage within the eucharistic sacrifice.

Appropriately, it is Jesus' mother, Mary, who calls upon him to bless family life by giving him the signal for which he has apparently been waiting to perform his first sign. John is evidently saying that, more than any other human being, Mary is the one who brings Jesus to us.

And so at Mary's signal Jesus goes public! He starts, says John, in Cana of Galilee, then goes on to Capernaum ''along with his mother and brothers''—the synoptics also tell of Mary and ''his brothers'' coming to see him in Capernaum, but under much different circumstances. Then John adds, "but they stayed there only a few days" (v. 12). According to the fourth gospel the opening Galilean ministry was very brief; it was rather in Judea, especially in Jerusalem, that the major part of Jesus' public ministry took place. Here then, is another seemingly major discrepancy between John and the synoptics. Yet, it does not affect the major thrust of all the gospels: Jesus is Lord wherever he works.

REFLECTION AND PRAYER

Mary, there are times when I have no wine, when I need Jesus to bring meaning into my life. I listen to your motherly bidding, "Do whatever he tells you." Lord Jesus, thank you for the beautiful sacraments by which you bless marital union and unite yourself to us.

Jesus Promises to Supplant the Temple (Jn 2:12-25)

"Since the Passover of the Jews was near, Jesus went up to Jerusalem" (v. 13). This is the first of three Passovers that John mentions during Jesus ministry (Jn 6:4, 13:1), in contrast to the synoptics' mention of only one. It is to John alone that we owe our knowledge that Jesus' ministry lasted about three years.

No sooner has this been said than we must note another discrepancy between John and the synoptics, this one apparently in favor of the historicity of the synoptics. John relates the cleansing of the Temple as taking place at the beginning of Jesus' public ministry. The synoptics put it at the end, where it does seem more probable as one of Jesus' final clashes with the Jewish leaders over authority. Perhaps John places it at the beginning of Jesus' public ministry as a sign that the whole of that ministry is oriented toward replacing the Temple with his body the church, and the animal sacrifices with his own sacrifice; he will fulfill the Old Testament Passover promise with the New Testament feast of resurrection.

All the gospels stress the zeal of Jesus for the purity of Temple worship. But only John relates that Jesus "made a whip out of cords and drove them all [the sellers and moneychangers] out of the Temple area, *with the sheep and oxen*" (v. 15). Isn't John telling us that Jesus is proclaiming the end of a Temple worship that consists in sacrificing animals? What a picture of Jesus' fury! He does not hesitate to use strong action to stop people from "making my Father's house a marketplace" (v. 16), action so vigorous that it reminds his disciples of a

266

line in a psalm they must have often prayed, "Zeal for your house will consume me" (Ps 69:10).

His authority questioned, Jesus speaks mysteriously of his own death and resurrection: "Destroy this temple and in three days I will raise it up" (v. 19). John comments that Jesus "was speaking about the temple of his body" (v. 21), referring this prediction to his bodily resurrection as a motive of faith in "the scripture and the word Jesus had spoken" (v. 22). In the context of Jesus' driving out the animals, John also seems to be suggesting that Jesus will replace the Temple with his body the church as the locus of true worship of God. John thereby ties this incident to the preceding one at Cana. Just as at Cana Jesus foreshadowed the sacramental change of wine into his own blood, now at the Temple cleansing he symbolizes the change from old covenant Temple sacrifices to new covenant eucharistic sacrifice of his own body and blood. Doesn't such powerful insight justify John's tampering with chronology to juxtapose these symbolic events?

John also sees this incident as a sign of Jesus' power; he remarks that "many began to believe in his name, when they saw the signs he was doing" (v. 23), suggesting that Jesus offered many other signs, too numerous to relate. Then follows that penetrating insight into the mind of Jesus, who "knew them all, and did not need anyone to testify about human nature. He himself understood it well" (vv. 24-25).

REFLECTION AND PRAYER

Do I believe that participation in Jesus' eucharistic sacrifice is the greatest worship that I can offer to the Father?

Dear Lord, let me share in your zeal for our Father's house and for the temple of your body, of which I am privileged to be a member.

Jesus Tells Nicodemus the Importance of Baptism (Jn 3)

Chapter 3 begins with Jesus' private conversation with Nicodemus about another Christian sacrament: baptism. That this "ruler of the Jews" (v. 1), in the sense of member of the Sanhedrin, comes to Jesus at night clearly indicates the hostile view of Jesus already taken by the Jewish leaders. Only John mentions Nicodemus and relates this conversation, which Nicodemus opens by praising Jesus as a true teacher "come from God" (v. 2).

Jesus declares that "no one can see the kingdom of God without being born from above" (v. 3), a mysterious expression that will lead the conversation into baptism. Nicodemus takes him literally, asking how a man can be born again. Jesus, the great teacher, has prepared his pupil psychologically for his instruction on the need of being "born of water and Spirit" (v. 5), whose freedom of action he likens to the wind that "blows where it wills" (v. 8).

Again Nicodemus wants to know *how this happens*. As Jesus responds, we suddenly sense that there is more here than a simple conversation between two men:

> "Amen, amen, I say to you, *we* [the solemn or royal plural that Jesus never uses elsewhere?] speak of what *we* know and *we* testify to what *we* have seen, but *you people* do not accept *our* testimony" (vv. 10-11).

Doesn't it sound here as though the community of John is speaking to a neighboring community of Jews? Scholars point to this passage as evidence that this gospel was probably composed by John's school, and that his community had special difficulties with a nearby Jewish community that had excommunicated these Christians from the synagogue for continuing to speak about the need to be "born of water and Spirit."

Indeed, verse 13 refers to the ascension as having occurred by the time of this conversation: "No one *has gone* up to heaven except the one who came down from heaven, the Son of Man." This sentence is a strong clue that Jesus did not actually speak these words and that John's school has composed this part, perhaps the whole conversation, for dramatic effect. What better way to write a catechism for their community than to compose it in the form of questions proposed by a sincere inquirer (who may really have been a Jewish leader) and answers from the lips of the greatest teacher of all—Jesus? There is certainly plenty of evidence throughout the New Testament that Jesus must have spoken to his disciples in terms similar to these about baptism of water and the Spirit. To give this instruction a striking literary form would not have bothered John or the other evangelists in the least, so why should it bother us?

The instruction continues with another reference to a future event, the crucifixion, which would seem a very unlikely prophecy for Jesus to make in this private conversation, but which fits very well into post-resurrection catechesis. Moses' act of lifting up the bronze serpent upon a pole saved repentant Israelites from dying of snakebite (Nm 21:6-9); Jesus' submission to being "lifted up" (v. 14) on the cross will save for "*eternal* life" (v. 15) *all* who believe in him.

Then follows one of those golden sentences, the fruit of John's long years of inspired meditation on what he had heard and seen of Jesus: "God so loved the world that he gave his only Son, so that everyone who believes in him might not perish but might have eternal life" (v. 16). This single sentence captures the very essence of the good news, the gospel revelation: The one God is not a vengeful God like the gods of the Gentile pagans, or even the primarily just God of most of the Jewish leaders of Jesus' time. Most of Nicodemus' brother Pharisees so insist upon faithfulness to the Mosaic law and to their own expansion of it in multiple observances that they have lost sight of the loving mercy of God, highlighted by many prophets.

The God that John's Jesus here reveals so clearly is above all the God who loves! He loves this whole world of his own creation and each of the men and women with whom he has populated it. He loves Nicodemus so much that he has sent his only Son to talk to him personally—as he will do for any of us! This God reveals his love not only in the words of his Son Jesus but even in his very person as his *only Son*. In fact, his love is so great that he "gave" his only Son up to death for the dying world, not to condemn it, "but that the world might be saved through him" (v. 17), saved not just in this temporal life, but for *"eternal life"* (v. 16). The present life that we call "real" is but a shadow of eternal life. And, just as we found in the synoptics, this salvation is appropriated by faith: "Whoever believes in him will not be condemned" (v. 18).

Jesus closes the conversation with a contrast that this gospel will play upon repeatedly, the contrast between the *darkness* of evil—especially the evil of refusing to believe in Jesus—and the *light* of truth. "Whoever lives the truth comes to the light, so that his works may be clearly seen as done in God" (v. 21). A conversation that ostensibly began as a discussion of baptism has developed into a theology of salvation.

Having spoken of the vital importance of baptism, Jesus now spends "some time with them [his disciples] *baptizing*" (v. 22). But, as we find out in the next chapter (Jn 4:2), Jesus himself did not baptize; rather, he had his disciples baptize new followers. This passage is significant witness to the importance that the first Christians placed upon this sacrament of initiation into the Christian community. It also suggests that Jesus gave his disciples the authority to make new disciples even before his resurrection.

Nearby John the Baptist is still engaged in his ministry (v. 23). His disciples, aroused by news of Jesus' superior following (v. 26), jealously complain. Again the Baptizer flatly denies any claim to be the Messiah, defining his mission as that of precursor, "sent before him" (v. 28). Only the Messiah is Israel's groom (remember, the prophets had spoken of Yahweh in this symbolism!), and the Baptist is his "best man" (v. 29), joyful at the wedding (Jesus' entry upon his public ministry), for "he must increase; I must decrease" (v. 30). Here we glimpse the true greatness of the Baptist in his humble acceptance of his inferior role.

The final passage of this chapter, verses 31-36, could be the comment of either the evangelist or the Baptist. Since scholars are divided on this point and ancient writers used no quotation marks, translators and commentators must use their own best judgment. Notice again the emphasis on the importance of testimony and the point that only "the one whom God sent speaks the words of God" (v. 34). Moreover, Jesus speaks with *full* authority, for God "does not *ration* his gift of the Spirit." The passage ends with a powerful repetition of the Johannine theology of salvation: "Whoever believes in the Son has eternal life" (v. 36).

REFLECTION AND PRAYER

Do I cherish my own baptism as birth in the Spirit of freedom?

Do I cherish it as a gift of Jesus?

Lord Jesus, give me also the gift of living a life of light so that my works may be clearly seen as done in God. And, as you did for the Baptist, increase your life in me, even though it means that my life for myself must decrease.

Jesus Reveals His Identity to a Samaritan Woman (Jn 4:1-42)

John implies that Jesus now leaves Judea to avoid any further confrontation with the Pharisees (vv. 1-3). On his way back to Galilee he passes through Samaria. The Samaritan woman at Jacob's well is doubly shocked that Jesus should ask her for a drink: first, because Jews considered Samaritans unclean, not to be dealt with under pain of becoming unclean themselves; second, because men of the time considered it beneath their dignity to ask a favor of a woman.

Jesus' reply further baffles her, especially that expression "living water" (v. 10). Her question indicates that she thinks he is speaking of flowing water. To provide such water would indeed show him to be greater than Jacob, to whom was attributed the origin of the well at Sychar.

Jesus makes it clear that what she thinks of as real water is only a symbol of his "living water," the water that John's readers will associate with baptism, continuing and deepening the theme struck in the previous chapter. This living water creates a new spiritual reality within the recipient—eternal life, a new quality of life wholly satisfying (v. 14). *Eternal life* is becoming one of the major themes of this gospel.

The woman does not understand the figurative language, but she expresses a desire for this living water. So Jesus leads her toward repentant reform by revealing that he knows how immoral her life has been and still is. At last he has struck the personal note that calls forth from her secret suffering an answering chord as she confesses her guilt (v. 18).

Convinced that he is a prophet, she asks about the true place to worship God. This is all the opening that Jesus needs to instruct her (and John's readers): The old religions, both the authentic Jewish religion centered in Jerusalem and the deviate Samaritan variety at Mount Gerizim, are giving way to the new worship of "the Father in Spirit and truth" (v. 23).

When the woman exclaims that the Messiah will clear up all these squabbles about which is the true religion, Jesus replies, "I am he, the one who is speaking with you" (v. 26)! By synoptic standards this is a most uncharacteristic thing for Jesus to say to anybody, especially to a Samaritan woman in a private conversation! It is becoming more and more evident that the author of this gospel has arranged the events and at least parts of the conversations in such a way as to advance gradually the development of his major themes concerning salvation and how it is granted through the new life ("living water") given us by Jesus, the Messiah and Son of God.

As in the conversation with Nicodemus, Jesus is again the great teacher who knows how to disclose just enough of his mysterious message to provoke the curiosity of the inquirer into questions that lead on toward an ever deeper level of spiritual understanding. Whether such a conversation really took place or the evangelist composed it as a dramatized catechetical lesson is secondary. That such a conversation *could* have taken place would seem to be justification enough for the writer to report it as he has. He is clearly telling us: This is the kind of person Jesus is; these are the things he said, whether more implicitly than reported here, or just as explicitly.

On their return the disciples do not question Jesus, an indication of their deep trust and reverence. Meanwhile the woman becomes a witness for Jesus, testifying to her people that he is the Messiah (v. 29). When the disciples urge Jesus to eat, his reply reveals that he has a food greater than any that they can imagine: "My food is to do the will of the one who sent me and to finish his work [of salvation]" (v. 34). The real harvest is out there waiting—all those people waiting to find God. Jesus has sown the seed; his disciples must reap the harvest (vv. 35-38). And certainly John is thinking not only of Jesus' immediate disciples as the reapers, but also of his own Christian community and of us later Christians. He wants action! He wants it because he knows that Jesus wants action, not passivity.

Luke 9:51-56 gave us the impression that Jesus was completely unwelcome in Samaria. But John tells us he felt so well-received that he stayed there for two days (v. 40), and "many more began to believe in him because of his word" (v. 41). By now we are quite accustomed to such discrepancies. But this difference between the two gospels might not be a discrepancy at all; it is certainly possible that Jesus' initial effort in Samaria met with disdain, but that a later effort was successful.

REFLECTION AND PRAYER

Has John convinced me that Jesus is easily approached, that it is really he who approaches each of us?

My Jesus, let me speak to you as freely and confidently as did the Samaritan woman. Speak to my heart as you did to hers. Give me living water.

Jesus Works Two Cures as Further Signs (Jn 4:43—5:15)

Returning to Galilee, Jesus heads for Cana, perhaps to visit the newlyweds he recently blessed. A "royal official" from Capernaum (v. 46), probably the centurion of Matthew (Mt 8:5-13) or Luke (Lk 7:1-10), asks Jesus to cure his dying son. When the man passes Jesus' test, showing by his love for his son that he is not merely seeking a sign of Jesus' power, Jesus cures the boy, as the trusting official is told on his way home. John points out that "this was the *second sign* Jesus did" (v. 54), the second sign in Cana of his power.

In chapter 5 Jesus is again back in Jerusalem for a feast. He visits the pool called "Bethesda" (v. 2), a pool with "five porticoes." Archaeologists have uncovered a pool near the Temple site surrounded by four porticoes with a fifth crossing the center of the pool, dividing it in half. Here is one of the apparently obscure passages that have led modern scholars to believe that John was better acquainted with the details of the Jerusalem of Jesus' time than were the other evangelists.

Compassionately, Jesus picks out a man who has been ill for 38 years, apparently hoping all that time to be first into the pool after it is stirred, perhaps by an intermittent spring popularly interpreted as an angelic visitation. Touched by the man's plight, Jesus cures him and tells him to take up his mat, even though it is the sabbath. This time the Jews object not only to curing on the sabbath (v. 16) but also to the work of carrying the mat (v. 10). Again avoiding direct confrontation Jesus "slipped away" (v. 13). But he makes it a point to find the cured man and warn him, "Do not sin any more, so that nothing worse may happen to you" (v. 14).

John ends this account with the remark that the man "informed the Jews that Jesus was the one who had made him well" (v. 15), thus setting up the controversy that follows.

REFLECTION AND PRAYER

Dear Lord, I believe that you cured many people of all kinds of ills. I, too, have weaknesses—physical, mental, spiritual. Cure me, too, my Lord. Cure especially my petty prejudices.

First Controversy: Jesus Is the Son of God (Jn 5:16-47)

Why did the Jewish leaders turn against their greatest teacher? According to John, it was because he opposed their interpretation of the Mosaic law, especially concerning the sabbath observance (v. 16). But even more, he "called God his own father, *making himself equal to God*" (v. 18). Jesus has declared: "My Father is at work until now, so I am at work" (v. 17). The sabbath rest was based on God's rest after the six days of creation. But does God really rest if he continues to hold the world in existence by his Providence? And if God gives life during his long sabbath, is not his own Son justified in giving it as well through such cures as that of the man at the pool? Thus the real issue has become Jesus' identity.

In his answer to the Jews, therefore, Jesus likens himself to "a son [who] cannot do anything on his own, but only what he sees his father doing" (v. 19). In this context, Jesus declares that even as his Father raises from the dead and gives life, so does the Son give eternal life (v.

21). He is also pointing ahead to his climactic signs, his raising of Lazarus and his own rising from the dead. He declares that the Father has given the power of judgment to him as Son, so that he deserves equal honor with his Father (vv. 22-23). Hence, judgment will be based on belief in the identity of Jesus as Son of the Father: "Whoever hears my word and believes in the one who sent me has eternal life" (v. 24). In fact, those who are spiritually dead are already being brought to life in Jesus by hearing his word (v. 25), for he is Life itself (v. 26). Verse 25 may also refer to those who have physically died; they too "will hear the voice of the Son of God, and those who hear will live" (v. 25).

Verse 26 constitutes one of the most profound statements in John's gospel: "Just as the Father has life in himself, so also *he gave to his Son the possession of life in himself*" (v. 26). This sentence defies analysis. It is obviously contradictory to say that the Father *gives* the Son *life in himself*. In attributing these words to Jesus, John must know that "life in himself" can only mean that life of God that is given by no one, the divine life that he possesses of himself, always. How then can the Son have *life of himself* if he has been *given* it by the Father? John is trying to make human language do what it cannot do— express the infinite—and of course his human language breaks down in the attempt, as must all theological language that tries to express divine mystery. Yet even in his failed logic John has sent our minds soaring into a new realm of insight. He is saying that by generation the Son derives his life from the Father and that, nevertheless, this divinely generated life is the very life of God, the very being of God, absolute equality with the Father.

Insight follows upon insight: "He [the Father] gave him [the Son] power to exercise judgment, because he is *Son of Man*" (v. 27). Here is the second part of Jesus' claim to be the true and only mediator between God and humanity. As Son of God he not only represents God, he *is* God; as Son of Man he not only represents humanity, he *is* a human. Hence he alone can truly unite God and humankind. He alone can truly judge the living and dead (vv. 28-29), being himself a human being, yet also God. Nor will his judgment be arbitrary; it will accord with "the will of the one who sent me" (v. 30).

Jesus bases the truth of these astounding statements not only on his own testimony, but also on that of others, following the Jewish tradition. Just as two witnesses were required for an important judgment (Dt 17:6), Jesus now offers two witnesses for the truth of what he says: John the Baptist (vv. 33-35) and his Father, in "the works that the Father gave me to accomplish" (v. 36) and in the Father's voice in the scriptures that also "testify on my behalf" (v. 39).

Jesus declares that the Jews do not accept him because they do not really love God (v. 42). Their accuser before God will be the man in whom they have placed their hope, Moses, "because he wrote about me" (v. 46).

How different is this long discourse from others like the Sermon on the Mount! Can we imagine the Jesus of the synoptics speaking so directly of his own identity? Who was right about the way Jesus spoke, the synoptics or John? The early Christians thought they were both right, accepting both as authentic expressions of what they believed about Jesus. The synoptics were right historically: Jesus did keep his identity a secret during his public life; his revelation of his true identity was a gradual process. But John was also right; he was theologically right. If Jesus really is the divine human being described in this discourse, he could have said these things. This was justification, by historical and literary standards of the first century, for attributing such a discourse to Jesus himself.

REFLECTION AND PRAYER

My Jesus, I believe that you are truly the Son of God, that he has given you his own life and power from all eternity, that you came to do his will in continuing his work of creation and salvation, and that he has given you all judgment. O Son of Man, have mercy on me! I adore you as the only Son of God!

Second Controversy: Jesus Is "the Bread of Life" (Jn 6)

The scene now shifts back to a mountain in Galilee. In preparation for Jesus' next great controversy John gives his version of the multiplication of loaves, significantly introducing this new sign of Jesus' identity by remarking that the "feast of Passover was near" (v. 4). Jesus' action of taking the loaves and giving thanks foreshadows the Eucharist, which he will administer to his disciples on the following Passover feast.

Many of the details in this account suggest that John knew at least one of the synoptic gospels. His account agrees with Mark's first miracle of the loaves (Mk 6:35-44) in all the numbers: Two hundred days' wages would hardly buy sufficient food; only five loaves and two fish arc available; 5,000 men are fed; the generous miracle provides 12 baskets of leftovers. But the aftermath of the miracle is much different in John; since the people want "to make him king, he withdrew again to the mountain alone" (v. 15).

Though the next sign of Jesus' identity differs from the synoptics in some details, it agrees basically with Mark 6:45- 51: Jesus walks on the water to rescue his disciples in the boat.

Next day the crowd, not finding Jesus, crosses to Capernaum looking for him (vv. 22-24). The question about when Jesus arrived is evidently prompted by the recollection that he did not leave the place of the miracle of the loaves with the disciples (v. 22). He knows the people are looking for him, not because they have seen signs of who he really is, but because they want more free meals (v. 26).

Accepting them as they are—still on the physical level—he endeavors to bring them toward a more spiritual aspiration. He speaks to them of working for "the food that endures for eternal life" (v. 27). They understand enough of what he says to ask how they can perform "the works of God" (v. 28) that will win "food that endures for eternal life" (v. 27). His answer repeats the theological point of the preceding chapter: The only work required is that they "believe in the one [Jesus] he [God] sent" (v. 29).

This brings them to their demand for another sign of his being sent by God. They remind him of one of the signs of Moses' mission from God, the gift of the manna in the desert, the "bread from heaven" (v. 31), obviously challenging Jesus to go one better, another handout.

He assures them that it is God, not Moses, who gives "the true bread . . . which comes down from heaven [Jesus himself] and gives life to the world" (vv. 32-33). The manna that they think is real bread from heaven is only a shadow of this "bread of God."

Still thinking that Jesus is referring to the bread that he gave them the day before, they ask that he give them this bread always. They want earthly bread forever instead of eternal life with God.

Weak as their understanding is, Jesus takes advantage of their reference to manna and their desire for a lasting bread to reveal more completely his true identity: "*I am the bread of life*" (v. 35). He tells them plainly he has come down from heaven to do his Father's will (v. 38), to save all whom the Father has given him (v. 39)—all who believe in him as God's own Son (v. 40). The reference in verse 38 to the Father's will relates this passage to that other in which Jesus spoke of the doing of the Father's will as the food that sustains him (Jn 4:32-35).

Just as Jesus' food is to do his Father's will, so those who fulfill the Father's will by believing in Jesus as the Son find him to be the food of eternal life.

The Jews have finally understood his claim to have *come down from heaven* as a statement of divine origin. Thinking that they know his human parents, they scornfully reject this claim (v. 42).

Undeterred, Jesus repeats his claim in stronger language: "No one can come to me unless the Father who sent me draw him" (v. 44). In verse 45 Jesus freely quotes Isaiah 54:13: "They shall all be taught by God." And what is God now teaching them? By showing the sign of his approval of Jesus in the multiplication of loaves, the Father is teaching them to come to Jesus as the bread of eternal life (vv. 47-48).

Up to this point, Jesus' references to himself as "the bread of life" could be understood as purely figurative: Just as bread sustains our earthly life, so Jesus imparts eternal life to those who believe in him. But as he speaks figuratively of himself as "the living bread that came down from heaven" (v. 51), he suddenly adds a new literal meaning: "The bread that I will give is *my flesh*, for the life of the world."

The Jews can see no more than a cannibalistic reference in "his flesh to eat" (v. 52).

Nevertheless, Jesus plunges on:

"Amen, amen, I say to you, unless you eat the flesh of the Son of Man and drink his blood, you do not have life within you. Whoever eats my flesh and drinks my blood has eternal life, and I will raise him on the last day. For my flesh is true food, and my blood is true drink. Whoever eats my flesh and drinks my blood remains in me, and I in him. Just as the living Father sent me and I have life because of the Father, so also the one who feeds on me will have life because of me" (vv. 53-57).

This last sentence, in simple, straightforward language, powerfully links the inner meaning of the Incarnation with that of the Eucharist: As the Father is the source of Jesus' divine life, so Jesus, in what was later called the sacrament of the Eucharist, is the source of our eternal life of sharing in the divine life already given to us during our mortal life. Just as the Word-become-flesh finds the food of his life in doing the will of his Father by revealing him to us, so does he give us his own flesh to be the food that nourishes our life of eternal union with him and the Father.

Evidently the crowd does not accept these words of Jesus in the synagogue at Capernaum; even many of his disciples, apparently in a subsequent meeting, murmur in protest (vv. 60-61).

Instead of assuring them that he does not mean to be understood as speaking literally, Jesus appeals to his coming ascension into heaven (v. 62) as proof that he really has come down from heaven with the message he has just given them, a message that they will grasp only through the inspiration of the Holy Spirit (v. 63). It is again evident that John is addressing post-resurrection Christians with a dramatized theology of the Eucharist and its necessity for salvation. No one can approach Jesus with faith "unless it is granted him" by the Father (v. 65).

Although many now leave him, refusing to believe in the truths presented in the above discourse, Jesus will not change his message. For the integrity of that word, he is even ready to lose the Twelve: "Do you also want to leave?" (v. 67). Peter speaks up for the first time in this gospel: "You have the words of eternal life. . . . We have come to believe and are convinced that you are the Holy One of God" (v. 69). Jesus, the Word, speaks words of eternal life! This staunch confession of faith in Jesus is John's equivalent of the synoptic passages in which Peter answers Jesus' question: "Who do you say that I am?" (Mk 8:29). But counter to this confession runs the undercurrent of rejection: "Yet is not one of you a devil?" (v. 71). John insists that Jesus reads people's hearts, and one of his own is already breaking his heart!

Let us sit back for a moment to appreciate the depth of this remarkable chapter. It testifies to the faith of the early Christians that this Jesus, who has received the very life of God, gives a share of his eternal life to those entrusted to him by the Father, both by his word and by the sacrament of his flesh and blood. It organically connects the truths later defined as the doctrines of the Incarnation, sacramental communion and salvation by demonstrating in simple language their intimate relationship with one another.

How did early Christians understand this passage about flesh and blood—literally or figuratively? Did they think that when they received the bread of life it was the very flesh and blood of Jesus or simply a community ceremony to remember together that the Word had become flesh and lived among us for a time? Verses 54-58, reinforced by verses 62-64 could be taken as figurative only by imposing an interpretation obviously foreign to the intention of the author. Christian tradition, from as far back as it can be traced, held firmly to the literal interpretation until the sixteenth century when some of the Protestant leaders broke with it in favor of a figurative interpretation more or less equivalent to saying: "This bread symbolizes my body."

In the present passage John is reflecting upon the event that Paul, the first to report Jesus' words at the Last Supper, had already reported long before him:

> The Lord Jesus, on the night he was handed over, took bread, and, after he had given thanks, broke it and said: "This is my body that is for you. . . . This cup is the new covenant in my blood. Do this, as often as you drink it, in remembrance of me" (1 Cor 11:23-25).

That Paul took these words literally is obvious by what he immediately adds as his own reflection:

> For as often as you eat this bread and drink the cup, you proclaim the death of the Lord until he comes. Therefore whoever eats the bread or drinks the cup of the Lord unworthily will have to answer for *the body and blood of the Lord.* . . . For anyone who eats and drinks *without discerning the body, eats and drinks judgment on himself* (vv. 26-29).

Both Paul and John manifest the same early faith that Jesus truly gives his own flesh and blood as the food of the Christian who receives the bread of eternal life. The eating and drinking are physical actions that are real, yet also symbolize the spiritual nourishing of the Christian's life in Jesus. In chapter 6 John has made it crystal clear that he considers the Eucharist to be the true encounter of later Christians with the living, resurrected Jesus, as real as that enjoyed by the disciples who walked with him.

REFLECTION AND PRAYER

Lord Jesus, I believe that you are the bread of life, the bread of my life! I cannot live without you.

Third Controversy: Jesus Is "the Living Water" (Jn 7:1—8:11)

Chapter 7 begins with a preparation for renewed controversy. Jesus stays in Galilee "because the Jews were trying to kill him" (v. 1). His "brothers" advise him to go to Judea for the autumn feast of Tabernacles (booths or tents) commemorating the Exodus, but they really don't believe in him (v. 5), though John is not so emphatic on this point as Mark 3:21. Jesus' mysterious answer introduces a new gospel meaning of the word *world* (v. 7), which we will see with increasing frequency in John. In Jn 3:16 *world* had a positive meaning: "God so loved the world. . . ." But now it has taken on a sinister meaning: The world cannot hate Jesus' worldly minded relatives, but it does hate Jesus because "I testify to it that its works are evil" (v. 7).

Although he delays, Jesus finally goes up to Jerusalem secretly (v. 10). The crowd is sharply divided as to whether he is a troublemaker or "a good man" (v. 12). Against this background Jesus enters the Temple. As in the synoptics, the crowd is amazed at his powerful teaching.

An action-packed controversy begins, moving at a breathless pace. Jesus declares that anyone can know that his teaching is from God, anyone who chooses God's will (v. 17). Those who fail to see that Jesus seeks not his own glory but God's break the law of Moses by seeking to kill him (vv. 18-19).

The Jews consider him mad ("possessed") for saying that they want to kill him. Jesus refreshes their memories about the violent reaction he stirred up by curing the man at the pool on a sabbath (Jn 5:18). If they can circumcise on the sabbath in fulfillment of the Mosaic law, why do they oppose him "for curing a whole person on the sabbath" (v. 23)?

They take pause, but end by rejecting him because they think they know his parentage. Jesus repeats his claim to be sent by the One who "is true" (v. 28).

They try to seize him but fail "because his hour [of sacrifice] had not yet come" (v. 30). The crowd wavers, but some believe in him. So the Pharisees send the Temple guard into action. Jesus stays them with the promise that he will bother them "only a little while longer" (v. 33). But where he will go they cannot follow.

They mull over his words, wondering if he means to go "to the dispersion" (v. 35) to visit the Greek-speaking Jews and Gentiles outside Palestine.

Apparently this is a running controversy that goes on for days, for "on the last and greatest day of the feast" (v. 37) Jesus cries out in grand climax to the controversy:

> "Let anyone who thirsts come to me and drink. Whoever believes in me, as scripture says:
> 'Rivers of *living water* will flow from within him' "
> (vv. 37-38).

Jesus offered to give the Samaritan woman "living water" that would become in her "a spring of water welling up to eternal life" (Jn

4:14). Now he declares himself to be the source of this living water, symbolized by the harvest-giving rain water poured on the Temple altar during the harvest feast of Tabernacles that they are presently celebrating (Jn 7:2).

The source of the Old Testament quotation in verse 38 is uncertain. The life-sustaining quality of water became a strong theme from the time of the Exodus when, through Moses, God gave his people water from the rock (Ex 17:6; Nm 20:11). Isaiah 12:3 therefore speaks of the Lord as "the fountain of salvation" and Jeremiah 17:13 as "the source of living waters" (Jer 17:13).

In the context of Jesus' climactic statement his reference to his cure of the paralytic by the pool (v. 21) suggests that he is the life-giving water replacing the curative waters of the pool. And the theme that Jesus replaces the Temple, developed in John's version of the cleansing of the Temple (Jn 2:19-22) and in the conversation with the Samaritan woman (Jn 4:22-26), points strongly to a passage in Ezekiel:

> I saw water flowing out from beneath the threshold of the Temple toward the east [a stream that grew into a mighty river]. . . . Wherever the river flows, every sort of living creature that can multiply shall live. . . . Fishermen shall be standing along it . . . spreading their nets. . . . Along both banks of the river, fruit trees of every kind shall grow; their leaves shall not fade, nor their fruit fail (Ez 47:1-12).

In John's gospel living water has become a prominent theme to express the abundance of life that Jesus offers to those who believe in him. The evangelist himself further interprets Jesus' climactic declaration as a prediction that the Holy Spirit will be the living water poured out upon Jesus' followers after his glorification (v. 39). The gift of the Spirit is promised to anyone who truly seeks Jesus!

Again the people are divided over Jesus' identity. Their discussion of his human origin indicates the emphasis that was given to the prophecies concerning the Messiah's Davidic lineage. The Temple guards are so impressed by Jesus' discourse that they fail to apprehend him. But among the chief priests and Pharisees only Nicodemus defends Jesus' right to a hearing before they condemn him (v. 51).

Chapter 8 begins with a short episode that seems to have been inserted some time after this gospel was completed. It might fit better in Luke's gospel of forgiveness. At any rate, it certainly gives us a beautiful picture of Jesus that fits well into any of the gospels.

As Jesus is teaching in the Temple the scribes (this is the only mention of them in John) and Pharisees bring to him a woman "caught in adultery" (v. 3). They pretend to let Jesus be the judge as to whether she should be stoned in accordance with the law of Moses. If he tells them to stone her, he appears heartless before the crowd; if he tells them not to, they can find him guilty of opposing the law held sacred by every Jew (Dt 22:22-24).

Instead of entering into controversy, Jesus merely writes in the sand with his finger. As they insist on a judgment, he gives a surprising one: "Let the one among you who is without sin be the first to throw a stone at her" (v. 7). Then they seem to perceive what he is writing, apparently their names, in accord with a passage from Jeremiah: "Those who turn away from thee shall be *written in the earth*, for they have forsaken the Lord, the *fountain of living water*" (Jer 17:13, *RSV*). Now we see why this passage was added here after Jesus' declaration: "Let anyone who thirsts come to me and drink" (Jn 7:37). The woman's accusers fade away, "beginning with the elders" (v. 9).

Alone with the accused, Jesus is tender yet firm: "Neither do I condemn you. . . . From now on do not sin any more" (v. 11).

Much different from the rest of John, this passage is a short, self-contained episode, so typical of the synoptics that such incidents practically identify the "gospel genre" as a literary form. Too much insistence on this identification would lead us to question whether John can be considered to be a gospel at all, for as we have noticed by now, the fourth gospel is composed of lengthy discourses and more amply developed events than the short self-contained episodes typical of the other gospels.

REFLECTION AND PRAYER

Jesus, I believe that you are the One sent by the Father. You are my living water refreshing me with forgiveness and the promise of salvation.

Fourth Controversy: Jesus Is "The Light of the World"
(Jn 8:12-59)

Whether the rest of chapter 8 is to be considered a new controversy or simply a continuation of the one interrupted by the insertion of the episode about the adulteress, the situation, the time and the opponents seem to be the same as those in the preceding controversy.

Jesus renews his revelation of his true identity by applying to himself another symbol of the Feast of Tabernacles, the special torches used to illuminate the Temple during the feast: "I am the light of the world . . . the light of life" (v. 12).

The Pharisees are not going to let that claim go unchallenged. They discredit this testimony as given in his own behalf.

Jesus contrasts his own clear-minded witnessing—"I know where I came from and where I am going" (v. 14)—with their witnessing according to "appearances" (v. 15). He responds to their objection about lack of witnesses: "My judgment is valid, because I am not alone, but it is I and the Father who sent me" (v. 16). Thus, there are two who give witness that Jesus is the light of the world: the Father and Jesus. The Mosaic law requiring two witnesses for important matters (Dt 17:6) stands fulfilled after all.

They demand to see the Father.

Jesus ends this part of the debate by giving them proof that they really don't know God; they have not recognized Jesus as a man of God. In spite of his amazing teaching, a teaching that must reverberate in the very depths of any man or woman of God; in spite of his amazing works, which could only spring from divinity as ultimate source; in spite of the testimony of the Baptist, a man whom simple people recognized as a great prophet; in spite of all these witnesses, they have not known him. Hence, they have not known his Father either: "If you knew me, you would know my Father also" (v. 19).

Stung by his words, they still do not arrest him: "His hour had not yet come" (v. 20).

Whether immediately or sometime later the debate continues with Jesus' provocative statement: "Where I am going you cannot come" (v. 21).

They wonder if he means that he will commit suicide (v. 22), another supposition based upon their worldly judgment, as he quickly points out, warning them: "If you do not believe that *I AM*, you will die in your sins" (v. 24). "I AM"! By this daring expression John attributes to Jesus the claim to the name by which Yahweh revealed himself to Moses at the burning bush:

> "I am who am. . . . You shall tell the Israelites: *I AM* sent me to you . . . . The LORD, the God of your fathers, the God of Abraham, the God of Isaac, the God of Jacob, has sent me to you. This is my name forever; / this is my title for all generations" (Ex 3:14-15).

Jewish tradition considered this passage the source of the name Yahweh, by which God identifies himself as the almighty Creator: I am who am, the One who always is, with no beginning and no end; I am the One who possesses being of himself, not derived from anyone else; I am the source of all that exists. This name became so sacred to the Jews that they would not even pronounce it, substituting for it *Adonai* ("Lord"). In the Hebrew Bible it was written *YHWH*. Modern scholars reconstruct the name as *Yahweh*. It is clear, then, that in John 8:24 Jesus is quoted as attributing the name Yahweh to himself and declaring that our salvation depends upon our belief that Jesus is Yahweh.

No wonder the Jews ask in amazement: "Who are you?" (v. 25).

The first part of Jesus' answer is not clear, even to scholars. "What I told you from *the beginning*" (v. 25) seems to refer to the opening of all these controversies, but probably also echoes Genesis 1:1, "In the beginning. . . ." Jesus is apparently saying: "I have been manifesting who I am from the beginning of creation." As matrix of all creation, Jesus is revealed by the world itself. The sense becomes a bit clearer in verse 28: "When you lift up [on the cross] the Son of Man, you will realize that I AM, and that I do nothing on my own, but I say only what the Father taught me."

John tells us that "because he spoke this way, many came to believe in him" (v. 30). This believing would almost certainly have to be post-resurrection faith, for it is hardly possible that any of the Jews witnessing this debate would suddenly be converted by a statement that, in the atmosphere described thus far, would have seemed to them even harder to accept: "When you crucify me, you will know that I am Yahweh"! Yet that is exactly what did happen in those who became Christians: When he was crucified, they finally came to know him as the one who did and said only what the Father willed; and when he was also "lifted up" in the resurrection, they came to believe that *HE IS*!

Jesus then proclaims the consequence of faith in him: "You will know the truth, and *the truth will set you free*" (v. 32).

As usual the Jewish leaders misunderstand him: "We are descendants of Abraham and have never been enslaved to anyone" (v. 33). In the heat of argument they seem to have forgotten Egypt and Babylon!

Jesus clarifies that the freedom he extols is freedom from the darkness of sin: "Everyone who commits sin is the slave of sin" (v. 34), as we have all come to know by bitter experience. Then, playing on their image of physical slavery, Jesus declares that as Son in the free family of God, he himself can free them (v. 36). Yes, they are of Abraham's stock, Jesus reflects, but they are not true children of Abraham, for they want to kill him (v. 37). He adds that while he tells them only what he knows from God his Father, they act according to instructions from a different father: "You do what you have heard from *your father*" (v. 38, *RSV*; see the note in *NAB*).

They catch his implication that their father is Satan and proudly declare: "*Our father* is Abraham" (v. 39), implying that Jesus is the one who is not a true son of Abraham.

Jesus insists that they are not true children of Abraham. By their evil intent to kill him they do the works of a different father (v. 41).

They resent his indirect way of declaring them illegitimate and indignantly claim even God as their father.

"If God were your father, you would love me" (v. 42), Jesus replies. "You belong to your father the devil" (v. 44). Then comes a sentence that reveals the admiration of Jesus' followers for his human integrity: "Can any of you charge me with sin?" (v. 46).

Continuing the name calling, the Jews try "Samaritan," probably voicing one of the ways in which the Jews of John's time were trying to discredit Jesus' Jewish background, for they considered the Samaritans traitors to true Judaism by deviating from orthodoxy. But they immediately go much further by accusing Jesus of being possessed (v. 48).

Jesus' denial adds a promise: "Whoever keeps my word will never see death" (v. 51).

This assertion really raises their scorn: "Are you greater than our father Abraham, who died?" (v. 53). His answer strikes them dumb:

> "Abraham . . . rejoiced to see my day; he saw it and was glad. . . . Amen, amen, I say to you, *before Abraham came to be, I AM*" (vv. 56-58).

Having lost the battle of words, they stoop to stones.

John has presented us with a catechism of deep theology in a setting of breathless drama. The great truth that climaxes this confrontation of Jesus with the Jewish leaders and of John's Christians with the local synagogue—Jesus is divine!—was certainly not an empty formula to these early Christians. It was their battle cry!

REFLECTION AND PRAYER

Is Jesus the light of my world, the real sunshine of my life?

Do I try to see all the circumstances of my life in the light that is Jesus?

Jesus, my true Lord, I adore you as Son of the Father, equally Yahweh himself! *YOU ARE!*

Jesus Cures the Man Born Blind (Jn 9)

John has by no means exhausted his theme of the divinity of Jesus and the blindness of the Jews. He again shows us that Jesus reveals his identity not only in speech but also in action. He now presents another of Jesus' great "signs" in one of the most dramatic dialogues of the gospels.

Seeing a man blind from birth, the disciples ask Jesus to tell whose sin was to blame for his blindness. The notion that physical ills are due to sin is frequently expressed in the Old Testament, especially in the Book of Job. Jesus declares that sin is not the cause of this man's blindness; the man's misfortune provides an opportunity to make visible "the works of God" (v. 3) in Jesus' healing ministry. The cure that follows is connected to the preceding confrontation with the Jews by Jesus' repetition of the sentence that opened it, "I am the light of the world" (v. 5), now demonstrated in action.

Instead of "putting spittle on his eyes," as in Mark 8:23, Jesus spits on the ground to make a mud paste, which he then smears on the man's eyes (v. 6). This act must have evoked in the biblically trained mind of the first century the picture of Yahweh stooping down to form man "out of the clay of the ground" (Gn 2:7). But in making the mud pack, Jesus is breaking one of those many sabbath rules of the Pharisee's oral tradition.

Jesus elicits the blind man's collaboration in the cure by sending him to wash in the Pool of Siloam. John's parenthetical remark that the name means "sent" (v. 7) reminds us that Jesus has been sent by the Father, but it may also refer to the blind man as one sent by Jesus, illustrating the many sayings in John's gospel culminating in that ultimate expression of vocation: "As the Father has sent me, so I send you" (Jn 20:21).

Thus cured, the man identifies himself to his acquaintances as one cured by Jesus (v. 11). They take him to the Pharisees to authenticate the cure. More inquiry, more answering by the beggar. As always, the Pharisees overlook the good done: "This man is not from God, because he does not keep the sabbath" (v. 16). When the cured man declares that Jesus is a prophet, they summon his parents to testify whether he was really born blind. No satisfaction here, either; the parents assert that he is really their son who was born blind.

Verse 22 clearly shows that the evangelist is writing about his own time as well as that of Jesus, for the decision to put out of the synagogue anyone who acknowledged Jesus as the Messiah had to be made after the resurrection when the Christians began to speak of Jesus in Temple and synagogue (see Acts 3).

Back to the cured man! They can't get him to admit that Jesus is a sinner; he annoyingly keeps saying, "I was blind and now I see" (v. 25). Himself annoyed by the repeated questioning, the man sarcastically blurts out, "Do you want to become his disciples, too?" (v. 27). Having lost the round about Abraham, they now declare that it is Moses who speaks for God, not Jesus. This calls forth more biting sarcasm from the cured man and even a demonstration of reason that might be expressed as a syllogism:

God does not hear sinners, but only the devout;
God did hear this Jesus;
Therefore, Jesus must be devout (a man of God).

Their answer is physical; they throw him out of the synagogue.

As sequel to the story Jesus invites the cured man to pronounce his confession of faith. Jesus' statement, "You have seen him [the Son of Man]" (v. 37), carries two layers of meaning: You have seen Jesus with your new sight, and you have seen who he really is, even though the Pharisees haven't.

The Pharisees overhear his implication that they are blind (vv. 29-40). Certainly they have proved that point more than amply in this chapter. But Jesus remarks that they are worse than blind; they deliberately refuse to see the obvious, a sin that "remains" (v. 41), for God will not violate their free will to continue refusing to see.

REFLECTION AND PRAYER

To what extent am I blind to the light that is Jesus?

Do I see all things and especially all people in his light?

Lord Jesus, grant that I may really see who you are. Be the light of my life!

Jesus Is the Good Shepherd, True Leader of the Jews (Jn 10:1-39)

Without any transition chapter 10 proceeds with that beautiful instruction in which Jesus likens himself to a good shepherd, an image that communicates gentle leadership and constant care. The image of the good shepherd is enhanced by many Old Testament references to Yahweh as shepherd of his people, most cherished of which is Psalm 23:

> The Lord is my shepherd; I shall not want.
> In verdant pastures he gives me repose;
> Beside restful waters he leads me;
> he refreshes my soul (vv. 1-3).

Jesus begins by picturing a simple routine well known to his audience: The true shepherd, known to the gatekeeper, leads his own sheep out to pasture, calling them by name. They will follow him alone because they recognize his voice (vv. 2-5).

Jesus' listeners fail to catch his meaning, so he changes the figure or parable and clearly applies it to himself: "I am the gate for the sheep" (v. 7). All those who pretended to be this gate before him were "thieves and robbers" (v. 8). In the preceding passage the Pharisees expelled from the synagogue the man cured of blindness. Having become a closed gate for that man, they aren't going to like being called "thieves and robbers"! Then comes that marvelous promise: "Whoever enters through me will be saved" (v. 9). The thief seeks his own advantage, but "I came so that they might have life and have it more abundantly" (v. 10).

In verse 11 Jesus returns to the first figure: "I am the good shepherd [who] . . . lays down his life for the sheep." Jesus wards off the wolf (Satan) that scares away the hired shepherd.

In the midst of this simple parable comes an astounding sentence: "I am the good shepherd, and I know mine and mine know me, *just as the Father knows me and I know the Father*" (vv. 14-15). At the Last Supper Jesus will explain further. Besides this fold (of Jews) Jesus speaks of other sheep (Gentiles) that he must also lead: "There will be one flock, one shepherd" (v.16). The Father loves him because for all these sheep he will freely lay down his life and freely "take it up again" (v. 17).

Whether these are Jesus' actual words or John's literary device for expressing Christian faith, it is very clear that Jesus is here presented as universal Savior who knows and loves each individual personally, and who *of his own free will* dies for every one of us and by his own power rises again.

The division of the people over the true identity of Jesus persists; in their eyes he is either a possessed maniac or a wonderworker (vv. 19-21).

Again John mentions a feast, this time a December celebration of the Maccabees' rededication of the Temple after it had been desecrated by Antiochus IV. Notice how much more precise John's time markers have been than those of the synoptics. His memory seems to work from feast to feast. At a deeper level we may perceive that he is using these feasts to symbolize that Jesus is himself the new cause of festive celebration in the church.

The Jews demand to know whether Jesus is the Messiah. Of course, he just told them so in the preceding parable, but they are never satisfied. Jesus refers them to his "works" and reviews the shepherd parable, ending with another astounding statement: *"The Father and I are one"* (v. 30).

They understand very well that he is claiming to be one God with the Father, for they reach for stones and accuse him of blasphemy by "making yourself God" (v. 33).

Jesus points out an irony: Their own scriptures call their judges "gods" (Ps 82:6) merely because they exercise a function that ultimately belongs only to God (Ex 21:6), yet they lay this charge of blasphemy against "the one whom the Father has consecrated and sent into the world" (v. 36). The use of "consecrated" here suggests that Jesus is the real Temple of which the reconsecrated Temple celebrated on this feast is but a pale foreshadowing.

Again Jesus appeals to his performance of "my Father's works" (v. 37) as proof of his claim to be "the Son of God" (v. 36). And he does not hesitate to declare: "The Father is in me and I am in the Father" (v. 38). This powerful theological statement climaxes the incident. They try to arrest him, but he escapes.

REFLECTION AND PRAYER

Do I often think of Jesus as my Good Shepherd?

Do I trustingly place my life, my future, in his care?

Jesus, you have laid down your very life for me. I thank you and worship you as my own Good Shepherd and the Son of God.

Jesus Raises Up Lazarus, His Climactic Sign (Jn 10:40—11:57)

John reports that Jesus returns to the place across the Jordan where the Baptist had been ministering and where many people now accept Jesus, because of his signs, as the one the Baptist foretold (vv. 40-42).

Martha and Mary send word to Jesus that their brother Lazarus, "the one you love," is ill (Jn 11:3). This message is obviously an implicit request, like that of Mary at Cana. And just as at Cana, Jesus seems at first to refuse the request; he purposely delays leaving "that the Son of God may be glorified through it [Lazarus' illness]" (v. 4). Finally he decides to return to Judea despite the fears and protests of his disciples. Figuratively he tells them that he must work before his night of death comes upon him (vv. 9-10). When he tells them that Lazarus sleeps they fail to understand his symbol. He must use literal language: "Lazarus has died" (v. 14). Thomas, whom John will later report as the doubter, shows the courage to be willing to die with Jesus in Jerusalem. They are well aware of the danger of continuing to follow Jesus! Behind Thomas' literal meaning John may be suggesting the Christian belief that we die with Jesus in order to be raised up to new life with him. The raising of Lazarus from the tomb will become a symbol in action of our final resurrection.

As in Luke, Martha is the more active of the two sisters, coming out to meet Jesus on his way. Her request is more explicit than before: "I know that whatever you ask of God, God will give you" (v. 22). But she takes his assurance that Lazarus "will rise" (v. 23) as a reference to the last day (v. 24), and thus elicits from Jesus one of the most vivid expressions in the gospels of his power over death: "*I am the resurrection and the life*; whoever believes in me, even if he dies, will live" (v. 25).

This statement is a clear example of what scholars call realized eschatology in John's gospel. The synoptics speak of eternal life as realized in us only after the eschatological (end of the world) events of the second coming of Christ and the last judgment. Without denying that eternal life will be ours *definitively* only after these future events, John frequently implies that eternal life is already ours *incipiently*, insofar as Christ lives in us even now. This is the truth that later theology also expresses as the indwelling of the Holy Spirit in sanctifying grace.

Jesus then gives Martha the opportunity to declare her faith in him as Messiah and Son of God. Mary, the more profound of the sisters, moves Jesus deeply: "He became perturbed and deeply troubled" (v. 33). His tears attest his great love for Lazarus and his sisters (v. 36). Twice John reports that Jesus is "perturbed" (vv. 33, 38) to stress the intensity of Jesus' emotions. John is concerned to show us how human Jesus really is, how warm his friendship for Lazarus, even as we approach his most awesome sign of divine power.

To Jesus' order to roll away the stone, Martha objects that the body is already decaying. She apparently thinks that Jesus merely wants to see once more the body of his friend. Her mention of *four days* since Lazarus' death sets this miracle apart from the synoptic resuscitations, reported as taking place shortly after death. This will be a sign that nobody can doubt!

Jesus proceeds with his plan to display ''the glory of God'' (v. 40). Before the whole crowd he publicly prays to his Father ''that they may believe that you sent me'' (v. 42). Clearly the inner purpose of the miracle is here stated as a sign of Jesus' true identity.

The drama builds toward climax with the cry of Jesus: ''Lazarus, come out!'' (v. 43). Like a ghost the mysterious figure appears, still wrapped in burial cloths. What a climax to all the signs of Jesus' identity related in John! In this last sign the evangelist skillfully shows us both the human nature and the divine nature united in the one person of Jesus in action.

Any wonder, then, that Lazarus becomes a living witness arousing the faith of many of the Jews in Jesus? Ironically the living Lazarus becomes such a threat to the influence of the chief priests and the Pharisees that Caiaphas can now persuade them to take that final step of deciding upon Jesus' death. John sees in Caiaphas' pronouncement of doom an unwitting prophecy ''that Jesus was going to die not only for the nation, but also to gather into one the dispersed children of God'' (v. 52).

Again John presents Jesus as avoiding direct confrontation by withdrawing toward the desert. The atmosphere in Jerusalem is boiling with anticipation; people wonder whether Jesus will come for the feast of Passover, for they know the peril he would run by such an appearance.

In relating this miracle of the raising of Lazarus, does John intend to tell a historical event or is he dramatizing the Christian belief in the efficacy of Jesus' approaching resurrection for our own? Scholars are divided in their answer. If this event really happened, why did the synoptics fail to mention it? Would not such a spectacular event have been well- known to them? Would it not have fit very well into their general plan of presenting Jesus as Son of Man, Son of God, Savior of all? The name Lazarus is mentioned in Luke 16:19-31. The rich man asks Abraham to send Lazarus, now in heaven, to warn the rich man's brothers to repent. Could John be transforming this parable into a breathtaking dramatization?

John may very well have had both purposes in relating this event; that is, to tell a historical event in such a way as to bring out its inner significance. But historical event or not, we can be certain that this passage is an inspired expression of the faith of the early Christians that Jesus is the resurrection and the life—our resurrection, our real life!

REFLECTION AND PRAYER

Jesus, in you I ground all my hopes for the present and the future. You are my hope for a future life, my resurrection into the real life with the Father!

Jesus Announces That His Hour Has Come (Jn 12)

Chapter 12 begins with the anointing of Jesus at Bethany, probably the same incident as that related in Mark 14:3-9, but with a somewhat different cast of characters and certain details that suggest knowledge of the same tradition behind Luke 7:36-50. Instead of the house of Simon the leper (Mark) or Simon the Pharisee (Luke), John's setting is the house of Lazarus, with Martha serving (as in Luke 10:40). Instead of an unnamed woman, John speaks of Mary anointing Jesus. Instead of anointing Jesus' head, she anoints his feet, drying them with her hair (as in Luke 7:38), perhaps to express her loving gratitude to Jesus for raising her brother to life rather than as an act of penitence. Instead of attributing the criticism of Mary's act to the apostles in general, John names only Judas, whom he accuses of stealing the contributions (v. 6). John closes this event with his comment about the great crowd eager to see Lazarus as well as Jesus, and the expansion of the leaders' plot to include Lazarus.

Mark and Matthew place the anointing of Jesus after his entry into Jerusalem. By placing it before that event, John emphasizes the triumphal aspect of the entry as the public recognition of the already anointed "King of Israel" (v. 13), the expression that John adds to Psalm 118:26 as the crowd's greeting. Like Matthew, John is reminded of Zechariah 9:9, but gives a much freer translation that emphasizes Jesus' humble selection of "an ass's *colt*" (v. 15). Again John adds his own commentary, pointing out that the disciples understood the significance of this event only after Jesus' resurrection (v. 16).

The Greeks who ask to see Jesus are probably Gentile converts to Judaism, for they have "come up to worship at the feast" (v. 20). Jesus speaks a mysterious language to them in a discourse that explains his imminent passion as "the hour . . . for the Son of Man to be glorified" (v. 23). At last we know the meaning of *the hour* often referred to in John! Like a grain of wheat, Jesus must die before he rises; death itself is an essential element in his glorification! The figure of wheat also suggests the bread of life, already powerfully developed. Paradox follows paradox: Not only must we die to live, we must die to produce fruit; if we love (temporal) life, we lose (eternal) life; if we hate (temporal) life, we preserve it "for life eternal" (v. 25). "Hates" is here a deliberate exaggeration to emphasize the importance of preferring eternal to temporal life, even to the point of the sacrifice that Jesus himself will soon make.

The thought turns to discipleship: If you would serve me, follow me; if you serve me, the Father will honor you (with eternal life). But a shadow falls: "I am troubled now" (v. 27). John seems to have transferred the agony in the garden, which he otherwise skips, to this moment:

"Yet what should I say? 'Father, save me from this hour'?
But it was for this purpose that I came to this hour" (v. 27).

This perfect obedience to the Father is the source of Jesus' glory, as the voice from heaven immediately confirms (v. 28).

Only Jesus understands the voice; some of the bystanders think it is thunder, others the voice of an angel. Jesus explains that the voice is a testimony of God's judgment in Jesus' favor against Satan (v. 31). In this titanic struggle of Good against Evil, Jesus' crucifixion ("lifted up from the earth") will score the victory over "this world" (in the connotation of evil that John has already established) and its ruler (Satan): "I will draw everyone to myself" (v. 32). This is the greatest paradox of them all; in the moment of being vanquished in death, Jesus will triumph definitively over evil, over sin—even over death itself.

The crowd declares that the Messiah will not die, an idea that may have been derived from Psalm 89:37, which says that David's "posterity shall continue forever." They have evidently understood Jesus' reference to himself as "Son of Man" (v. 23) in the sense of a claim to be the Messiah, for they now demand to know how he can die crucified ("lifted up") if he is the Son of Man.

Jesus answers by obliquely referring to himself as the light by which they must walk while they still have it (vv. 35-36). Then he retires into hiding.

Drawing toward the close of his "Book of Signs," John reflects upon the results of all those marvelous signs by which Jesus manifested his loving power to bring joy to a wedding feast by changing water into wine, to a royal official by curing his son, to a paralyzed man by an instant cure, to a crowd of people in the desert by feeding them, to his endangered disciples by walking on the water to save them, to a man born blind by giving him sight, to Martha and Mary by bringing back Lazarus from the tomb. Seven great signs of divine love and power, yet the people "did not believe in him" (v. 37). Such incomprehensible disbelief reminds John of Isaiah 53:1, a passage in which the prophet foretells the disbelief of the people in Yahweh's suffering servant. John thinks also of that other prophecy of Isaiah that equally impressed Matthew: "He blinded their eyes" (Is 6:9, quoted in Mt 13:13). Evidently early Christian communities regarded Isaiah as the great messianic prophet. John even states that "Isaiah . . . saw his [Jesus'] glory" (v. 41).

Although the crowd in general does not believe in Jesus, John assures us that many individuals, even in the Sanhedrin, do believe in him (v. 42). But they fear to give testimony, preferring "human praise to the glory of God" (v. 43).

John ends his "Book of Signs" by reporting a summary of Jesus' proclamation during his public ministry. Jesus declares that faith in him is faith in the Father: "Whoever sees me sees the one who sent me" (v. 45). He is light for those who believe, escape from darkness. He comes not to condemn the world but to save it. Whoever rejects Jesus will be condemned by his word, which, as the very word commanded by the Father (v. 49), confers "eternal life" (v. 50).

REFLECTION AND PRAYER

Lord Jesus, I do believe in you. I believe that you have the words of eternal life. I welcome you into my heart as the crowd welcomed you into Jerusalem. May my own death participate in yours, and may my resurrection share your glory.

Jesus Prepares to Enter Into His Glory
(Jn 13—21)

Chapter 13 opens with nostalgic poetry: "Before the feast of the *Passover*, Jesus knew that his hour had come to *pass* from this world to the Father." This is the hour of Jesus' passage, the real Passover into his glory, which we will see anticipated in the very way that John relates the Last Supper and the passion. This is the hour in which Jesus will reveal the depths of his love: "He loved his own in the world and he loved them to the end." This main theme of the Last Supper will be repeated again and again as John's final characterization of Jesus on this last night before his death.

This bright peace is abruptly broken by a dark contrast, typical of John: "The devil had already induced Judas . . . to hand him over" (v. 2).

Jesus Washes His Disciples' Feet, Yet Is Betrayed (Jn 13:1-30)

The Last Supper begins with Jesus' prayer of awareness "that the Father had put everything into his power and that he had come from God and was returning to God" (v. 3). Like Luke, John would have us understand that the constant focus of Jesus' consciousness is his Father and his mission from him.

As guests arrived from the dusty streets for a Jewish supper, they could expect their host to receive them hospitably by providing servants to wash their feet. Jesus himself, the most hospitable of hosts, now provides this menial service. Love in action!

But Peter objects, declaring his unworthiness. When Jesus makes Peter's submission a condition for sharing in his heritage from the Father, the impetuous Peter wants to be wholly washed! Jesus patiently explains that one who has already bathed needs no more than the foot-washing.

This act of washing resembles baptism, especially when Jesus insists that Peter's acceptance of this washing is a condition for eternal life. But in verse 10 the Greek word used for *bathed* is from the same root as the word used for baptism in several Pauline letters; and the one who has "bathed" is said here to be "entirely cleansed." Since Peter has already been "entirely cleansed" (apparently through baptism at the Jordan, Jn 4:1-2), the present washing of feet seems to be a ritual washing foreshadowing the sacrament of penance or reconciliation. By obedient submission to Jesus' will, even as he humbly demonstrates his own submission to the Father's will, the disciples are cleansed of sins committed since they were first "entirely cleansed." But they have not all made this humble inner submission; the betrayer has not been washed clean (v. 11).

Jesus now makes his action lesson clear. As their teacher and master he has done them this service as an example of how they must serve one another (vv. 12-17). But Jesus knows that one of his disciples is not following his example of love: "The one who ate my food has raised his heel against me" (v. 18, quoting Ps 41:10). By thus foretelling the betrayal, Jesus is revealing "that *I AM*" (v. 19), appropriately repeating this most solemn revelation of his true identity at the beginning of the Last Supper.

Troubled, Jesus continues, "One of you will betray me" (v. 21). And now, for the first time, we meet "the one whom Jesus loved," reclining close to Jesus. As indicated above, strong traditions hold that this beloved disciple was either the author of this gospel or the author's eyewitness source. Peter and this beloved disciple are obviously good friends; a mere signal from Peter is enough to set him in motion: "Master, who is it [the betrayer]?" (v. 25). As partial fulfillment of the prophecy in verse 18, Jesus dips a morsel into a sauce and gives it to Judas. John comments, "Satan entered him" (v. 27); even as he receives Jesus' attentive offering, Judas makes his final decision to betray him.

Jesus seems to encourage him to execute his evil design quickly. Is this John's way of saying that Jesus freely accepts his passion as the Father's will? Or is he rather suggesting that Jesus mercifully covers up for Judas' sudden exit. John is probably suggesting both ideas, for he frequently gives two or more levels of meaning to a single expression. The cover-up is successful: "Some thought that since Judas kept the money bag, Jesus had told him . . . to give something to the poor" (v. 29). Poor as he is in the goods of this world, Jesus habitually gives alms to those poorer than his own band. Then another multilevel expression: "And it was night"— both in nature and in Judas' heart.

REFLECTION AND PRAYER

My Teacher and Master, give me a share in your immense love for all persons. Let me be unashamed to stoop to menial services for others just as you washed your disciples' feet. May I never betray you, never give myself to any cause or act that displeases you.

The Beginning of Jesus' Last Discourse (Jn 13:31—14:31)

Jesus is obviously relieved by Judas' exit. The means of salvation, at least in its initial phase, is at last in motion: "Now is the Son of Man glorified, and God is glorified in him" (v. 31). Jesus' glory is to suffer and die for our salvation; he thereby glorifies God in revealing him as the Father who "so loved the world that he gave his only Son" (Jn 3:16). He will soon leave them, and they will not be able to follow him. As his last will and testament, he gives them "a new commandment" to love one another, even *as he has loved them* (v. 34), a love just demonstrated in washing their feet. It will be by their mutual love that they will identify themselves before the world as his disciples!

Peter wants to know where Jesus will go. Jesus' answer that Peter will be able to follow him only later does not satisfy him. His boastful declaration that he is ready to die for Jesus brings only the prediction that he will deny Jesus three times before morning. Notice that many of John's details now begin to match those of the synoptics, an indication of the strength and relative agreement of the traditions regarding the passion.

Chapter 14 continues Jesus' last discourse, the longest in the gospels. For many readers it is the passage that most clearly reveals the identity and personality of Jesus. The literary pattern of this discourse is similar to many of the conversations that John has already reported: Jesus makes a profound statement, one of the listeners objects to it or questions it, Jesus clarifies the original statement by adding an even deeper one.

The disciples are obviously distressed when he repeats that he is taking his leave of them. He consoles them, urging them to believe in him, assuring them that his real purpose in leaving is to prepare a place for them in his Father's house to which he will bring them at a second coming (v. 3).

When he tells them that they know the way to this place, Thomas declares that they don't even know his destination, let alone the way to it.

Jesus answers that he himself is both the way and the destination (v. 6). For as truth itself, he illuminates the way to the *life that he also is*! To find Jesus, then, is to find the way to true life—life in and with the Father. He surprises them further by saying that they have already seen the Father (v. 7).

Philip pleads to be shown the Father.

Jesus responds: "Whoever has seen me has seen the Father" (v. 9). Jesus is the face of Yahweh! Verse 9 is one of the profound statements in this gospel that the church eventually elaborated into the dogmas of the Incarnation and the Trinity. Verse 10 adds another aspect of these dogmas: "I am in the Father and the Father is in me. . . . The Father who dwells in me is doing his works" (v. 10). Those works, recorded in the "Book of Signs," testify that Jesus speaks the truth (v. 11). He further promises that when he returns to the Father he will do whatever they ask of him "that the Father may be glorified in the Son" (v. 13). And they can ask anything in Jesus' name with assurance of being heard. John certainly wants his readers to feel free to address either the Father or the Son in prayer.

Moreover, Jesus promises that if they love and obey him, he will ask the Father to send them *"another* Advocate" (v. 16), in Greek courts a defense attorney. Jesus has been their first advocate interceding for them with his Father; this very night he will defend them from soldiers who will threaten to arrest them. By promising another Advocate, he assures them that he will not leave them alone, for this new Advocate will remain always with them as "the Spirit of truth" (v. 17).

Moreover, Jesus himself will come back to them. In light of verse 19, this return seems to refer to his resurrection as one who lives and who will give them new life in which they will be more fully aware that he dwells in the Father. They will even dwell in like manner in Jesus and he in them! This beautiful passage is one of the many seeds in John's gospel from which grew the church's doctrine that Christians live the very life of Christ. Jesus lays down a condition for this life: obedience to his commandments as proof of love for him. He does not say *"the* commandments" but *"my* commandments." And he promises a tremendous reward: "Whoever loves me will be loved by my Father, and I will love him and reveal myself to him" (v. 21).

Judas, perhaps another designation for Thomas, asks why Jesus will reveal himself to his disciples but not to the world.

Jesus answers that it is love that makes the difference. Moreover, he promises that whoever truly loves him enough to keep his commandment to love others will enjoy his abiding presence and that of his Father (v. 23), one of the most explicit statements of the theme that we have seen surfacing in the synoptics: Jesus still lives in his people. In a more complete sense than the synoptic writers, John is the theologian of the spiritual life, the eternal life, the very life of the Father and of the Son animating Jesus' faithful followers. It is also the life of the Holy Spirit, whose assigned role as Advocate is to preserve and increase this divine life of grace in us by teaching us everything we need to know (v. 26).

Jesus now seems to say his last farewell to his faithful disciples, a farewell of peace, the abiding peace produced by that indwelling of which he has just spoken—a gift far superior to the peace that the world offers. To console them for his imminent departure Jesus seems to contradict some of his former statements: "The Father is greater than I" (v. 28). Later theology offers a helpful distinction: Although the three Persons of the Trinity are equal, the Father is greater than the Son in his human nature.

Jesus' final conflict with evil is about to begin: "The ruler of the world [the world that refused to accept him] is coming" (v. 30). Jesus will appear to lose the conflict, for "the world must know that I love the Father and that I do just as the Father has commanded me" (v. 31). In other words, the only way the world could ever know the depth of God's love was the crucifixion. Jesus was crucified, not because the Father demanded this supreme sacrifice to satisfy his justice, but because Jesus remained true to his mission of revealing the Father's infinite love for his people, even when they, under the influence of hatred, would kill him for it!

With that, he leads them out of the supper room: "Get up, let us go"—to crucifixion and glory!

REFLECTION AND PRAYER

Jesus, with all my heart I want to respond to your love for me. Give me a love expansive enough to include all others, a love that the Father will recognize as your love operating in me, so that he will come to live in me, with you and the Holy Spirit. I rest in this love, in this triune life.

Last Discourse: On Love and Hatred (Jn 15:1-25)

Surprisingly, chapter 15 continues the Last Supper discourse in apparent disregard of Jesus' closing words at the end of chapter 14. A glance ahead to chapter 18 will detect a second closing of the discourse. These two closings are among the most obvious clues that this gospel has undergone revisions by another writer or writers, almost certainly of the same school of thought, so close are their theological and literary approaches. Chapters 15—17 repeat and develop many of the same themes that we have seen in chapter 14. These later chapters have apparently been added to clarify and expand those themes.

Perhaps the image of the vine beginning chapter 15 is meant to give the impression that Jesus continues his final discourse after leaving the upper room, as they pass a vineyard on their way to the Mount of Olives. It is certainly one of the most powerful sustained figures in all of scripture. Jesus likens himself to the vine, his followers to the branches that are alive and productive only by the life they receive from their union with him, and his Father to the vinedresser who cuts away the dead branches and trims the live ones to increase their yield of fruit. What deep meaning, then, in Jesus' urgent "Remain in me, as I remain in you" (v. 4)! And just as a vinedresser glories in the abundance of grapes on his vine, so does the Father glory in our intense living of the Christ-life (v. 8).

This thought leads naturally back to the main theme of love. Simply, yet with powerful logic, the theme is developed:

> "As the Father loves me, so I also love you.
> Remain in my love. . ." (v. 9).

> "This is my commandment:
> love one another as I love you.
> No one has greater love than this,
> to lay down one's life for one's friends" (v. 12-13).

That word "friends" leads into a related theme:

> "I have called you friends,
> because I have told you everything I have heard from my Father" (v. 15).

Lest they still haven't understood, he repeats his command to "love one another" (v. 17).

This is certainly one of the key passages in the gospel of John. It clearly and insistently proclaims that Jesus has established a new covenant with his own new commandments—really just one commandment, which replaces all the rest because it gathers them all up into the higher synthesis of fraternal love. It has sometimes been interpreted narrowly as a love only for fellow members of Jesus' band of disciples. But in the context of the rest of Jesus' teaching, the love that Jesus here commands of his followers must have that universal reach, out to the whole world, of the Father's love, of Jesus' love. This is basically the same synthesis of the commandments as the great commandments of the synoptics.

But in the real world, love is sometimes requited with hatred. The followers of Jesus must expect the same hatred that he is suffering (vv. 18-25). Here "world" has again become the evil world that rejects Jesus because its members "do not know the one who sent me" (v. 21). The strong parallelism between their treatment of Jesus and their treatment of his followers ties this passage firmly to the preceding passage identifying the life of the branches with that of their sustaining vine (vv. 1-8).

The tie is further strengthened by the stark contrast between the hatred of the world and the love of Jesus and his friends (vv. 9-17). If to love Jesus is to love the Father and one another, then to hate Jesus is to hate the Father (vv. 23-24) and Jesus' followers (vv. 18-21). In hating Jesus, they hate the Father, whose words Jesus has spoken to them (vv. 21-22) and whose works Jesus has performed (v. 24). Hence their sin cannot be excused (v. 22). The synoptics call the sin against the Holy Spirit the unforgivable sin. Both these versions of the inexcusable sin point to the same perverted use of free will in calling good evil. God will not undo the free will he has given us, even when we use it to turn away from him.

In verse 25, thinking of his coming trial, Jesus climaxes the passage by identifying the hostile world with the Jewish leaders who are violating their own law: "They hated me without cause" (Ps 69:5). The context implies that they will also hate Jesus' followers without cause.

REFLECTION AND PRAYER

Lord Jesus, let me remain in your love, even when I feel the disdain of others for trying to love you and be true to your love in my way of living—especially when I experience the hatred that you foretold as the lot of those who love you enough to live by that love.

Last Discourse: The New Advocate and Coming Joy (Jn 15:26—16:33)

For the second time Jesus promises the Holy Spirit. But this time he says "whom *I will send you from the Father*" (v. 26). Now we see more clearly why Jesus calls him the Advocate and the Spirit of truth: He will testify to the truth about Jesus, bolstering the apostles' faith and their testimony on behalf of Jesus (v. 27).

The theme of rejection continues in chapter 16. Jesus foretells that the apostles will be expelled from synagogues, something that has apparently happened to the Johannine community. The evangelist is anxious to brace up their faith (vv. 1, 4) either by recalling the exact words that Jesus spoke or by attributing to him words that he might very well have spoken. Some Christians, perhaps even of John's community, have been put to death by those who thereby claim to be serving God (v. 2).

In verses 4-16, Jesus returns to the theme of his imminent departure from them. His statement, "Not one of you asks me, 'Where are you going?'" (v. 5), ignores both Peter's question in John 13:36 and Thomas' in John 14:5. This seeming slip of the Johannine pen may not be a slip at all. It suggests that the final editor of John's gospel may very well have combined somewhat differing versions of the Last Supper discourse, handling each version with such respect that he did not try to reconcile them by ironing out minor discrepancies or eliminating the frequent repetitions that we are finding.

For the third time Jesus assures his disciples that the Advocate will come to them, this time intimating that the Advocate will take Jesus' place as their leader (v. 7-8). This new Advocate will convince the disciples that the world was wrong (v. 8). The world considered Jesus the sinner, the blasphemer; the Advocate will show that the real sinner was the world itself in its refusal to believe in Jesus (v. 9). The world thought itself righteous in condemning Jesus to death; the very presence of the Advocate sent by the Father and Jesus will prove that real justice has been achieved through the glorification of Jesus at the Father's side (v. 10). The world thought it was condemning Jesus; it is really Satan and his evil world that are doomed by the death of Jesus (v. 11).

Jesus declares that there is much more to tell them, but they are in no state of mind to "bear it now" (v. 12). When the Advocate comes—again identified as the Spirit of truth—he will be their guide to all the truth that the Father wants them to know (v. 13) and will thus give glory to Jesus, whose message he will continue to announce (v. 14). Verse 13 ends with the statement that the Spirit "will declare to you the things that are coming." The church has never understood this sentence to mean that the Spirit will be constantly foretelling future events; such an interpretation would run counter to Jesus' own message that the future lies in the Father's hands. The promise is that *the Spirit will continue guiding Jesus' followers through future times.* Thus questions like abortion or euthanasia that were not raised in Jesus' time can be addressed by the church today in the confidence that the Holy Spirit is still guiding its deliberations as Advocate on the side of truth. This promise is the basis for the church's claim to infallible truth in vital matters of faith and morals.

Verse 15 presents one of the key statements for the eventual formulation of the doctrine of the Trinity: "Everything that the Father has is mine." This is a clear declaration of the equality of the Son with the Father. A like equality of the Holy Spirit is implied in what follows: "He [the Spirit] will take from what is mine and declare it to you."

Thus the dogma of the Trinity holds that all three Persons are united and equal in their complete possession of the Godhead or divinity of the one God, yet distinct in their relationship to one another: The Father eternally generates the Son, and from the Father and the Son eternally proceeds the Holy Spirit. Or, to complete Augustine's analogy begun on page 257, just as the Father perfectly knows and expresses himself generating his personal Word, or Son, so Father and Son breathe forth perfect love for one another, a love that is Person like themselves, the Holy Spirit, equal Sharer in their Godhead. The eternal generation of the Son entered time and human history at the moment of the Incarnation of Jesus Christ in the womb of Mary. The eternal breathing forth of the Spirit by the Father and the Son will, after Jesus' death and resurrection, enter time and human history.

But before that "you will no longer see me [after my death and burial], and again a little while later and you will see me [after my resurrection]" (v. 16). Without the bracketed explanation implied by John's post-resurrection knowledge, the disciples ask one another the meaning of Jesus' strange statement. He assures them that although they will indeed mourn his death as others rejoice at it, they will soon after be filled with joy (v. 20). Their grief will be as short-lived as the labor pains of a woman, pains that turn into exquisite joy at the birth of her child.

Then there will be no need of questions, but there will be other needs for which the Father will provide if they but ask him in Jesus' name (v. 23). Jesus insists that the Father will give them anything that they ask for *in his name*. Implicitly that condition requires that their petitions be aligned with Jesus' own spirit of total dedication to his Father's will. This passage suggests that when the evangelist recorded these words, early Christian liturgy was already using a formula similar to the one so often used at Mass today: "in the name of Jesus Christ our Lord."

Jesus adds that he will soon tell them "clearly about the Father" (v. 25). Then his relay of their petitions will not be necessary (v. 26), for the Father even now loves them for believing in Jesus and loving him (v. 27).

Suddenly, John's Jesus reveals the grand trajectory of his own life:

"I came from the Father and have come into the world. Now I am leaving the world and going back to the Father" (v. 28).

The disciples thank him for this plain speaking and declare their complete faith in him: "Now we realize that you know everything" (v. 30). He knows their questions before they ask him, as he has just shown (v. 19), thereby demonstrating that he has come from the Father (v. 30).

But their faith is still immature, as Jesus now points out; when his hour comes, they will be scattered and leave him alone (v. 32). Yet he ends this depressing moment in high anticipation: "Take courage, I have conquered the world [which Satan ruled]" (v. 33).

REFLECTION AND PRAYER

Lord, I believe that you have conquered Satan's world. Continue to conquer it in me through the power of the Holy Spirit, whom you have sent to dwell in me. Come, Holy Spirit, fill the hearts of your faithful and enkindle in them the fire of your love!

End of the Last Supper: Jesus' Prayer to the Father (Jn 17)

Chapter 17 begins with a brief transition from Jesus' long discourse to his prayer concluding the Last Supper. The Passover meal ends with a ritual prayer, which Jesus now converts into a very personal conversation with his Father in the presence of his disciples. In John's gospel Jesus teaches his followers by demonstration. He looks "up to heaven" to address his Father in loving intimacy as he begins this longest Lord's Prayer.

"Father, *the hour* has come!" (v. 1). At last we have arrived at that frequently foretold hour of Jesus, the hour of his suffering, the hour of his glory! Father and Son mutually glorify each other: The Son glorifies the Father by suffering and dying to testify to the Father's love for us all; the Father glorifies the Son in his resurrection and ascension and by giving him authority over all, to give them eternal life (v. 2). Parenthetically John inserts a theological definition of eternal life as intimate knowledge (the biblical *knowledge* that includes love) of the Father and Jesus, who would hardly have spoken of himself at this point as "Jesus *Christ*" (v. 3).

Jesus declares his work of revealing his Father to the world to be complete (v. 4), and thereby lays claim to "the glory that I had with you before the world began" (v. 5). This statement implies that the Son had set aside that glory to become man. Perhaps it can best be understood in parallel with the hymn in Philippians:

> Christ Jesus,
> Who, though he was in the form of God,
>> did not regard equality with God something to be grasped (Phil 2:5-6).

Later Christian reflection would attempt to clarify the unchanging relationship between the Father and the Son by distinguishing two natures in the one Son; in his divine nature the Son never lost the eternal glory that he shares with the Father, but in the human nature that he took upon himself in becoming Mary's son he "gave up" that glory until his "return" to the Father's side after his death and resurrection. This clarification is far from complete. The Incarnation is still a divine mystery that we can try to express in our human terms only in what Aquinas called analogical language, indicated here by the use of quotation marks.

In verses 6-19 Jesus prays for his followers to whom he has revealed the name of God as *Father, Father-who-so-loved-the-world* (Jn 3:16); for these followers have "kept your word . . . and they have believed that you sent me" (vv. 6-8). Then comes that marvelous statement: "I have been glorified in them" (v. 10)! Think of it: Our loving faith in Jesus glorifies him! And in glorifying Jesus we fulfill God's plan in sending his Son, and we thereby glorify God himself. St. Ignatius of Loyola gave to the Society of Jesus the motto: All for the glory of God. It must become every true Christian's way of life.

On the point of leaving the world, Jesus prays for his followers who must remain in it: "Holy Father, keep them in your name that you have given me so that they may be one just as we are" (v. 11). The first part of this quotation suggests that, as Isaiah so often declared, the name of God is *holy*; God is *Holiness itself. Holy* is his very name, the name which Jesus has inherited as his Son, the holiness Jesus has imparted to his followers and now prays that the Father preserve in them despite the contrary influences they will experience in the world. The second part of the quotation defines the holiness of Christians as their unity, so strong that it can be compared to the unity of the Father and the Son.

Jesus declares that he has lost none of his close followers except Judas, an inevitable loss since it had been foretold in Psalm 41:10.

Here we see a conviction in John that we have already observed in the synoptics: It is not necessary to seek further explanation for events in Jesus' life than Old Testament prophecies that express the incomprehensible will of God. Later theology considers it legitimate to ask the further question of *why* this was God's will. Sometimes this more daring approach leads to striking new insights. But often it leads only to the same conclusion that we find implied here in verse 12: Even when God's will is beyond our grasp, we must trust that it is ultimately for our good, for God is holy.

Verse 13 introduces the most solemn part of Jesus' prayer, the consecration of his disciples as sharers in his own mission, and hence in his priesthood, in preparation for that moment after his resurrection in which he ordains them as his apostles by sending the Holy Spirit upon them (Jn 20:21-23). First he expresses his reason for making this prayer in their presence: "That they may share my joy completely." Then he repeats his petition that, since they are to remain in the world after he leaves it, the Father "keep them from the evil one" (v. 15). Finally, he prays:

"Consecrate them in the truth. Your word is truth" (v. 17).

Since Jesus has just spoken of the Spirit of truth (Jn 16:13), the phrase "in the truth" implies that he is asking the Father to consecrate them through the Holy Spirit of truth. And his addition, "Your word is truth," implies that the consecration is also to be accomplished through Jesus himself as the Word (Jn 1:1-18) of truth (Jn 14:5). Hence, this consecration is conferred by the three divine Persons.

And in what does the consecration consist? "As you sent me into the world, so I sent them into the world" (v. 18). They are consecrated to continue the very mission of Jesus. They are to be not merely disciples of Jesus but also his *apostles* to others.

"I consecrate myself for them" (v. 19) must mean that Jesus is in this moment expressing his definitive and utterly free acceptance of the suffering and death that await him, "that they also may be consecrated in truth." His suffering and death will win for them the grace of redemption and the vocation to share in his redemptive work and suffering.

In verse 20 Jesus broadens his prayer to include all who "will believe in me through their word," obviously down through the ages as their word is passed on and on. He prays for their unity, a unity so powerful that he again compares it to his own unity with the Father (v. 21).

306

That unity will eventually convince the world "that you [Father] sent me." It will be a reflection of the unity of the Persons in God himself. By Jesus' standard our parishes, dioceses—all our Christian churches— have a long way to go!

Verses 22-23, "I have given them the glory you gave me. . . . I in them and you in me," signify that the life of glory, eternal life, is in some way already theirs. They share Jesus' own life; their life with God has already begun, at least in embryo. Later theology would speak of this new life in Christ in many ways: the state of sanctifying grace, the Christ-life in us, the divine life in us, life in the Spirit, the spiritual life.

In verse 23 the Christian unity modeled on the unity of Father and Son in verse 21 has now become Christian unity *in* Father and Son, a unity of such love that it should be evident to the world "that you [Father] loved them even as you loved me."

Then Jesus prays that the completion of the life of glory be given his followers, its completion in heaven, that they may be "where I am, . . . that they may see my glory" (v. 24). Heaven will be the completion of our union with Jesus Christ, our union already begun here on earth!

Jesus ends this unique prayer of intimate communion with the Father who sent him with the promise to continue to reveal his name, evidently through the Holy Spirit whom he will send, "that the love with which you loved me may be in them and I in them" (v. 26).

In this chapter we have been granted the privilege of a most intimate glimpse into the very heart of Jesus in total communion with his Father. John does not relate the institution of the Eucharist, perhaps because the synoptics have already done so to his satisfaction. But in this chapter he has presented Jesus' truly eucharistic prayer, offering his coming sacrifice on the cross to his Father and gathering his followers into his own loving communion with the Father.

REFLECTION AND PRAYER

Thank you, Lord Jesus, for praying for me. Teach me how to pray. May my prayer imitate yours as a total self-dedication to the Father and to whatever his will holds out for me. Father, I thank you for sending us your only Son to show us how to live and bring full life to us. Increase his life, your life, in me.

The Arrest of Jesus and Peter's Denials (Jn 18:1-27)

In chapter 18 John reports Jesus' entry with his disciples into the garden that he often visited (vv. 1-2). John omits Jesus' agonizing prayer, probably considering that he has transformed it into the long prayer of the preceding chapter in accord with the theological perspective that he has expressed in 13:31: Jesus' glorification has already begun with his acceptance of Judas' betrayal. This perspective also helps to explain other differences between John and the synoptics in reporting the arrest of Jesus, especially John's strong emphasis on the majesty of Jesus during his passion.

John's report that Judas led not only Jewish guards but even "a band of soldiers" (v. 3), apparently a Roman unit of 60 to 600 men, suggests that the Romans were already cooperating with the Jewish leaders against Jesus. It emphasizes the courage of Jesus in stepping forward to confront his would-be captors, felled by his answer, "I AM" (v. 5), in bold assertion of his true identity as divine Lord of the universe. John is obviously suggesting that Jesus really has complete power over his enemies, if he chooses to use it. The majestic picture of Jesus standing over the prone soldiers recalls Daniel's vision of a "man dressed in linen with a belt of fine gold around his waist," of such awesome aspect that Daniel fell face forward before him and his men fled (Dn 10:5-9).

At the repetition of question and answer, Jesus deliberately hands himself over to the soldiers but demands freedom for his followers, thus fulfilling his word to his Father: "I guarded them, and none of them was lost" (Jn 17:12).

As do the synoptics, John reports the severing of the servant's ear, but unlike them, he names Peter as the swordsman and Malchus as the wounded man. Another Johannine transformation of the prayer in the garden reported by the synoptics is contained in Jesus' rebuke to Peter: "Shall I not drink the cup that the Father gave me?" (v. 11).

Only John reports that upon his arrest Jesus was led first to Annas, father-in-law of Caiaphas. Annas had been deposed by the Romans and replaced by Caiaphas as high priest. But since the Jews considered the office to be for life, this deference to Annas may be more than a preparation for the real trial before Caiaphas.

Meanwhile Peter, with "another disciple" (v. 15), followed Jesus. The minute details of verses 15-16, uncharacteristic of John's gospel, give the distinct impression of reflecting a personal experience and thus point to the unnamed disciple as the beloved disciple, John himself. This probability seems further enhanced by the identification of Peter's third questioner as "a relative of the man whose ear Peter had cut off" (v. 26).

In keeping with his picture of the majesty of Jesus in the garden, John presents Jesus' strong defense of his ministry in response to Annas' questions about his disciples and his teaching (vv. 19-21). Interpreting this strength as arrogance, a guard strikes Jesus. With impressive calm and dignity Jesus ignores his own hurt and challenges the guard to act according to reason: "If I have spoken wrongly, testify to the wrong; but if I have spoken rightly, why do you strike me?" (v. 23). As noted in the chapter on Matthew, the admonition of Jesus to turn the other cheek (Mt 5:39) should be interpreted in the light of his own conduct during such an incident: Break the chain of violence by rising above hurt feelings and challenge the offender to act like a rational human being. Annas apparently finds Jesus too much for him and sends Jesus to Caiaphas.

REFLECTION AND PRAYER

Dear Jesus, in my hour of trial, give me a share in your courage. Never let me deny you. Rather, help me defend myself with the dignity that you teach us. Help me rise above my own hurt to reach out to others.

Jesus' Trial Before Pilate (Jn 18:28—19:16)

John merely implies the trial before Caiaphas, leaving the impression that the real decision of the Sanhedrin has already been taken during the trial before Annas. Early in the morning the Jewish leaders bring Jesus to the praetorium, Pilate's place of judgment as Roman governor.

Verse 28 indicates that it is the day of the Passover meal. This chronology conflicts with that of the synoptic writers, who identify the Last Supper with the Passover meal (Mk 14:12). Whichever chronology is correct, John is probably implying a correspondence between Jesus' death and that of the paschal lambs sacrificially slaughtered in the Temple during the afternoon before the Passover meal.

Apparently in deference to the Jews' scruples about ritual impurity, Pilate overlooks the implication that he is unclean (after all, so was every non-Jew) and comes out of his residence to meet them more than half way (v. 29). However, the opening conversation discloses a note of hostility between Pilate and the Jewish leaders. When Pilate asks why they don't pass judgment on Jesus themselves, they give a reason not in the synoptics: "We do not have the right to execute anyone" (v. 31). Historians are uncertain as to whether at this time the Romans permitted the Jews to execute persons that the Sanhedrin found guilty of crimes. In any case, only the Romans could execute by crucifixion, the death by which the Jewish leaders want to disgrace Jesus' cause and his followers, in unwitting fulfillment of his prophecies about the manner of his death.

Perhaps as a sign of his impartiality, Pilate re-enters his residence where he can examine Jesus away from the Jewish leaders. Perhaps he has heard rumors that some of the Jews consider Jesus to be their king, for he begins his questioning on that point. John's picture of Jesus is worthy of his kingly dignity; he questions Pilate. Angered, Pilate demands to know what Jesus has done to bring upon himself the condemnation of the chief priests.

Unlike the synoptics, John's gospel has scarcely mentioned the theme of the kingdom of God, but here Jesus defines it as his own kingdom and as completely non-political, "My kingdom does not belong to this world" (v. 36). Though not *of* this world, it is already *in* it, for he speaks of "my attendants," his disciples who have shown their readiness to fight for him but whom he restrained in the garden. "Attendants" is a word that Pilate can understand, but "my kingdom is not here" leaves him confused.

When Pilate presses for greater clarity, Jesus gives the same obscure answer as that reported in Mark 15:2, "You say I am a king" (v. 37). He offers clarification of the sense in which he really is a king, but only the kind that can be understood by persons committed to the truth. That leaves Pilate out, for his sarcastic question reveals his cynical indifference about whatever Jesus might mean by truth.

Yet Pilate is convinced of one thing: The Jews have trumped up a case against Jesus, a case that in justice he cannot agree with (v. 38). So he offers to release Jesus as the Jew to be freed at Passover. But he makes the mistake of mocking the crowd by referring to Jesus as "King of the Jews" (v. 39). The result is predictable; they shout for the release of Barabbas instead.

Pilate seems to accept their decision, for he now has Jesus scourged, the ordinary preliminary to crucifixion (Jn 19:1). The soldiers improvise further indignities to fit the supposed crime of pretension to royalty: the crown of thorns, the purple cloak and their mocking servility.

310

But in verses 4-5 we see that the scourging was really a maneuver on Pilate's part. In now repeating that he finds no guilt in Jesus and in presenting him to the crowd in his present state, Pilate is evidently trying to move them to pity for Jesus: ''Behold, the man!''

''Behold, the man!'' How often we have tried in our imagination to see him! We picture his bleeding head and face under the cruel thorns, the tear-shot eyes looking straight ahead in utter agony, the sagging jaw and drooping mouth bespeaking bare survival, the open gashes on his chest set off by the purple robe. Certainly this image of the suffering Jesus is true as well as traditional. Yet this is an image more in keeping with the synoptic vision of the passion, and the present incident is presented only by John, who would obviously have us see it differently, if we judge by his context.

In John's immediate context we see ''the crown of thorns and the purple cloak'' (v. 5) as the symbols of his royalty. But we do not see any description of blood and tears. Indeed, if we look back to the garden scene of the bold Jesus, whose forceful personality throws his opponents to the ground (Jn 18:6), and if we look ahead to the strong Jesus ''carrying the cross himself'' (Jn 19:17), we can be quite certain that John wants us to ''Behold the man'' in the sense of ''What a man!'' Behold this Jesus, truly a man, yet certainly not an ordinary man. After the scourging, which John does not describe but which we know by Roman standards to have been an excruciating experience, after the crowning with thorns that must have pierced his skull, after the mockery of striking him repeatedly (v. 3)—after all this, he stands there erect, a truly noble figure proving himself the king he has just claimed to be. This inner power does not escape Pilate, and he hopes that it will not escape the crowd.

Two contradictory images of the suffering Jesus are held up to our view: the bleeding, agonizing Jesus of the synoptics, so exhausted and weakened by his passion that he cannot bear his own cross; and the noble, head-erect, kingly figure depicted by John! Which is the image that we should hold as Christians who contemplate this suffering Jesus? The early Christians decided in favor of *both*, for they considered all four gospels as vehicles of inspired revelation about Jesus Christ.

And both the synoptics and John must be valid for us today. The synoptic picture is what really happened, and so is John's picture. If we look at the whole gospel of John, we will see that, far from saying that the synoptics had it wrong, he is supplementing their work. He is not saying that Jesus did not suffer in the passion. Rather, he is telling us to

311

look beyond this agonized exterior, to remember that inwardly this man is suffering freely, nobly. In the manner that we have become accustomed to see in his gospel, he now makes exterior an inner reality so that we may see more clearly not only the meaning of the events, but also the inner quality of the person who endures these events as the king that he really is.

In one great essential both the synoptic picture and John's picture completely coincide: This is the man of complete love. In the synoptic view he is reduced to the edge of life by his love for us. In John's view he is the valiant king who nobly bears every indignity to show us how much he loves us. Behold the man who loves more than any other ever did or could!

Pilate appeals to the crowd's feelings and their admiration for a man who bears his sufferings so nobly. But the chief priests and the Temple guards seem to have no feelings but hatred: "Crucify him!" (v. 6). Pilate's retort, "Take him yourselves and crucify him," is not yet his capitulation but an expression of frustrated taunting, for they cannot crucify Jesus themselves; only the Romans can.

Also frustrated, the chief priests finally tell why they want to see Jesus crucified: "He made himself the Son of God" (v. 7). Though John has not reported the dramatic moment of the trial before the Sanhedrin in which Jesus affirmatively answered the question about his divine sonship, John here displays his basic agreement with the synoptics about the real cause of Jesus' condemnation. He died to uphold his true identity!

Now in fear (v. 8), Pilate renews the interrogation of Jesus: "Where are you from?" But Pilate's scornful attitude toward truth has shown him incapable of understanding any answer to this question, so Jesus offers none. Jesus does, however, answer Pilate's boast of power over his life, for Jesus alone has that power in his own freedom: "You would have no power over me if it had not been given to you from above" (v. 11). This statement is one of the bases for the Christian belief that all legitimate human authority is under the Providence of God. Then Jesus clearly indicates that, although the sin of the Jewish leaders in handing him over to Pilate is greater, Pilate's abuse of his authority in condemning a person he considers innocent is also sinful. Pilate doesn't understand much about sin, but his fear increases, for he now tries to release Jesus.

The Jews know how to get to Pilate: "Everyone who makes himself a king opposes Caesar" (v. 12). That is the final blow to Pilate's courage; he fears Caesar more than he fears God. He finally sits in the judgment seat "in the place called Stone Pavement." Archaeologists have found such a pavement under the fortress Antonia. At this solemn moment of Jesus' condemnation to death, the evangelist reminds us that "it was Preparation Day for Passover, . . . about noon" (v. 14), the hour when the priests begin to slaughter the lambs for the Passover meal that evening. Pilate tries to wring a bitter satisfaction from the moment by taunting the Jews: "Behold, your king!" (v. 14). In no mood for dallying, they call for Jesus' crucifixion. Pilate stoops to mockery, thus infuriating them to cry, "We have no king but Caesar," not only a burst of hypocritical subjection but even a blatant repudiation of their proudest heritage of recognizing God alone as their ruling Lord (see Jgs 8:23; Zep 3:15).

REFLECTION AND PRAYER

Lamb of God, condemned to be crucified for the sins of the world, for my sins, I humbly adore you! Let me truly look upon you as my King, my noble, admirable King!

Crucifixion and Death of Jesus (Jn 19:17-42)

Contrary to the synoptics, John insists that Jesus carries the cross *"himself"* (v. 17), still master of the situation, still the noble figure of kingly dignity. Only John mentions that the inscription on Jesus' cross proclaims him king in Hebrew (for the Jews), in Greek (for the Gentiles), in Latin (for the Roman Empire)—*universal King!* Pilate refuses the request of the chief priests to change what he has written. His show of strength at the end might be interpreted as a petulant effort to maintain what dignity he could or as a genuine conviction that he found more truth in Jesus than in the chief priests. Either way, it serves John's purpose in once more drawing attention to one of his main passion themes: Jesus is truly King.

Only John mentions Jesus' seamless garment, for which the soldiers gamble. In explanation, John quotes Psalm 22:19, the same psalm that Jesus quoted in the only word from the cross attributed to him by Mark and Matthew. Perhaps in mentioning that the soldiers decide not to tear the seamless garment, John is alluding to Leviticus 21:10, forbidding the tearing of the high priest's special garment; he thereby implies that Jesus is the true High Priest in the moment of his supreme sacrifice. John's gospel justifies the symbolic representation of Jesus on the cross dressed in priestly robes, arms outstretched in self-offering to his Father.

The central moment of the crucifixion in this gospel is Jesus' significant message to Mary and John. The synoptics mentioned a group of women at a distance from the cross. Only John places them by the cross and includes among them Jesus' mother. To her, John's Jesus now speaks his first word on the cross: "*Woman*, behold, your son" (v. 26); then to his beloved disciple: "Behold, your mother." The word *woman* propels our memories back to Cana where Jesus had said: "*Woman*, . . . my hour has not yet come" (Jn 2:4). Now that his hour has come, he thinks of her again, tenderly providing for her: "From that hour the disciple took her into his home" (v. 27).

Obviously there is great use of symbolism in this passage. Just as Mary is a key figure in John's gospel at the beginning of Jesus' public ministry as the person who launches him, seemingly against his will, into the first *sign* of who he really is, now at the end of that ministry, she is again associated with him in the very moment of his redeeming sacrifice. The *woman* of Cana and of the cross is Jesus' dying gift to "the beloved disciple"—and to all Jesus' beloved disciples. He proclaims her our mother, for as his own mother she mothers his life in us.

By again referring to her as *woman* John's Jesus moves our memories back to that moment in paradise when God spoke to the serpent that had tempted Eve:

> I will put enmity between you and the *woman* [at this point, Eve], and between your offspring [collective plural] and hers;
> He [dramatic shift to the singular] will strike at your head, while you strike at his heel (Gn 3:15).

Here on the cross hangs that promised offspring, Jesus the new Adam crushing the head of Satan, even as he seems himself stricken. And by the side of her offspring is the new Eve sharing in his suffering and in his triumph over Satan by undoing the harm wrought by the original Adam and Eve upon our race.

Another Johanine book, Revelation, refers once more to this cosmic *woman* of salvation history: "A great sign appeared in the sky, a *woman* clothed with the sun, with the moon under her feet, and on her head a crown of twelve stars" (Rv 12:1). The verses that follow describe how, after this woman gives birth to a child, a great seven-headed dragon (the Roman Empire) attacks her and her boy, "destined to rule all the nations" (Rv 12:5). Fathers of the church interpreted this pas-

314

sage primarily symbolizing the church, the woman beset by persecution as she tries to win the nations to Christ. But they also saw in the woman, Mary, mother of the ruler of the nations.

In view of these implications of John's use of *woman* in referring to Mary, it is not surprising that Vatican II declared: "The Mother of God is a model of the Church in . . . faith, charity, and perfect union with Christ" (*The Dogmatic Constitution on the Church*, no. 63). And Paul VI could therefore call Mary "The mother of the Church."

Continuing his narrative, John tells us that, having first looked to his mother and his beloved disciple, the dying Jesus now turns his thoughts to the scripture (v. 28). To fulfill Psalm 22:16, Jesus cries: "I am thirsty." A man bleeding to death suffers extreme thirst. But more than this physical thirst, Jesus is here expressing his burning desire to complete the work his Father has given him to accomplish.

This cry of Jesus again links John's account of the crucifixion to that of the synoptics, for it is the beginning of this same psalm that Mark reported on Jesus' lips: "My God, my God, why have you forsaken me?" (Mk 15:34). Fixing a sponge soaked in wine to the stem of a plant, someone offers him refreshment. Perhaps John wants us to see that even his executioners cannot watch him die without being touched to perform this last act of human kindness. Jesus does not refuse this offer (v. 30).

He dies declaring, "It is finished." His life of fulfillment of his Father's will, contained in the scriptures, has been completed. His head, held up nobly throughout his suffering, finally bows as "he handed over the spirit." By thus reporting his death, John highlights its redemptive value; Jesus is now ready to pass on his Holy Spirit to his followers (see Jn 7:39).

Though John disagrees with the synoptics about the identity of the Last Supper with the Passover meal, he agrees with them that the crucifixion took place on a Friday. For he now relates that the Jews want the bodies of the crucified taken down from their crosses before the sabbath, which will begin at sundown. Pilate grants their request to have the legs of the crucified broken, thus forcing their bodies so tightly against their crosses that they would quickly die of asphyxiation. When the soldier finds Jesus already dead, instead of breaking Jesus' legs he drives his lance into Jesus' side, apparently to make sure of his death. The evangelist insists that on the testimony of a truthful eyewitness—evidently the beloved disciple whom he has reported to be close to the cross—"blood and water flowed out" (v. 34). John thereby underlines the reality of Jesus' death, perhaps to refute the Docetists, who at the time of writing were contending that Jesus had only *appeared* to die because he did not have a real body. It is significant that the gospel that most strongly emphasizes the divinity of Jesus likewise insists so much on his humanity.

The mixture of blood and water would also be seen by the Christians of John's time as symbolically meaningful. From the side of Jesus flows forth the grace of salvation given in the sacraments of the church. The water suggests baptism, and the blood points to the Eucharist. That John really intends to be understood as using symbolism is confirmed by his reference to the scripture passage, ''Not a bone of it [the paschal lamb] will be broken'' (v. 36, referring to Ex 12:46). We have seen John's references to Jesus the true Paschal Lamb as one of his favorite themes.

John ends his contemplation of Jesus dead upon the cross with a reference to Zechariah's messianic prophecy:

> I will pour out on the house of David and on the inhabitants of Jerusalem a spirit of grace and petition; and *they shall look on him whom they have thrust through*, and they shall mourn for him as one mourns for an only son, and they shall grieve over him as one grieves over a first-born (Zec 12:10).

With John, we stand there, lost in deepest thought and feeling.

As in the synoptics, Joseph of Arimathea obtains Pilate's permission to bury Jesus' body. But unlike the synoptics, John says that Nicodemus brings the embalming materials (v. 39). Ironically, it is not Jesus' closest followers but these two members of the Sanhedrin who prepare Jesus' body for burial. Jesus' death has given courage to these secret disciples to minister openly. They lay Jesus' body in ''a new tomb, in which no one had yet been buried'' (v. 41). This last reverent detail agrees with Luke 23:53.

REFLECTION AND PRAYER

Lord Jesus, King of the Jews and my King, with Mary and John I look upon you ''whom they have pierced.''

Jesus' Resurrection Appearances in Jerusalem (Jn 20)

Attempts by scholars to harmonize the widely varying accounts of Jesus' resurrection appearances have not produced satisfying results. It seems better simply to accept it as fact that the disagreeing gospel accounts reflect the excited confusion that swept the first Christian community as it experienced the presence of the risen Jesus. Instead of trying to ascertain which account is more historically accurate, who first knew that Jesus was alive, what he did, how he really looked, and so forth, it seems better to admit that the difficulties are beyond our power to resolve, just as they obviously were for those who experienced them.

According to John, when Mary Magdalene comes to the tomb early Sunday morning and sees that the stone has been rolled back, she runs to tell the disciples. Excited by the unexpected news, Peter and the beloved disciple run to the tomb (v. 4). The older Peter falls behind. Out of fear or deference the beloved disciple, through whose eyes we now see "the burial cloths" (v. 5), waits at the tomb for Peter to enter first. As Peter enters the tomb, we continue to see through the eyes of the beloved disciple, and in such striking detail (the head cloth separate from the rolled-up wrappings) that it reinforces the impression that he must be the eyewitness for the events related here, and probably in the rest of this gospel.

This beloved disciple "saw and believed" (v. 8). That he now believes Jesus has risen from the dead is indicated by the comment that the disciples did not understand as prophecies of the Messiah's resurrection such scriptural passages as Psalm 16:10, Hosea 6:2 and Jonah 2:1. The disciples have simply not been expecting the resurrection.

Neither have the women. After the disciples leave, the weeping Magdalene sees "two angels" (v. 12) in the tomb. Her matter-of-fact answer to their question implies that she thinks they are ordinary men. Still not expecting anything extraordinary, she takes Jesus for a cemetery gardener—until he calls her by name! She immediately recognizes him, greets him with a title of deep respect, "Rabbouni," meaning "my master," and reverently embraces his feet (see Mt 28:9) to adore him as the Lord. But Jesus tells her that such adoration will be more fitting after the completion of his glorification when he ascends to his Father (v. 17). First, there is work to be done. He commissions her to tell "my brothers" of his imminent ascension to "my Father and your Father" (v. 17), truly "their Father," now that they will fully believe in him.

Jesus' final words to Magdalene imply that his ascension will take place before he appears again. In John's view Jesus' ascension is intimately linked to his resurrection as two moments in his glorification. Whether the ascension took place only 40 days after the resurrection as in Acts 1:2 or very soon after it, as implied here, both Luke and John agree that Jesus communicated several times with his followers after his resurrection. Hence, they also imply that during the intervals between these appearances Jesus was with his Father before his definitive ascension.

On the evening of that same day Jesus appears to Magdalene, he comes through locked doors (v. 19) to visit his brothers. He greets them with that special peace that he spoke of as his gift to them (Jn 14:27) and identifies himself by showing them his wounds. How much in need of peace they are after abandoning him, denying him, perhaps losing their faith in him as they watched him die from their safe distance!

But their grief is now turned into joy (Jn 16:20) at sight of him. He repeats his blessing of peace as he proceeds to the solemn ordination for which he prepared them in his prayer after the Last Supper (Jn 17:17-19): "As the Father has sent me, so I send you" (Jn 20:21). He *breathes* on them in the act of re-creating them, even as God breathed upon Adam's clay to send spirit into him bringing him alive (Gn 2:7). The Spirit Jesus now sends them is not their own souls; it is his Holy Spirit bringing them new Life in Jesus!

And through the Holy Spirit he gives them a share in his own mission, authority and more specifically his power to forgive sins (v. 23). Such power implies judgment, a judgment of the penitent's sincerity. In the practical life of the church this judgment has traditionally been exercised through the confession of sins. The Council of Trent quoted this passage as evidence that Jesus established the religious rite later called the sacrament of penance or reconciliation (*The Teaching of the Catholic Church*, p. 312).

According to John, the Holy Spirit was given to 10 disciples on the evening after the resurrection. According to Luke, the Holy Spirit came upon 11 apostles and other followers of Jesus on Pentecost (Acts 2:1-4,38). Pentecost may therefore be considered the confirmation of this original gift of the Spirit related in John and the publicizing of it to the whole world.

Thank God for doubting Thomas! Absent at Jesus' first appearance, Thomas refuses to believe without putting his finger in the nail marks and his "*hand* into his side" (v. 25), thus giving us an idea of the size of that lance wound for which this gospel claims an eyewitness.

Next Sunday Jesus returns just for Thomas. He blesses them all with his peace, and invites Thomas to do just what he had demanded as his test of truth. John seems to be telling us that even our frivolous requests are heard if they are somehow prayers for faith. Jesus' return for this wayward disciple is clearly stated: "Do not be unbelieving, but believe!" Thomas' brash front crumbles as he exclaims, "My Lord and my God!" (v. 28), paraphrasing Psalm 35:23, addressed to Yahweh. Adoring the risen Jesus as the living God has now become the most natural thing in the world for the men and women who have lived with him and experienced his complete humanity.

Jesus accepts Thomas' worship, but also declares as even more worthy of blessing the faith of those who believe in him without having seen him in his risen splendor. John is evidently including this episode in his gospel as a special message to later generations of Christians who may have already been wavering in their faith with the excuse that they had not been gifted with the sight of the risen Jesus as had that first generation. This episode demonstrates dramatically that the divine glory of Jesus constitutes the very center of the Christian's faith in him.

What seems to have been the original version of the gospel of John concludes with the remark that what he has written is only a cross section of Jesus' signs, presented "that you may . . . believe that Jesus is the Messiah, the Son of God, and that through this belief you may have life in his name" (v. 31). Again the importance of faith, its *vital* importance for *living Jesus' life*.

REFLECTION AND PRAYER

Do I consider Jesus' resurrection the source of deepest peace?

My risen Lord, I believe in your divine glory. Like Thomas, I prostrate myself before you and proclaim you "my Lord and my God!"

Jesus' Resurrection Appearance in Galilee (Jn 21)

After the conclusion of John's gospel at the end of chapter 20, still another chapter appears. Because its style is different, modern scholars consider it the product of some other writer, probably also of the Johannine school, for it displays many of the same characteristics. It has been added as an appendix by someone who evidently thought there was still more to relate about Jesus that is of great importance to the church. And because it appears in all surviving manuscripts of the gospel of John, chapter 21 has always been accepted by the church as possessing the same inspired value as the rest of the gospel.

319

Chapter 21 tells only one long incident, the appearance of Jesus to seven disciples in Galilee. In Mark 16:7 a heavenly visitor reported that Jesus would appear to his disciples in Galilee but Mark did not relate the appearance. Matthew's gospel supplies a Galilean appearance (Mt 28:16-20). John's gospel now ends in Galilee with a much different event.

Led by Peter, seven of Jesus' disciples fish all night in vain. At dawn a stranger on shore directs them to cast their nets "over the right side" (v. 6). When the light was right, a person on shore could sometimes detect the movement of fish better than could those in a boat. In this case the result is so spectacular that they look back at that stranger; but, significantly, it is only "the disciple whom Jesus loved" (v. 7) who can recognize Jesus.

Impulsive Peter cannot wait for the boat to pull ashore; he reverently tucks in his garment and plunges into the water to swim to Jesus. When the others arrive in the boat, they find that Jesus has already prepared a meal for them of bread and fish (v. 9), reminiscent of his miraculous feeding of the crowd and, like that incident, suggestive of the Eucharist. Jesus calls for some of their fish to add to those he is cooking; their catch will contribute to the banquet, symbol of the heavenly banquet.

Of course it is Peter who drags in the net. They count 153 fish, probably symbolizing the abundant fish of all kinds that would be found, according to the prophecy of Ezekiel 47:10, in the wonderful stream to flow from the Temple entrance, the new fountain of living water that Jesus offered the Samaritan woman (Jn 4:10). All these symbols point to the writer's intention of illustrating Jesus' commissioning of his disciples to be fishers of people of all nations. The remark that such a large number did not tear the net suggests that this net symbolizes the unbroken, unified church.

Even as they draw near at Jesus' invitation to eat, they do not seem to recognize him; yet they realize it is "the Lord" (v. 12). Isn't the writer implying that when we approach the Eucharist we know we are receiving Jesus even though we do not recognize him? Just as Jesus had served them at the beginning of the Last Supper by washing their feet (Jn 13:4-11), he now serves them bread and fish. It is really he who, through the church, provides the Christian's spiritual sustenance.

After their meal Jesus gives Peter three opportunities to declare his love for him, obviously in reparation for his three denials. Notice that Jesus does not call Peter by the name that he has given him but by

Peter's own name and parentage: "Simon, son of John" (vv. 15-17), indicating that this is a solemn moment in the history of the church. Peter thrice declares his love, but without boasting—as has until now been his tendency—that his love is greater than that of the others. It is significant that Jesus tells him to care for his lambs and his sheep, even though, after the first time, he drops the demand for greater love "than these." It is sufficient for his office as chief shepherd that Peter truly love Jesus with a love strong enough to die for him (v. 18).

Evidently Jesus is entrusting to Peter the greatest share in his own office of Good Shepherd (Jn 10:1-18) and the highest responsibility among the apostles to care for the spiritual needs of his flock. The First Vatican Council quoted this passage as one of the chief bases for its declaration of the primacy of the pope as successor of Peter in jurisdiction over the whole church (*The Teaching of the Catholic Church*, p. 222).

In veiled language, Jesus tells Peter that he will be led to death for following him. The comment in verse 19 indicates that Peter had already been martyred by the time this chapter was written. In this context Jesus' "Follow me" takes on the significance of a specific invitation to follow him in a death that would be faithful to his role as shepherd. Perhaps a literal interpretation of this invitation accounts for an early tradition that Peter was crucified upside down. Whether by crucifixion or not, Peter died in Rome as a martyr, about the year 64, during Nero's persecution.

The theme of death continues, but now in reference to the beloved disciple. The author carefully shows that Jesus' question, "What if I want him to remain until I come?" (vv. 22-23), should not have been interpreted "among the brothers" to mean that the disciple would not die before Jesus' second coming. The author's effort to explain this statement suggests that his community has been surprised and perhaps shocked that this disciple has died despite a belief that Jesus had promised the contrary. The writer does not pretend to know what meaning the statement really has, but is content to insist that it does not mean what some have thought.

Once more the gospel of John is brought to its conclusion, this time definitively with the declaration that this beloved disciple, now dead, is the eyewitness upon whose testimony this gospel is based, a witness whom the members of the Johannine community have all learned to trust implicitly as a man of truth (v. 24). The new writer repeats, even more forcefully, that not all that Jesus did is related here:

321

"If these [other things] were to be described individually, I do not think the whole world would contain the books that would be written" (v. 25).

Is not this still the case? We will never be able to say the last word about Jesus Christ!

REFLECTION AND PRAYER

Lord Jesus, continue to nourish me with your word in scripture and your very self in the Eucharist. Help me follow you in my life and in my death.

SUGGESTIONS FOR FURTHER READING OR REFERENCE

Brown, Raymond E. *The Gospel of John*, 2 vol. Anchor Bible Series. Garden City: Doubleday, 1970. Very thorough and scholarly commentary.

Flanagan, Neal M., O.S.M. *The Gospel According to John and the Johannine Epistles*: Collegeville, MN: The Liturgical Press, 1983. A short, well-presented commentary.

Kirk, Albert and Obach, Robert E. *A Commentary on the Gospel of John*. New York: Paulist Press, 1979. A good, readable commentary.

McCool, Gerald A., ed. *A Rahner Reader*. New York: Seabury Press, 1975. See especially, "The Knowledge and Self-Consciousness of Christ," pp. 159-166.

Moody, Smith. *John*. Philadelphia: Fortress Press, 1976. Fairly easy-to-read treatment of major themes of John.

Schnackenburg, Rudolph. *The Gospel According to St. John*, 3 vol. New York: Crossroads, 1982. Excellent, but sometimes tedious.

EPILOGUE

Have We Found Jesus in the Gospels?

In our reading of the gospels we have discovered that Jesus is too much for any one evangelist. He is a figure so complete that no single spotlight can capture his full dimensions, grace and strength. We have found the synoptics lighting up his figure from below: Mark illuminated for us his human features; Matthew, his messianic mission; Luke, his compassionate love. John, like a beacon from above, highlighted his divine power and his absolute love for us.

But have we found Jesus himself? As your reading companion, I certainly hope so. Yet I'm not surprised if, even after getting this far, you feel somewhat disappointed. We are still struggling with the problem of *the identity of Jesus as the person who is totally human yet totally divine*, the central unresolved problem of the gospels. Be consoled; neither the evangelists nor nearly 20 centuries of theologians have solved all the problems relating to the identity of Jesus, for that identity is a divine mystery fully accessible only to the mind of God. Yet we must let that mystery intrigue us into an incessant quest to enter into it ever more fully, according to our limited capacity. Meanwhile, with our faith we must bridge the gap between the reality of Jesus' identity and our own understanding of it. Only through faith can we truly embrace and love Jesus Christ in the mystery of his identity.

The gospels can set us on the path, but to reach Jesus we must do more than simply read them; we must *live* them. The gospels themselves called upon us to *imitate Jesus*. They carefully delineated for us the character traits that, to become true Christians, we must strive to acquire.

With Mark we contemplated the truly human Jesus as our model, the man who experienced all our emotions and endured the pressure of the crowd, yet dedicated himself completely to his Father's mission by dedicating himself completely to all with whom he came into contact, especially to his uncomprehending disciples—even unto exhaustion and ignominious death.

With Matthew we listened to Jesus, the messianic teacher of God's perfect holiness who embodied that holiness in his own life and called us to imitate it in ours by renouncing anger, lust, retaliation, and instead loving all our brothers and sisters—even our enemies.

With Luke we listened to the compassionate Jesus tell us about the absolute goodness of our Father and call us to imitate his own special love of the poor and the suffering. We saw Jesus' mother keeping in her heart all the events that revealed his person. And we watched him direct his life toward his Father—and all humankind—from the age of 12 until his death on the cross and his ascension into heaven.

With John we were blinded by the wisdom of Jesus, Light of the world, yet thrilled by his attractive personality and deeply moved by his assurances of his abiding presence with us. We knelt with Thomas and adored his glorified majesty.

To follow the Jesus of the gospels is indeed a great ideal, an ideal that demands a constant return to the gospels in daily reading and daily efforts to live what we read. In moments of discouragement, we must call to mind that Mark's Jesus will come walking even over the waters that threaten to engulf us, that Matthew's Jesus will be with us always, "until the end of the age," that Luke's Jesus walks at our side, even when we don't recognize him, and that John's Jesus dwells within our very hearts.

And when we are most sorely tempted to think that we will never really find Jesus, *he will find us*.